The Blackwell Guide to Plato's *Republic*

Blackwell Guides to Great Works

A proper understanding of philosophy requires engagement with the foundational texts that have shaped the development of the discipline and which have an abiding relevance to contemporary discussions. Each volume in this series provides guidance to those coming to the great works of the philosophical canon, whether for the first time or to gain new insight. Comprising specially commissioned contributions from the finest scholars, each book offers a clear and authoritative account of the context, arguments, and impact of the work at hand. Where possible the original text is reproduced alongside the essays.

Published

Forthcoming

THE BLACKWELL GUIDE TO

PLATO'S
Republic

EDITED BY GERASIMOS SANTAS

Blackwell
Publishing

BLACKWELL PUBLISHING
350 Main Street, Malden, MA 02148-5020, USA
9600 Garsington Road, Oxford OX4 2DQ, UK
550 Swanston Street, Carlton, Victoria 3053, Australia

First published 2006 by Blackwell Publishing Ltd

1   2006

Library of Congress Cataloging-in-Publication Data

The Blackwell guide to Plato's Republic / edited by Gerasimos Santas.
p.   cm. – (Blackwell guides to great works)
Includes bibliographical references and index.
ISBN-13: 978-1-4051-1563-6 (hard cover : alk. paper)
ISBN-10: 1-4051-1563-7 (hard cover : alk. paper)
ISBN-13: 978-1-4051-1564-3 (pbk. : alk. paper)
ISBN-10: 1-4051-1564-5 (pbk. : alk. paper)   1. Plato. Republic.   I. Santas, Gerasimos
Xenophon.   II. Series.

JC71.P6B58 2006
321′.07–dc22
2005004895

A catalogue record for this title is available from the British Library.

Set in 10 on 13pt Galliard
by SNP Best-set Typesetter Ltd, Hong Kong
Printed and bound in the United Kingdom
by TJ International, Padstow, Cornwall

The publisher's policy is to use permanent paper from mills that operate a sustainable forestry
policy, and which has been manufactured from pulp processed using acid-free and elementary
chlorine-free practices. Furthermore, the publisher ensures that the text paper and cover board
used have met acceptable environmental accreditation standards.

For further information on
Blackwell Publishing, visit our website:
www.blackwellpublishing.com

Contents

Notes on Contributors

Mariana Anagnostopoulos received her PhD from the University of California, Irvine, in Ancient Philosophy, held a post-doctoral fellowship at UCLA, and is currently a lecturer in the Philosophy Department at California State University, Fresno. Her primary research interests are in ancient Greek philosophy, ethics, moral psychology, and theory of action. She is the author of the paper "Desire for good in the *Meno*" and is currently at work on Aristotle's and subsequent analyses of the problem of *akrasia*. Her teaching interests include the history and application of ethics and twentieth-century analytic philosophy.

Rachel Barney is Canada Research Chair in Classical Philosophy at the University of Toronto, and Director of its Collaborative Programme in Ancient and Medieval Philosophy. She did her undergraduate work at McGill and Toronto and her PhD at Princeton; she has also taught at the Universities of Chicago, Ottawa, Harvard, and McGill. She has published papers on Plato and on Hellenistic epistemology and ethics, and the book *Names and Natures in Plato's* Cratylus (2001); her current research is focused on Plato's ethics.

Michael Ferejohn is Associate Professor of Philosophy at Duke University. He has held visiting positions at the University of Pittsburgh and Tufts University and a Mellon Faculty Fellowship at Harvard University. He is the author of *The Origins of Aristotelian Science* (1991) as well as numerous articles on early Platonic ethics and metaphysics, and on Aristotelian metaphysics, epistemology, and philosophy of science. He is currently working on a book on the place of definition in ancient epistemology.

David Keyt is Professor of Philosophy at the University of Washington in Seattle. He is the author of *Aristotle:* Politics *Books V and VI* (1999) and co-editor with Fred D. Miller, Jr. of *A Companion to Aristotle's Politics* (Blackwell, 1991). He has held visiting appointments at Cornell University, the University of Hong

Kong, Princeton University, and the Los Angeles and Irvine campuses of the University of California, and has had research appointments at the Institute for Research in the Humanities at the University of Wisconsin, the Center for Hellenic Studies in Washington, DC, the Institute for Advanced Study at Princeton, and the Social Philosophy and Policy Center at Bowling Green State University.

Gabriel Richardson Lear is Assistant Professor of Philosophy at the University of Chicago. She is the author of *Happy Lives and the Highest Good: An Essay on Aristotle's* Nicomachean Ethics (2004).

Jonathan Lear is the John U. Nef Distinguished Service Professor at the Committee on Social Thought and the Department of Philosophy at the University of Chicago. He is the author of *Aristotle and Logical Theory* (1980), *Aristotle: The Desire to Understand* (1988), *Love and its Place in Nature: A Philosophical Interpretation of Freudian Psychoanalysis* (1998), *Open Minded: Working Out the Logic of the Soul* (1998), *Happiness, Death and the Remainder of Life* (2000), *Therapeutic Action: An Earnest Plea for Irony* (2003), and *Freud* (2005).

Hendrik Lorenz is Assistant Professor of Philosophy at Princeton University. He is author of *Desire Without Reason in Plato and Aristotle* and of several articles on Plato and Aristotle.

Mark L. McPherran is Professor of Philosophy at the University of Maine at Farmington. He is the author of *The Religion of Socrates* (1996), the editor of *Wisdom, Ignorance, and Virtue: New Essays in Socratic Studies* (1997) and *Recognition, Remembrance, and Reality: New Essays on Plato's Epistemology and Metaphysics* (1999), and author of a variety of articles on Socrates, Plato, and ancient skepticism.

Terry Penner did his apprenticeship as an analytical philosopher studying Plato and Aristotle at Oxford with Ryle, Owen, and Ackrill; and at Princeton, where he was Gregory Vlastos's junior colleague. He taught philosophy for 34 years (and, for some of that time, Greek) at the University of Wisconsin-Madison. His main interests are Socratic ethics, Platonic metaphysics, Socratic/Platonic dialectic, Frege, and modern analytical philosophy. He was A. G. Leventis Visiting Professor of Greek at the University of Edinburgh for 2004/5. He hopes shortly to publish his long complete *Plato and the Philosophers of Language*.

Christopher Rowe is Professor of Greek at the University of Durham, UK. He has published several commentaries on Platonic dialogues, and has edited (with Malcolm Schofield) *The Cambridge History of Greek and Roman Political Thought* (2000), and (with Julia Annas) *New Perspectives on Plato, Modern and Ancient* (2002). An extensive monograph on Plato's *Lysis*, by Terry Penner and Christopher Rowe, is due to appear in 2005.

Gerasimos Santas is Professor of Philosophy at the University of California, Irvine. He is author of *Socrates: Philosophy in Plato's Earlier Dialogues* (1979), *Plato and Freud: Two Theories of Love* (Blackwell, 1988), and *Goodness and Justice: Plato, Aristotle, and the Moderns* (Blackwell, 2001).

Christopher Shields is Fellow of Lady Margaret Hall and University Lecturer at Oxford University. He has previously taught at the University of Colorado at Boulder and has held visiting posts at Stanford, Cornell, and Yale. He is editor of the *Blackwell Guide to Ancient Philosophy* (Blackwell, 2003), co-author of *The Philosophy of Thomas Aquinas* (2003), and author of *Order in Multiplicity: Homonymy in the Philosophy of Aristotle* (1999) and *Classical Philosophy: A Contemporary Introduction* (2003). He is also editor of the forthcoming *Oxford Handbook on Aristotle*, and author of the forthcoming *Aristotle*, De anima: *Translation and Commentary*.

Rachel Singpurwalla is Assistant Professor of Philosophy at Southern Illinois University, Edwardsville. She has written numerous articles on Plato's moral psychology and ethics. Her current research explores the links between Plato's conceptions of the good, aesthetic value, and moral motivation.

Introduction

Gerasimos Santas

The *Guide* presents thirteen new essays by established scholars and younger investigators on some of the main themes and arguments in Plato's *Republic*. They are all intended to throw light on Plato's important and influential discussions in that work, and to guide the reader through the subtleties of his unusual philosophical style, the breadth and depth of his theories, and the reasoning of his arguments. Many of them also discuss some of the best recent secondary literature on their subjects. And all of them are living philosophical engagements with the dialogues in the *Republic* that made Plato the father of philosophy. Almost twenty-four centuries after its composition the *Republic* continues to be one of the most – some say *the* most – influential and best-selling philosophical books of all time. What makes it such an important book?

Its style is no doubt one of the major reasons. It begins with an easy and charming conversation between Socrates and Cephalus about the burdens of old age and the advantages of wealth. Cephalus' renewed fears of what might happen to him in the afterlife if he has done injustice leads Socrates to ask him about justice. This launches a series of more and more vigorous and searching dialogues between Socrates and passionate opponents and proponents of justice and injustice and their benefits and evils. We don't know for certain who represents Plato. We don't know for certain who wins. But if we persist to the end, we know that we have been in the middle of the most fascinating intellectual battle about things no human being can be indifferent to. Even if we don't understand half of what is going on, Plato pulls us right along with every device, weapon, or stratagem known to a writer, be he or she a poet, philosopher, psychologist, or storyteller.

Christopher Rowe helps us understand the style of the *Republic*, its dialogue form, the uncertainty about who speaks for the author in the conversations; and he suggests explanations of these unusual literary devices for a philosopher, with which Plato tries to persuade us of his own unusual views. Rowe also sketches various historical and contemporary readings of the whole work: is it doctrinal, skeptical, or perhaps even an open text? He argues that the *Republic* contains "a hard core of connected ideas" continuous with the so-called Socratic dialogues. "Challenge, provocation, paradox: the purpose is to shock us out of our current ways of thinking, yes, but *into* considering certain other ways." The hard core is that "justice pays" but understood in terms of "a particular conception of what justice is and of a particular conception of what it is for something to 'pay'."

Jonathan Lear shows us Plato as a master proto-psychologist, illuminating the subtleties of Plato's approach to his interlocutors and his readers through the use of myths and allegories. The *Republic*, he tells us, "is a work of astonishing depth . . . and it can certainly be read as an occasion to work through the power of allegories and myth." Beginning with the childhood stories that came back to terrorize Cephalus, Lear helps us understand Plato's educational and therapeutic uses of stories about gods and heroes, of the Noble Falsehood and the allegory of the Cave. The myth of Er with which the *Republic* ends, Lear argues, is both therapeutic and argumentative about the main theme of the work: it serves to cover "all the possibilities." Plato's arguments try to show that we are better off being just in this life; the myth covers the possibilities of life after death and returning to life after that.

In the *Republic* the style, the myths, the allegories, and the psychology are beautifully integrated with the vigorous and lively investigations about justice and our good. Plato was the first to ask what justice is and to discuss, critically and more systematically than might appear at first sight, major answers to the question. Rachel Barney discusses Socrates' examination of the first major answer, that of Thrasymachus, who claims that justice in a society is the advantage of the ruling party in that society, and that justice is not the good of the subject who is just by obeying the laws of the rulers, but the good of another, the ruler and the stronger. Barney's article helps us understand better Socrates' main arguments against this view, and she shows that, viewed charitably, they are more persuasive than usually supposed, though not perfect. Equally important, she discusses how the arguments of Book I are related to the rest of the work, and combines "grains of truth" from different traditional interpretations – that they are deliberate rhetorical failures or that they are intended as markers of the essence of justice – to show how the first book is a good introduction to the rest of the work.

Socrates himself is not satisfied with his refutations of Thrasymachus. Neither are Plato's brothers, Glaucon and Adeimantus, who reopen the issues of justice and its benefits. Christopher Shields shows us what a powerful challenge they work up against the desirability of justice, and what an "utterly foundational question" they pose for Socrates: why should I be just? Is it anything more than a "mere instrumental" good, which we accept from fear of what would happen to us if we did not? Shields illuminates "a series of engaging and trenchantly put thought-experiments" by which the brothers try to "separate our motives" and show us that we do not prize justice for itself, as an intrinsic good, but only out of fear of punishment. If the prospect of punishment were to disappear would *we* do what is just?

Socrates does not try to refute the two brothers directly, as he did with Thrasymachus. Instead, he makes a new start of his own, first with the fundamental question, What is justice? Only after he has sketched an answer to it (Books II, III, IV), does he take up Glaucon's challenge: Wouldn't I be better off or happier being unjust, if I could get away with it?

Socrates divides the first question into two: what is justice in a city-state? What is its counterpart in a person? He takes up social justice first, proceeds to sketch a "completely good" city, and then tries to locate social justice in it. But by what method is he trying to answer this question? I argue that Plato not only sketches three major theories of what justice is, but also displays three different methods by which these theories are expounded and defended: the empirical method of Thrasymachus, the social-contract method of Glaucon, and the functional method of Socrates. Three different methods give three different results. I try to throw light on the significance of such methods, by discussing whether each of these three characters would have reached his results had he used either of the other two methods.

On the way to outlining in speech "the completely good city," Socrates sees that he needs to discuss a program of early education for its citizens, an education that would aim at making them good citizens and inculcating the virtues of courage, temperance, wisdom, and justice (which are eventually defined in Book IV). What stories about gods – role models by definition – should be included in such early education? Are the popular stories of Homer and Hesiod about the gods and their attitudes to justice to be admitted in the curriculum? Mark McPherran's article helps us understand Plato's dissatisfaction with such stories, and explains what Plato thought was true about god: Plato's new canons of theology. More broadly, he argues that the *Republic* as a whole is a work of theology as well as of political and moral philosophy; he compares Cephalus' conventional piety, Socratic piety, and Platonic piety, and shows that Plato did not reject, but reinterpreted, the religious practices of his day in the service of philosophy.

Gabriel Richardson Lear's essay takes up another, less obvious centerpiece in Plato's theory of education, the love of beauty. Plato's Socrates claims that the young guardians' musical-poetic education culminates in the love of beauty, a result crucial to being just. But how so? Richardson Lear argues that Plato thinks the beauty of poetry subtly shapes young people's presuppositions about reality on the basis of which they later deliberate; "a proper sense of beauty aids the development of moral knowledge." Further, "beauty as such" is attractive to the spirited part of the soul, and the virtuous person will take care to present to the spirit images of the beauty of justice and strengthen the passion for beauty rather than for some other spirited object. To support her argument Richardson

Lear offers us an analysis of Plato's conception of beauty and its relation to goodness and to Plato's moral psychology.

After Socrates has defined the virtues of the city, with social justice as the foundation of the other virtues, he takes up the second question about the nature of justice: what is justice in a person? On the unusual assumption that justice in a person is isomorphic to justice in a city, and given that justice in a city required division of the citizens into three groups on the basis of what social role (or function) each is suited by nature to do best, he now sees that he is faced with the question whether the human soul has three corresponding parts. Though proceeding from such a motivation, Hendrik Lorenz shows that Plato's analysis of the human psyche has an importance of its own, both as a theory of human motivation and as a theory of what constitutes the embodied human soul. He discusses carefully the three arguments by which Plato divides the soul, in Book IV, and shows how Plato's psychological portraits of unjust persons, in Books VIII and IX, illuminate further Plato's conception of the capacities and the roles of reason, spirit, and appetite. He also considers the problems that a composite soul presents for Plato's views about the immortality of the soul.

During his analysis of the human psyche, Socrates seems to reject the earlier Socratic view that all desires of everyone are for good things (438a); yet in the famous passage about the Form of the Good in Book VI, Socrates tell us that the good "every soul pursues and does everything for its sake, but [it is] puzzled and unable to see adequately what it is" (505e). Mariana Anagnostopoulos helps us understand different interpretations of this contrast between Socratic views in Plato's earlier dialogues and the view of the *Republic*. She disputes the dominant interpretation, that Plato now recognizes the anti-Socratic possibility "of acting in pure pursuit of some goal other than one's good (say, pleasure)," and the accompanying view that parts of the soul are agents with desires and beliefs. She argues that Plato is able to "identify the domain of appetite" as distinct from reason, by identifying "mere thirst" and other such simple desires, "basic psychic forces" which neither conceive nor pursue the good. Ordinary motivating desires are more complex; "reason's role in their development serves to make them part of the agent's pursuit of the good," though reason can be disturbed by appetite and mistake, say, pleasure for the good. Thus Plato can say that every soul does everything for the good and still hold that not every desire is for the *truly* good (as distinct from what appears good).

But can we *know* the good? When Glaucon asks Socrates whether the completely good city can be realized, Socrates replies that an approximation of it can be realized, but only if political power is based on wisdom: knowledge of what is good for the parts of the city and the city as a whole, which is not possible without knowledge of the Form of the Good. The paradox of the philosopher-king was implicit in the wisdom of the rulers of the completely good city, and now Socrates is faced with new challenges: what is knowledge as distinct from opinion, and how is knowledge possible, especially knowledge of the good? In the middle books of the *Republic* Plato sketches the epistemology and meta-physics that he thinks are a necessary foundation for his ethics and politics.

Mike Ferejohn's chapter helps us understand Plato's conception of knowledge. He traces the practical roots of concerns about the nature of knowledge in Socrates' earlier attempts to distinguish "genuine experts" from "mere pre-tenders." Ferejohn then turns to the *Republic* and presents the Theory of Forms as Plato's completion of an epistemological project initiated in the *Meno* (where Socrates distinguishes between knowledge and true opinion by reference to causal reasoning), "by establishing the theoretical possibility of an exceptionally reliable human capacity to make correct ethical judgments, which are to be implemented in the governance of a well-functioning political state or a well-developed ethical agent." Plato's Forms provide the reliable objects which persons of exceptional ability and education can know. But Ferejohn also argues that the allegory of the Cave provides evidence that Plato believes prenatal acquaintance with the Forms plays a key role in even uneducated people's ability to form fairly reliable judgments about the world of sense experience.

Terry Penner's chapter helps us understand Plato's Theory of Forms and to "see what the Forms are within the context of the overall project of the *Repub-lic*." This overall project, Penner says, is to show that the just person is happier than those completely unjust persons who are Thrasymachus' heroes. The point of most of the metaphysical books (VI, VII) is to take "the longer road" for specifying the parts of the soul (and presumably the virtues), which Plato alluded to in Book IV. The longer road is necessary, Penner suggests, because of the need for a fuller specification of the function of the rational part of the soul: to seek the good or the Form of the Good. As what the guardians must gain for the ideal city is the good of the three classes of the city and for the whole city, so what the rational part must gain for the soul is the good for the three parts of the soul, both separately and as a whole. Plato's Forms, Penner suggests, are the objects of the sciences: health is what medicine studies, number what arith-metic studies, and so on. As sciences presuppose that the laws and real natures they study exist antecedently to our thought and language, so Plato takes the Forms to exist antecedently to our thought and language. Plato's fundamental argument for the Forms, Penner argues, is anti-reductionist, showing that it cannot be the case that all there is to beauty is beautiful perceptible objects. Penner extends this anti-reductionism to his explanation of the great central pas-sages containing the images of the Sun, the Divided Line, and the Cave.

Plato's simile of the Ship of State in the sixth book of the *Republic* is famous in political philosophy, but it has not received the attention commentators have accorded the Sun, the Line, and the Cave. David Keyt undertakes for the first time a full analysis of the simile "in light of what can be gleamed about ancient ships and seafaring." He shows that the Ship of State is "a potent emblem of Plato's political philosophy," which complements the Sun, the Line, and the Cave – emblems of his epistemology and metaphysics. Plato may have thought that as a ship with an unruly crew is a good image of many existing Greek cities, a ship with an orderly crew and a competent steersman may be a good image of his ideal city. There are two parts to the simile of the Ship of State as there are two parts to the simile of the Cave. Keyt also explores problems which make the simile a dubious support for Plato's ideal city, ending with the suggestion that the Socratic method of cross-examination (the "elenchus") is presupposed, in the *Republic*, as a test of any king who claims to be a true philosopher ready to start the ideal city.

After Socrates sketches a most demanding higher education for the rulers-to-be of the ideal city, he returns to justice and injustice and their relations to our happiness. He now sketches various kinds of injustice, in cities and individuals, and argues with all his might that justice in the soul is better for us than any of these injustices. Rachel Singpurwalla's article helps us understand Socrates' defense of justice throughout the work and the controversies that have swirled around it since the mid-twentieth century. Recent commentators have tended to concede that the state of soul Socrates defined as just (and temperate, brave, and perhaps wise, in Book IV) is better for us than the states of soul he describes as unjust in the later books: perhaps because, unlike unjust souls, his just soul is well-functioning, like a healthy body, harmonious and at peace with itself. But since Socrates defined the just soul without reference to conduct or the good of others, why should he think, as he explicitly claims, that such a just soul would refrain from typically unjust actions such as embezzling, breaking promises, and so on? Plato may have secured a connection between his justice in the soul and happiness, but he seems to have lost any significant connection between his just soul and the typically just and unjust actions Thrasymachus and Glaucon had in mind in their challenge. Such a defense of justice suffers from a fallacy of irrelevance. David Sachs pressed this objection in 1963, and there has been no consensus on a good answer since then. Singpurwalla discusses the main answers that have been proposed: relying on the motivations of Plato's just person, or on an analysis of our desire for the Form of the Good as an objective good. She also points to some problems with these solutions; and suggests a positive answer of her own, relying once more on our desire for the good but interpreting that good to be unity or harmony within ourselves and with other persons.

With the Theory of Forms, the possible knowledge of them, and the analysis of the soul at hand, Socrates returns to the discussion he had initiated earlier (in Books II and III) of poetry and other works of art and completes the analysis and valuation of them on the basis of these new theories. He seeks to replace poetry as a teacher of what is real, true, and valuable, and place philosophy – love and knowledge of the Forms – in that role. And finally, through the great myth of Er about the possibility of an afterlife and even a return to life, he seeks to place our lives here and now in a larger perspective and, with the new theology also at hand, to suggest a defense of justice even in the possibly much greater life spans of our souls.

1

The Literary and Philosophical Style of the *Republic*

Christopher Rowe

1 Introduction

The *Republic* is by any standards a large work, occupying ten "books";[1] it is the second longest, after the *Laws*, which has twelve books, and it is very nearly four times the length of the next longest of Plato's works, the *Timaeus*. The *Republic*, however, considerably exceeds even the *Laws* in the sheer number of the topics it touches on, and in the overall complexity of its argument: themes, arguments, apparent digressions appear in such rapid succession that it is easy for the reader to lose his or her way. And yet this is no mere random or accidental pile. Far from it: explicit and implicit references forwards and backwards within the dialogue, and the way that the overall argument loops back on itself, make it clear that this is in fact – for all the apparent informality of its style – a work that was both designed and executed with extreme care.[2]

This complexity, and intricacy, of the *Republic* go some way towards explaining why, in the modern period,[3] it has tended to be regarded as Plato's masterwork. But that is not inevitable: as we move back through the 2,500 years that stretch between us and Plato's lifetime, we find other periods preferring the *Timaeus*, Plato's account of the physical universe (emblematic of Plato for the Italian Renaissance), or the *Phaedo* (centered on the soul's immortality, and on metaphysics, subjects particularly dear to "Middle Platonism"), or the inquiry into the nature of knowledge in the *Theaetetus* (a natural choice at a time when Plato's Academy took a skeptical turn). What particularly makes the *Republic* seem so central to us moderns is probably its peculiar combination of the ethical, the political, and the metaphysical, which seems alternately to resonate with or – more frequently – to provide a counterpoint to our own twentieth- and twenty-first-century preoccupations, particularly in ethics and politics.

Yet at the same time the interpretation of almost any aspect of the *Republic* remains more or less controversial. This is not just because of the difficulty of tracking its overall argument, but also because of the form in which it is written: as a *conversation*, reported by an "I,"[4] who turns out, some lines after the beginning of the work, to be Socrates; and a conversation whose direction, for all the reader knows, is partly determined by the other interlocutors: in the first book old man Cephalus, Cephalus' son Polemarchus, and above all the rhetorician Thrasymachus; in the remaining nine books Plato's elder brothers Glaucon and Adeimantus. Where Plato stands in relation to this – imaginary – conversation that he constructs, we the readers have no way of telling in advance. It is a fair guess that his viewpoint is, by and large, represented by Socrates' "I"; yet at the same time it is not at all obvious even where Socrates himself stands in relation to everything he says, among other reasons because he uses many different tones and registers. Moreover, any reader of the *Republic* who comes to it from other Platonic dialogues will find that the Socrates of this dialogue at least *seems* often to be saying things that are different from what his counterpart Socrates says in other dialogues.

One response is to try to prescind from any knowledge we have of what "Socrates" says elsewhere, and to focus exclusively on what he says in *this* dialogue; but then we have still to decide on the degree of firmness and seriousness with which he says it. (Maybe it is all just a provocation to us, to think things through for ourselves? Or on the other hand, maybe it is more than that, as comparison with other dialogues will in fact usually show: the more often a claim shows up, the less likely it is – one would suppose – to be a mere thought-experiment.) Another approach is to try to reconcile the Socrates of the *Republic* with other Socrateses, and then, when this fails, to explain apparently significant differences as changes of mind on Plato's part. Or – the alternative that comes closest to my own view – might it just be that, underlying the play of each and every dialogue, there is a kind of subterranean flow of thought that is forever – by and large, more or less – constant? Every reader of the *Republic*, on every reading, is forced to make such choices, and there is no set of instructions there to help us: Plato is happy to disappear behind his characters, leaving no explanatory notes or essays. Nor does it necessarily help very much to look at what *ancient* readers of Plato made of him. One might easily suppose, and indeed it has sometimes been supposed, that the greater nearness of Plato's ancient readers to the man himself, both in time and in terms of their philosophical and cultural assumptions, would make them better readers of his texts. But it is plain enough from the wide range of interpretations of Plato already available less than a century or two after his death that ancient readers too were faced with exactly the same sorts of choices that face us, and that they got things neither more right nor more wrong than we moderns do.[5]

So, given such an abundance of hermeneutical choices, which way should one turn? The approach I shall adopt in this chapter is to reject absolutely the possibility that Plato intended to leave his readers with an open text, that is, a text on which the reader is free to place his or her own interpretation. Given the current popularity – at least in some parts of academe – of varieties of relativism in literary theory, such a reading of the *Republic* might seem attractive enough; yet it does not square at all with Socrates' general tone in the dialogue as a whole. Whatever else we may want to say about the work, this much is incontrovertible: that the *Republic* is absolutely serious about the main proposal that formally shapes, or rather embraces, its whole structure – that is, the claim that *justice pays*, or in other words that the just person will be happier than anyone else, by virtue of being just. There are other Platonic dialogues that on the surface reach no conclusion, and are often taken to be specifically designed not to do so. These are mainly shorter dialogues, often labelled as "Socratic" (because they allegedly reflect more closely the ideas and methods of the historical Socrates, that master of dialectical examination: small wonder that his victims so often fail to come up with the goods!), but they also include the weighty *Theaetetus*, that favorite of the Academic skeptics. In such cases, the idea that Plato's main aim is to get the reader to *think for himself or herself* has real purchase, even though here too I myself think its attractions ultimately little more than superficial. But in the *Republic* the idea is a complete non-starter. Even at those many moments when Plato is setting out to challenge and provoke us, in the way that – and by virtue of the fact that – his character, Socrates, challenges and provokes his interlocutors, the purpose is not merely to shake us out of our existing assumptions, and get us thinking some other way (no matter which way). No: underlying the whole grand edifice is a substantive, and connected, set of ideas, which needs to be carefully excavated and reconstructed. For otherwise there is no accounting for the *passion* with which Socrates expresses himself. Among those many features that mark off the *Republic* from other philosophical works that we recognize as classics – its indirection, its tangled plot, and so on – is that its main speaker is plainly talking about things that not only matter to him, but evidently matter more to him than anything else. Further than that, he talks as if he thinks that they matter in the same way to *us*. Challenge, provocation, paradox: the purpose is to shock us out of our current ways of thinking, yes, but also *into* considering certain other ways. The only difficulty is to determine exactly what these are. What exactly, by way of substantive thoughts, does Plato want us to carry away from the *Republic*?

I shall go on to suggest certain fairly specific answers to this question. But first we need to answer an obvious objection (obvious, indeed, to anyone who even begins reading the *Republic*). If Plato is so anxious to communicate, or at any rate get us thinking about, certain substantive theses, why does he go about it in so roundabout a way? Why use dialogue, and dialogue of such informality (so closely mirroring, or pretending to mirror, the unpredictabilities of a real conversation), that we are left uncertain, by the time we have finished reading the whole, precisely what – beyond that claim that "justice pays" – we are meant to carry away with us from what we have just read? To answer such a question adequately would require at least a separate paper to itself. However I hazard the following thoughts as the basis of a proper answer. Plato's use of the dialogue form reflects his recognition of the distance that separates his own assumptions from those of any likely reader, and of the consequent requirement, if any effective communication is to take place at all, to find methods of mediating between apparently different starting points.[6] The underlying point here is that Platonic dialogue is as much a matter of dialogue between *positions* as it is between individuals: for all that Socrates tends to personalize his conversations with others ("Say what *you* think, not what others say!"), it is not persons but ideas that interest him, if only because he thinks that either the main or the only thing persons need is to get their ideas sorted out. And so it is with the *Republic*. The first book ends with what may look like a rather unsatisfactory defeat for Thrasymachus – defender of the advantages of injustice – at Socrates' hands; Plato then, at the beginning of the second book, has Glaucon and Adeimantus restate the case for injustice; they do not believe it themselves, but want to hear it answered. Yet, again, Plato (or his Socrates) has more than a merely theoretical interest in the issues he discusses. His aim is to draw *us* over from where we are now to where *he* is; and to that end he employs a variety of persuasive devices, including, where it suits him, the use of his (Socrates') interlocutors' or opponents' premises. (One clear example in the *Republic*, an example to which I shall return: when in Book II he is outlining the origins of cities, Socrates arrives at a community which lives the simplest of lives – the "true" city, he calls it at 372e, and "a healthy one, as one might put it"; but he is then forced, or pretends to be forced, by Glaucon to consider a "luxuriant" city, one "with a fever." This is what generations of modern readers, puzzlingly, have come to identify as the "ideal" city of Plato's *Republic*, when actually, if we take Socrates seriously at 372e, it is nothing of the sort: it is Glaucon's city, if also Glaucon's city radically transformed, its "fever" cured or held in check by the institution of philosopher-rulers.) In every context, I propose, even when he is beginning from assumptions that are not his own, there is a genuinely Platonic argument, and a genuinely Platonic position, in the offing. But the author rarely gives it to us straight – and how can he, when the kinds of ways in which he wants to talk about the world are so radically different from the ways we naturally talk about it, and the ways his immediate, contemporary Greek audience talked about it?[7] It is Plato's sense of that radical difference of perspective, combined with the urgent requirement to communicate (to change others' perspectives) that is the real, and deepest, explanation of his use of the dialogue. In the remainder of this chapter, I hope among other things to put some flesh on this so far rather bare, or inchoate, assertion.

2 New Beginnings, or Continuity? Contrasting Readings of the *Republic*

Serious modern readers of the *Republic* – from whom I exclude those who merely cherry-pick certain contexts or aspects, without taking account of the whole of which they form a part[8] – tend to treat the *Republic* as self-standing; and reasonably enough, given that that is how it is written, with no more than implicit reference to any other Platonic writing.[9] Of course, it is hard to ignore the fact that Plato did in fact write numerous other works. Yet the very tendency to treat the *Republic* as the, or a, master-work tends to reinforce the expectation that it should be readable, and intelligible, by itself. This, we tell ourselves, is the *mature* Plato, superseding and overpowering anything that went before. And then, since what went before was, in the main, that group of dialogues labelled "Socratic," we immediately have a new opposition, a new kind of contrast: the *Republic* – so the story goes – gives us a Plato breaking free from his master Socrates (or up to a point), becoming his own man. Indeed, some have thought this process visible in the *Republic* itself, for the first book looks very like a typical "Socratic" dialogue: a close encounter with a series of interlocutors, on a moral subject, ending in *aporia* or impasse. Just as Plato wrote a *Laches*, on courage, a *Euthyphro* on piety, a *Lysis* on "friendship" . . . so (the hypothesis runs) what we know as *Republic* Book I was originally – to invent a notional title – a *Thrasymachus* (on justice), which Plato then used as a kind of preface to the real *Republic*: nine books that show the way out of *aporia*, in a way that Socrates in those other dialogues seemed so reluctant to do.

This modern narrative, however, carries no necessity with it. It is certainly likely that *something* new is occurring with the *Republic*: Plato appears to be writing on a scale that he had not previously done, and to be allowing his Socrates to develop themes on a scale greater, and with a tone apparently more didactic, than more or less anything we find in those dialogues that can plausibly be dated earlier than the *Republic*.[10] Yet this *is* only a matter of scale, for in one way or another Socrates was always – even in the "Socratic" dialogues, and even while preserving his position as someone who knows nothing – prone to helping his interlocutors along, hazarding guesses, making proposals, and, most importantly, using his own convictions as premises in his arguments. The real difficulty for the modern narrative in question is that it tends to ignore all this, and to treat the "Socratic" dialogues as each consisting of a series of arguments that are either mainly destructive in intent (and anyway issue in impasse) or even if not, are ultimately unsatisfactory as a method for finding the truth. Small wonder, from this perspective, that Plato should have come to feel he had done all he could with the "Socratic method," and needed a different approach; the passage between the "Socratic" Book I and Books II–X of the *Republic* neatly marks the transition. But if the starting point for such a perspective on the *Republic* is false, and the Socrates of the earlier dialogues is neither primarily a destroyer, nor a man failing in his search for a satisfactory method, then there will be room for a reassessment. What if – and I here state one of the main premises of the present chapter – the presence of Book I in the *Republic* is intended to mark the *continuity*, not the discontinuity, between its style, and approach, and that of the rest of the work?

To begin to make sense of this proposal, the reader will need some kind of description of what is in Book I, and of what we find in the other books. I shall first give a fairly neutral description of the whole, and then give two alternative readings of that whole: first a more standard reading, then the one that I prefer – the one, that is, which emphasizes the *unity* of the *Republic*.

A neutral summary

Book I: Socrates goes to the house of the elderly Cephalus, and the conversation between the two of them comes round to the subject of justice: Cephalus suggests what he thinks justice is (telling the truth and paying one's debts), and Socrates raises some objections to the suggestion. Cephalus' son Polemarchus then takes over the discussion, and Socrates argues against various suggestions *he*, Polemarchus, makes about what justice is; finally Thrasymachus erupts into the conversation, and proposes that justice is whatever is to the advantage of the stronger – which has the effect of identifying justice with what is commonly called injustice. The discussion between Thrasymachus and Socrates, in which Socrates means to refute Thrasymachus' position, gradually turns to the question: which is better for the agent, justice or injustice? Socrates comments at the very end of the book that they really needed to establish, first, what justice actually is, for if they don't know that, how can they tell even whether it is a virtue, or whether it makes a person happy or unhappy?

Books II–IV: Glaucon and Adeimantus establish that Socrates thinks justice one of those things that are desirable both in themselves and for the sake of their consequences, whereas (they say) most people think it only desirable for its consequences, not in itself. They then restate the case for injustice, and challenge Socrates to show that justice is desirable even apart from its consequences. Socrates accepts the challenge, but proposes first to search for the nature of justice. This he means to do by looking for justice on the larger scale: by constructing a just *city*, seeing in what feature, exactly, of such a city justice lies, then applying the same kind of analysis to the just individual, on the basis that what justice is should be the same everywhere (whatever the scale of what instantiates it). Socrates' first stab at such a city, based on a strict separation of functions, Glaucon describes as a city of pigs; allowing it more luxuries then leads to the requirement for a police- and warrior-function – for "guards," the description of whose nature, education, and way of life takes us already well into Book IV. (Some of the "guards" will be selected as rulers, and these become the "guards" proper: Plato's legendary "Guardians.") Because – it is agreed – the city that Socrates, with Plato's brothers, has constructed is good, it must possess the virtues of a city: wisdom, courage, "self-control," and justice. Wisdom will be found in the rulers, courage in the warrior-class, "self-control" in the agreement between these two groups and the third and largest group in the city, the producers, as to who should rule (who would want to be ruled by the ignorant rather than the wise?); justice, for its part, is identified with that very principle with which Socrates started his construction of the city, the separation of func-

tions – the city is just in virtue of the fact that each group keeps to its own function (and in particular that ruling is restricted to the group qualified by nature
and upbringing to rule). So to individual justice: the soul is found to consist of
three "parts," corresponding to the main divisions of the city, and thus Socrates
can apply the same analysis to justice in the individual (soul) as he has to justice
in the city: a soul will be just if its three parts each perform their proper functions. Glaucon is ready even now to declare the case for justice made, but
Socrates suggests that there is much more ground still to be covered: in particular, they need to examine other, diseased, types of city and individual.

Book V: But before he can embark on that task, Socrates is now forced to
explain a remark he made about the need for the guards to hold their women
and children in common; first, he argues that women, so far as nature allows,
should be required to share the ruling function – and so the education that goes
with it – with the men. Just one change, he suggests, will be needed to bring
about this radical new society: kings must become philosophers, and philosophers kings (and queens). The book ends with a justification of this proposal:
only philosophers have access to true reality (the Platonic "Forms") and so to
true knowledge; non-philosophers are perpetually in a state of mere *belief.*

Books VI–VII: Socrates contrasts real philosophers with those currently called
"philosophers"; he then describes the subjects they will need to study –
including the highest subject of all, the Form of the Good, of which he can only
give an indirect account, by means of similes. This completes his account of the
good city and the corresponding individual (the philosopher).

Books VIII–IX: Socrates turns to the task he would have taken up at the
beginning of Book V had he not been prevented. He describes four inferior types
of city, and four inferior types of individual that correspond to them – all in
terms of a mock-epic story of decline from the good city and the kind of individual that gives it its character. First there is "timocracy," and the "timocratic"
individual, whose sights are set on honor; then oligarchy and the oligarchic individual, whose life revolves around material possessions, but in line with the
"necessary" sort of appetites; then democracy and the democratic individual, who
has no fixed aims but flirts with one kind of life after another, and is ruled by
"unnecessary" appetites; and finally tyranny, and the tyrannical sort of individual, himself ruled by an all-consuming master-lust. This tyrannical type is the
supreme representative of injustice, and can now be compared with the good
individual – the philosopher: the tyrannical life, as Socrates confirms by means
of a series of three arguments, is many (actually 729) times less happy than the
good man's.

Book X: Socrates picks up once more (from Book III) on the subject of the
place of the arts, and especially of poetry, in the good city – but now in light
of the division of the soul in Book IV, and the metaphysical ideas introduced in
Books V–VII. He then offers a kind of proof of the immortality of the soul,
before rounding off the whole with a myth: the myth of Er, who came back

from the dead to give a perspective on human existence from the standpoint of eternity, and to describe the fate of human souls after their separation from the body at death. The souls of the unjust will be punished, those of the just rewarded. Human rewards and punishments will be distributed similarly. So from every point of view justice pays, and injustice does not.

A standard reading of the argument of the Republic[11]

In Book I, Socrates attempts to refute first Polemarchus, then Thrasymachus, by means of a set of arguments none of which is clearly successful, although they are together sufficient to send Thrasymachus packing. Starting in Book II, Plato then tries to do better: he has Glaucon and Adeimantus restate the case for injustice, after which he sets out to define justice, the job he failed to do in Book I, as a necessary preliminary to answering the main question, now properly set up by the two brothers, about the benefits of justice. The answer he now gives – through Socrates – is much longer and more elaborate. While it is, ultimately, no more successful than what he had to offer in Book I, the attempt provides an opportunity for him to develop a new and specific, if sketchy and preliminary, account of what justice is, and to deliver an explicit account (or as explicit as anything is in Plato) of a new and distinctive moral theory and a distinctive moral psychology, based on the idea of a tripartite soul (Book IV), and an apparently new kind of metaphysics[12] (Books V–VII), along with a sketch both of an ideal form of state (Books II–III), and of existing, rival forms (Books VIII–IX), and much else besides.[13] The arguments of the latter and main part of Book IX begin to round off the case for justice, which is completed by the end of Book X. Here, finally, the external rewards – the "consequences" – of justice can be added in, the case for its inherent desirability having been completed in Book IX. The outcome of the whole is as complete a picture of Plato's view of human nature, of the individual in society, and of the place of humanity in the grand scheme of things,[14] as we may find anywhere in the corpus of his writings.

An alternative reading of the argument of the Republic

In Book I, Socrates deals first with Polemarchus, then with Thrasymachus, partly by using their own premises (especially when it is a matter of clarifying what exactly they are saying), partly by tacitly using premises of his own: Polemarchus is induced to accept these, on the basis of analogies, whereas Thrasymachus tends rather to try to hold out and stick to his own perspectives. Among those peculiarly Socratic premises[15] are: that a friend is someone useful (334e–335a: actually a premise volunteered by Polemarchus);[16] that harming someone means making them worse (335b–c);[17] that it does not belong to a just person to harm anyone (335e);[18] that justice is a kind of cleverness or wisdom (350a–c); and that the unjust are at odds even with themselves (351e–352a).[19]

At the beginning of Book II, Socrates says what kind of good he thinks justice is,[20] and Glaucon and Adeimantus restate the case for injustice. Socrates is at a loss, or says he is: he actually thought that what he was saying to Thrasymachus showed that justice was a better thing than injustice. He also knows that the brothers are unconvinced by the case they have just presented. But he can't stand by and see justice attacked, so he'll do his best (368b). (Evidently, then, the arguments he put to Thrasymachus were not really disabled by his failure to say first what justice is; and it seems to follow that the account he will go on to give of it in Book IV will be of that very thing he was defending in Book I.) Now he begins his construction of a good city – and arrives, first, at what Glaucon describes as a "city of pigs" because of the simple life Socrates envisages its citizens as living.[21] Once again Socrates marks the distance between himself and the others: *he* thinks this kind of city the "true" one. But he will discuss the "luxuriant," modern kind that Glaucon has in mind "because by looking at such a city we might actually see how justice and injustice are engendered in cities" (372e), i.e., presumably, what causes a city to be just and what causes it to cease to be so. The "true," "healthy" city, which satisfied itself with necessities, would itself have been a good and just one; in Glaucon's "fevered" city, by contrast, with its requirement for all sorts of luxuries, justice will require additional measures in order to cure, or check, the "fever." Somehow or other, says Socrates, it is the pursuit of things beyond the bare necessities from which "evils come about for cities, both on the individual and the public level" (373e); even the need for soldiers ("guards") – whether war is good or bad – comes about from the same source.

A discussion of the qualities required from this new addition – soldier-guards – to the strength of the city (they must among other things be spirited, and philosophical) then leads Socrates and Glaucon to ask, in the remainder of Book II, and in Book III, what sort of *education*, and way of life, will produce such paragons: in short, one that will teach them to love and hate the right things even before they know the reasons for loving and hating them (see, e.g., 401e–402a). Some of them will rule, others will be ruled: the rulers will be chosen according to their ability to withstand the involuntary loss of their true beliefs (for who would want to lose beliefs that are actually *true*?), especially the belief that their main aim must be to pursue what benefits the city, on the basis that this is also what will benefit themselves, for this will be the basis of the wisdom needed for their function of guarding (412c–414a).

Book IV starts with an objection from Adeimantus, that Socrates' "guards" will not get anything out of their rule, in the way other rulers do: land, big houses, furniture, money. Socrates responds that he wouldn't be surprised if they were actually better off as they are, without such things (420b: an echo of his praise for the "city of pigs"), but in any case his purpose was to construct a city that was happy (happy, on his account, because just), not a city that merely contained some happy people – and wealth and poverty both interfere with people's capacity to fulfil their functions. So: the city has wisdom (in the ruler-guards), courage (in the "auxiliary" guards, the fighters), and "self-control" (insofar as rulers, auxiliaries and the rest, the producers, all agree about who should rule); it is also just, in virtue of the fact that the rulers rule, the fighters fight, and the producers produce: each "does his (or her) own." Or, in other words, the city is just because wisdom – as described, in terms of an understanding about what is truly good for oneself – is in charge, and not the rather different virtues of the warrior and producer classes. Next, the *soul* is found to fall into three analogous "parts," each with its own qualities, and each capable in principle of lording it over the others; and, again analogously with the city, the *just* soul will be the one in which reason, and a reasoned view of one's proper ends, governs the whole, while the other parts both perform their own properly assigned roles (providing the competitive and the more basic appetitive drives), under the control of reason.

Book V starts with women and children, and then goes on to that most provocative of all proposals, that *philosophers should rule* (though in effect this point has more than once been allowed to slip in already, almost unnoticed). Why? Because they have *knowledge* where others merely have *belief*. Or, more specifically, because they are concerned with beauty and ugliness, just and unjust, good and bad, "in short, all kinds of things"[22] *in themselves*, not merely as they are instantiated, or appear to be instantiated, in particular things and actions. (Socrates has already given us two implicit examples of this kind of approach, first when he asked whether Adeimantus was right to identify land, big houses, etc. as happy-making, and so good: the question about what particular things are good will come after discovering *what it is* for something to be good[23] – something on which the ruler-guards are already required to have a handle at the end of Book III. The second example lies in Socrates' insistence, in Book IV, that justice is not a matter merely of performing just actions; it is rather a state of the soul that leads to certain sorts of actions – or, better, that feature in virtue of which individual souls are, or might be, just.)

Books VI–VII: The central topic is now *the good* – through which, somehow, "both just things and the rest become useful and beneficial" (505a)[24] – and the higher education of the ruler-guards that revolves around it. Curiously, although Socrates describes the acquisition of knowledge of the good in terms of vision, of seeing a special kind of object (i.e., with "the mind's eye"), he has nothing to recommend by way of a method of acquiring such knowledge beyond a kind of process that looks remarkably similar to the sort of dialectic with which he himself operated in the "Socratic" dialogues (and in *Republic* Book I).[25]

Books VIII–IX: A description of the four inferior types of city and individual, followed by clinching arguments for the superior benefits of the just life, based on the tripartite division of the soul. But now the just life is represented by the life of the philosopher: the just person *is* the philosopher, because it is in the philosopher, and only in him (or her) that reason properly rules over the irrational, and each part of the soul "does its own." The philosopher, Socrates claims to show, enjoys pleasures that far outweigh those of the "victory-lover" (representing those dominated by their higher irrational, or "spirited," part) and of the "money-lover" (money being the chief means by which the appetites belonging to the lowest part are most readily satisfied: 580e–581a). In fact, providing that the rational part enjoys its proper pleasures, so will the other two parts enjoy theirs; whereas if one of the other two parts gets control, then all three will find themselves going after "alien and untrue pleasure" (587a).

Book X: After the second treatment of poetry and the arts, Socrates turns to the beneficial consequences of justice: the just will be rewarded by men and gods alike, while the unjust, if they do not suffer human punishment, will get more vicious and miserable (IX591a–b), and finally will be found out and punished by the gods. The greatest reward, and the greatest punishment, have to do with the choice of future lives: philosophers will choose wisely, others will make the wrong choice. So it is up to us: "let us do well" (the closing two words in the Greek text).[26]

3   Plato and his Audience, Plato and Socrates

On this third (and my preferred) reading the various, and otherwise apparently diverse, parts of the *Republic* hang closely together; the Socrates of Books II–X is still recognizably the same as the Socrates of Book I. That itself should probably count in favor of the reading proposed; if it is true of artistic products in general, and of Platonic dialogues in particular, that they should possess some kind of unity. As for the reason why Plato left us having to dig so hard to find that unity, I have already given the outline of an explanation (at the end of 1 above): because he is perpetually moving, and trying to mediate between, his own (Socratic) perspective and that of his audience; or, to put it another way, he tends to be arguing simultaneously on two different levels. Here are two further examples:[27]

(A)   At the end of Book X, as we have seen, Socrates claims that he is now licensed to add in the "consequences" of justice, having met the challenge to show its benefits "in itself." This he does in a rather complex way: he first asks if he can have back the rewards that tend to go to those who merely *seem* just (612d); then suggests that, since the gods both see everything and care for justice, whatever in fact happens to the just – whether "poverty, disease, or some other seemingly bad thing" – must be or turn out good for them (612e–613b); then proposes that the really just will after all do better, even in terms of human rewards, than the merely "clever but unjust" (613b–c); finally he asks to be allowed to *say* the things about the just that Glaucon said about the unjust: that they'll achieve power (if they want it), marry whomever they want to marry, and so on (613c–d). Glaucon is impressed, but it hardly seems as if he should be so impressed, not just because there is no guarantee that the just will in fact get the things in question, but because – as Socrates reminds Glaucon even as he proposes them[28] – it is not at all clear that they are good things at all (and from Socrates' point of view they are not). So *these* aren't the beneficial consequences *Socrates* has in mind. For those, we need to turn to the ensuing myth about the afterlife, in which we seem to be told that those who have lived a life without injustice will (a) spend some time seeing wonderful sights (Platonic Forms?) in the heavens (614e–615a), and (b), if they have lived *philosophical* lives, will be best placed to make an intelligent choice of the life to live when next they return to a physical body – because they are best able to understand what is truly beneficial (618b–619e). Quite how much, if any, of the myth we are to take at all literally is uncertain (though we should not by any means dismiss out of hand the possibility that Plato believed not only in an immortal soul, but in an eternal cycle of death and rebirth). However we should note that the one reward that will be guaranteed – for the ideally just person, the philosopher, and in virtue of his philosophy – is that he is best able to make the best choice of life, i.e., whether after death or (if we take the myth as allegory) in life. And this is the kind of "consequence" to which Plato, and his Socrates, commit themselves elsewhere;[29] one of a very different sort from the one Glaucon has in mind here in Book X, or back at the beginning of Book II.

(B) When in Book IV Socrates arrives at his analysis of the various virtues (wisdom, courage, "self-control," and justice), he seems at first sight to be treating them rather differently from the way in which he tends to treat them in the "Socratic" dialogues: there the other virtues themselves tend to be *identified* with wisdom, whereas in *Republic* IV they are clearly separated from it, insofar as they are made to belong either to groups of individuals who specifically are what they are (warrior-auxiliaries, producers) because they lack wisdom, or to parts of the soul that lack reason altogether. However, as I suggested in section 2 above, the idea of justice as wisdom appears, however inconspicuously, in *Republic* I. Furthermore, the Book IV treatment of the virtues comes heavily qualified as provisional: at 504a Socrates tells us that "we said that it was another longer way round to see [the virtues] as perfectly as possible"[30] – and this in a context where he also tells us that it is "by means of [the good that] both just things and the rest become useful and beneficial" (505a), and that a guard who doesn't know "how it is that just and fine things are good" will not be worth much (506a). By the time we learn, in the myth, that those who "partake in virtue by habit, without philosophy' make especially bad choices (619c–d), we surely have sufficient grounds for suspecting that no one apart from the guards can, strictly, be virtuous at all, and that the accounts given of the virtues are not only provisional but (strictly) inadequate. They are, one might say, Glauconian rather than

Socratic virtues, just as Kallipolis is more Glaucon's kind of city than it is Socrates': see section 1 above. The argument works, if it works at all, because the account of *justice* is good enough for its purposes: not merely in the sense that it allows the argument to go through, but insofar as it is sufficiently close to what Socrates would want to say about justice on his own account – provided that reason's "doing its own" is a matter of its ruling with *wisdom*. That makes it not merely an argument to satisfy, persuade, Glaucon and people like him, but also – up to a point – an argument that interests Socrates (and Plato).

I propose that two main conclusions should be drawn from all of this. The first is that the reader must be perpetually aware of the need, in principle, to distinguish between what Socrates says when speaking with his own voice (or, perhaps to put it more strictly, since "Socrates" is always under his author's control: Plato's), and what he says when speaking to the assumptions and perspectives of others, perhaps including ourselves. The point, to repeat, is that Plato is not in business merely as a philosopher, but also to *persuade* us (as Socrates tries to persuade his interlocutors in the written text). Keen though Plato often is, by implication, to distinguish what he does from what orators and rhetoricians do, there is undoubtedly a rhetorical aspect to his writing, insofar as it is designed specifically to address an audience of a certain kind (that being, at the least, one unfamiliar with, and more than likely to be hostile to, his own starting points). The resulting mixture, between what he is prepared to own and what he merely borrows or appropriates, is nowhere clearer than in his use of myths like that in *Republic* X: using basic themes that will have been utterly familiar to his original audience, but then adapting these, and using them for purposes that are his and absolutely no one else's. It has commonly been supposed that Plato uses myths as a kind of last-ditch appeal when all rational argument has been exhausted; the truth is rather that myth is just one of the many persuasive devices Plato has at his disposal – argument being another. This is not to say that there is no difference between "rational" argument and telling stories, just to emphasize that there can be a persuasive (rhetorical) element to philosophical argument too: everything depends on the premises that are chosen.

The second conclusion to be drawn is that beneath the general flow of the argument – and rhetoric – of the *Republic* there lies a hard core of connected ideas. But this point needs to be taken in a very particular way. The point is not just that Plato has a set of ideas that he happens to believe in, and to which he gives us some sort of limited access.[31] (Nor, I should add, does it preclude the possibility that the dialogue is sometimes experimenting, exploring: if nothing else, dramatic dialogue is a highly versatile form.) Rather, the point is that a claim like "justice pays" is to be understood in terms of a *particular conception of what justice is*, and of a *particular conception of what it is for something to "pay."* Justice will be something along the lines of the rational part's ruling rather than the irrational parts (perhaps equating with wisdom's rule, but evidently on condition that "spirit" and "appetite" are also in the right condition[32]); in turn, a thing's "paying" will be a matter of its being good for the agent, according to Socrates' unusual notion of what that good is (certainly not land, big houses, power, or anything of that sort).

In general, I claim (and this is likely to be the most controversial aspect of this chapter), that what I have called the "hard core" of ideas at the center of the *Republic* is absolutely continuous with those ideas that surface, and dominate, in the so-called "Socratic" dialogues and elsewhere – including (as I have suggested) the first book of the *Republic* itself: ideas such as that virtue is knowledge, that a just (wise) person will harm no one, even – in the words of that other famous Socratic paradox – that "no man goes wrong willingly."[33] (These, for convenience, I label as "Socratic" ideas; there is in fact a good chance that they go back to the historical Socrates.) What cannot be shown here, and will have to be taken on trust, is that this is no mere succession of adventitious thoughts, but rather constitutes aspects of a systematic theory about human action and motivation.[34] It is this ("Socratic") theory that, by and large, forms the background to, and from time to time surfaces in, the overt argument of the *Republic*; and it is his allegiance to that theory that causes Socrates to step back – as my third reading of the dialogue in section 2 above shows him sometimes doing – from that argument. All the more reason, then, to start (as I proposed doing in that same third reading) from this *Socratic* point of view when we are trying to understand those numerous aspects of the *Republic* that Plato seems to leave relatively indeterminate: especially, but not exclusively, its metaphysical aspects. But it follows that we need to learn to give up calling that point of view "Socratic." Plato and Socrates – who is, at the very least, that Socrates of the (so-called) "Socratic" dialogues – are so much at one that there is little purpose in continuing to contrast them. Some aspects of the *Republic*, and other (so-called) "middle" dialogues – especially their sheer scale, and the fact that Socrates suddenly seems to have so much more to say – tend to make these works seem a world apart from the generally shorter dialogues that evidently preceded them. If we look more closely, however, the style – philosophical, literary, and also rhetorical – is not so different; and neither, once we have come to understand that style, is the content it is designed to convey.[35]

Notes

1 The division into "books" no doubt once reflected a physical division into manageable papyrus rolls; they sometimes but not always mark off sections of the argument of the whole. (The division into *ten* books may well in fact not be original.)

2 Cf. Dionysius of Halicarnassus, *De compositione verborum*, p. 208 in Reiske; Diogenes Laertius III.37. (I owe both references to Hackforth 1952: 165 n. 2.)

3   The "modern period" in Platonic criticism is usually counted as beginning in the nineteenth century: see Taylor 2002: 73–84.

4   The dialogue begins "I went down yesterday to the Piraeus with Glaucon [Plato's brother] son of Ariston [Plato's father]."

5   Ancient readings of Plato are often different from modern ones, though the latter usually turn out to be special variants of the former: the *skeptical* reading of the so-called New Academy, for example, has a counterpart in the kind of modern reading that likes to stress the aporetic and dialectical aspects of the dialogues, while modern accounts of Plato that stress its *doctrinal* content often hark back deliberately to Plato's immediate successors in the Academy, or else to the Middle Platonists or to Neoplatonism.

6   We may compare here some of the things Socrates has to say, at the end of the *Phaedrus*, about the need of the expert speaker or writer to adapt what he says to the souls of his audience (*Phaedrus* 270a–271b; 277b–c). One standard explanation of Plato's use of dialogue form is that it is the only form that would have been consistent with his view of the nature of philosophy, and of true learning and understanding: as a matter not of absorbing *ex cathedra* statements, but of coming to see things for oneself. This is surely *part* of the explanation, and an important part, but only at a very general level; there is much more to be said about the particular strategies, and goals, that are facilitated by the dialogue form.

7   Take as one central example talk about "goods": we would likely take it for granted that health, and life itself, are inherently good, as Plato's original audience would have done; Plato's Socrates thinks it false that they are inherently – always – good. The problem, for Plato, is how to set up a conversation between two sides who differ so radically in what they say, and think – or, as he would have preferred to put it, between himself, Socrates, and a world that managed to get things so very badly wrong. For the very large theoretical issues all this will raise, see Penner and Rowe, forthcoming.

8   "Literary" and "philosophical" style in Plato come together, in the sense that the philosophy – the argument – is never intelligible in separation from its full context: it always requires taking into account who is speaking, to whom, in what circumstances, in what tone, and so on (for some of the reasons why this is so, see the last paragraph of section 1 above, and section 3 below).

9   That, of course, is consistent with its dramatic form, of an orally reported conversation. Any explicit reference would mean keeping at least some of the same *dramatis personae*; that Plato rarely does this between any two dialogues is perhaps one mark of how little interested he is in cross-references. But we should not overdo this argument: mere overlap of ideas between dialogues will already tend to give us such cross-references – just without that reference to the *personae* to whom they happened to be attached. For one such central case see n. 24 below.

10 On the dating of Plato's dialogues, see Kahn 2002: 93–127.

11 What follows will be something of a caricature: no interpreter has ever read the *Republic* quite like this. My aim, however, is no more than to give a flavor of a typical *sort* of (modern) reading of the dialogue.

12 A metaphysics, that is, which also provides a basis – though Plato does not himself spell this out – both for the basic claim about justice (that it pays) and for the moral theory of the *Republic* in general.

13 Especially an account of primary education (Books II–III, perhaps with the first part of Book X), then of a special and higher kind of education, designed to produce philosopher-kings (Books VI–VII).

14 This especially in the myth in Book X, which includes a cosmic aspect.

15 The evidence for Socrates' acceptance of these premises comes from outside the *Republic*; here in *Republic* I, they are introduced by a variety of different means. However, it seems not unreasonable to suppose that it is more than a coincidence that he now happily uses the same premises to refute a position he clearly wants to reject.

16 See, e.g., *Lysis* 214e–215c.

17 An idea implied *passim* – if virtue is wisdom, and wisdom is the only thing unconditionally good (*Lysis*, *Euthydemus*, *Apology*).

18 See *Crito* 48e–49d.

19 See *Lysis* 214b–e.

20 It is natural to suppose that when he says he thinks justice good both in itself and for its consequences, he has the same sorts of consequences – i.e. external consequences, e.g. in terms of reputation – as the brothers; and indeed in Book X he will claim that justice will have such consequences. But we need not assume that that will impress Socrates as much as it will impress Glaucon and Adeimantus. In fact, on the reading I am here proposing, Socrates has a quite different sort of "consequence" in mind. See below.

21 What immediately sparks off Glaucon's description is Socrates' provocative suggestion that the citizens will roast *acorns* over their fire (372c–d).

22 The Greek has *kai pantôn tôn eidôn*, where *eidos* is one of the usual terms for a Platonic "Form." That is how it is usually translated here; however, at least for a Thrasymachus, who is still there and listening, the word is most likely to read in a quite untechnical sense ("kind of thing," "sort"); and in fact there are good reasons for not supposing that Plato believed in forms of ugliness, injustice, and bad. No doubt the whole context is *ultimately* about "Forms" of a Platonic sort (whatever a Platonic Form might be), but the immediate point that is being made does not require anything but the elementary assumption that it is not only possible but useful to think about something like beauty or justice or good without identifying these with particular (allegedly) beautiful, just, or good things.

23 This is a central Socratic point: other things are *made good* by knowledge (*Apology*), or are not good without it (*Euthydemus*) – because their usefulness depends on our knowing how to use them rightly.

24 Specifically, what is involved here is the *idea* – I here transliterate the Greek word – of the good, *idea* being the other Greek term Plato uses for "Form" in his special usage. But the fundamental conception involved is one that Glaucon has heard about "not infrequently" (504e), and "often"; it is also one that is familiar to readers of Plato's "Socratic" dialogues. See further section 3 below. (This is one case of the "overlap of ideas" between dialogues referred to in n. 9 above, one to which Plato carefully draws our attention.)

25 See especially 534b–c: "whoever is not able to mark off the Form [*idea*] of the good, separating it in his account [*logos*] from everything else, and as if in battle coming successfully through all challenges [*elenchoi*: "attempts at refutation," "test"(?)],

eager to test [*elenchein*, that is, "refute," "test"(?) what he is saying] not according to opinion [*doxa*] but according to being [*ousia*], and makes his passage in all of this with his account [*logos*] still standing – you'll not say that a person in this condition knows either the good itself or any other good at all."

26 I.e. let us do the right thing for ourselves (for which we need wisdom), and so be happy ("fare well").

27 The first consisted in the contrast between the "city of pigs" and the "feverish" city (which he nevertheless goes on to call Kallipolis, "Beautiful City"; and after all its fever *is* under control).

28 "They'll achieve power (*if they want it*)."

29 See n. 23 above: the acquisition and possession of goods, and so of happiness, flows from wisdom (even if, as the *Lysis* suggests, happiness is in fact also identical to wisdom: see Penner and Rowe, forthcoming).

30 The reference back is apparently to IV.435d, where in fact the "longer way round" is not so much to the virtues but to answering the question whether the soul has three parts or not. However the two subjects are, in the *Republic*, vitally connected.

31 This is the outcome of the kind of approach that tends to treat Plato's famous "unwritten doctrines" as central to the understanding of the dialogues; see, e.g., Szlezák 1999.

32 That is, because wisdom will depend on the irrational parts being kept down. In any case, justice is still wisdom; which is to say, just acts (the ones we ordinarily call just: see 442b–443b) are properly understood as wise acts. Socrates is not here talking about some kind of "justice" known only to himself, but the justice we all talk about, and Thrasymachus, Glaucon, and Adeimantus are talking about, even if they are not clear about it (see Penner and Rowe, forthcoming, esp. Part II).

33 See *Republic* 505d–506a, where every soul is said to pursue, and do everything for the sake of, the good, where the context makes clear that it must be the real good that is being talked about.

34 For a full justification of this particular claim, see Penner and Rowe, forthcoming.

35 An important qualification is needed here: at least one of the central ideas in the *Republic* is quite distinctly *non*-Socratic. In what I am choosing to treat as the "Socratic" theory, all desire is for the real good; if we go for what is in fact bad, that is simply because of ignorance. But in *Republic* IV, Plato's Socrates specifically argues, and goes out of his way to argue, for the existence of desires that are not for the real good: the desires of the two irrational parts. What is more, this is no flash in the pan, for the argument of the dialogue continually presupposes that the desires of the lower parts can not only counteract, and nullify, rational desires, but can actually pervert reason, so that the agent comes to devote himself to *their* projects (or what would be their projects, if they could devise any such things for themselves). True, Book X does suggest that in its "true" state, uncorrupted by association with the body, the soul is a unity (611b–d). But that hardly helps, since the argument of the dialogue is either primarily or exclusively concerned with the soul as it is in a body. It seems a plain fact that the *Republic* abandons this one particular aspect of the Socratic theory – the one that has it that all desire is good-directed. (For one statement of the possible, and considerable, consequences of this shift, see Rowe 2003: 17–32.) And yet, in a way, that only serves to make it all the more

striking how much else of the theory Plato actually preserves – even the claim that no one goes wrong willingly (see above); for in the *Republic*, as much as in the "Socratic" dialogues, and indeed as in the *Laws* (860a–861a), any action that does not in fact contribute to the agent's good is unwilling or involuntary (cf. *Republic* 505d–e and "every soul pursues the good in everything"; also 412c–414a, on the involuntary nature of any loss of true beliefs). So actions done under the influence of irrational desires are involuntary, as are even actions done on the basis of false beliefs; what the agent still wants is what is really good for him – what reason, uncorrupted, would tell him is really good for him.

References

Hackforth, R. (1952) *Plato's* Phaedrus, Cambridge: Cambridge University Press.

Kahn, C. (2002) "On Platonic chronology," in J. Annas and C. Rowe (eds.) *New Perspectives on Plato, Modern and Ancient*, Cambridge, MA: Harvard University Press (for the Center for Hellenic Studies).

Penner, T., and C. Rowe (forthcoming) *Plato's* Lysis, Cambridge: Cambridge University Press.

Rowe, C. (2003) "Plato, Socrates, and developmentalism," in N. Reshotko (ed.) *Desire, Identity and Existence: Essays in Honour of T. M. Penner*, Kelowna, BC: Academic Printing and Publishing.

Szlezák, T. A. (1999) *Reading Plato*, trans. G. Zanker, London: Routledge (*Platon lesen* first published 1993).

Taylor, C. C. W. (2002) "The origins of our present paradigms," in J. Annas and C. Rowe (eds.) *New Perspectives on Plato, Modern and Ancient*, Cambridge, MA: Harvard University Press (for the Center for Hellenic Studies).

2

Allegory and Myth in Plato's *Republic*

Jonathan Lear

I

It is by now a terrifying commonplace – agreed to by people across the political spectrum, indeed across the divide of civilizations – that our future well-being, and that of future generations, depends on shaping the hearts and minds of the young. Why do we think this? And do we have any idea how to do it well? Plato is the first person in the western tradition to think seriously about these questions and it is worth going back to him; not only as a return to origins, but because there are aspects of his thought which are still not well understood.

Plato's famous account of how to educate youth comes in the immediate aftermath of a spectacular breakdown of rational argument between two adults. In *Republic* I, Socrates and Thrasymachus argue over whether it is best to be just, even if one could get away with being unjust – and by the end Thrasymachus is reduced to sarcastic silence, while Socrates "wins" what he himself recognizes as a hollow victory. It has often been suggested that Plato is here dramatizing a failure of the Socratic method, the elenchus. And, no doubt, Socrates does adapt his method in the remaining books of the *Republic*. But looking at the breakdown, it seems clear that what is at stake is not some *particular* form of argument – as though if we made a few adjustments, it would come out all right. Rather, the problem seems to be that rational argument itself is coming too late. Thrasymachus already has an outlook on the world, and he will tend to recognize good and bad arguments in terms of that outlook. The problem then is not just the limitations of elenchus: there is a question of how any good argument could properly influence someone whose outlook is distorted and distorting.

So the pressing questions become: How are outlooks formed? What is it to have a good outlook? How might one go about shaping one? To address these questions, Socrates not only changes his method, he changes his interlocutors. Glaucon and Adeimantus are young, and they are exceptional (II.367e–368b).

They are able to pose a stunning challenge to justice, and yet are not convinced by their own arguments. Socrates suggests that there is something divine about their characters that leaves them open to conduct a genuine investigation with him. We shall investigate what this openness could be, but for the moment, it is Adeimantus who makes clear what a remarkable achievement this is. Glaucon has already challenged Socrates with an argument that what matters for happiness is only *appearing* to be just, not really being just. But it is Adeimantus who shows how this outlook is already built into normal ethical education. Fathers encourage their sons to be just because of all the societal benefits they will acquire by being known to be moral (II.363a–b). But these rewards are compatible with simply appearing to be just. And the poets suggest that the gods do not themselves behave justly. Indeed, according to the poets, rich people can buy off the gods with sacrifices (II.363e–366d). In short, the ethical outlook being instilled in contemporary Athens is unknowingly hypocritical: on the surface justice is being praised, while just under the surface is the cynical message that all that really matters is appearance.

Note what a challenge this is for the idea of reflective equilibrium as a test for one's ethical beliefs. If in raising the question of how to live, we reach out to the "wisdom" of our parents, indeed to the "wisdom" of the most highly respected cultural sources, we may simply be reaching out to the accumulated prejudice of our age. And if we test it against our own sense of right and wrong, we will unwittingly be "testing" it against the same outlook – albeit one that has been instilled in us when we were young. It will *seem* to us that we will be asking and answering reflective questions, but we will simply be reinforcing the prejudices of the day.

Even philosophical debate – at least, of a familiar sort – isn't going to help. So, to take a salient example, if we want to test our ethical commitments against an imaginary opponent, whom we might call "the skeptic," can we think of a better example than Thrasymachus? As we debate with "the skeptic," we *think* we are confronting a radical alternative. This encourages the illusion that we are investigating all the possibilities there are. It becomes hard to see that these positions are of a piece. Thus once an ethical outlook has been instilled, it is difficult to induce reflective discomfort. For all the debates that have occurred, Adeimantus tells us that no one has *ever* questioned justice and injustice except in terms of the reputation, prestige, and rewards they bring (II.366e).

II

For Plato, the human psyche is itself a psychological achievement. The infant does not have a fully formed psyche; at most he or she has the capacity to acquire and develop psychological structures. And this formation is crucially shaped by the social environment. Cultural messages penetrate and mould the psyche in ways that are often not well understood (II.377b; III.401c–e). So we need to understand what these meanings are and how this process works.

There is no need to dwell on Socrates' well-known critique of content: we are to eliminate tales of the gods fighting amongst themselves, especially inter-generational conflicts; tales which suggest that the gods are responsible for any-thing but the good; tales which suggest that gods change form or deceive; we are also to eliminate tales of heroes fearing death or lamenting the loss of loved ones. Socrates says that these tales turn children into cowards as well as loosen the bonds of family and citizenship (III.387). But how? That is, what is the process by which these objectionable contents take hold? Socrates gives this reason for banishing these objectionable stories: "The young cannot distinguish what is an allegory (*hyponoia*) from what is not, and the opinions they form at that age tend to be ineradicable and unchangeable" (II.378d–e). That is, youth lacks the capacity to recognize allegory as such.

But what is this capacity which youth lacks? The Greek word *hyponoia* is cor-rectly translated as "allegory," but it also means the deeper or real meaning which lies at the bottom (of a thing). It is the deeper sense or hidden meaning: it is that which lies at the bottom of a myth or allegory.[1] *Hyponoia* is quite literally the under-thought. Indeed, it is an "under-thought" in another sense: it enters the psyche beneath the radar of critical thought. (Think of the way a *hypnotist* influences another by encouraging her to suspend critical judgment.) Precisely because the child lacks the capacity to recognize allegory as such, he cannot grasp the deeper meaning of the story that is entering his soul, and thus he cannot subject it to critical scrutiny. And so, it would seem that the young can take in the surface story, but they cannot recognize it *as* a surface. That is because they cannot recognize the deeper meaning nor can they recognize that the allegory is allegorical *of* this deeper meaning. Thus they are unaware of the place of alle-gory in the larger structure of things. I shall therefore call this lack of capacity, which is constitutive of youth, *lack of orientation*.

This lack of orientation lends extraordinary power to the stories one hears. Once one has acquired the capacity to recognize allegory as such, one can rec-ognize a story as a surface-story, and then go on to inquire into its deeper meaning. But before one acquires the capacity, it is not merely that one cannot recognize the surface-story as such, the very idea of surface is unavailable. For one has no idea of depth with which to contrast it. It is precisely this capacity to distinguish surface from depth that one acquires as one acquires the capacity to recognize allegory as such. Thus without this capacity, the surface-story takes on a weird "reality" of its own. It is too quick to say that the young treat alle-gories as though they were true. For we are trying to capture a state of mind in which the concept of truth itself is not yet firmly established. Part of what it is to have the concept of truth is to have acquired the capacity to discriminate reality from appearance – and in certain crucial dimensions, this is what young people lack. But precisely because they lack this capacity, the experience of allegories has a kind of power which we (loosely) associate with the experience of reality.

It is difficult to capture this childhood state of mind with precision. In part, this is due to the fact that once we acquire the capacity to recognize allegory as such it becomes difficult for us to remember the subjective quality of earlier states of mind when we lacked this capacity. Thus it is difficult for us to say retrospectively what it was like. In part, it is because the childhood state of mind itself lacks a certain definiteness. Clearly, children do have a symbolic capacity, they can distinguish symbol from thing symbolized. And they can recognize a difference between a story told and the report of a real-life event. But what difference do they recognize? Obviously, Plato was not as interested as we are in capturing the precise nature of childhood subjectivity. But he is, I think, pointing to an important characteristic of childhood experience: that even if children can *in some sense* recognize that they are being told a story, part of its thrill, part of the thrall in which it holds them, derives from the fact that they can't quite locate the story as such.

Precisely because childhood stories float in a sea of imaginative life that they exercise a certain power, a power which inclines us to to describe stories as "having a reality of their own." Now if a particular story terrifies a child, parents might try to calm her by saying, "It's only a story." However, if the child lacks the capacity to recognize an allegory as such, then these words cannot be understood by the child in the way that the parents mean them. The child may be calmed by her parents' words, not because she understands the words, but because she trusts and loves her parents – and accepts that they are providing some sort of explanation why she shouldn't be scared. Indeed, the child may learn to repeat to herself, "it's only a story," and she may thereby develop a capacity to calm herself. Still, the mere repetition of the words does not *on its own* instill the capacity to recognize allegory as such. These words can make the right kind of difference, but only when they are embedded in the process of acquiring the capacity to recognize allegory as such. At that point the words can be used to utter a judgment, and thereby locate the story as such.

And what is shocking is that even though people eventually acquire the capacity to recognize allegory, the fact that there was a youthful period in which they lacked this capacity casts a shadow over an entire life. The *Republic* begins with a fascinating conversation between Socrates and Cephalus, a wealthy merchant of ripe age, who has the wisdom and moderation that would exemplify the best kind of a life that was nevertheless organized around accumulating wealth. Socrates asks him directly what he thinks is the greatest benefit of having great wealth. Cephalus answers:

> What I have to say probably wouldn't persuade most people. But you know, Socrates, that when someone thinks his end is near, he becomes frightened and concerned about things he didn't fear before. It's *then* that the stories we're told about

Hades, about how people who've been unjust here must pay the penalty there – stories he used to make fun of – twist his soul this way and that for fear they're true. And whether because of the weakness of old age or because he is now closer to what happens in Hades and has a clearer view of it, or whatever it is, he is filled with foreboding and fear, and he examines himself to see whether he has been unjust to anyone. If he finds many injustices in his life, he awakes from sleep in terror, as children do, and lives in anticipation of bad things to come. But someone who knows that he hasn't been unjust has sweet good hope as his constant companion – a nurse to his old age, as Pindar says . . . Wealth can do a lot to save us from having to depart for that other place in fear because we owe a sacrifice to a god or money to a person. It has many other uses, but, benefit for benefit, I'd say that this is how it is most useful to a man of any understanding. (I. 330d–331b)[2]

In other words, the stories he heard in youth were absorbed and retained by Cephalus throughout his life. They were taken in as allegories-not-recognized-as-such, and even after Cephalus acquired the capacity to recognize allegory, these stories remained for most of his life dormant within him, with little significance for him. Indeed, for much of his life, he makes fun of them. However, as he enters old age and starts to face the prospect of death, these old stories come back to haunt him with uncanny power. Here is a man who has organized his entire life around acquiring wealth, but when asked in old age what has been the value of it all, his answer is that its greatest benefit is to ward off the fears that are only now arising around stories he heard in childhood.

Cephalus is describing the structure of a traumatic cocktail.[3] The childhood stories were taken in before he had the capacity to recognize their allegorical status – and thus before he had the capacity to grasp their deeper meanings. They may provoke childhood fears but, in childhood at least, they have nothing to latch onto. However, in old age it seems that Cephalus' emerging anxiety over death needs the childhood stories to give it form and content. The elderly anxiety combines with the early childhood stories, and together they disrupt any previous self-understandings and give a new, anxious meaning to Cephalus' life. Note that Cephalus is unable to remain with Socrates and inquire into what justice really is: he has to go off to make a sacrifice (I.331d).

One would like to think that as one gets older one matures and, in particular, one leaves childhood stories behind. Plato's picture, as described by Cephalus, is darker. There seem to be three developmental stages: a childhood stage where the stories are taken in but not recognized as such; young adulthood, when the stories are both recognized as such and ridiculed; old age, when the stories come to inform an otherwise amorphous anxiety over death. And so, retrospectively, we can see that childhood is a time when the seeds are planted for a terror that will explode only in old age.

Socrates is also clear that the un-oriented tales we hear in youth are actually *dis*orienting. The heroic tales provide paradigms for imitation which, through the imitation, shape the psyche (III.395c–d, 401c–e; II.377b, 378b). For they facilitate the establishment of structures of repetition: habits and dispositions whose full meaning cannot be understood at the time they are being formed. So, for instance, a little boy hears heroic tales of Achilles at a time when he lacks the capacity to recognize allegory as such. When he goes out to play his version of *hoi agathoi kai hoi kakoi* (good guys and bad guys), he assigns himself the role of Achilles. He acts out a certain image of courage before he is able to understand what courage is. This image is enacted over and over again in play, and in this way his psyche gets "Achillized." He becomes accustomed to see the world and act in it from an "Achillized" perspective. And so, by the time he does acquire the capacity to recognize allegory as such, it is in an important sense too late. He can now recognize the Achilles tale as a story, but the tale has already done its psychic work. And by the time he tries in adulthood to think about what courage is, he is already looking out from Achilles' perspective.

III

It is important to recognize that lack of orientation has the same formal structure as dreaming. In dreams, we experience images without recognizing them as images and without understanding their deeper meanings. It is not quite correct to say that in dreams we think we are awake. Part of what it is to think we are awake is to exercise the capacity to distinguish between waking and dream states, and it is this capacity that goes to sleep when we sleep. Thus dream states do have a reality and power for us, *not* because we think we are awake, but because the capacity to distinguish between waking and sleeping has temporarily shut down. So again there is disorientation: we lose the capacity to recognize our dream as a dream and thus to determine what it is about.

Socrates assigns exactly this structure to dreaming. He is talking about the lovers of sights and sounds: those who recognize many beautiful things but are ignorant of the beautiful itself. And, he asks, isn't such a person – whether asleep or awake – really living in a dream? For isn't dreaming this: "thinking that the similar thing is not similar but that it is the thing to which it is similar" (V.476c, my translation)? Here the "dreamer" lacks orientation: he cannot recognize the place of the many beautiful things in the larger structure of the world. He cannot recognize a beautiful thing as an imitation of the Form nor does he know what it is an imitation of. Thus he cannot understand its deeper meaning. This condition is thus structurally analogous to lacking the capacity for recognizing allegory as such. In this lack of orientation, it is as though these sights and sounds are reality. This is the nature of dream experience.

It follows from these reflections that, for Socrates, entering conscious wakeful life is tantamount to entering a dream. Even if we leave aside Plato's metaphysics for the moment, it is his view that it is constitutive of youth to lack the capacity to recognize allegory as such. Entering conscious life is entering into an awareness that lacks the capacity to recognize the similar thing (the allegory) as similar. But without this capacity life has the character of a dream. And now if we do take Platonic metaphysics into account, it turns out that as young men and women acquire the capacity to recognize allegory as such, they "wake up" from one dreamlike state only to enter another. Ironically, the newly acquired sense of reality – "that was only a story!" – is precisely that which disorients us all over again. For we now plunge into the adult world of cultural artifacts, social practices, and physical objects – and we take it to be the real thing. As we acquire one version of the capacity to recognize the similar as similar, we enter a new level of experience where there is another version of the capacity that we lack.

IV

It is time to take another look at the Noble Falsehood. Socrates thinks that the inability to recognize allegory as such is constitutive of childhood. Thus for him the task cannot be to avoid all allegories – that is impossible – but to find the right kind of allegory that will not be recognized as such.[4] That is, in choosing which stories to tell children, we ought to make use of our knowledge that, in the first instance, they will not be able to recognize the allegory for what it is. Obviously, there may be various grounds for criticizing Socrates' candidate, but by now it should be clear that, given the overall outlook, there is one position that is not available: simply speak the truth to our children. This is not due to lack of fortitude on our part, nor to dishonesty. It is *constitutive of the adult–child* situation: children cannot possibly understand our words as we mean them. Either we remain unaware of this ourselves, or we try to take it somehow into account. Our children lack orientation; so can we tell them things that at least won't disorient them? Even better, can we orient them in the right sort of way?

Socrates distinguishes a verbal falsehood (*to en tois logois pseudos*) from "true falsehood" (*alēthos pseudos*), and it is clear that a verbal falsehood has essentially the same structure of an allegory-not-recognized-as-such. For a verbal falsehood is basically a form of words that comes to rest in the soul *without* being connected to its "deeper meaning." Plato calls it an imitation or image of a "true falsehood." Now a true falsehood is like that "deeper meaning": it is actually a condition of a person's soul when she is living in falsity. And it is a condition everyone wants to avoid. A verbal falsehood, like an allegory-not-recognized-as-such points to – or imitates – this deeper meaning *without* actually being connected to it. That *lack* of connection is what keeps the falsehood in its verbal form. And as such, Socrates thinks it can be used as a medicine (*pharmakon*). Clearly, this is a potentially dangerous drug; how can we use it for medicinal purposes? To answer this question, perhaps it is useful to ask, what is the "disease" from which children need to be "cured"?

The aim is to implant an allegory not recognized as such which will help children with the fact that they live in a condition of not being able to recognize allegories as such.

> I have to try to persuade first the rulers themselves and the soldiers, and then the rest of the city, that the entire upbringing and education we gave them was after all merely a dream" (III.414d).

In other words, we are to implant an allegory not recognized as such which in effect "says" that the entire content of our experience up until now has been in a condition where we cannot recognize allegories as such. It is a dream about dreaming and waking up. And unlike standard myths about the gods or ancient heroes, this myth is explicitly about the people to whom it is being told. As such it serves as a dreamlike wake-up call *for them*.

It is important to recognize that this Noble Falsehood is proto-philosophical in two ways. First, it attempts to give an account of the totality of our experience (up until now). It claims that *all* experience (up till now) can be understood under the concept "dream." Insofar as philosophy attempts to comprehend the whole, this myth is an imitation of that aspiration. Compare that to the familiar Homeric myths from which this aspiration is absent. There is thus reason to think it would have a very different effect on the young psyche from the standard fare of the day. Second, the myth inherently sows the seeds of discontent. It opens us to the idea that all our experience until now is somehow inadequate. And although we do not yet know precisely what this allegory means, we do know that it is classifying all our experience (until now) as somehow second-rate with regard to being well-oriented to reality. Thus it is a myth which introduces the philosophical distinction between appearance and reality – and it tells us firmly that up until now we have been living in appearance. In this way, the myth prepares us for philosophy.

It has often been remarked that the Noble Falsehood is a politically conservative myth: it claims in essence that people are born with innate and distinctive natures, suited for different social and political roles.[5] It also reinforces the idea that citizens are indebted to the existing political order, the beautiful city or kallipolis. However, what is less well understood is that while the Noble Falsehood may be *politically* conservative, it is *epistemically* revolutionary. It is meant to instill discontent with one's entire current epistemic condition. Moreover, the allegory is authored by someone who explicitly understands that children lack the capacity to recognize allegory as such. Thus one should expect the myth to be tailored to play to this lack of capacity. At the end of the Noble Falsehood, Socrates asks Glaucon "Is there any way of persuading them of this myth?" And Glaucon responds, "No way with those people you tell it to; but with their sons and with future generations" (III.415.c–d; my translation). Glaucon recognizes that the proper way to "believe" a myth is to hear it before one acquires the capacity to recognize allegory as such. For once one acquires that ability, allegories lose their "quasi-realistic" power. Thus there is no way you can get an adult to "believe" your myth.

At first one might think that from the perspective of living within the truth, the original adults who hear this myth are the best placed. For they can immediately recognize the allegory as an allegory – and, after all, that is what it is. The succeeding generations will all in some sense be misled: for they will all take in the allegory before they can recognize it as such. And the power that the myth will have for them will depend essentially on having heard it before they were in a position to understand its true nature.

But, for Socrates, the situation is the reverse of what it seems. For while the original adult generation will immediately be able to recognize the allegory as such, that recognition will occur in a life that is fundamentally disoriented. For this is a generation that assumes that the physical objects and artifacts in its midst are the real thing. They lack the capacity to recognize the familiar couch on which they lie as an imitation of the Form (X.596–8). Thus they are in a position structurally analogous to the child who cannot recognize allegory as such. They cannot recognize the "deeper meaning" of the familiar couch, they cannot even recognize that it has a deeper meaning. Thus the physical couch will inevitably seem more real to them than it in fact is. As we have seen, Socrates says that such people are in effect dreaming. And the Noble Falsehood cannot, for them, function as a wake-up call precisely because they immediately recognize it as an allegory. Ironically, the allegory gets located as such, but in a sea of disorientation.

But for the children, grandchildren, and subsequent generations, we should expect the myth to have the kind of two-stage effect we saw in the case of Cephalus. In childhood, the myth is laid down as an allegory-not-recognized-as-such. But even as a surface-story, the myth begins to teach the child to be hermeneutically suspicious of the other myths he has heard in childhood. After all, it's all been just a dream up till now. Thus one can think of the Noble Falsehood (told in childhood) as itself beginning to inculcate the capacity to recognize allegory as such. For it is an allegory told to us when we cannot recognize allegory as such but which *right on its surface* tells us that the other allegories we've already heard (and by hypothesis have not yet recognized as such) are really only dreams. In that way, the Noble Falsehood embeds an anti-fundamentalist message about all other myths: none of them should be taken literally.

Now we have reason to think that the Noble Falsehood will be told to *all* the children in the polis: for it is told to the rulers, soldiers, and *the rest of the city*. But we can imagine it having a special belated effect on the future rulers of the city. The Noble Falsehood sets them up for a later aha!-experience. Just as the stories Cephalus heard in childhood set him up for a later explosion in old age of terrible fears about death, so the Noble Falsehood one hears in childhood sets one up in adulthood to be open to the reality of the Forms. Think of young men and women who have the same outstanding character as Glaucon and Adeimantus, but who have been brought up since childhood in the right sort of way. In particular, they were exposed in childhood to the Noble Falsehood. As they grow up, the finest young men and women amongst them will be exposed in their education to the reality of the Forms. Because earlier, in childhood, they had been told the Noble Falsehood, they are now also in a position to feel "Aha! So *that's* what the myth was really about." In their education, they are being exposed to the true nature of reality for the first time, but their souls have already been set up to embrace it with gusto. It's like getting a joke many years after you've heard the punch line. Only in this case the joke is the idea that ordinary physical objects constitute reality. From a certain Platonic perspective, that is very funny. And if you've heard the Noble Falsehood in childhood, you're in a position to let out a real belly-laugh as an adult. (If that seems implausible to you, you can reflect on the fact that you didn't hear the Noble Falsehood as a child.)

Thus it is superficial to think of the Noble Falsehood *simply* as a myth that is designed to make children loyal to the established political order in the kallipolis. It may in fact do this, but it is also concerned with orienting children towards the truth. Socrates is trying to take explicit account of the fact that we are born into a culture, and that by the time we can reflect on it that culture has already shaped our souls. In particular, it has shaped our souls in ways that will influence the reflection. What is striking about the Noble Falsehood, in contrast to other myths and ideologies that are meant to legitimate the status quo, is that this allegory does its work by generating dissatisfaction. It teaches us to be dissatisfied with all the myths we've heard, at least insofar as we've taken them to have more than dreamlike status. Indeed, it teaches us to be dissatisfied with all of our experience up until now insofar as we have taken it to be experience of reality. This is not how legitimating myths normally work.

V

It is now possible to see that Socrates' account of the Cave is a repetition and re-creation of the Noble Falsehood. As is well known, this image is meant to characterize us in terms of "the effect of education – or lack of it – on our nature" (VII.514a). Again, it is essentially about those to whom it is being told: it is designed to describe their fundamental condition. And it is proto-philosophical in the same ways as is the Noble Falsehood. First, it is trying to capture the totality of our experience up until now, the moment when this story is introduced. It claims that all of our experience till now can be understood under the concepts *seeing shadows* or *hearing echoes* (and mistaking them for reality). Second, the account is designed to instill dissatisfaction with the current level of experience. It introduces in imagistic terms the philosophical distinction between appearance and reality, and it gives us "grounds" for "thinking" both that we are living in appearance and that we should be unhappy about that. The dissatisfaction is thus not about this or that belief – this is not a process of rejecting false beliefs – it is dissatisfaction with the sum total of experience (up till now).

Both the Noble Falsehood and the Cave thus intentionally create reflective disequilibrium; they build an inherent discontent with the current level of experience. Unlike existing myths – say Homer's presentation of Achilles, which, in Plato's view, gives a fixed, false, and thus imprisoning image of courage – the Socratic allegories encourage the idea that the current state of experience, "knowledge," etc. is unsatisfactory. Life up until now has, unbeknownst to us, been a dream. Life up until now has, unbeknownst to us, been a prison in which we are mistaking shadows for the real thing. The Socratic allegories unlike the Homeric myths inherently encourage dissatisfaction with the existing state of affairs. They thus motivate us to try to go on in some different way. If Socrates is right that we have been living in a dream, then these allegories serve as a wake-up call. If he is right that unbeknownst to ourselves we have been living in prison, then in becoming aware of that we begin to chafe at the chains.

Note that the problem we began with was the idea that our best attempts at achieving reflective equilibrium might be a sham. This was in effect Adeimantus's challenge: as we try to test our ethical beliefs we end up reaching out to the (disguised) prejudices of the day. But here are finally allegories that are not intended to legitimize the values of the day, but rather to instill suspicion with respect to them. It does this not by criticizing this value or that, nor by taking on the role of "moral skeptic," but by making us uncomfortable with our entire mode of acquiring beliefs and values. Whatever else might be said about these myths, they are clearly not meant to keep us locked into current images of goodness, beauty, courage. Rather, they create an inchoate sense of discomfort with those images.

After Socrates describes the Cave, Glaucon says "A strange picture. And strange prisoners." Socrates responds, "No more strange than us" (VII.515a). The Greek word for "strange" is *atopos*, which means more literally *out of place*; most literally it means *without a place, unlocated*. But "unlocated" is precisely the "position" of an allegory-not-recognized-as-such: we do not yet know its place in the scheme of things. Insofar as we, as children, lack the capacity to recognize allegory as such, *we* shall be unlocated, for we cannot orient ourselves with respect to these allegories. Now the story of the Cave is ostensibly being told to Glaucon, who does have the capacity to recognize allegory as such. But he stands in relation to ordinary experience – to physical objects, artifacts, contemporary beliefs about the good life – as children stand to allegories: he cannot yet locate them as imitating the Forms. As a young adult he lacks the capacity to recognize the allegorical nature of ordinary experience. He cannot locate his experience in relation to reality – to the Forms – and thus he remains unlocated, *atopos*. The Cave is an allegorical attempt to get him to recognize that.

As such, the Cave seeks to instill a new form of Socratic ignorance. As is well known, in the *Apology* Socrates says that he discovered he was the wisest among humans because he knew that he didn't know. But the Cave is a story that is designed to put Glaucon, and anyone else ready to hear it, into a position where they can begin to recognize that they don't know. Socrates says that education is not a matter of putting knowledge into souls, but of turning the whole soul away from the darkness towards the light (VII.518c). Certainly, what we are turning away from are images, shadows, echoes, allegories *not recognized as such.* Thus we are turning away from a dreamlike state. And what we are turning towards is a recognition that if we are to understand these images we must grasp that they are images, and we must struggle to understand what these images are images of. Indeed, the process of turning away is constituted by coming to recognize the "allegorical" nature of ordinary experience. We may not yet be able to say what the deeper meanings are – thus we remain ignorant – but we are able to glimpse that they are pointing towards deeper meanings – and thus we at least know that we are ignorant. Thus the allegory of the Cave facilitates a Socratic movement from being ignorant, yet ignorant of one's ignorance, to being ignorant but aware that one is ignorant. And insofar as ordinary life is like a dream, then as we move towards Socratic ignorance, we begin to wake up.[6]

It is important to keep in mind to whom the Cave allegory is addressed. Ostensibly it is addressed to Glaucon and Adeimantus, and it is addressed *directly* to them. That is, the Noble Falsehood is told to Glaucon and Adeimantus, but in the context of an inquiry into what stories we should tell the members of the kallipolis. The Cave, by contrast, is told directly to Glaucon and Adeimantus and it is explicitly for them. I suspect that in this way the Cave is addressed to the ideal reader of the *Republic.* For, as we have seen, Glaucon and Adeimantus are exceptionally fine people who have had the historical bad luck to have been born into a bad society. The *Republic* is a book for such people. There are two features of such readers that command our attention. First, they have already been exposed in childhood to the misleading myths and stories of their culture – though given their fine natures they have not been as misshapen by them as other members of society. In particular, they are capable of going through a process of questioning their myths, much as Glaucon and Adeimantus do in Books II and III. Second, by the time they are told about the Cave, it is too late for them to experience the allegory in the way that a child does. They already have the capacity to recognize allegory as such. So there is reason to think that the allegory is meant in the telling to be essentially denatured: it is not meant to have on the intended recipients the kind of power it would have had if it had been told in youth. But, then, what kind of effect is it supposed to have?

Earlier in the day – or earlier in the reading of the book – Glaucon, Adeimantus and the ideal reader have been exposed to the Noble Falsehood. They are in a position to recognize that it could not possibly affect them as it is meant to affect the young members of the kallipolis. At best, they are left to imagine what effect it might have on a young soul in a good society. But now, when they hear the Cave, they are hearing basically the same story for the second time – only now they are hearing an age-appropriate version. I am going to indulge the fantasy that we are ideal readers of the *Republic*. Obviously, it is too late for the Cave – or any other story – to have the same effect on us as it would have had if told to us in youth.

Nevertheless, the fact that we are first told the Noble Falsehood, then the Cave, means that we are put in a position where we can re-enact in adult life a process by which a child acquires the capacity to recognize allegory as such. Ostensibly the Noble Falsehood is *for them*; the Cave is *for us*. But what is really for us is *the movement* by which we go from hearing the Noble Falsehood (which is for them) to the Cave (which is for us). For the fact that we have just heard the Noble Falsehood sets us up for an aha!-experience when we hear the Cave. Retrospectively we can say with emotion and conviction, "So *that's* what the Noble Falsehood is about!" We are now able to locate the Noble Falsehood in a way we couldn't earlier – and this is an adult surrogate to the childhood process by which we first learned to recognize allegory as such.

Prospectively, the Cave gives us an inkling of something which we recognize we can at best only glimpse. In effect, the story tells us that as we leave childhood behind and enter adulthood we are, in effect, entering a second childhood. For the Cave invites us to picture our situation as one of seeing images and shadows and mistaking them for reality. It is an imagistic story in which we are told that we lack the capacity to recognize *reality* as such. Just as the children in the kallipolis will be told the Noble Falsehood *before* they have acquired the capacity to recognize allegory as such – and thus are left with an uncanny sense that they will soon be experiencing things in non-dreamlike ways (whatever that means) – so we will be told the Cave allegory before we have acquired the capacity to recognize reality as such. And thus we are left with an uncanny sense that we may soon be experiencing reality in non-dreamlike ways (whatever that means). The Cave intimates to us our own future selves. At least, it intimates our own best possible future selves.

Note also that someone in Glaucon's position who had been exposed to the allegory of the Cave would be in a better position to tell the Noble Falsehood to children. If the kallipolis is ever going to be established it will have to be by someone like Glaucon, though someone who is better placed in terms of power and historical opportunity. So it is someone like Glaucon who is the projected inaugural teller of the Noble Falsehood. Now the founder of the kallipolis will be the first-generation teller of the Noble Falsehood, so he is not in a position where he can believe it, nor was he ever in a position where he did "believe" it. By contrast, the children who hear the Noble Falsehood will be able to transmit it to their children with added verve.[7] Thus this original transmission will be the weakest in terms of producing the intended effect. However, if we arm the founder of the kallipolis with the picture of the Cave, we have, as it were, given him an age-appropriate allegory – and one that has the same basic structure as the Noble Falsehood he now has to tell. This puts the original teller of the Noble Falsehood in a position where he himself has accepted an allegory that has the same basic structure as the one he is about to tell. And thus he can speak with a conviction which might otherwise be lacking. Although this is the first transmission of the Noble Falsehood to children, the earlier transmission of the allegory of the Cave to adults secures as much efficacy as is possible within the context of this original telling.

VI

The *Republic* is a work of astonishing depth, so there are obviously a number of ways to read it. But it certainly can be read as an occasion to work through the power of allegories and myth. At the very beginning, we the readers are exposed, through Cephalus, to the uncanny power that childhood myth can have later in adult life. Insofar as Cephalus's situation is not unusual, we have reason to feel vulnerable. What myths that *we* have heard in childhood are ticking away, deep inside our souls, ready to explode our happiness at some future date? The myths Cephalus heard disturbed Cephalus, but the fact that he was disturbed should disturb us.

It is in such a disturbed state that we come to the Noble Falsehood – which we recognize as a cure that couldn't possibly help us. The Noble Falsehood itself provides a prophylactic *for children* against all the other misleading myths they might have heard. For it claims that all their experience up until now has been a dream. But the myth is useless when told to adults. Many students who come to the *Republic* for the first time express pleasure that they have not been subjected to such "lies," and that response is understandable. But when we come to understand the deeper motivation of the Noble Falsehood, there is also room for a certain wistfulness that such lies could no longer do us any good.

But then there is the Cave, an allegory specifically designed for a young adult reader or interlocutor. At last we have an allegory that is *for us*, yet it is also a re-creation of the Noble Falsehood to which we have already been exposed. As we have seen, even in our original encounter with the Cave we are coming to it for the second time. There is thus reason to think that the *Republic* is not merely an account *of* the proper mythic education of youth – an education we could never experience – it is also a form of mythic therapy for us. For we are told a story (the *Republic*) of being told a myth in childhood (the Noble Falsehood), followed by being told an allegory (the Cave) of the same basic structure that is appropriate for us as adults.

It is this whole movement that *for us* does the therapeutic work. For although it is impossible for us to create a myth that would have the effect on us that it would have had if we had heard it in youth, there is reason to think that the allegories we do create – in particular, the Noble Falsehood and the Cave – will be prophylactic against the untoward effects of the myths we have heard in youth. For the allegories we are now hearing are essentially *reactive*. They are not myths about the creation of the universe nor are they about the gods or heroic ancestors who founded civilization as we know it. Rather, they are about our epistemic condition; and they say that all previous myths we have heard are really only a dream, a shadow, an echo. Insofar as we take the earlier myths to have more reality than that, we are deluded. The Noble Falsehood and the Cave are allegories to correct for all previous myths. We first see this corrective in a version that, we imagine, we would have heard if only we had been children at the founding of the kallipolis. Later we encounter a version which is more appropriate to our age and actual historical circumstance. In short, we move from the ideal to the real, from a fantasy of what a great childhood would be like, to a more realistic appraisal of what our actual condition is. But all this is accomplished within the movement of allegory. I suspect Plato thought it would work like an antidote: the outcome of this movement is to put ourselves in the best possible position we could be in – given the realities of our early life in a flawed culture – to counteract the later effects in adult life of early childhood myths. This cannot all be accomplished at the level of reasoned arguments: we need to use imagination to counter the belated ill effects of earlier imaginative products. But with the prophylactic tales of Noble Falsehood and Cave, we have done the best we can to avoid the kind of horror that, in late age, struck Cephalus.

Having accomplished this, we are in a position to re-visit a healthy version of the type of myths that came to torment Cephalus. This, in effect, is the myth of Er. Thus the *Republic* ends as it began, with a myth of justice and retribution in the afterlife. Er was supposedly a hero from a foreign land, killed in battle, who twelve days later came back to life and thus was able to report on life after death. There are two important emendations that Er makes to the myths that torment Cephalus. First, the myth confirms Cephalus' fear that he would be punished for his injustices, but it is worse than he feared (X.615a–b). For not only is a person punished ten times – indeed, punished ten life times – for each offense, there is no hope of buying off one's injustices with money. The idea that in this life Cephalus could buy his way out of punishment in the next is exposed as a merchant's fantasy. Second, the myth reveals that Cephalus' version is only partial. Cephalus can't get beyond the punishments he might suffer in the next world. But Er declares that after an extended period of punishment, there is then another chance to re-enter life. Only one must choose lots for what kind of a life one shall lead. This is the most dangerous and fraught part of the cycle, for even the shape of one's soul is at stake. For the soul is affected by the kind of life it chooses to live (X.618b).

Now what role does this myth play in the closing moments of the *Republic*? It seems to me that the myth is both therapeutic and argumentative at the same time. Therapeutically speaking, we know from the case of Cephalus that we ourselves have been implanted with childhood stories of retribution which are set to "go off" in old age. We need to do something now that will prevent these stories from later having a deleterious effect upon us. This is just what the myth of Er is designed to do. For it takes up the stories that come to haunt Cephalus, but it points us in a different direction.

> It looks, my dear Glaucon, as if that is where the whole danger lies for a man. It is why the greatest care must be directed towards having each and every one of us disregard all other branches of study, and be a follower and student of this branch of ours, in the hope that he can learn and discover who it is who will give him the ability and knowledge to distinguish the good life from the bad, and choose always and everywhere out of all those possible, the life which is better. *He must take into consideration all the things we have talked about here today* . . . (X.618b–c).[8]

The day began with everyone hearing of Cephalus' fears, but by the end of the day we can see that these fears led him off in the wrong direction. The late-blooming effect of childhood myth on Cephalus was to make him anxiously try to pay off debts and make (no doubt expensive) sacrifices to the gods. And this prevents him from doing the one thing he should be doing if he wants to make a genuine contribution to his future happiness: spending the day with Socrates to inquire what a good life might really consist in. Cephalus can't stick around for the discussion because "It's time I was doing something about the sacrifices" (I.331d).

By the time we hear basically the same kind of myth at the end of the day we are ready to move in a very different direction. The therapeutic action of the myth of Er runs along two dimensions, conscious and unconscious. Consciously, the myth sheds light on all the previous myths and allegories we have heard in this remarkable day. Not only does it illuminate what is going wrong in Cephalus' reception of his myth, it sends *us* back to the Noble Falsehood and the Cave. For if the all-important task is to be able to determine what is (and what is not) a good life, these earlier myths help free us from the illusion that we already know the answer. And the myth of Er is there to show us how important that is.

But it is reasonable to assume that the myth will also have unconscious effects on us. Yet, if the effects are unconscious, how are we to investigate them? Obviously, the route needs to be indirect and can be no more than hypothetical. My hypothesis begins with a conscious phenomenon, and treats it as a symptom: I have often heard readers express disappointment that the *Republic* ends with a myth. My suggestion is that the experience of disappointment is in some sense correct, but that it has fastened on to the wrong object. For if we are ideal readers of the *Republic*, then part of the process of coming to grips with the text must be the realization that *we* are in various ways flawed. After all, if we have grown up in less-than-ideal historical and social circumstances, there is now reason to think that this has taken a toll on our souls. To give one salient example: it is likely that in childhood we too were subject to terrifying stories of a terrifying place, just as Cephalus was. For Cephalus it was Hades, in the Christian tradition it is hell, in a secular context there will some version of going over to "the dark side." In each case the reader would be living with an unconscious "time bomb" that might "go off" in old age. The myth of Er takes up these childhood stories and diverts them down a different stream. We now have implanted within us a story which takes up previous punishment stories and emends them – locating them in a larger story of coming back to life, of personal responsibility, and of the importance of choosing well.

Thus there does seem to be some basis for the experience of disappointment – but we haven't thought through our own relation to the book if we experience it as disappointment with the book, rather than with ourselves. What *is* disappointing – though to dwell on it would be self-indulgent – is that by the end of this marvelous book we, even as ideal readers, still need a myth.

I have heard readers complain that, by ending the book with a myth, Plato is admitting a kind of argumentative defeat. After all, wasn't the challenge to Socrates to argue that the just life is the best one? And if his argument has succeeded, why does he need a myth to prop it up? This complaint does not take sufficient account of the role a myth might play inside an argument. It seems to me Plato could have reasoned like this: when it comes to justice, the universe of possibilities breaks up into three broad classes. Either we live in this life and when we die, that's the end of it; or, after we die we go into some kind of afterlife; or, after we die we go into some kind of afterlife and somehow return to this life. Those are all the possibilities there are. The main argument of the *Republic* covers the first possibility, and the main argument plus the myths covers the other two.

And one should not be surprised that an argument that includes possibilities of life after death would make recourse to myths, for the actual conditions of life after death are not something we can know anything about. From an argumentative point of view, the recourse to myth itself is not problematic just so long as it covers all the possibilities there are. This, I suggest, is precisely what the myths of the *Republic* set out to do. *If* there is life after death, the unjust will be punished; *if* there is life after that, the just will be better off.[9] Thus Plato's recourse to myth at the end of the *Republic* in no way gives up argumentative rigor, and disappointment with the book on that basis is thus misplaced.

Plato has used myth not to argue for an actuality, but to cover the universe of possibilities. One way or another, these are the ways things have to be – unless, that is, there is a fourth possibility: namely, that the world is essentially a bad place, an occasion for despair. In this world there would be an afterlife in which the just would be mocked and tortured by malevolent gods. Virtually all of the rhetorical power of the *Republic* – the allegories and myths, the arguments and images – is designed to cure the reader of the temptation to think this is a real possibility. Reality and intelligibility itself are structured by the Good. Thus while there may be grounds for *pessimism*, there can never be grounds for *despair*. How successful Plato was in eliminating this temptation is a task for each reader to decide: less as an academic exercise than as an approach to the question of how to live.

Notes

1 See the entry *hyponoia* in Liddell and Scott 1977: 1890.
2 Plato, trans. Grube and Reeve 1999.
3 This is basically the structure that Freud assigns to trauma. See, e.g., Freud 1981: 347–59. See also Jacques Lacan, e.g. 1988: 34–5, 189–97, 232, 283.
4 This is what Jean Laplanche would call a seduction. See Laplanche 1999 and Lear 2000.
5 I take it that Plato thought that these claims were true. Thus the Noble Falsehood is at worst a verbal falsehood, not a true one. If one is capable of grasping the true allegorical meanings of the Noble Falsehood, one can grasp its truth: that people are "rooted" in the polis – in the sense of political obligation – that they do have different innate natures, and that their experience until now has been "dreamlike" in the sense elaborated in this paper. However, the Noble Falsehood is to be told to children who do not yet have the capacity to grasp the allegorical meaning, and insofar as it is grasped literally, the claims are false. (Obviously, this interpretation requires its own argument which is beyond the scope of this essay.)
6 One can now see in a new light why Socrates, at the end of the *Republic*, wants to expel imitative poets from the kallipolis. For the poets have the effect of recreating this childhood condition in adults. The imitative poet does not act as though he is narrating a story about Achilles, he speaks as though it is Achilles himself who is speaking. Thus the literary form induces a dreamlike state: instead of our thinking that A (Homer) is similar to B (Achilles), it is as though A is B. Thus the imitative form collapses spatial, temporal, and narrative distances. Every time someone re-enacts Homer's poem, he will not only be saying the same words as Homer, it will again be as though Achilles is speaking. Thus the imitative form again pulls us in the direction of taking in an allegory not recognized as such. That is, it is a regressive force, pulling us back to the incapacities of childhood.
7 Think about the difference between adults who never believed in the Santa Claus myth versus adults who in childhood were in the myth's thrall each telling their children about it a generation later.
8 Plato, trans. Griffith 2000; my emphasis.
9 And if after death it is neutral – neither better nore worse – for the just and the unjust, it is still better to live a just life. For, by the first argument, it is better to be just in this life. So if it is neutral in the next life, it is still better to be just overall.

The ideas presented in this paper have been in gestation for several years, and an earlier version appeared in the Boston Area Colloquium in Ancient Philosophy. G. R. F. Ferrari, Charles Griswold, Gabriel Lear, Glenn Most, Jane Mueller, and David Sedley read a previous draft and offered valuable comments. I should also like to thank my students at the

University of Chicago who participated in various seminars I have taught on the *Republic* over the years. Their conversation has been an invaluable source of stimulation.

References

Freud, S. (1981) "Project for a scientific psychology," in *The Standard Edition of the Complete Psychological Works of Sigmund Freud*, vol. I, London: Hogarth Press.

Lacan, J. (1988) *The Seminar of Jacques Lacan*, Book I: *Freud's Papers on Technique, 1953–1954*, Cambridge: Cambridge University Press.

Laplanche, J. (1999) "The unfinished Copernican revolution," in *Essays on Otherness*, London and New York: Routledge.

Lear, J. (2000) *Happiness, Death and the Remainder of Life*, Cambridge, MA: Harvard University Press.

Liddell, H. G., and R. Scott (eds.) (1977) *A Greek-English Lexicon*, Oxford: Clarendon Press.

Plato (1999) *Republic*, trans. G. M. A. Grube and C. D. C. Reeve, Indianapolis: Hackett Publishing.

——(2000) *The Republic*, trans. T. Griffith, Cambridge: Cambridge University Press.

——(2004) *Republic*, trans. C. D. C. Reeve, Indianapolis: Hackett Publishing.

3

Socrates' Refutation of Thrasymachus

Rachel Barney

Nobody is very satisfied with the arguments Socrates presents against Thrasymachus in Book I of the *Republic*.[1] Certainly not Thrasymachus, who is left grumpy, rude, and obviously unconvinced. Not Glaucon and Adeimantus, who, equally unconvinced, demand that Socrates begin all over again at the start of Book II. And not Socrates himself: he not only accepts their demand, but complains of frustration with his own procedure and results at the end of Book I (354a13–c3). Plato must share the discontent of his characters: for if the Book I arguments really did what they purport to, namely show that "the just person is happy, and the unjust one wretched" (354a4), the *Republic* could in principle have ended there.[2] Given this consensus, it is no surprise if most interpreters have agreed that the arguments fall somehow short.[3]

But what *exactly* is wrong with Socrates' arguments? Clearly they are rhetorical failures: they fail, that is, as attempts at persuasion directed towards Thrasymachus (and Glaucon and Adeimantus, and most readers). But whether this is due to their being *philosophical* failures – by being logically invalid, say, or based on false premises, or irrelevant or question-begging – is another question. I will try to show that Socrates' arguments are somewhat more promising than interpreters have tended to suppose. Some of their premises are controversial, and a few key inferences confused or under-argued; but there is no obvious fatal flaw with the basic line of argument. Moreover, the arguments are not the disconnected grab-bag of objections they might seem, nor do they depend on assumptions peculiar to Plato's Socrates. Rather, they work through a systematic chain of reasoning intended to show that Thrasymachus' own commitments – in particular, his claim that ruling is a craft, *technê* – should lead him to consider justice preferable to injustice. This defense will suggest that Plato intends Socrates' arguments to be read as *in a way* philosophically successful and satisfactory. However, our sense that the arguments fall short, and that Plato recognizes as much, is not an optical illusion: we will see at the end why their strengths are still not enough.

Thrasymachus on Justice

Before turning to Socrates' arguments, we need to be clear about the position he is attempting to refute. Exactly what Thrasymachus means to claim about justice has been much discussed by interpreters.[4] He enters the discussion with what is clearly intended as a startling and impressive pronouncement: "Justice is the advantage of the stronger" (338c2–3). What he means by this, he explains, is that different ruling parties in each city make the laws for their own advantage, and decree that following those laws is "just." So Thrasymachus treats "the advantage of the stronger" and "the advantage of the ruler" as equivalent (338e6–339a4); later, he adds a third formulation, claiming that justice is "the advantage of another person" rather than oneself (343c3–4). In a general way his point is clear: if you behave justly, others will reap the benefits of your behavior, the "stronger" ruling faction above all. The problem is that Thrasymachus' three formulations are not really equivalent, if taken strictly as definitions of justice. There are cases in which they seem to conflict: for instance, if *you* are the ruler, is it just for you to act for your own advantage or that of "another person"? Thrasymachus' opening slogan might suggest that he holds a conventionalist or positivist account of justice: justice is whatever the rulers decree through their legislation, and an examination of the evidence shows that they decree whatever is to their own advantage. But in that case the decrees of a tyrant would be as just as any others; yet later on Thrasymachus will go on to describe tyranny as "the most complete injustice" (344a4).

There has been much scholarly debate over what to make of Thrasymachus' formulations. The solution, I think, is to see that Thrasymachus is not giving a definition of justice, but rather is debunking it by pointing out the standard *effects* of justice as usually understood (see Chappell 1993; Barney 2004). He is in fact presupposing a commonplace and traditional conception of justice, one famously set forth by the early poet Hesiod in one of the central works of the Greek moral tradition, *Works and Days*. One of Hesiod's concerns in the *Works and Days* is to denounce unjust behavior: he condemns a range of misdeeds including bribe-taking, dishonesty, cheating one's neighbor, perjury, and fraud. In general, injustice seems to be behavior which, motivated by greed (*pleonexia*; see below, and also Balot 2001 for discussion of this concept) and arrogance, involves violating laws and social norms (*nomoi* or sing. *nomos*, "law"). Justice is understood to be a matter of obeying the law, practising honesty and self-restraint, and keeping your hands off the property of others; it is the virtue which makes us good citizens and neighbors.

Now as David Furley (1981: 81–2) has pointed out, there are two different ways in which ancient thinkers may challenge a normative concept like Hesiodic "justice." One is to revise the scope of the term; for instance, Callicles in Plato's *Gorgias* argues that really, "according to nature," it is just for the strong to take whatever they want from the weak (482c–486d). The other option is to leave the traditional extension of the term in place while changing its *value*. This second operation is what Thrasymachus is up to here. When he speaks of "justice" he has in mind the same behavior as Hesiod has when he uses the word: his point is that justice so understood is *worthless* to the person who possesses it. This is a radical rejection of Greek moral tradition. According to Hesiod, justice is the key to a good and successful life: for law (*nomos*) was allocated to humans by Zeus, and he rewards those who uphold it and punishes the unjust.[5] Thrasymachus not only says nothing about any divine status for justice, he implicitly suggests that the tradition is something of a scam: when the ruling faction dictates that to follow its laws is "just," they are relying on credulous citizens thinking that Zeus will reward their obedience. The moral tradition represented by Hesiod is merely a tool of exploitation used by the ruling power.

Thus it seems fair to class Thrasymachus as an "amoralist" or "immoralist":[6] i.e., someone who argues that we have no good reason to abide by the dictates of justice or morality as such (that is, in the absence of punishments or restraints), on the grounds that it is injustice which contributes to making a person *eudaimôn* or happy.[7] He presents this position as a matter of cynical realism and sociological insight. Just look around, he says, and you will see that the unjust flourish while the just harm themselves (a point vividly hammered home by Glaucon later on), and further that talk of "justice" is no more than a tool of exploitation. However, it is important to see that there is a gap between these cynical observations and the immoralist conclusion. Thrasymachus presents himself as a tough-minded, realistic observer, impatient with abstractions (336c6–336d4), but like most people who strike that pose he is enslaved to philosophical assumptions he has never really thought about. His central assumption is that a person's "advantage," "good," and "happiness" (all are equivalent terms in this context) must be understood in worldly terms, and in particular as a function of money and power. Moreover, these goods are assumed to be "zero-sum": that is, for one member of a community to have more of them is for another to have less, so that if my justice serves your advantage it must work against my own. Thrasymachus also seems to assume that everyone is naturally motivated by *pleonexia*, the drive to "have more" (*pleon echein*) of these goods – indeed to have as much of them as possible, which given their zero-sum nature can only be at others' expense – a principle made explicit in Glaucon's more systematic account in Book II (359c4–6).[8] That is why governments, according to Thrasymachus, uniformly make laws to serve their own (perceived) advantage, and why justice can only be a kind of simple-mindedness (348c12). (Thrasymachus actually waffles on the rather important question of why anyone is just. At another point he suggests that justice is more a matter of hypocrisy than gullibility: "Those who reproach injustice do so because they are afraid not of doing it but suffering it" (344c3–4).) This cluster of assumptions about the good explains why for Thrasymachus the tyrant represents an ideal: for the tyrant has

succeeded in acquiring *all* the political power in his city, which enables him to monopolize its wealth as well (344a4–344c9).

Thrasymachus thus silently excludes two related possibilities. One is that justice might have other effects as important as those he reports. He says nothing about the psychological effects of justice on the just person, or its operation within the family and on personal relations, or how it affects our relations with the gods. This is perhaps natural enough if our horizons are restricted to wealth and power, but what if (and this is the second possibility) other goods matter at least as much to us? Thrasymachus is simply assuming – and this is really his most bold and important claim, unstated though it is – that his analysis of justice captures the most important facts about it. The following nine books of the *Republic* will be, among other things, a demonstration of just how much he is leaving out.

Thrasymachus and the Ruler in the Strict Sense

Before Socrates' arguments against this position can get underway, an important clarification is called for. Socrates begins by getting Thrasymachus to agree that, according to him, (1) justice is the advantage of the stronger, aka the rulers; (2) it is just to obey the rulers (this is part of Thrasymachus' claim about the language of justice serving as a tool of exploitation: because of the traditional association of justice with *nomos*, what counts as "just" in a community depends on what the rulers decree); (3) rulers sometimes err, and command what is not to their own advantage. This yields the contradictory result that (4) it both is (because of (2)) and is not (because of (1)) just to do what the rulers command in such a situation (339d–e).

This is a classic Socratic elenchus, i.e., an argument which, using only premises endorsed by the interlocutor, derives a contradiction from them. In Plato's early "Socratic" dialogues, such as the *Laches*, the elenchus is used to show that since Socrates' interlocutor is committed to claims which entail a contradiction, at least one of which must therefore be false, he cannot be wise on the subject in question. In this case, however, it is not hard for Thrasymachus to adjust his statements so as to avoid self-contradiction; so here the elenchus functions as at best a preliminary refutation, and a tool of clarification. In fact, Plato indicates that there are several escape routes available to Thrasymachus. Two young bystanders to the argument, Polemarchus and Cleitophon, leap into the fray, and Cleitophon supplies the obvious way out: surely what Thrasymachus means is that justice consists in what the stronger or ruler *believes* to be his advantage, since this is what the weaker is commanded to do (340b6–8).

But Thrasymachus pointedly rejects this option. Instead, surprisingly, he eliminates the contradiction by rejecting the indisputable-looking (3). Strictly speaking, he claims, a "ruler" is an expert, like a doctor or grammarian, and an expert as such never makes a mistake: "each of these, insofar as he is what we call him, never errs, so that, in the strict sense (since you are a great one for speaking strictly), no craftsman ever errs" (340d8–340e3). So too in the case of ruling: "a ruler, insofar as he is a ruler, never makes errors and unerringly decrees what is best for himself" (340e8–341a2).

This is a fascinating twist. For Thrasymachus has now changed the subject, and is no longer offering to describe the empirical realm – how actual rulers behave – in value-neutral "sociological" terms. Instead, he is putting forward a norm for our approval: he turns out to be a kind of idealist, full of admiration for the perfect scientific tyrant of his imagination. This concept of the "real ruler" or ruler in the strict sense of course points forward to the rest of the *Republic*: Plato's own version of the real ruler is eventually revealed as the Guardian of Books III–IV and the philosopher-king of Books V–VII. The fact that Plato's version of this ideal is completely different makes it all the more interesting that he uses Thrasymachus to introduce the concept in the first place. He shows that while Socrates and Thrasymachus are polar opposites, they can agree on a single crucial point: ruling is a craft (or art, or area of expertise: *technê*), and only the ruler who exercises power in a fully expert way deserves the name. This shared hypothesis that ruling is a craft provides Thrasymachus and Socrates with a way of bringing the immoralist challenge into focus. The question raised (and answered in the affirmative) by the immoralist is whether it is rational for us, in order to pursue our self-interest, to reject the demands of justice or morality. For Thrasymachus and Socrates, the crafts provide a model of expert, fully informed rational action. The real ruler is imagined by both as having the kind of knowledge, decision-making ability, and power to attain his ends as ordinary craft-practitioners do – not about some specialized area, though, but about the general conduct of life. So the immoralist challenge can be posed as the question: *what would the expert ruler do* – in particular, would he be just or unjust? The answer will at the same time be an answer to the more general question of which way of life it is rational for all of us to prefer. As Socrates says, in urging Thrasymachus to continue the debate, "do you think it is a small matter to determine which whole way of life would make living most worthwhile for each of us?" (344d7–344e3). And lurking underneath this debate about rational agency is a dispute about the nature of happiness or the good, which is understood to be the rational person's aim.

Socrates' Refutation of Thrasymachus

In the remainder of Book I, Socrates and Thrasymachus explore these issues through five arguments. The first group (arguments I–III below) investigate the shared hypothesis that ruling "in the strict sense" is a craft; in them Socrates sets out the features of craft so as to show that they belong to the just person rather than the unjust Thrasymachean tyrant. The second round of arguments (IV and V) then set out some central properties of justice which explain why this is so. Taken collectively, the arguments are thus an ambitious, systematic attempt not only to undermine Thrasymachus' attack on justice but to establish the opposed Socratic position: it is justice, not injustice, which makes us happy. As we will see, however, the arguments stop short of *defining* justice, and in Plato's eyes this means that they can only have a preliminary status.

I The "nature of craft" argument (341c–342e)

Socrates begins by getting Thrasymachus to agree, on the basis of the examples of medicine and being a ship's captain, that every craft has a distinctive object or subject matter (e.g., the human body in the case of medicine), and is "by nature set over this to seek and provide what is advantageous to it" (341d8–9). Like Thrasymachus, Socrates is happy to talk of the real ruler as being "stronger" than his subjects, but he thinks that strength properly understood means self-sufficiency: the craft-practitioner shows his "strength" precisely by serving the advantage of the "weaker" subject rather than his own.

With a little tidying up, Socrates' argument can easily be represented as a valid one:

1 Every craft has a distinctive end, which consists in serving the good of its subject matter; thus the craft-practitioner "in the strict sense" serves the good of the subject matter, not his own.
2 A Thrasymachean ruler (i.e., an unjust, self-serving tyrant) serves his own good, not that of his subject matter (the ruled).
3 Therefore, a Thrasymachean ruler is not practicing a real craft.

The crucial thesis here is clearly (1), with its claim that crafts as such have "ends" distinct from the particular motivations which might lead individuals to practice them. This seems reasonable enough: while one doctor might be driven to his work by a sense of religious obligation, another by money, and a third by a craving for praise, the end of medicine is not any of these things, but the health of the patient. We might say that this end is *internal* to the practice of medicine, whereas the motivations that drive people to take it up are (or may be) *extrinsic* to it. Whatever her motivations, a doctor *qua* doctor, i.e., one acting as the craft of medicine prescribes, takes for her goal in acting the health of the patient. Of course she *may* benefit from her work in various ways, but that is incidental; she acts as a doctor just as much if she does it to her own detriment. Real craft is not self-interested but *disinterested*; therefore, Socrates concludes, Thrasymachus' self-serving ideal ruler is not practicing a craft.

One reason Socrates' concept of the internal end seems plausible is that we do treat categories like "doctor" and "captain" as establishing norms of their own: a "good doctor" is the one who is good at serving the end of medicine, rather than a good person who happens to be a doctor, or somebody who is good at using medicine to get whatever he wants. Nonetheless, (1) is eminently debatable. Socrates depends heavily here on the examples of the doctor and the ship's captain, presented in a brief *epagôgê* or "induction": that is, a survey of cases belonging to some general kind, leading to a general conclusion about that kind (or, via an implicit general conclusion, to a conclusion about another, more controversial case); for instance, a survey of a few kinds of craft used to support a claim about crafts in general. Aristotle speaks of this method as one of Socrates' specialities (*Metaphysics* 1078b28), and it is used frequently in Plato's early dialogues (e.g., *Apology* 25b; *Gorgias* 460a–461a). The limitations of induction are obvious, however: unless every possible case is covered, it can never have the status of a demonstrative proof. The fact that a few examples of crafts are disinterested does not entail that *all* crafts are – as Thrasymachus now argues.

Thrasymachus responds with a powerful tirade (343b–344c) in which he works himself up into a sort of frenzied hymn to tyranny. Practiced on a grand scale, injustice is not scorned but envied, and "injustice, if it is on a large enough scale, is stronger, freer, and more masterly than justice. And, as I said from the first, the just is what is advantageous to the stronger, while injustice is to one's own profit and advantage" (344c5–9). Thrasymachus' rant confirms that he is not a mere sociological observer, but has strong views about how an intelligent man *should* live. It also includes a powerful rebuttal of Socrates' argument (I). Thrasymachus sarcastically accuses him of childishness and naïveté: "You think that shepherds and cowherds seek the good of their sheep and cattle, and fatten them and take care of them looking to something other than their master's good and their own" (343b1–4). The shepherd shows that Socrates' induction was unreliable. Shepherding is not a version of zookeeping or animal rescue, aiming at the welfare of the sheep themselves; it is a practice in which the sheep are exploited for the benefit of the shepherds or their masters. This shows that there are crafts in which the end is the advantage not of the "subject matter" operated upon, but of the practitioner; and Thrasymachus is free to maintain that ruling is one of them. Moreover, the ruler is sometimes symbolized as a shepherd in ancient Greece, as in ancient Judaism and many other cultures; so this is not just a random counterexample, but one with a built-in claim to relevance.[9]

In response, Socrates refuses to budge: he insists that even in the case of shepherding, any benefit to the practitioner of the craft is incidental to it (345c1–345d5). Thrasymachus cannot really refute this, as opposed to ridiculing it; so we are left with a stalemate between two radically different conceptions of craft, each of which can call on plausible supporting examples. And it is striking that, although we now phrase the issues somewhat differently, the conflict – and the stalemate – between these conceptions of craft endures today, with real social battles being fought over a number of professions.[10] A good example is journalism. What is the end of the craft of journalism, which the good newspaper editor (for instance) successfully serves? Is the good newspaper the one which maximizes its own financial health, or the one which serves some disinterested end distinctive to journalism, such as making the public better informed about important political and social questions? Most journalists hold the latter, Socratic view; but proprietors, publishers, and the investors increasingly take the Thrasymachean one. Medicine too is now in practice a contested field, with doctors and profit-oriented healthcare companies often dividing along Socratic and Thrasymachean lines. Plato was not in a position to have Thrasymachus use the jargon of "maximizing return to shareholders," but he would easily recognize it as an updating of the Thrasymachean ideal, with the difference that instead of the individual, the agent practising the craft of journalism or medicine is now often a corporate entity whose "advantage" is construed in terms of profit margins and stock price. Socrates is here taking what seems to be the normal standpoint of individual craft-practitioners themselves (at least in such fields as journalism and medicine), and arguing for the autonomy of the crafts: they serve distinctive ends of their own, he insists, which impose certain goals on their practitioners and set norms for what counts as success. For Thrasymachus the crafts are heteronomous, all identical in their subordination to the extrinsic self-interested motivations reliably supplied by human *pleonexia*. He stands for those who see all lines of business as just business, with the "bottom line" the same in every case.

To reaffirm and clarify his conception of craft, Socrates now offers a supplementary argument.

II The "wage-earning" argument (345e–3457d)

Real crafts (such as medicine and, Socrates insists, shepherding too) only benefit their practitioners if extrinsic "wages" are given in return: that is why craft-practitioners get paid. In the case of rule, Socrates adds, the best "wage" for a ruler is not to be governed by someone worse than himself. The crucial move is to establish that wage-earning is distinct from the crafts it accompanies:

1 Every distinct craft has a particular distinctive end, different from the ends of the others.
2 Medicine and navigation are distinct crafts.
3 Wages can result from the practice of both medicine and navigation.
4 Therefore, wages are the end of neither medicine nor navigation.
5 Therefore, wage-earning must be the end of a third craft distinct from medicine and navigation, and practiced by the doctor and navigator in common, namely wage-earning.

There are a few steps missing here: notably, (4) does not follow from the previous premises without some further assumptions, and (5) bypasses the obvious possibility that, though wages may *result* from the practice of various crafts, they are not the *end* of any craft at all. (This is in fact the option Socrates should prefer, given the difficulties with wage-earning as a craft, which I will note in the next paragraph.) Still, the argument raises a telling point: if crafts as such were beneficial to their practitioners, why *would* they get paid? Thrasymachus' assumption that crafts are self-interested seems to be based on a sloppy failure to distinguish the craft itself from its incidental rewards.

On the other hand, the argument does not really do anything to disarm Thrasymachus' counterexample of the shepherd. Worse, the introduction of "wage-earning" as a distinct craft creates more problems than it solves. For Socrates' central thesis about craft is his opening claim in argument I, that every craft benefits not its practitioner but what it is "set over." And for the craft of wage-earning to fit that model, it would have to somehow, mysteriously, benefit the wages themselves. If instead it is admitted to be an instance of a Thrasymachean craft, one which directly benefits its practitioner, why should ruling be any different?

So taken together, arguments I and II are fraught with difficulties and deficiencies. Still, they do succeed in showing that an alternative to Thrasymachus' conception of craft (and of ruling "in the strict sense" in particular) is available, if not that it applies to every case. What Socrates now needs, and attempts to provide, is an argument which breaks the stalemate by showing that what the Thrasymachean tyrant practices *could not* be a craft.

III   The "non-pleonectic" argument (349b–350c)

Socrates argues, with appeal to examples from medicine and music, that a craftsperson does not seek to "outdo" or act pleonectically towards fellow craft-practitioners, but rather to do the *same* as they do, i.e., to perform whatever action the craft requires (I will discuss just what *pleonektein* means in a moment). Thrasymachus had presented his "ruler in the strict sense," the infallible tyrant, as the practitioner of a craft – as someone who literally raised injustice to an art form. Socrates' claim is that injustice is structurally or formally unlike a craft precisely inasmuch as it is pleonectic, whereas justice *does* have the structure of a craft. He then (in (4)–(6) below) presses the point, edging down a slippery slope from the likeness of justice and craft to an identification of justice with wisdom.

1   In practicing the recognized crafts, one expert does not act pleonectically in relation to another, but only in relation to the non-expert; the non-expert acts pleonectically in relation to everyone.
2   An unjust person acts pleonectically in relation to everyone, whereas a just person is pleonectic only towards the unjust.
3   Therefore, the unjust person is not the practitioner of a craft; and inasmuch as he resembles the expert, a just person is like a good and a clever one, and an unjust person like an ignorant and a bad one.

4 Each person, the just and the unjust, "is such as the one he resembles" (349d, 350c7–8)
5 Therefore the just person is good and clever, and an unjust one ignorant and bad.
6 Justice is virtue and wisdom and injustice is vice and ignorance.

This argument is probably the most confusing and least satisfactory of the whole series. An initial problem is that Socrates may seem to be claiming that craft-practitioners are not competitive with each other. That is obviously false, and the truth had been recognized in Greek culture ever since Hesiod, whose *Works and Days* opens by praising the "strife" involved in productive competition. Part of the solution is to see that *pleonektein* is here not simply to outdo in competition but to maximize one's possession of some good in a zero-sum context – to have more (*pleon echein*), that is, or to strive to have more, *by virtue of someone else's having less* (see LSJ, under *pleonekteô*, esp. senses I.3, II.1–2). And so understood, Socrates seems to be right that craft-performance is not pleonectic, however competitive it may be in a broader sense. If one musician plays in tune, so may another; if I navigate safely to shore, so can you. Since the goals aimed at in the practice of a craft do not exclude each other, craft is not competitive in the "win/lose" or "zero-sum" way characteristic of Thrasymachean *pleonexia* and the practice of injustice.[11]

What remains puzzling is that in Socrates' examples, "acting pleonectically" seems to be a matter of somehow overshooting the mark in the performance of a craft itself, as by tuning the strings of a lyre too high (349e). This suggests that expert action is here to be understood as involving the attainment of some kind of natural measure or limit, like the "mean" in Aristotle's doctrine of the virtues (*Nicomachean Ethics* II.6; and cf. Plato, *Philebus* 24e–26d, 55d–58d). But this raises as many puzzles as it solves. It is odd to describe the non-expert who fails to hit the mean as "acting pleonectically," as if novice doctors always prescribed *too much* (which is anyway straining the possible meaning of *pleonektein*), and odder still to describe the expert as pleonectic in relation to the non-expert (349e15, 350b7–8). Moreover, Socrates repeatedly speaks of agents as being "willing" (*ethelein*) to *pleonektein* (349e11, 350a1, 350a7, 350b7), as if it were a choice or decision. But the non-expert misses the mean involuntarily, because he makes mistakes in trying to do what the expert does successfully; pleonectic and non-pleonectic agents differ, by contrast, in their motivations and aims (cf. Annas 1981: 51–2).

Perhaps these oddities are deliberate, though, and designed to draw attention to a valid contrast lurking here: the contrast between a genuine craft-practitioner and one corrupted by *pleonexia*. For what the argument brings out is that, since the internal ends of crafts are not possible objects of pleonectic action, to "act pleonectically" *within* the actual practice of a particular craft could only mean to deviate from those ends because of the extrinsic motivation of *pleonexia*, in a way which would be indistinguishable from making a mistake: a doctor who orders irrelevant tests or pointless surgery out of greed is behaving exactly as a non-expert might do inadvertently. Socrates' examples are misleading in that not all non-experts are pleonectic (and experts are not really pleonectic towards non-experts at all); but he may reasonably insist that the pleonectic person, when acting as such, acts like a non-expert.[12] So once again, Thrasymachean tyranny does not fit the profile of a craft; whereas, Socrates now claims, justice does.

With the corollaries added in (4)–(6), Socrates gradually pushes Thrasymachus from the admission that the just person is *like* the clever one to the conclusion that justice *is* wisdom. Thrasymachus may be powerless to draw the line here, but for us to have confidence in Socrates' inferences he would have to tell us much more about exactly how craft, cleverness, and wisdom are related. As it stands, his sleight of hand is an important source of Thrasymachus' and the reader's dissatisfaction: for the final argument of Book I (argument V below) will rely crucially on this claim that justice is virtue, and Thrasymachus seems to have simply made a mistake (as a non-expert attempting to act pleonectically against an expert might do?) in assenting to it.

At any rate, Socrates now takes these arguments about craft to have shown that it is justice, not injustice, which is to be classed with the virtues (see Socrates' summary of the debate quoted in the Conclusions of this chapter, below). He now turns to consider the "power" (*dunamis*) of justice, taking on Thrasymachus' claim that injustice is "stronger and more powerful" (351a2, cf. 344c5–6).

IV The "gang-of-thieves" argument (351b–352b)

Socrates argues that injustice is, in groups, a cause of disunity, conflict, and impotence. Whether joined together in a city, an army, or a band of thieves, a group of human beings can only function successfully when they treat each other justly. (This would have struck Thrasymachus, and Plato's readers, as a truth vividly taught by history: in Greek warfare, every *polis* risked being undermined by factions among its citizens who felt unjustly treated by the status quo, and who might ally themselves with the enemy to gain power.) And, Socrates continues, similarly within the human soul: justice is what unifies and empowers us in action. The argument is thus a simple one:

1　In groups, justice unifies, empowers, and enables successful action, while injustice does the opposite.
2　Justice within a single individual must have the same effects on the soul as it does in groups.
3　Therefore, justice within a single person must unify and empower that person's soul, while injustice does the opposite.

The most obviously questionable move here is (2). The problem is not that we can never draw inferences from groups to individuals (often such analogies are fair enough) but that in this particular case the inference requires a large unstated assumption. Socrates' argument distinguishes between what we may call *internal* and *external* justice, and his thesis is that internal justice is what makes for successful action (just or otherwise) externally: the gang members must be just towards each other in order for the gang as a whole to be successfully unjust towards everyone else. Internal justice is thus the state of a system each of whose parts is *externally* just to the others: the members of the gang must each show justice towards each other, where that justice is the same property the gang as a whole lacks towards the rest of the world. So Socrates' thesis can apply to an individual only on the assumption that a human being is a system with component parts, analogous to the members of the criminal gang, each of which can be just or unjust towards the others. Book IV will of course argue that our souls do have three such parts, and the argument serves to spur us into thinking about the question; but Socrates does not here defend this crucial assumption, nor is it yet clear what it would *mean* for psychological parts to practice justice. (And he had better not be assuming that *anything* capable of external justice must be capable of internal justice, since that would lead to an infinite regress of parts.) A further problem is that this shift to internal justice leaves it unclear what has really been proven. Justice as commonly understood – as praised by Hesiod and denounced by Thrasymachus – is justice towards others, external justice; and the gang of thieves case shows that internal justice does not imply the external kind. So Socrates' argument that we need internal justice has not shown that justice in the traditional, external sense is empowering or otherwise useful for us as individuals. (When Socrates turns to explain internal justice in Book IV, many commentators would say that this problem only gets worse, and that the relation of Platonic internal justice to justice as traditionally understood remains unclear; however, Plato does there provide some argument that an internally just person will behave in an externally just way (442d11–443b6).)

At any rate, Thrasymachus responds with bad-tempered irritation (352b4–5): defeated in argument, and forbidden to launch into the speech-making he prefers, he has now largely given up, and has already made several sulky remarks to the effect that he is merely humoring Socrates (350d8–350e4, 351c5, 351d6). So Socrates may as well complete his argument with a proof of the superiority of the just life:

V The "function" argument (352d–354a)

This argument begins with a long induction to support the claim that the function of anything is "that which one can do only with it or best with it" (352e3–4, 353a9–11). From there, its structure is simple:

1 The virtue of anything is what enables it to perform its function well.
2 The function of the human soul is "taking care of things, ruling, deliberating and the like," and indeed living itself (353d3–10).
3 Justice is the virtue of the human soul (conclusion of argument III).
4 Therefore, justice enables a human soul to deliberate and live well.
5 Whoever lives well is happy.
6 Therefore, "the just person is happy, and the unjust one wretched" (354a4).

This argument completes the transition begun by the gang-of-thieves argument, placing the focus firmly on the effects of justice *within* the human soul.[13] The functional theory of virtue announced in (1) seems to be introduced largely for its intrinsic interest and importance later on;[14] the heavy lifting of the argument is done by (3), the claim imported from the conclusion of argument III, that justice is the virtue of the soul. The major weakness of the argument is imported with it, for as I noted at the time, more needs to be done to show why Thrasymachus, or we, should accept it. However, argument IV should have served to make this claim much more plausible: for it argued that justice is what enables human beings to act effectively, which is close to what (1) claims the virtue of anything does for that thing.

To sum up, I have tried to bring out that Socrates' arguments are organized around a series of claims which are both plausible and important: that the crafts have internal ends distinct from their wages or the motivations of their practitioners; that injustice or tyranny, since it is pleonectic, cannot be counted as a craft; and that human virtue, as what enables us to function effectively, may plausibly be identified with "internal" justice, which unifies and empowers its possessors. Still, we have also seen a number of points which give grounds for dissatisfaction. Socrates' account of the nature of crafts leans heavily on induction over a few examples, and his notion of a craft of wage-earning actually undermines it. The crucial assumption that justice can operate the same way in the soul as it does in society is never defended. Worst, the all-important thesis that justice is a (or even the) virtue of the soul is slipped in as a corollary to argument III, which does not directly establish it. These are serious weaknesses, and although most of them look like errors of omission I would not want to maintain that Plato is aware of them all or would find them easy to repair. Still, as we will see, they are less significant than another, more general weakness to which he himself draws our attention.

Conclusions: The Function and Limitations of the Arguments

Nothing in Plato is simple, and the debate between Socrates and Thrasymachus can be read on many levels. One could read it as merely a trailer for the arguments to come in the rest of the *Republic*.[15] The ideal of the "real ruler" as the rational expert (arguments I–III); the understanding of justice as what unifies and empowers, both in human society and in the individual soul (argument IV); the claim that it is what enables someone to function well and be happy (argument V) – these are more than nods and gestures forward, they are the central planks of the moral and political theory to come in Books IV–IX.

Another way to read the arguments is as a deliberate exercise in failure. Every reader notices a radical change of method between Books I and II of the *Republic*, and Glaucon's challenge to Socrates makes it explicit that we are to see Book II as a necessary fresh start (357a–b, 358b). The change is epitomized by the change in interlocutors: in place of the opinionated, arrogant, and bad-tempered Thrasymachus, we have the talented and tractable youths, Glaucon and Adeimantus, who share Socrates' fundamental moral allegiances and are eager to help him construct his theory. Obviously Thrasymachus would be a hopeless interlocutor for the kind of slow, constructive exposition that will occupy most of the *Republic*. So one might think that Book I is as it were programmed to fail, the better to illustrate the need for a radically different method with an essentially different interlocutor. (An extreme version of this reading is that Book I was actually first written as an independent dialogue – the *Thrasymachus*, say – and that only later did Plato's dissatisfaction with it lead him to write the rest of the *Republic*, for which he retained it as a sort of springboard.[16])

Both these readings have a grain of truth; but they need to be made more precise. To do that, we need to look more closely at the clues Plato gives us. He twice suggests that the arguments are impaired by a general flaw. When Adeimantus urges Socrates to offer a more convincing argument in Book II, he says: "Don't, then, give us only a theoretical argument (*endeixê monon tô logô*] that justice is stronger than injustice, but show what effect each has because of itself on the person who has it – the one for good and the other for bad – whether it remains hidden from gods and human beings or not" (367e1–4). And Socrates himself ends Book I with a complaint about his method. He has behaved like a glutton at a banquet, he says, snatching at each new dish before properly enjoying the previous one. With a somewhat misleadingly tidy summary of the discussion so far, he complains that they have come to be distracted from the fundamental question of *what justice is*:

> Before finding the answer to our first inquiry about what justice is, I let that go [at 347e, presumably] and turned to investigate whether it is a vice and ignorance or a kind of wisdom and virtue [argument III]. Then an argument came up about injustice being more profitable than justice, and I couldn't refrain from abandoning the previous one and following up on that [at 350d5–7, but hearkening back to 344c5–7, 347e2–7, and 348b8–10]. Hence the result of the discussion, as far as I'm concerned, is that I know nothing, for when I don't know what justice is, I'll hardly know whether it is a kind of virtue or not, or whether a person who has it is happy or unhappy. (354b3–354c3)

Now Socrates' arguments, as I have read them, have offered us plenty of important information about justice, notably that it is unifying, craft-like, the virtue of
the soul, and is what enables us to live happily. We might say that the arguments
set out significant clues or *markers* for justice: features or properties which justice
must possess, and roles it must be able to play. They do so, however, without
identifying *what justice consists in* or essentially *is* (Socrates' point at the end of
Book I), and therefore without showing in a vivid and convincing way *how* it is
able to do these things (Adeimantus' complaint). Contrast the account to be
given in Book IV of the *Republic*. Here we do learn what justice is: it is the
state in which each part of a complex system (a city or a soul) does the work
for which it is best suited without interfering in the work of the others, and, in
particular, one in which the non-rational parts of the system accept the rule of
a rational part. And because this account specifies the nature or essence of justice,
it enables us to see *how* justice is indeed a virtue, beneficial, and so on.

This contrast between the "markers" and the essence of a thing has a
profound role to play in Plato's epistemology. Socrates' complaint at the end of
Book I is familiar to readers of Plato's earlier dialogues as the principle that until
I know *what* something is – its nature or essence, as expressed in a definition –
I cannot know anything about it (cf. *Meno* 71b; *Euthyphro* 11a–b; *Protagoras*
361d).[17] This principle, taken strictly, threatens to land Plato with the "problem
of inquiry" expressed by the famous paradox in the *Meno* (80d–e): how can I
inquire so as to gain knowledge about something if I don't already know it? For
how can I recognize what I have been searching for, if I haven't encountered it
before? Plato's solution to the paradox, I believe, leans heavily on distinguishing
between the *knowledge* that we have of a thing when we have grasped its essence,
and the merely true beliefs we have about its roles, properties and effects (the
"markers") which may lead us to that essence.[18] I can gain knowledge about the
natures of things by using the markers as specifications, and looking for what
possesses them – just as I can find Meno in the market place, without having
met him before, if I correctly believe that he is the tallest man there (cf.
Aristotle, *Eudemian Ethics* II.1, 1220a15–22).

Without a full, Book IV-style account of the essence of justice, we cannot
really *know* that justice is what enables us to function, or that it is the virtue of
the soul, or even that it is better than injustice. But conversely, without some
grasp of the properties of the thing, how can any account of it ever be developed and assessed? Socrates does not exactly prove in Book IV that justice must
be what he says it is; but whatever plausibility his account has comes from the
fact that justice so defined can be seen as having all the "markers" set out in the
arguments with Thrasymachus. (And, for that matter, those set out elsewhere in
Books I–IV. For instance, the pre-philosophical definitions of justice offered by
Cephalus and Polemarchus both revolve around the intuitive notion that justice
is somehow a matter of *rendering what is due*, whether that means straightforwardly paying your debts (Cephalus) or giving friend and enemy the differing
treatment they deserve (Polemarchus). And in Book IV, justice turns out to be

the state in which each part of the soul or city is given the role which is due to it.)

This is the grain of truth in the "trailer" reading, which was however too general and weak. The Book I arguments are not just gesturing towards Book IV as a nice artistic touch, or softening us up for it as a rhetorical gambit: they are a philosophically necessary preparation for us to recognize justice when we encounter it there. And the grain of truth in the "programmed-to-fail" reading likewise can now be put in its place: the defects of the arguments, and in particular their failure to address the essential nature of justice, are intrinsic to them precisely because of this role as preparation for the essential account. According to Aristotle, Plato thought it was important to distinguish between arguments "on the way to first principles" and "from first principles": it is like the difference between the race to the turning point and then back to the finish line (*Nicomachean Ethics* I.4, 1095a30–30b4). The Book I arguments are arguments on the way to the first principles (that is, the full account of justice in Book IV), and we can only really appreciate them when we have seen how they serve that function – which means, when we come to them again *after* reading the book as a whole. They show that the *Republic* is (as you already knew) a book to be read more than once.

Notes

1   Thrasymachus was a real person, a famous sophist (i.e., a professional intellectual and teacher, especially of public speaking). However, we have no evidence that the position of Plato's character was ever advanced by the historical Thrasymachus. His views sound rather (but not exactly) like the beliefs of another contemporary Sophist, Antiphon, in the surviving fragments of his *On Truth*. (For the fragments of *On Truth*, see Gagarin and Woodruff 1995 or Pendrick 2002.)

2   Quotations are in the translation by G. M. A. Grube, revised by C. D. C. Reeve, in Cooper 1997, in some cases with revisions.

3   E.g. Annas: "Socrates' arguments . . . [against Thrasymachus' principal thesis] are all weak and unconvincing to an amazing degree" (1981: 50); and Reeve: "Book I emerges as a brilliant critique of Socrates, every aspect of which is designed to reveal a flaw in his theories" (1988: 23).

4   See e.g. Chappell 1993, which includes a survey of other possible interpretations. An earlier version of the interpretation which follows is presented in Barney 2004; this includes a comparison of Thrasymachus to Plato's other great spokesman for immoralism, Callicles in the *Gorgias*.

5   However, it is not always the unjust individual who is singled out: a man's descendants, or his whole community, may be punished for his behavior (*Works and Days* 276–327). Later poets relocate these rewards and punishments to the afterlife of the unjust individual; in Book II of the *Republic*, part of Adeimantus' case against justice is that the poets are not consistent about this, and that loopholes are left for the unjust to bribe the gods or for cult initiates to get special treatment (362d–366e).

6 On the philosophical significance of immoralism, see Williams 1985: 22–32; 1993: 3–13.

7 Two clarifications are called for here. First, ancient Greek has no word exactly corresponding to "moral" or "morality." However, ancient concerns about "justice" often overlap with modern philosophical discussions of "morality," since justice is the virtue which requires that we restrain our self-interest and respect the rights and interests of others. Second, the Greek concept of *eudaimonia* is rather different from our "happiness." It is a long-term condition, involving much more than conscious feelings and moods: to say that someone is *eudaimôn* is to say that she is flourishing and successful, that as a matter of objective fact her life is going well. So Thrasymachus' version of the "immoralist" claim, more precisely put, is that injustice promotes the flourishing of the person who practices it, and that we therefore have no good reason to be just.

8 Socrates and Plato may agree with Thrasymachus, not that human behavior is always pleonectic (that is, aimed at maximizing wealth and power and the goods they can provide), but that it is in a more general way self-interested or egoistic. For Socrates' argument about wage-earning seems to assume that no one would practice a craft unless it did benefit him through "wages" of some sort (347a–d). Moreover, the argument of the *Republic* as a whole is framed in egoistic terms: it aims to vindicate justice by showing that it benefits the just person. It is debated among scholars whether Plato thinks that our reasons for action could ever be *ultimately* disinterested – in particular, whether a Guardian might act simply to further the good as such, rather than his own good or happiness.

9 Cf. Adam 1902 on 343a7. For Plato's own use of the image, and his reservations about it, see *Statesman* 265d–268d, 274e ff.

10 See Gardner et al. 2001.

11 Of course, we can specify the aims of the craft-practitioner in ways which *sound* exclusive; for instance, a doctor might strive to be the *best* doctor in her city. But consider what forms this "competition" might take. First and most obviously, she might compete simply by practicing medicine as well as she can. For under normal circumstances, she can have no effect on whether other doctors do their work well or badly: she can only strive to be the best she can be, letting the comparative results take care of themselves. This sort of normal and healthy craft-competition then turns out to be no different from the non-comparative efforts of practitioners to attain the end of the craft. If alternatively she decides to compete by hiding her rivals' medical equipment or teaching them nonsense, it seems fair to say that she is no longer acting *qua* doctor at all – for she would be acting *against* the end of medicine, which is the patients' health.

12 I here pass over the question of how particular craft-operations (prescribing the right dosage, hitting the right note) relate to the higher-order internal ends of the crafts (health, beautiful music). Perhaps we are to assume that those higher-order ends are also to be understood in terms of a mean. This is not an unreasonable assumption: Plato might well think that the *reason* there is a right dose in medicine is that health itself consists in a mean state, so that the right dose is one which establishes it in the patient.

13 It is odd that Socrates here speaks of the soul as if it were an instrument which "we" use: for who are "we," anyway, if not our souls? In other dialogues Plato is more

inclined to suppose that the soul *is* the person, and the *First Alcibiades* explicitly argues for this (130a–c). (The *Alcibiades* may well not be an authentic work of Plato; perhaps a later Platonist noticed that Plato relies on this identification without ever arguing for it, and set out to make good the deficiency.) But perhaps we are to see Socrates as here playing fair with Thrasymachus; *he* could not be assumed to share this conception of the self as the soul, especially since for Plato it entails that the good of one's soul is far more important than physical health or wealth. So what Socrates shows here is that *even if* you think of yourself as something distinct from your soul, using it as a tool, you must admit that the soul is such an *important* tool that your welfare depends on its being in a good state.

14 For an account of the *Republic* which brings out the centrality of the idea of function to its moral and political theories, see Santas 2001. Aristotle will explicitly use the idea of a human function as the fundamental principle of his account of virtue and happiness in the *Nicomachean Ethics*, in the famous "function argument" of *NE* I.7. (However, Aristotle's understanding of a function differs importantly from Plato's concept, as I hope to show in a future paper.)

15 E.g., White 1979: "Book I is a kind of prologue to the *Republic*" (p. 61); "the purpose of Book I is to raise issues" (p. 65).

16 For the history of this hypothesis, and a convincing refutation of it, see Kahn 1993.

17 Confusingly, Plato seems to see this as true on two levels, which he does not always keep distinct. First, if I have no acquaintance *at all* with something, I can know nothing about it. If the name "Meno" means nothing to me, I cannot know, or even believe, that Meno is handsome or rich (*Meno* 71b). More interestingly, knowledge (not mere belief) about the properties of something depends on knowledge of what it really, by nature is – in Aristotelian terminology, its "essence." Plato seems to think of this knowledge of essences as also a kind of acquaintance – as if only by knowing Meno first-hand can I really know that he is handsome, and as if knowing the essence of something is somehow first-hand in the same way.

18 This is a controversial claim, and would have to be supported by a full interpretation of the *Meno*; it is fairly explicitly Aristotle's solution to the problem in the *Posterior Analytics*.

I would like to thank Tad Brennan, Stephen Menn, and Gerasimos Santas for extremely helpful comments on an earlier draft of this paper. I am particularly grateful to Tad Brennan for forcing me to confront some of the inadequacies of my reading of argument III.

References and further reading

Adam, J. (ed.) (1902) *The Republic of Plato*, 2 vols., Cambridge: Cambridge University Press.

Adkins, A. W. H. (1960) *Merit and Responsibility: A Study in Greek Values*, Oxford: Clarendon Press.

Algra, K. (1996) "Observations on Plato's Thrasymachus: the case for 'pleonexia'," in K. Algra, P. Van der Horst, D. Runia (eds.) *Polyhistor*, Leiden: Brill.

Annas, J. (1981) *An Introduction to Plato's* Republic, Oxford: Clarendon Press.

Balot, R. K. (2001) *Greed and Injustice in Classical Athens*, Princeton, NJ: Princeton University Press.

Barney, R. (2004) "Callicles and Thrasymachus," in *Stanford Encyclopedia of Philosophy* (http://plato.stanford.edu/entries/callicles-thrasymachus/).

──(forthcoming) "The sophistic movement," in M. L. Gill and P. Pellegrin (eds.) *The Blackwell Companion to Ancient Philosophy.*

Bett, R. (2002) "Is there a sophistic ethics?," *Ancient Philosophy* 22, pp. 235–62.

Chappell, T. D. J. (1993) "The virtues of Thrasymachus," *Phronesis* 38, pp. 1–17.

──(2000) "Thrasymachus and definition," *Oxford Studies in Ancient Philosophy* 18, pp. 101–7.

Cooper, J. M. (ed.) (1997) *Plato: Complete Works*, Indianapolis: Hackett Publishing.

Dover, K. (1974) *Greek Popular Morality in the Time of Plato and Aristotle*, Oxford: Blackwell.

Everson, S. (1998), "The incoherence of Thrasymachus,", *Oxford Studies in Ancient Philosophy* 16, pp. 99–131.

Furley, D. J. (1981) "Antiphon's case against justice," in G. B. Kerferd (ed.) *The Sophists and their Legacy*, Wiesbaden: Steiner.

Gagarin, M., and P. Woodruff (eds. and trans.) (1995) *Early Greek Political Thought from Homer to the Sophists*, Cambridge: Cambridge University Press.

Gardner, H., M. Csikszentmihalyi, and W. Damon (2001) *Good Work*, New York: Basic Books.

Gifford, M. (2001) "Dramatic dialectic in *Republic* Book I," *Oxford Studies in Ancient Philosophy* 20, pp. 35–106.

Kahn, C. (1981) "The origins of social contract theory in the fifth century BC," in G. B. Kerferd (ed.) *The Sophists and their Legacy*, Wiesbaden: Steiner.

──(1993) "Proleptic composition in the *Republic*, or Why Book 1 was never a separate dialogue," *Classical Quarterly* 43/i, pp. 131–42.

Kerferd, G. B. (1981a) *The Sophistic Movement*, Cambridge: Cambridge University Press.

──(ed.) (1981b) *The Sophists and their Legacy*, Wiesbaden: Steiner.

Liddell, H. G., R. Scott, and H. S. Jones (LSJ) (1996) *A Greek-English Lexicon*, with revised supplement, Oxford: Clarendon Press.

O'Neill, B. (1988) "The struggle for the soul of Thrasymachus," *Ancient Philosophy* 8, pp. 167–85.

Pendrick, G. (ed. and trans.) (2002) *Antiphon the Sophist: The Fragments*, Cambridge: Cambridge University Press.

Reeve, C. D. C. (1988) *Philosopher-Kings*, Princeton, NJ: Princeton University Press.

Roochnik, D. (1996) *Of Art and Wisdom*, University Park, PA: Pennsylvania State University Press.

Santas, G. (2001) *Goodness and Justice*, Oxford: Blackwell.

White, N. (1979) *A Companion to Plato's* Republic, Indianapolis: Hackett Publishing.

White, S. A. (1995) "Thrasymachus the diplomat," *Classical Philology* 90, pp. 307–27.

Williams, B. (1985) *Ethics and the Limits of Philosophy*, Cambridge, MA: Harvard University Press.

──(1993) [1972] *Morality*, Cambridge: Cambridge University Press.

4

Plato's Challenge: the Case against Justice in *Republic* II

Christopher Shields

What reason remains for us to prefer justice to the greatest injustice? ... By what route will anyone with any resources of mind or wealth or body or birth set any value on justice, rather than simply guffawing when he hears someone praising it?

Plato, Republic 366b3–366c3

Why be moral? Why, more particularly, be just? On some occasions, I feel inclined to act against the demands of justice as I understand them. I may want to pilfer just a bit of cash from the till; or I may prefer to avoid reporting some of my income in order to move myself into a lower tax bracket; or I may want to drive a bigger and more luxurious car, even though I fully appreciate that my doing so will leave the environment slightly less well off for future generations. Why should I not indulge these and other like inclinations when I am so disposed? If I do not on each occasion of my acting want to abide by the dictates of justice as I conceive them, then perhaps I would do better to ignore the pangs of conscience when they prick me, to deride them as having only a spurious claim on my motives. Perhaps, indeed, I should pattern all of my behavior and indeed structure my entire life so as to maximize my own self-indulgence and pleasure, even though I know that others will suffer in little and large ways for my doing so. What matters to me in the end, after all, is my own supreme self and not the claims of those so remote from me in time and place that I need never hear or heed their pleas.

I cannot, of course, indulge my every fancy: very often I know that I will be punished if caught, and made to feel shame if my conduct is brought to light. If I steal cash from the till, then I risk being fired and prosecuted for embezzlement; if the tax man investigates me and exposes me as a fraud, then I will pay heavy fines, far in excess of what I would have had to pay had I simply reported my true income in the first place; and while I will probably never be made to feel sufficiently ashamed for driving a big car that I will actually stop doing so, I may find myself having to avoid some circles of environmentalists who will forever make themselves unpleasant to me with their ceaseless harping and who will thus at the very least inconvenience me on my way to refuel. For these reasons, at least, I may deny my impulses towards injustice and conform to a comfortable social norm, but only because I regard doing so as in one way or another advantageous.

So, one motive for deferring to the demands of justice, as I understand them, may simply be *calculative*. Although if left to my own devices, I might not want to bother about justice, I am in point of fact not left to my own devices in this world: there are others whose demands impinge upon my predilections and who can and will make me uncomfortable if I ignore them for too long. Rational egoism thus dictates that I follow the strictures of justice at least to the extent that I must do so to avoid detection. To that extent, at least, perhaps I have some reason to be just.

Socrates' interlocutors in *Republic* II, Glaucon and Adeimantus,[1] who introduce themselves as the mouthpieces of common sense and common conception, are willing to concede at least that motive to be just (358a2–6).[2] Most people, they allow, understand that they must be just in order to avoid suffering the consequences of *detected* injustice. They quickly point out, however, that any such motive is extrinsic, that in fact any such motive is really rather a motive to *seem to be just*, and not any sort of a motive to *be just for its own sake*. The question with which we began, however, concerned why we ought to *be* just. Anyone can allow that it might be prudent to seem to be just, and even further that in order to seem just it will be necessary to be just at least some of the time; but so much says little to our initial question, unless it is to say in fact that we have no reason at all to be just for its own sake.

Glaucon and Adeimantus also, however, show themselves to be alive to a question which is properly prior to the question with which we began. Each of us may ask: why defer to the demands of justice – as I understand them? The prior question pertains to our understanding of the character of these demands, and so ultimately to the character of justice itself. If I suppose that justice demands that I grow my own vegetables instead of supporting globalized agribusiness, then perhaps I am simply confused. It may be the case that globalized agribusiness begets injustice; or it may not. Beyond the many and complex empirical and economic questions pertinent to this matter there lies a purely philosophical question, an analytical question concerning the nature of justice itself, namely: *what is justice?* That is, even after we have agreed about all the empirical and economic facts, we might yet disagree about whether they constitute an injustice. If we disagree about the nature of justice itself, then our dispute will rage on even after we have come to an agreement about the non-evaluative facts, until, finally, we analyze the nature of justice to our mutual satisfaction.

This is why Plato does not rest content in *Republic* II to pose a question concerning whether we have any good reason to be just, or more generally, to be moral. If we want to answer these questions properly, if we want to know whether we should be just, if we want to know why we should be moral, then we will want to know in the first instance what it is that we should want to be. For it may well turn out – and in subsequent books of the *Republic* Plato will argue stridently that it does turn out – that most people have a false conception of justice and a false conception of morality. It follows that when most people say that they have no reason to be just, then perhaps what they fail to respect is not in fact justice, but rather something else altogether, perhaps conventional social norms or local law, which upon a careful consideration might or might not turn out to be just. If Plato is right, and most people misunderstand justice, they also misunderstand its demands; it remains a possibility, consequently, that when they come to understand justice rightly, most people will come to appreciate why they should want to be just after all.

Thus Plato sets himself a two-part challenge in *Republic* II, a challenge which will chart the course for most of the rest of the *Republic*.[3] He must: (1) define justice (*dikaiosunê*);[4] and (2) show that justice is desirable for its own sake, and not merely for its consequences (358b4–7). Much of *Republic* II makes vivid why most people think – whether they admit it in public or not – that justice (as they conceive it) is a waste of time, not to be prized in itself, for its own sake, but is rather something to be avoided so far as is possible. The book closes with Plato making the perfectly plausible observation that when most people take such an attitude towards justice and its demands, their doing so reflects a particular understanding of justice, one which may well prove incorrect when unearthed and analyzed. This is why, he says, it is necessary to begin carefully and slowly, constructing a perfect city whose justice is manifest to all (368d1–369a3). Only then, he implies, will we find ourselves in a position to understand the true nature of justice, which, when understood, will prove to be something we all do and should prize for its own sake.

The Situation of Republic II

Although Glaucon and Adeimantus had been present throughout the conversation reported in *Republic* I, neither had played a very substantial role in the refutation of Thrasymachus. The second book of Plato's *Republic* opens to find them regrouped and ready to take up the campaign to discover the nature of justice afresh. *Republic* I had ended on something of a dispiriting note: Thrasymachus, having been silenced but hardly satisfied, withdrew with a sneer; the discussion, like those of so many of the early, Socratic dialogues, ended aporetically, without any positive resolution.[5] At the end of the book, Socrates reports:

> The result of our conversation is that I know nothing; for so long as I do not know what justice is, I shall hardly to know whether or not it is a kind of virtue, or whether the one who possesses it is unhappy or happy. (354c1–4)

In so speaking, Socrates effectively calls for an analysis of justice.[6] If we want to know whether justice really is a virtue, as we have all supposed until Thrasymachus called even that platitudinous-sounding contention into question (344c2–7, 354b3–9), or if we want to show that the presence of justice in a person's life will make her happier than she would have been in its absence, then first we shall have to know *what justice is*. If we cannot say at all what justice is, then we will hardly be able to characterize its relation to other qualities or to specify what its significance in a person's life may be.

As *Republic* II opens, Socrates reports that he thought that the discussion regarding justice had reached its conclusion. Instead, as it turns out, the first book of the *Republic* proved only a prelude to what followed (357a1–2). In fact, the challenge with which Socrates finds himself faced in *Republic* II is far more serious, and far more engagingly put, than anything he had encountered in the first book. In this sense, the opening of *Republic* II serves as a second and improved introduction to the dialogue.[7] For just as the chapter opens, Glaucon asks Socrates a rather Socratic-sounding question: does Socrates want all present to be genuinely convinced that justice is better than injustice, or will he rest content with having simply silenced Thrasymachus? Socrates, unsurprisingly, responds that he wants the genuine article: he wants to persuade others that justice really is better than injustice (357a4–357b3).

What Kind of Good is Justice?

If he is to succeed in his aims, Socrates will have to begin by coming to terms with a distinction drawn by Glaucon between three classes of good things and to show where justice fits among them. The classes delineated are in some ways clear and in some ways perplexing. They are clear insofar they reflect an immediately intuitive way of dividing up the kinds of things we value. At the same time, some of the examples Glaucon uses to illustrate the division he has in mind suggest that this initially intuitive divisions may not correspond precisely to those he has in mind. The three types of goods are (357b–d): I Things valued for their own sake, and not for their consequences. II Things valued both for their own sake and for their consequences. III Things valued only for their consequences and not for their own sake.

Initially, the division thus drawn seems to correspond to a straightforward distinction between *intrinsic* and *instrumental* goods. Some things, like happiness, are intrinsic goods, never wanted for anything beyond themselves (and so seem to correspond to type-I goods); other things like money, are purely instrumental, valued only for what they can procure and never in themselves (and so seem to be of type-III); still other things, like health, appear both intrinsically and instrumentally valuable (and so to correspond to type-II goods). Looked at this way, type-I goods are surely superior to type-II and type-III, at least inasmuch as items in the latter two categories are subordinated to items in the first. We desire money, rightly or wrongly, for the sake of happiness; we do not seek happiness in order to have more money.

The first indication that this natural way of thinking about Glaucon's classification of goods cannot be exactly what he intends emerges when he suggests, to Socrates' immediate agreement, that the best sort of good thing belongs not to type-I but to type-II. This indicates that we should perhaps not regard type-I as supreme, a conclusion further reinforced by the examples of that type provided by Glaucon. He claims that type-I goods comprise "harmless pleasures" and other simple enjoyments of the moment (357b7–9), modest delights which though valued for their own sakes hardly constitute the highest good for a human being. Further, if we conclude that good things of type-II cannot be ultimate, on the grounds they are valued not only for themselves but for their consequences, then it will follow that Glaucon's list is not intended to be exhaustive. Rather, the good things taxonomized are evidently understood by Glaucon as subordinate to some further good, the ultimate good, whatever that may be.[8] Among the goods listed, type-II goods are the most prized, because they are more closely connected than any other kind of good to the ultimate good not listed. Passing pleasures are fine, but they are far removed from what is of ultimate value for a human being; and mere instruments are sought only for their consequences and thus do not even command our interest as what they are in themselves.

This explains why Glaucon wants justice praised as a type-II good, rather than a type-I good. It also shows how our initial intuitive reading of the division, while not wholly incorrect, can be a bit misleading. If we were thinking of the intrinsic goods of type-I as ultimate as well as intrinsic, then we have misunderstood Glaucon's request. Whatever the ultimate good may be, it does not find its way into Glaucon's taxonomy of goods, but rather stands behind it.

If that is so, however, there immediately arises another, more troubling puzzle regarding Glaucon's three-part classification and the request he structures in its terms. He asks Socrates to show that justice is a type-II good, something valued both for itself and for what flows from it. Glaucon very clearly wants justice praised in itself and not merely for its consequences. If, as suggested, type-II goods are not ultimate, if they are good in part because of their relation to some further good standing beyond them, like happiness, then Glaucon seems guilty of an incoherence in demanding simultaneously that justice be praised in itself *and* for its contribution to a good beyond itself. Indeed, he seems to be asking Socrates to praise justice in itself *by* praising it for its contribution to something beyond itself, namely happiness. That then comes perilously close to a request for justice to be praised as intrinsically good on the grounds that it is instrumentally good. That would be an odd, or even incoherent, request.

Indeed, even if we do not accept the suggestion that Glaucon's three-part classification of goods is subordinate to a further good whose end they serve, there is already some peculiarity in his asking to have justice praised in itself by being identified as a type-II good; for those goods, according to our intuitive taxonomy, are both intrinsic and instrumental. While showing justice to be a type-II good would thus suffice to show that it has intrinsic value, it would also needlessly locate its value in its consequences, perhaps in the very rewards or reputations Glaucon and Adeimantus avowedly want set aside in the appraisal of justice they request. Looked at this way, there seems to be an independent tension inherent in their challenge. Glaucon says in a number of different ways that he wants justice praised in isolation from its relation to other goods. He says that he wants it praised "itself, on its own account" (*auto hautou heneka*; 357b6), "itself, in terms of itself" (*auto kath' houto*; 358b5), and "itself, because of itself" (*autêdi' hautên*; 367b4). At the same time, Adeimantus says in simple terms that in praising justice as a type-II good, he expects Socrates to focus on how "justice, in itself, benefits the man who has it in him . . . leaving rewards and reputation for others to praise" (367d3–5; cf. 366e5–9, 367b2–9, d3–4, e3–5).[9] If they want it praised as an intrinsic good by pointing to its *benefits*, then Glaucon and Adeimantus evidently want something rather odd. Theirs may seem, accordingly, an unfair, even incoherent, demand upon Socrates, as if they were requiring him to prove that pleasure is an intrinsic good by pointing to some good residue of value left behind after it has gone. Socrates would be right to respond that whatever its after-effects, pleasure is not shown to be intrinsically good by specifying what further good we might expect to obtain by means of its presence. In the same way, we might now expect him to respond that if Glaucon and Adeimantus are seeking to have the *benefits* of justice identified, then they are not asking to see it praised in itself, as they claim to be.

That Socrates does not respond along these lines suggests that he understands Glaucon and Adeimantus' request in a different sort of way, that he shares with both of his interlocutors an understanding about the challenge they mean to put to him. They are not asking him to prove that justice should be praised as an ultimate good, as something whose possession can make no contribution to anything beyond itself. Certainly they want some predictable effects of possessing justice set aside. We have already seen that Adeimantus expressly forbids Socrates to praise justice for the rewards or reputation it may procure for its possessor (367b5–7). This does not preclude its being praised for its effects upon a just person's soul. Socrates might legitimately focus on the contribution justice makes to the happily lived life, if it makes any contribution to such a life, without focusing on its purely extrinsic benefits, such as reputation or public accolade – or eventual sainthood for that matter.[10]

Still, one might want to press the point. If it is to be praised for its benefits, then justice is not strictly being praised for itself, as an intrinsic good. What is it exactly, one may yet want to know, that Glaucon and Adeimantus expect of Socrates? Do they want justice shown to be choiceworthy for its benefits or for itself? If we attend once again to the illustrations employed by Glaucon in his initial classification of goods, we can see that the answer is, in a sense, *both*. That is, the question presents a false dichotomy, a point evidently appreciated by all of the participants in the discussion of *Republic* II. According to Glaucon, whose division we are considering, the best examples of type-II goods are health, knowledge, and vision (358c1–3). Health is praiseworthy in its own right, by itself, and on its own account. We brush our teeth and floss in order to have dental health; we do not seek dental health so that we might floss and brush twice a day. In general, we desire health and do things for its sake. Even so, we also desire health for the contribution it makes to be best kind of life we can lead. Health is, however, not something left behind or discarded as without value once we come to procure the greater good sought via it. Health contributes to a good life in the way that a well-tuned violin section contributes to the playing of a symphony: part of what it is for the symphony to be well played *is* for the violin section to perform well. We might reasonably praise the playing of the violin section in tonight's concert by commending the sharpness of its entrances and the precision of its pitch, and for the contribution it has made to an overall beautiful orchestral performance, all as a way of praising the playing itself, in its own terms. This would be a far cry from praising the members of the section for being nattily dressed at tonight's concert. In the same way, we value health as something contributing to a good beyond itself insofar as it *partly constitutes* that good. So, we might well praise health both as something good in itself and because of its contribution to the best sort life available to us. Indeed, it is something good in itself at least in part because of that very contribution.

Or again, suppose that someone drives alertly and cautiously, obeying posted speed limits and paying heed to all regulations of the road. When a flashing light indicates that she should proceed with care, she does so, when she hears emergency sirens, she pulls to the side of the road, and so on. When asked why she is driving within the speed limit, she will rightly answer that she drives slowly in order to drive well and safely. Her goal is safe driving; and she realizes this goal partly by driving within the speed limit. Clearly her driving well and safely is not an end reached by a means, driving slowly, which is then set aside, as money is once spent. Rather, intrinsic to her reaching her aim is precisely her executing the activities which constitute it.[11]

In the same way, Glaucon and Socrates can safely agree that acting justly might be a type-II good as something valued both for itself and for something beyond itself, namely the best life which it partly constitutes. There is, then, nothing incoherent in Glaucon's request or in Socrates' response. There is, rather, a formidable challenge to be met by that response. Why should acting justly be thought to constitute the best life available to us, even in part? Many people, as Glaucon notes, regard living justly as a severe impediment to their private aims.

Taken together, these observations suggest that Socrates understands the task he is to undertake, the task of praising justice as a type-II good, in a highly specific way. He is expected – and understands himself to be expected – to show that justice, like health, is something good in itself, and so something choice-worthy in itself, precisely because it is partially constitutive of an overarching good which is still more ultimate than it is itself considered alone, bereft of the role it plays in the best lived life. Here too, then, Glaucon's illustration proves telling: Socrates is asked to show that justice is the kind of good which health is (357c1–4), the sort of thing we prize both for its own nature and for the contribution it makes to the life which embraces it as a constitutive component. It is fair and appropriate to appreciate this shared understanding when we come to evaluate the success of Plato's response as its unfolds in *Republic* IV and beyond.[12]

The Origin and Nature of Justice

Although they repeatedly disassociate themselves from the views advanced by Thrasymachus and espoused by the many, Glaucon and Adeimantus nevertheless take it as their brief to put the strongest version of their cases forward (358c6–358d3, 367a9–367b2).[13] For only by their doing so will Socrates be positioned to achieve his aim of convincing his interlocutors that justice is preferable to injustice. He can genuinely persuade others only by entertaining and refuting the most forceful and plausible versions of their theories.

Glaucon and Socrates agree at the outset that most people regard justice as a type-III good, as something tedious like exercise, to be practiced only to the degree that some extrinsic good to it can be extracted from doing so (357c5–358a9). We exercise for the sake of health. Why, then, are we just? According to Glaucon, most people practice justice only because they understand its origin and nature in a certain way. Justice, think most people, arose out of coordinated rational self-interest. People sign on to the dictates of justice because – and only to the degree that – they must in order to lead relatively tranquil lives. This can be appreciated by considering, suggests Glaucon, the very origin of justice; for when we focus on its origin, we also uncover its true nature (358e3–359b5).

Imagine a historical or quasi-historical period which existed prior to the organized societies in which we now live. In that world, there were no laws, no police or judicial systems, no state-sponsored armies, and no recourse against aggression beyond brute strength and still fiercer aggression. In that world, says Glaucon, most people found themselves, in the absence of laws, defenseless against aggressors capable of overpowering them. Some people, those superior in strength and wit, dominated completely; others, the very weak and the very stupid, were utterly dominated; most of us, though, were somewhere in the middle, sometimes dominating and sometimes being dominated in turn. In this stateless state of nature, most people feel both the sting of abuse and the power of subjugation in turn. They take what they are inclined to take when they are able and feel the pleasure of their conquest, but they also suffer at the hands of those whose aggression they cannot turn back. In this condition, the vast major-ity of humanity quickly realizes that is in its interest, having tasted the extremes of domination and subordination, to move out of the lawless state, to make laws and compacts which constrain the actions of the strongest. This they do, and call the laws they create *just* (359a2–5). Such, then, is the origin and nature of justice:

> This is the origin and essence of justice: it is between what is best, doing wrong without paying the penalty, and what is worst, being wronged without the power to exact revenge. So, as something mid-way between these extremes, justice is accepted not as something good, but is honored rather because of powerlessness to do wrong ... That, Socrates is the nature of justice and such are the circum-stance in which it arose. (359a4–359b5)

In fact, no one capable of perpetrating harm with impunity would ever dream of signing on to such a compromise. To do so, says Glaucon, would be madness (359b3–4). Only abject losers and we mid-level weaklings, the vast majority of humankind, incapable of unfettered domination, find such a bargain attractive.

Importantly, in this account Glaucon makes claims both about the *nature* of justice and about its origins. He in fact implies that the nature (*phusis*, 359b4–5) and essence (*ousia*, 359a4–5) of justice is determined by its origins.[14] He sug-gests that the nature of justice is simply determined by the compacts of com-promise we find attractive and necessary in order to avoid a state of complete lawlessness. It is, then, relative to this understanding that justice can readily be seen as a type-III good. The argument implicit in his account is then:

1 If the nature of justice is revealed by its contractual origin, then people will (rightly) practice justice only unwillingly and to the extent they must in order to escape the lawless state.
2 The nature of justice is revealed by its contractual origin.
3 Hence, people (rightly) practice justice only unwillingly and to the extent that they must in order to escape the lawless state.
4 If (3), then justice is a type-III good.
5 So, justice is a type-III good.

The condition (4) seems fair enough. If it has been shown that justice is akin to foul medicine or exercise, then it will be a type-III good. So, (5) will follow from (3), if (3) is established. The interim conclusion (3), in its turn, plainly follows from (1) and (2), and so is itself true if they are true.

The initial premise (1) has at least some initial plausibility, if only in view of its conditional character. If the very nature of justice is revealed as contractually begotten, if justice is a product of our coordinated agreements and is even coextensive with the laws we create for the purpose of escaping the state of nature (359a2–4), then it may well be true that our motives for justice extend only so far as those laws are arrayed in our interest. Still, much more would need to be said on behalf of (1) in order to show it to be ultimately defensible, though in the present context, that of setting a prima facie challenge about the kind of good justice can be supposed to be, it can be provisionally admitted.

In the present context, then, everything hangs on (2). In order to show that (2) is true, Glaucon need not maintain that the story told about the origin of justice is historical fact. It suffices to show (2) holds counterfactually, that even now we are motivated to follow the prescripts of justice only because we fear statelessness, that we would prefer to sacrifice a hypothesized ability to perpetrate wrongdoing in order to stave off the threat of real suffering at the hands of those we cannot fend off.

That said, Glaucon's presentation of what most people say about justice does not suffice to make what most people say true. Indeed, interestingly, Socrates might even be willing to agree that *if* justice had the nature that Glaucon says most people think it has, then they might well be right to treat it as a type-III good. After all, if we think that justice is restricted to what we say is just when we codify our laws, and our sole motive for being lawful resides in the fact that we think we must do so in order to avoid detection, then why should we not look upon justice as an instrument akin to exercise or medicine? We will take it if we must, but only because we must as a means to something we antecedently desire.

Looked at in this way, Plato would do well to dispute the claims about the *nature* of justice made and repeated in the course of Glaucon's characterizing its contractual origin. This he will eventually do. Indeed, while Plato will agree that justice has a nature, he will deny that it has an origin in any contractual agreement, historical or counterfactual. On the contrary, the nature he will argue belongs to justice reveals it to be a virtue without any origin in time or place. Importantly, if Plato can later show that it lacks the nature Glaucon ascribes to it on behalf of the many, then it will remain at least an open question as to whether justice is best understood as a type-II or a type-III good. To this extent, Glaucon's claims about the origins of justice serve only as an invitation to Plato to dig more deeply into its essence and nature. We should expect the account he articulates in *Republic* IV to constitute Plato's acceptance of this invitation.

The Tale of Gyges

Having advanced these claims about the origin and nature of justice, Glaucon has not rested his brief on behalf of Thrasymachus and the many. In what is certainly one of the most striking and memorable episodes of the entire *Republic*, Glaucon presses on by recounting the story of a mythical ring said to belong to the ancestor of the Lydian, Gyges,[15] a ring which bestowed the power of invisibility, and so of undetectability, upon its wearer. Gyges was a shepherd working in the service of a king. One day while attending his flocks he discovered a ring on a shimmering, larger-than-life corpse exposed in a chasm opened by a violent storm. Naturally, he appropriated the ring for himself. When some time later he met with others in the king's employment, he discovered, while fiddling with the ring, that it had the power to make him invisible. When he turned the setting inward, he disappeared; when he turned it around again, he became visible once more. Upon making this astonishing discovery, Gyges lost no time in using the power of the ring to advance his interests as he conceived them. As Glaucon reports, Gyges in swift order seduced the queen and with her complicity killed the king, thereby establishing himself as ruler rather than ruled (360a4–360b2). Clearly, what Gyges stumbled upon was not just the power of invisibility. The real power he gained was the power of undetectability, which carries with it the power to decouple two things we normally find inextricably intertwined: (1) the motive to avoid injustice because it is an injustice and (2i) the motive to avoid injustice because we may well be punished if we are caught being unjust.

So far, then, the tale off Gyges' ring is a story about Gyges and his course of action when liberated from the fear of detection. Glaucon makes the story more piquant when he generalizes its results. Some would say, concludes Glaucon, that this story is really in essence a "great proof [*mega tekmérion*] that no one is just willingly" (360c5–6). This is a striking expansion, and one which commends a certain amount of skeptical resistance. To begin, how could this simple story constitute a "great *proof*" of anything at all? Moreover, even if it can be seen to constitute a proof of something or other, how can it be taken to establish so sweeping a conclusion, that *no one* is willingly just?

In the face of these questions, two features of the tale of Gyges' ring are immediately noteworthy. The first is precisely that the story can be framed as a *proof*. Glaucon intends the tale to encode an argument for a conclusion, one which he has readily extracted for our consideration. The second feature is connected to the first. The story encodes an argument because it is expressly introduced as a certain kind of *thought-experiment* (359b7–359c1), perhaps the first of its kind in the history of philosophy. Plato asks us in the telling of this story to separate two things which normally march hand in hand in our lives as we in fact live them: (1) our engaging in wrongdoing; and (2) the strong possibility of being caught for doing wrong. Because in fact we need to fear being caught on almost every occasion of wrongdoing, our motives for avoiding wrongdoing may never be completely transparent to us. For example, a woman may entertain cheating on her husband with an attractive co-worker, only to decide against doing so on the grounds that it might jeopardize her position in the firm, but also because she knows deep down that she has promised fidelity, that it would be wrong to indulge her appetite in this way. One motive is largely narrowly prudential, the other more broadly moral. Which, if either, is her real motive? Which, if both are in fact in play, is her dominant motive? She may satisfy herself that her moral motive was her real or dominant motive, and she may be right. Or she may be wrong. She may simply be comfortably self-deceived. We are mistaken if we believe that when our motives are mixed we can be confident in every instance about which among them has proved our most salient at the moment of action or forbearance.

For this reason, Plato is right to urge, as he does in the tale of Gyges' ring, that it is sometimes helpful, or even necessary, to isolate real-world motivational concomitants from one another in the laboratory of the mind in order to become as clear as we can be about what really matters to us at the moment of choice. The tale of Gyges makes a stark claim about our real, if hidden, reasons for choosing justice: we are just, ultimately, only because we are afraid of being caught. For this reason alone, the story is valuable. It boldly introduces a method into philosophy which, for better or worse, has remained with the discipline ever since.

Be that as it may, a thought-experiment is successful only to the extent that it helps shore up its intended conclusion. Glaucon is clear about his own intended conclusion: if two people were granted the same power, each would, whatever his or her initial proclivities, in the end march down the same road towards injustice (359c2–6, 360b2–360c5). If Glaucon is right, then although some of us may be loathe to admit it, even to ourselves, when freed from the fear of detection we are simultaneously freed from the constraints of justice. We are free to do as we wish; and what we wish, according to Glaucon, is the power to perpetrate injustice with impunity. In this sense, his attitude towards justice when telling the tale of Gyges' ring merely reproduces what he had already suggested in his analysis of its origin and nature: no one is just without compulsion. Justice is an unpleasant but unavoidable burden.

When encountering the tale of Gyges and its proclaimed purport for the first time, Plato's readers rather predictably divide into three groups: (1) those who concede with a smirk that Glaucon is clearly right, thus admitting that they themselves would use Gyges' ring as Glaucon predicts they will, while insisting that those who resist this conclusion are self-deceived or otherwise blinded by a foolish, self-abnegating ideology of one form or another; (2) those who insist that they would not use the ring for devious purposes, often pointing out that we all already have some occasion to perpetrate wrongdoing with the reasonable expectation of avoiding detection, but that many of us forbear nonetheless; and (3) those, mainly committed theists, who insist that it is in the end impossible to detach the consequence of punishment from the commission of evil acts. Glaucon has already won over the first group, if they have needed any winning over at all; and he has something compelling to offer the third, who are reluctant to engage the terms of the thought-experiment. The interesting and difficult question concerns whether he has anything forceful to offer his detractors in the second group.

To the third group, those who refuse in principle to entertain what is asked of them in the thought-experiment, Glaucon can politely request that they stop evading the issue. If the circumstance envisaged is not merely counterfactual, but counter to what someone regards as necessary (perhaps because they believe that God exists of necessity, knows all of necessity, and cannot in any way be blind to the events of the actual world), then the decoupling requested by Gyges' ring is not therefore inaccessible to the imagination or without any home in rational argumentation. After all, mathematical proofs sometimes proceed by assuming something impossible only to conclude something actual and important about what is real as a result. Indeed, even the metaphysical theist currently under consideration might accept as true and informative what she regards as predicated upon a metaphysical impossibility, e.g. that if *God did not exist, then there would be no possible foundation for morality*. The point here is not that the detractor in question would be right or wrong to support this, so to speak, countermodal hypothesis. The point is rather that when confronted with the tale of Gyges' ring she should simply try harder. Doing so might well lead her to discover something actual and important about her own motivational structure.

In any event, it is really those belonging to the second group of respondents who pose the most difficult challenge to Glaucon. Those in this group play along with the terms of the story, and so allow that it is in principle possible to separate motives of fear from motives of justice in reasonably clean and instructive ways. They simply deny that they would themselves act as predicted. More narrowly, they need only insist that not everyone would act as predicted. They think it is possible, because it is actual, that some people will avoid injustice even when they can reliably predict that they will avoid detection.

What, then, is Glaucon's response to them? What is the argument encoded in the tale? If the tale of Gyges' has a clear and stated conclusion, for which it is itself supposed to be a great proof, then we need only work backwards to see how Glaucon takes himself to arrive at his final destination. The conclusion, again, is "no one is just willingly" (360c5–6). Although there are in fact various routes to this conclusion, most prominent in Glaucon's telling of the tale seems to be this one, where S is any arbitrary individual:

1   If it were possible to isolate S's true motives for acting justly, then it would be revealed that S regards justice as having purely instrumental value.
2   It is possible by means of a thought-experiment (namely, the tale of Gyges' ring) to isolate S's true motives for acting justly.
3   So, S regards justice as having purely instrumental value.
4   If S acts justly while regarding justice as having purely instrumental value, then S does what is right only under compulsion and no one is willingly just.
5   So, S does what is right only under compulsion and no one is willingly just.

Since S is just any arbitrarily selected individual, it follows no one – not Gyges, not Mother Theresa, not me, not you – is motivated to act because of a desire to be just for its own sake. So, what most people think, that justice is a type-III good, proves true.

We are now, however, wondering whether someone disposed to resist this conclusion ought to be persuaded. Such a person is, of course, being asked to concede something about his own motives, against his protestations to the contrary. At least now with the argument put thus clearly, someone reluctant to accept the putative results of the tale of Gyges' ring is in a position to see where best to disagree.

A detractor might at this stage put pressure on a number of different places. First, and perhaps least significantly, someone might comfortably reject (4) as it is stated. Some things have, let us allow, only instrumental value. We submit ourselves to sometimes considerable pain in the dentist's office because we think that on the balance it is a good thing to do so. Unless we are masochists, we regard the value of such a visit as wholly instrumental: we simply would not go at all if we did not think that long-term dental health was worth the short-term discomfort we expect to suffer. Still, no one compels us to visit the dentist. On the contrary, we go voluntarily, having determined that it is good thing for us to do so. So, Glaucon should not feel sanguine about (4) as stated.

That said, Glaucon can soften (4) a bit and yet achieve his ultimate goal, which was, after all, simply to show that most people are right to regard justice as a type-III good, as having only instrumental value. For he can simply point out, by appealing to yet another counterfactual, that were it not for the benefits of going to the dentist, no one would willingly suffer the pain that is sometimes unavoidable. That then would show that other things being equal, no one would willingly choose such discomfort, and, by parity of reasoning, that given the alternative no one would willingly choose justice. That in turn would suffice to show that justice has only instrumental value, that is, that it is a type-III good.

Allowing that much, however, Glaucon's detractor should not now concede his overarching conclusion. For even granting (2), the suggestion that a thought-experiment of the sort we encounter in Gyges' ring does succeed in allowing us to clarify matters in the aetiology of action, we move from to (2) to (3), the claim that justice is valued only instrumentally only if (1) is true. The first claim (1) evidently relies upon two distinct thoughts. The first is that once we get clear about such matters, we come to appreciate that our true motives in acting are in every instance calculated to advance our narrow self-interest. The second is that given the nature of justice, we in fact have no reason to regard it in any way other than instrumentally.

One might take exception to Glaucon's assertion of (1) by taking issue with either one or the other of these contentions, or indeed with both. The first contention is subject to doubt insofar as it may accept without argument a highly controversial form of psychological egoism, roughly the thesis that we all act selfishly at all times. Someone who at this juncture wishes to resist Glaucon's conclusion would rightly and defensibly call that assumption into question. The second contention, that given the nature of justice we really have no self-interested reason to pursue it for its own sake, is at best premature at this juncture. As we have seen, Socrates ended *Republic* I by insisting that he had no firm grasp on the nature of justice (354c1–4). Inasmuch as Glaucon allows that as dialectically acceptable, because he has in fact asked Socrates to define justice (358b4–7, 368c3–7), he cannot regard it as a settled matter that the nature of justice is clear to all or even broadly accepted. For this reason, Glaucon cannot expect any such implicit assurance to escape unchallenged. Taking that much together, then, however engaging and formidable the tale of Gyges' ring may be, and however much it may resonate with certain of Plato's readers, a critical reader need not, and should not, at this juncture feel compelled to accept its intended conclusion.

Indeed, readers of Plato's *Republic* will find at the core of his gambit to show that justice is a type-II good lies an arresting, because non-standard, analysis of justice. His account may or may not be correct and defensible; but surely it is open to him to mount his case. Nothing internal to the statement of the problem of justice forecloses upon his doing so. We can appreciate the force of the problem without regarding it in advance as intractable.

In any event, given that Plato himself retails the story of Gyges' ring with the ultimate aim of rejecting the conclusion to the argument it encodes, it will prove instructive for his readers to return at the end of the *Republic* to this very argument in order to determine precisely how – and how well – he succeeds. While no one at this juncture can insist a priori that our actions would head in one direction or another if we should believe ourselves permanently immune from detection, Plato is nonetheless right to encourage each of us to ask and answer a simple question in the privacy of our own reflections: what would *I* do if I were in possession of Gyges' ring?

Life Choices

The tale of Gyges' ring holds open a door normally closed to us in our actual lives: we are offered the opportunity to act unjustly without the least fear of reprisal. In that scenario, then, we entertain the possibility of living unjustly with impunity, without any concern at all for the usual bad effects associated with such conduct.

In a final counterfactual scenario, Plato adjusts alternatives somewhat. Suppose, Glaucon suggests, that you are offered one of two lives. You can have either the life of perfect injustice, not only without the expected attendant unhappy consequences but with the good reputation and rewards normally offered only to the very just, *or* the life lived with perfect, unwavering justice, not only bereft of the normal accolades offered the just but with an unearned and unfair reputation for injustice. To make the point graphic, in one sort of life, you can imagine yourself as a person of the highest ideals, forever trying to do what is right and good, and usually succeeding. In this life, however, though you have done nothing but serve justice, everyone regards you as a liar and an untrustworthy creep, indeed as someone guilty of the vilest crimes: of rape, vicious and violent robbery, of murder for profit. In the other sort of life, you would indeed be guilty of all manner of self-promotion, of double-dealing, cheating, theft, and other sorts of nastiness. In this life, though, no one knows your true self: you enjoy the finest reputation available. People esteem you and treat you well, as an honored citizen and a decent person, as someone always considerate and other-regarding, as an exemplar and a paragon. In the first scenario you are burdened with unfair punishments; in the second, you escape punishment and reap rewards for deeds not done.

These are the only two lives available to you. Which would you choose? Glaucon suggests that when faced with this choice, most people would prefer the life of real injustice accompanied by the reputation for perfect justice. This may suggest, then, that most people only want to *seem* to be just, and not really to *be* just. If we think back to the putative origin of justice in a social compact designed to move us out of the state of nature, a place brutal to all save the utterly dominant, then we can appreciate why he might think this way. For in this scenario, we sign on to the edicts we call just so that we may avoid suffering the indignity of subordination to the dominant. Our doing so, upon reflection, gives us reason to seem just, so that others will regard us as complying with our agreements, but no real reason to be just, except insofar as it is necessary for us to be just in order to seem just. The current thought-experiment helps make this vivid: in a forced-choice situation, we appreciate that we have reason to seem just and no reason to be just, and so upon reflection we come to see that we really and rightly regard justice as a type-III good. Its instrumental value lies in part in the reputation it secures for us. Glaucon supposes, perhaps incautiously, that we can see this all the more clearly when faced with a choice of lives. If we acknowledge that most people would choose the life of injustice, we also understand why and how they regard justice as a type-III good; and if we admit to ourselves that we are like most people, then we too follow them in so regarding it.

Like the tale of Gyges' ring, however, this thought-experiment is only as successful as its implicit claims are shown to be once unearthed and considered on their own merits. In the choice of lives, Glaucon seems to make two related claims.

First, he suggests that many people would choose the life of injustice over the life of justice. In so doing, he makes a bald assertion to which he is not entitled, a claim offered both as a description of people's true motives and as a prediction of their likely conduct in counterfactual circumstances. In neither case does his assertion alone show him to be justified. Here, as in the case of Gyges' ring, we are each of us best left to our own reflections. Plato is implicitly asking us to ask ourselves how we might react if offered non-standard choices in life, and encouraging us not to be immediately self-indulgent or self-flattering in our responses to ourselves.

Second, Glaucon suggests something more, something neither descriptive nor predictive (368c). He implies that the thought-experiment itself provides some grounds for supposing that people would be right to choose the life of injustice when presented with it on the terms offered. We might now wonder whether he has overstepped the bounds of the experiment itself. For now he seems committed to a positive conception of justice in terms of which this sort of choice might be made. We have seen, however, that the nature of justice is as yet an open question (unless we are accepting that nature as given by its alleged origin, something we are still well placed to doubt). To this extent, it may yet be the case that when people say that they would prefer the life of injustice over the life of justice, they are operating with a false and indefensible conception of justice. If they are, as they may be, then their stated preferences may reveal less about their own real preferences about justice than they themselves suppose. If I say that I prefer baseball to cricket, because I have mistaken croquet for cricket and I find croquet dull, then my stated preferences, rooted in this confusion, may well not reflect my true preferences and are surely subject to revision once I have learned what cricket in fact involves.

Reflecting further on this final thought-experiment, we might also wonder whether Glaucon is right even to put such a request to Socrates. His goal has been to show that people reasonably regard justice as a type-III good, as a prefatory to having Socrates define it and show that it is in fact a type-II good. If Socrates could show that the just person is always happier than the unjust person, come what may in terms of reputations and rewards, then he would indeed provide a good reason for choosing the life of justice over injustice. If the just life is a happy life and also always happier than the unjust life, then if we choose happiness for ourselves we should likewise choose justice. That said, if our goal is to prove that justice is a type-II good, it is not *necessary* that we should prefer a life wretched in reputation and punishment but perfectly just to a life rich in reputation and reward though perfectly unjust. This is something Gluacon's original illustration already makes perfectly clear: if we wish to show that health is a type-II good, we need not also show that we would always choose a healthy but wretched life over an unhealthy but otherwise rewarding life. In making such a choice, we would no doubt consider the relevant degrees and thresholds involved and make our decisions accordingly.

To that extent, Glaucon's presentation of his final thought-experiment may be misleading. Even so, the considerations he places before us by means of this experiment are not therefore irrelevant. If Plato could meet the demand Glaucon seeks to impose upon him, then his case for justice would be utterly overwhelming. Readers should remain alert to a matter left unstated in Plato's response to this final challenge: if sufficient for the task of showing justice to be a type-II good, meeting it in its own terms is not therefore necessary.

Socrates' Reaction and Ours

With the end of this final thought-experiment, Glaucon and Adeimantus' challenge concerning the desirability and nature of justice comes to its conclusion. Socrates admits to feeling overwhelmed and inept: "I am at a loss as to what I am to do. Nor am I able to help in any way, since I regard myself as incapable" (368b3–5). How, he wonders, can he possibly respond? Needless to say, any response to so fundamental a challenge will perforce be complex and protracted. For the challenge set and made vivid in *Republic* II is utterly foundational: Why, after all, should I be just? Why should I regard justice as something to be sought for its own sake?

When embarking upon so great a task, Plato will not shy away from the difficult task of analyzing the nature of justice itself. For he is right to suppose that questions about the value and desirability of justice are posterior to questions about its nature and essence; and he is certainly right to resist the conceptions of justice presupposed by some of those who doubt its intrinsic value in *Republic* I and II. As we have seen, each of the thought-experiments considered has revealed its author to be relying upon a conception of justice which is well open to question. It may, accordingly, yet transpire that those who doubt its desirability doubt the desirability of something other than justice itself. If that proves correct, then the confidence they display in their own conclusions has been misplaced, because they have been predicated upon a mistake.

Readers of the remainder of Plato's *Republic* should consequently remain alive to the possibility that justice is not as justice has sometimes seemed. The force and innovation of the engaging challenge put to Socrates by Glaucon and Adeimantus will ultimately bring into sharp relief something upon which Plato will ultimately want to insist: justice may be desirable as something valuable in itself in much the same way that health is desirable as something valuable in itself (444c5–444d6, 591a10–591d3; cf. 441e1–442a1). If that is so, then justice cannot be what Glaucon and Adeimantus, speaking on behalf of the many, have readily and naturally supposed it to be. In this respect, their challenge to move justice from a type-III to a type-II good is also and at the same time precisely a challenge to show that the nature of justice diverges from the conception unreflectively accepted by the unschooled.

Thus, when they challenge Socrates to praise justice, Glaucon and Adeimantus also challenge him to analyze justice; and they simultaneously challenge us to do the same. Why should we want to be just? Why in the first instance should we even care about this question? What, moreover, is it that we mean to ask when we pose this question to ourselves? It is permanently admirable, even awe-inspiring, that Plato should frame his challenges about justice so engagingly and so trenchantly in *Republic* II. For the challenges he poses are challenges not only to us: they are equally challenges to himself, made in a public forum, challenges which Plato regards himself as capable of answering to the satisfaction of even the severest critics. If his answer is complex, requiring the entire edifice of the *Republic* as the framework for its articulation, then this can only be due to the hidden complexity of the question itself, as Plato rightly understands it. In *Republic* II, he makes vivid that however simple the question of whether we should be just may appear in its initial formulation, if when considering it we wish truly to be satisfied and not merely silenced by a superior dialectician, we must then expect a response at the level of complication delivered by Plato's *Republic*.

Notes

1 The historical Glaucon and Adeimantus were Plato's brothers, though Plato's presentations of them in the *Republic* need not be understood as representing their actual views. That said, the praise Plato offers them at 357a2–3 and 367e6–368a7 seems entirely genuine.

2 They also several times report that they are renewing the argument of Thrasymachus (358b7–358c1, 367a6, 367c2). It is not clear, however, that they can be understood, except in a very general way, as taking up his rather distinctive conception of justice. It is still less clear how they might be thought to represent the views of the many and of Thrasymachus at the same time, since the many do not share Thrasymachus' highly idiosyncratic approach.

3 Throughout this chapter I refer indifferently to "Socrates" and "Plato," thinking of Plato as the author of the *Republic* and of the character of Socrates who appears in the dialogue as his dominant spokesman. This is in part because I accept a dating of Plato's dialogues according to which the *Republic* is comfortably Platonic rather than Socratic, so that the Socrates who appears is not intended to represent the views of the historical Socrates. Although this matter is much disputed, not much will turn on my being correct for the present purposes. For a succinct introduction to some issues pertaining to the dating of Plato's dialogues, see Kraut 1992a: 1–24. For a fuller treatment, see Fine 2000. There is, however, an interesting question pertaining to whether *Republic* I was written as a self-contained Socratic dialogue, perhaps some years before the composition of Republic II–IX. See n. 5 below for more on this matter.

4 Throughout, "justice" renders *dikaiosunê*. For some orientation to the various connotations of the word rendered, see Vlastos 1971: 70–2, 75 n. 28.

5 It is for this reason, among others, that it is sometimes speculated that *Republic* I was written and completed as a self-contained Socratic dialogue, only to be revived and made to preface *Republic* II–X at a later date. Opinions on this matter vary widely, some supposing it as effectively incontrovertible, others regarding as wholly implausible. For a brief overview of the issue, see Guthrie 1975: 437–8. I regard it as likely that the first book was written earlier than the rest of the *Republic*, but do

not suppose that this affects the organic unity of the work or presents any obstacles to our interpretation of it taken as a whole.

6   For more on the Socratic impulse to analysis and Plato's own reliance upon it, see Shields 2003: 33–95.

7   The challenge brought forward by Glaucon and Adeimantus extends from 357a1 to 367e5. Plato begins his response at 368c7.

8   Irwin (2000: 647) reasonably cites 358a2–3 as a different sort of evidence for this claim.

9   On the relation between the various challenges of Glaucon and Adeimantus, see Kraut 1992b: 313.

10 This last possible benefit is worth mentioning since Plato does come around in the end of *Republic* X to a discussion of the possible payoffs and punishments we might expect in an afterlife for just and unjust behavior on earth. See 614b2–621a3.

11 See Irwin 1995: 192–3 for a discussion of this sort of approach to the relations between justice and happiness.

12 For more detailed discussion of issues pertaining to Glaucon's classification of good things, see, Foster 1937; Kirwan 1965; White 1979: 75–9; White 1984; and Irwin 2000.

13 Cf. n. 2 however.

14 Note, though, that he also suggests that there can be injustice in the state of nature (359e3, 359a3–6). Perhaps he has contradicted himself. Or perhaps he is characterizing the actions in the state of nature in terms of what we now call justice, in the way in which we might say that Germany was long ago inhabited by nomadic tribes. In any event, if we suppose that there is injustice only if there is justice, as seems reasonable, Glaucon cannot consistently speak of there being injustice before the origin of justice as arising in a social compact.

15 Strictly speaking the tale is not the story of Gyges' ring, but of an ancestor of Gyges who remains nameless. Cf., though, 612b4. Perhaps, as one tradition holds, the ancestor was also named Gyges. In any event, custom treats the story as given in Plato as the tale of "Gyges' ring." See Adam 1902: 126–7 for a brief introduction to some questions regarding the identity of the Gyges of Plato's text.

I thank Gerasimos Santas and Rachel Singpurwalla for their comments on an earlier draft.

References

Adam, J. (1902) *The Republic of Plato*, vol. I, Cambridge: Cambridge University Press.

Fine, G. (2000) "Introduction," in G. Fine (ed.) *Plato*, Oxford: Oxford University Press.

Foster, M. B. (1937) "A mistake of Plato's in the *Republic*," *Mind* 46, pp. 386–93.

Guthrie, W. K. C. (1975) *A History of Greek Philosophy*, vol. IV, Cambridge: Cambridge University Press.

Irwin, Terence (1995) *Plato's Ethics*, Oxford: Oxford University Press.

——(2000) "*Republic* 2: questions about justice," in G. Fine (ed.) *Plato*, Oxford: Oxford University Press.

Kirwan, C. A. (1965) "Glaucon's challenge," *Phronesis* 10, pp. 162–73.

Kraut, R. (1992a) "Introduction to the study of Plato," in R. Kraut (ed.) *The Cambridge Companion to Plato*, Cambridge: Cambridge University Press.

——(1992b) "Plato's defense of justice in the *Republic*," in R. Kraut (ed.) *The Cambridge Companion to Plato*, Cambridge: Cambridge University Press.

Shields, C. (2003) *Classical Philosophy: A Contemporary Introduction*, London: Routledge.

Vlastos, G. (1971) "Justice and happiness in the *Republic*," in *Plato: A Collection of Critical Essays*, vol. II, Garden City, NY: Doubleday Anchor.

White, N. P. (1979) *A Companion to Plato's Republic*, Indianapolis: Hackett Publishing.

——(1984) "The classification of goods in Plato's *Republic*," *Journal of the History of Philosophy* 22, pp. 393–421.

5

The Gods and Piety of Plato's *Republic*

Mark L. McPherran

The first sentence of Plato's *Republic* is itself concerned with beginnings, as Socrates recounts how he left the walls of Athens to celebrate the introduction of a new worship:

> I went down yesterday to the Piraeus with Glaucon, the son of Ariston, to say a prayer to the goddess [Bendis], and because I was also curious to see how they would conduct the festival, since this was its inauguration (327a1–3).[1]

With this religious beginning – and continuing on through to its eschatological ending (614b–621d) – Plato's *Republic* announces itself to be a theological work as well as a political and moral one. This opening also suggests what the text goes on to confirm, namely, that its purpose is to introduce a new worship outside the walls of the traditional dispensation. The divinity of this worship proves not to be a Thracian night-goddess, however, but the reality of the Form-world, and the new worship involves not nocturnal horse races (328a), but the intellectual activity of philosophizing the sacrificial reward of which is three-fold: wisdom, happiness, and the assurance of immortality. However, we should not think that Plato is prepared to dispense with the religion of his contemporaries. Rather, it seems evident that here, as in all of his dialogues, Plato follows the path of his teacher by appropriating, reshaping, and extending – but not rejecting – the religious conventions of his own time in the service of establishing the new enterprise of philosophy.[2] In what follows, I will spell out the place of the *Republic* in this Platonic reformation by paying close attention to the role it assigns piety and the gods.

Cephalus and Socratic Piety

Plato's *Republic* is counted as a middle dialogue by those who differentiate his authorship into early, middle, and late periods, but its first book is also thought to be early.[3] Whether or not that is right, Book I does serve as an introduction to the rest by recalling for readers the Socrates of the *Apology* and its companion, aporetic dialogues (e.g., *Euthyphro, Laches*).[4] This observation is not incidental to the religious opening of the dialogue and all that follows. For the active interest in Bendis that Socrates displays should make us equally curious as to why this figure – indicted and executed on a charge of impiety – would want to travel to the Piraeus to offer prayers and sacrifices to a new foreign goddess or, for that matter, any gods at all. We are, moreover, reminded of Socrates' distinctive view of piety toward the close of Book I, when Socrates prods weary Thrasymachus into affirming the *complete justice* of the gods (352a–b). This justice is clearly Socratic: Socrates holds that no one, not even a god, should do injustice, and from that it follows that no one should ever return evils done to one (335a–d; cf. *Crito* 48b–49d, 54c; *Gorgias* 468e–474b). Thus readers can rightly object on behalf of Thrasymachus that the gods of popular imagination are hardly models of non-retaliatory justice; rather, they act with duplicity and violence, are neither omniscient nor omnipotent, and regularly intervene in human affairs for good and ill (cf., e.g., *Euthyphro* 6e–9d; *Memorabilia* 1.1.19). Their behavior is just only insofar as justice consists in repayment in kind, good for good, and evil for evil (i.e., the *lex talionis*). Hence, calamities such as famine, war, and plague are to be understood as expressions of divine vengeance.[5]

What these gods care most about is behavior, not belief or psychic justice, and so what marked out a fifth-century Greek city or individual as pious (*hosios; eusebês*) – that is, as being in accord with the norms governing the relations of humans and gods – was therefore primarily a matter of correctly observing ancestral tradition. The most central of these activities consisted in the timely performance of prayers and sacrifices.[6] Such practices, however, typically assumed that justice consists in *do ut des* reciprocation (cf. *Euthyphro* 14c–15c; Yunis 1998: ch. 3.5). Socrates' affirmation of the completely Socratic, hence, non-retaliatory justice of the gods (352a–b), then, is at odds with the poetic tradition of warring divinity. His assertion of that justice ought to recall the way in which he implicitly connected justice to piety in the *Euthyphro*, by suggesting that (P) piety is that part of justice that is a service of humans to gods, assisting the gods in their primary task to produce their most beautiful product (*pagkalon ergon*, 12e–14a) (McPherran 1996: ch. 2.2). Since Socrates affirms that the gods are entirely good (because they are wise) and that the only true good is virtue/wisdom (e.g., *Apology* 29d–30b; *Euthydemus* 281d–e), he likely thinks that the only or most important component of the gods' chief product is virtue/wisdom.[7] Thus, since piety as a virtue must be a craft-knowledge of how to produce goodness (e.g., *Laches* 194e–196d), our primary service to the gods would appear to be to help them produce goodness in the universe via the improvement of the human soul (*Apology* 29d–30b). Because philosophical self-examination is for Socrates the key activity that helps to achieve this goal, through the improvement of moral-belief-consistency and the deflation of human presumptions to divine wisdom (e.g.,

Apology 22d–23b), philosophizing is a pre-eminently pious activity. However, as a result, it thus would appear that for Socrates, time spent on prayer and sacrifice is simply time stolen from the more demanding, truly pious task of rational self-examination. More threatening still, a theology of entirely just, "relentlessly beneficent" gods who distribute goods whether they are requested or not, and who cannot return evil for evil, would seem to make sacrifice and prayer (especially curses) entirely useless.[8]

Nevertheless, the opening of the *Republic* now indicates (as part of Plato's defense of his teacher perhaps) that Socrates does not reject conventional religious practices in general.[9] Arguably, then, we should hold that although Socrates cannot consider prayers or sacrifices to be *essentially* connected to the virtue of piety, their performance is nonetheless compatible with the demands of piety reconceived as philosophizing.[10] True to his concern with producing virtue in the soul, however, he would object to the narrowly self-interested motives underlying their popular performances (McPherran 2000a). Plato now displays such motivations and connects them with his larger concerns by presenting us with Cephalus – a paradigm of non-Socratic, conventional piety.

After paying his devotions to Bendis, Socrates is enticed by the prospect of further religious novelties to go to the home of Polemarchus and his wealthy old father Cephalus, who has just finished offering up a sacrifice in his courtyard.[11] Although Plato's portrait of Cephalus is not entirely negative, this first interlocutor serves as the starting point of the *Republic* by displaying the key faults of conventional Greek religion and morality. Cephalus initially secures Socrates' admiration by praising moderation in the enjoyment of pleasures such as sex and wine (329a–d), but he then goes on to reveal that his life has been dominated by the pursuit of money. The underpinnings of Cephalus' moral and religious scheme are then made clear, for when asked to explain the goodness of money, he replies:

> when someone thinks his death is near, he becomes frightened. . . . The tales that are told about Hades and how the men who have done wrong here must pay the penalty there . . . begin to torture his soul with the doubt that there may be some truth in them. . . . he begins to consider whether he has ever wronged anyone. . . . But someone who knows he hasn't been unjust has sweet good hope as his constant companion . . . It is for this . . . that the possession of wealth is of most value . . . Wealth can save us from having to cheat someone unintentionally and from having to depart for that other place in fear because we owe sacrifice to a god or money to a person . . . for a man of sense this is the chief use of wealth. (330d–331b)

Cephalus' value system is traditional and transparently externalist: for him justice is the performance of those debt-repaying actions prescribed by the *lex talionis*. That is why he finds it conceivable that a virtuous but poor man might still be punished in Hades: since the requirements of justice and piety are for

Cephalus simply matters of behavior motivated by fear of punishment and the hope of rewards, the failure to fulfill a sacrificial obligation can result in divine retribution in the afterlife irrespective of one's good intentions or excuses (Annas 1981: 20–1). Of course, the moment this conception of justice is put to the test of a counterexample it collapses (331c–d), with justice, not piety, then taking center stage for the remainder of the text. Cephalus hurries off to look after his courtyard sacrifice, while Polemarchus is forced to inherit the explanatory debt Cephalus incurred but cannot repay.

Plato encourages us to see Cephalus' values as a product of the old educational system that frequently portrayed the works of Homer and Hesiod. These authors were recognized as having established a kind of "canonical repertory of stories" that frequently portray the gods as indifferent to the inner, psychic justice to which Socrates later refers (351a–354a) (Vernant 1980: 193). It was on the basis of this literary repertory that "the elegiac, lyric, and tragic poets drew unstintingly while simultaneously endowing the traditional myths with a new function and meaning" (Zaidman and Pantel 1992: 144). Some of this probing was influenced by the investigations of those thinkers working within the new intellectualist traditions of nature philosophy (e.g., Xenophanes) and sophistry (e.g., Protagoras), and so in the work of authors such as Euripides even the fundamental tenets of popular religion became targets of criticism.[12] Plato now joins and extends this tradition as he considers the place of the gods and piety in his Kallipolis.[13]

Plato's New Gods

There are over a hundred occurrences of "god" or "gods" spread through each of the *Republic*'s ten books, with most occurring within the outline of the educational reforms advanced in Books II and III.[14] The gods are first brought into the conversation in their guise as enforcers of morality by Glaucon, and then, in greater detail, by his brother Adeimantus (357a–367e). These gods are rumored to repay injustice with frightful post-mortem punishments; hence, this threat to immoral behavior must be neutralized so that Socrates can be compelled to establish the merits of the just life independent of all extrinsic considerations.

Glaucon does so by postulating that the unjust person does whatever he or she desires, outdoes all opponents, and so becomes wealthy and thus able to benefit friends and harm enemies (362b). Such a person is consequently able to make the most lavish sacrifices to the gods, and to these they respond with rewards that exceed those given to those who are just (362c). To complete this portrait, Adeimantus spells out what those opposed to this conception would say, using Hesiod (*Works and Days* 332–3), Homer (*Odyssey* 19.109), and Musaeus to catalogue the rewards allotted to the pious. These include trees that are heavy with fruit, a long line of healthy offspring in this life, and drunken symposia in the life to come (363a–d). The impious and unjust, however, will suffer in this life, and then in Hades will be buried in the mud and forced to carry water end-lessly in a sieve (363d; cf. *Gorgias* 493b–c; on which, see n. 15 below). Never-theless, these stories are effectively opposed by many contrary popular stories that make the life of justice both difficult and uncertain in its rewards, while por-traying the unjust life as one that is easy and profitable. Other tales (e.g., *Iliad* 9.497–501) allege that

> the gods assign misfortune and an evil life to many good men, and the opposite fate to their opposites. Begging priests and soothsayers frequent rich men's doors and persuade them that by means of sacrifices and incantations . . . they can fix with pleasant rituals the injustices of a man . . . And they present a noisy throng of books by Musaeus and Orpheus . . . in accordance with which they perform their rituals . . . And they persuade . . . whole cities . . . that the unjust deeds of the living or the dead can be absolved or purified though sacrifices and pleasant games . . . These ini-tiations . . . free people from punishment in the hereafter, while a terrible fate awaits those who have not performed rituals. (364b–365a; cf. *Laws* 909a–b)[15]

According to Adeimantus, then, ambitious people can create a façade of illu-sory virtue that will allow them to lead the most profitable lives here and in the afterlife, despite the live possibility that the gods are aware of their misdeeds. For (a) if the gods do not exist or (b) if they are indifferent to human misconduct, we need not fear their punishments, and (c) even if they are concerned with us, given "all we know of them from the laws and poets," they can be persuaded to give us not penalties but goods (365c–366b, 399b). No wonder, then, that in the view of the many "no one is just willingly," but every person behaves properly only through some infirmity (366d). The challenge that Socrates must now meet by constructing Kallipolis is to demonstrate the superiority of justice to injustice independent of any external consequences (366d–369b). Then, when at last Kallipolis is established, he must explain how the required philosophical character traits of its rulers are to be produced (374d–376c).

Socrates asserts that it would be hard to find a system of education better than the traditional one of offering physical training for the body and music and poetry for the soul, but he quickly finds fault with its substance.[16] We expose the young to music and poetry that employ two kinds of story, the true and the fictional (*pseudeis logoi*), and of these two, it is best to begin with entertaining fictions of the kind provided by Homer and Hesiod (376e–377b). This form of education moulds the character of the young by using such stories to shape their "patterns of aspiration and desire (the elements of *thumos* and *epithumia* in Plato's tripartite model of the psyche)" (Gill 1993: 42) in ways conformable to the development of their rational intelligence. However, although such stories are false, some approximate the truth better than others and some are more con-ducive to the development of good character than others (377a, 377d–e, 382c–d). Plato assumes that the most accurate representations of the gods and heroes will also be the most beneficial (e.g., by providing good role models), but the converse is also true, and – famously – this means that there will have to be strict supervision of the poets and storytellers of Kallipolis. Moreover, much of the old literature will have to be cast aside because of its lack of verisimili-tude and its debilitating effects (see Janaway 1995: 89–91).

First on the chopping block is Hesiod's *Theogony*, with its deceitful, harmful tale of Kronos castrating Ouranos at the urgings of his vengeful mother Gaia (earth), then unjustly swallowing his own children at birth to prevent his over-throw by Zeus (377e–378b).[17] Poetic lies of this sort, which suggest that gods or heroes are unjust or disagree, hate, and retaliate against each other, must be suppressed. To specify with precision which myths are to be counted false in their essentials, Socrates offers the educators of Kallipolis an "outline of theology" (*tupoi theologias*, 379a5–6) in two parts, establishing a pair of laws that will ensure a sufficiently accurate depiction of divinity (379a7–9) (L1, L2a, L2b below):

1. All gods are [entirely] good beings (379b1–2).[18]
2. No [entirely] good beings are harmful (379b3–4).
3. All non-harmful things do no harm (379b5–8).
4. Things that do no harm do no evil, and so are not the causes of evil (379b9–10).
5. Good beings benefit other things, and so are the causes of good (379b11–14).
6. Thus, good beings are not the causes of all things, but only of good things and not evil things (379b15–379c1).
7. Therefore, the gods are not the causes of everything – as most people believe – but their actions produce the few good things and never the many bad things (379c2–8; 380b6–c3).

> L1: God is not the cause (*aitia*) of all things, but only of the good things; whatever it is that causes bad things, that cause is not divine (380c6–10; 391e1–2).

This is a reasonably cogent inference, but we are bound to ask how Plato's Socrates can simply presuppose the truth of the non-Homeric premise 1 which, once granted, drives the rest of the argument (premise 2 is also questionable). He can do so, I think, because of his inheritance of both popular and Socratic piety: the gods are good because they are wise, and they are wise because of their very nature (see n. 7). That said, however, we are left wondering how the new poetry is to depict the causes of evil, what those causes might be, and how they could coexist within a cosmos ruled by omni-benevolent gods. On that score, at least, Socrates appears to have been silent, whereas the traditional stories of the poets were able to give satisfying and cathartic shape to the fears of their audiences (e.g., *Works and Days* 58–128, *Odyssey* 1.32–79). In any case, the practical upshot of L1 is clear: stories of the gods' injustices like those at *Iliad* 4.73–126 and 24.527–32 must be purged. If the poets insist, they may continue to speak of the gods' punishments, but only so long as they make it clear – as Plato himself does later in Book X (614b–621d) – that these are either merited or therapeutic for those individuals who should pay penalty for their crimes (380a–b; cf. *Gorgias* 525b–c).

Next up for elimination are all those tales that portray the gods as changing shape or deceiving us in other ways. By means of two further arguments Socrates establishes a law with two parts: (L2a) No gods change (381e8–9) and (L2b) The gods do not try to mislead us with falsehoods (383a2–6). This second law will allow Kallipolis to purge traditional literature of all variety of mythological themes, ranging from the shape-shifting antics of Proteus (381c–e), to the deceptive dreams sent by Zeus (e.g., *Iliad* 2.1–34) (383a–b). Book III continues with further applications of Laws 1 and 2 to popular literature, and by its end – and without overtly signaling the fact – the popular gods of Cephalus have been demoted to the status of harmful fabrications.[19] Although the revisionary theology that results puts Plato at striking variance with the attitudes of many of his fellow Athenians, there is nothing in his theology that directly undermines the three axioms of Greek religion to which Adeimantus alluded earlier (365d–e): the gods exist, they concern themselves with human affairs, and there is reciprocity of some kind between humans and gods.[20] Moreover, it would have been no great shock for Plato's audience to find his Socrates denying the poets' tales of divine capriciousness, enmity, immorality, and response to ill-motivated sacrifice. They had been exposed to such criticisms for years by thinkers such as Xenophanes (DK 21 B11, 14, 15, 16), and Euripides (see, e.g., *Herakles* 1340–6), while others such as Pindar could speak plainly of "Homer's lies" (*Nemean* 7.23) without incurring legal sanctions.

In any case, the providential gods left for use in the educational literature of Kallipolis can still be called by their proper civic names and must be continuous with those referred to in Kallipolis' rituals. But that is all one can say for certain at this juncture. Before we can flesh out these new gods, we need to learn how Plato proposes to incorporate them and their rites into Kallipolis.

Platonic Piety

The key obstacle to understanding the place of piety in the *Republic* is the need to account for Plato's decision in Book IV no longer to count piety as a cardinal virtue (427e–428a).[21] A plausible explanation for this move can be found by attending to the more developed analysis of the soul we find in this section (435c–441c) (cf. Annas 1981: 110–11). Although both the Socratic dialogues and the *Republic* try to account for the apparent distinctness of the virtues in the face of the tenet that "the virtues are one" (e.g., *Protagoras* 329c–d; *Laches* 198a–199e), they do so in different ways.[22] In the former case, the Socrates of the *Euthyphro* is inclined to say, for example, that person S is "pious by piety," and given his account of piety (P), that means one needs to specify the *external* intended referent of S's action as we begin to characterize S's behavior – and thus, the psychic power of the soul "responsible" – as being pious (as opposed, say, to being secularly just or courageous). Plato in *Republic* Book IV, on the other hand, focuses directly on providing an internalist analysis of virtue-as-justice-in-the-soul, and so proceeds to emphasize the relationship between psychic virtue and the now clearly-located *internal*, non-rational sources of correct behavior. On his more complex analysis of the soul, each genuine virtue must correspond to a distinct type of correction of different psychic tendencies. Courage, for example, is not identified in the fashion of Socrates with the knowledge of good and evil and the struggle against externally generated fears, but is a condition of the spirited part that holds on to the right beliefs about what we should do in the face of danger (429a–430c). Thus courage is the virtue that corrects tendencies towards fear in the spirited part of us (Irwin 1995: 239). This sort of analysis, however, forces the recognition that there is little real *internal* difference in the soul between the expertise that contributes to doing what is pious and just toward gods and the expertise that contributes to doing what is just towards mortals. As a result, piety as a form of psychic virtue seems more clearly now to be nothing other than justice *simpliciter*, only aspectually differentiated by reference to its external expression (e.g., funding a festival, in the case of a pious action). Hence, although Plato speaks of pious actions in the *Republic* (e.g., 395b–d, 463c–d, 479a–b, 615b–c) he must now leave piety off the list of cardinal virtues. On his primarily internalist account, "piety" is now seen to name nothing other than justice-in-the-soul.

Although Plato, like Socrates, vigorously rejects the idea that gods can be magically influenced (363e–367a; cf. *Laws* 885b–e, 888a–d, 905d–907b, 948b–c), it is clear that he retains a role for pious, traditional-appearing religious practices. There will still be sacrifices (419a) and hymns to the gods (607a), along with a form of civic religion that features temples, prayers, sacrifices, festivals, priests, and so on (427b–c; Burkert 1985: 334). Plato also expects the children of Kallipolis to be molded "by the rites and prayers which the priestesses and priests and the whole community pray at each wedding festival" (461a6–8). The *Republic* is lamentably terse on the details, however, but this is because its Socrates is unwilling to entrust the authority of establishing these institutions to his guardians or to speculative reason ("We have no knowledge of these things"; 427b8–9).[23] Rather, the "greatest, finest, and first of laws" (427b3–4; cf. 424c–425a) governing these matters will be introduced and maintained by "the ancestral guide on such things for all people": Delphic Apollo (427a–c; cf. 461e, 540b–c).[24] This fact alone suggests that the ritual life of Kallipolis will – with the exception of its cult for deceased philosopher-kings (540b–c) – be very hard to distinguish from that of Plato's Athens. Confirmation of this occurs when we are told that the citizens of Kallipolis will "join all other Greeks in their common holy rites" (470e10–11 [and note the warning against innovation at 424b–c]; cf. *Laws* 848d). However, we are later given reasons for thinking that the inner religious life of Plato's philosophers will be vastly different from that of a Cephalus.

Plato holds that worship is a form of education that must begin in childhood, where it can take root in the feelings; thus, he finds charming tales, impressive festivals, seeing one's parents at prayer and so on to be effective ways of impressing upon the affective parts of the soul a habit of mind whose rational confirmation can only be arrived at in maturity (401d–402b; cf. *Laws* 887d–888a). Most citizens of Kallipolis, however, will be non-philosophers who are unable to achieve such confirmation, but who will still profit from the habitual practice of these rites insofar as they promote the retention of their own sort of psychic justice. For philosophers, however, such pious activity is quite secondary to the inwardly-directed activity which it supports; this is their quest for wisdom – for direct apprehension of the Forms – that focuses directly on making oneself "as much like a god as a human can" (613a–b).[25] The education given to these future philosopher-kings of Kallipolis will thus take them far beyond the limitations imposed by the anti-hubristic tenets of Socratic piety. For by coming to know the Good itself they will no longer be regarded as servile assistants of the gods, but will serve Kallipolis as the gods' local representatives (540a–b).[26]

The educational plan for the rulers of Kallipolis stems from Plato's optimistic epistemology, which in turn is stimulated by his era's growing dissatisfaction with the traditional gap separating the human from the divine (testified to by the increasing influence of ecstatic rites and salvation-oriented rituals that aimed in various ways at the human-initiated passage into the realm of the gods).[27] Reacting to the epistemic pessimism exemplified by Socrates' account of piety (P) as involving subservient, anti-hubristic self-examination on the one hand (*Apology* 20c–23d) and the achievements of contemporary mathematics on the other, Plato was led to philosophize convinced of the possibility of an ascent to a newly-conceived heaven and an apprehension of its Forms that is both cognitive and mystical (e.g., 490a–b).[28] As a corollary of this epistemic hope, Plato also added the doctrine of recollection and its postulations of a pre-natal existence and immortality (*Meno* 81c-d; *Phaedo* 76c ff.).[29] He then used ecstatic religious terminology to extend the traditional notion of the divine to include our ruling part (590c–d, 589e), describing how philosophers will be led up "into light, as some are said to have gone up from Hades to the gods" (521c2–3) by imitating the divine (500b–d), thus becoming "divine" (611e–612a, 613a, 540b–d, 557e, and 469a–b), and offeriing images of the soul's return to whence it came (614b–621d; cf. *Phaedo* 66e–67b).

Forms and Gods

Plato's Kallipolis, then, accommodates the virtue of piety and religious myth and ritual by harnessing them to its central project of producing rulers who will be "as god-fearing and godlike as human beings can be" (383c4–5). The nature and activities of these gods is only sketched out in Books II and III, however, and so readers might reasonably expect to learn more of them in the central metaphysical books' account of their heavenly abode: the realm of Forms (Books V, VI, VII). However, despite this section's discussion of these non-spatio-temporal objects of knowledge, the gods hardly appear at all (e.g., 492a; except for the brief mention of that physical god, the sun [508a]). As G. M. A. Grube puts it, "when the Ideas are fully developed, we get the impression that they and the gods are never on the stage at the same time" (1968: 158). Some scholars have concluded on this basis that although Plato is willing to retain morally uplifting, fictional talk of all-good gods for the children and non-philosophers of his Kallipolis, when he turns to the serious business of educating his philosophers he reveals that the only true divinities are the Forms.[30]

This reading may be too extreme. After all, justice-enforcing gods are redeployed as real features of the cosmos in Book X. Secondly, Plato frequently alludes to genuine gods in dialogues contemporaneous with, and later than, the *Republic* (e.g., *Phaedrus, Parmenides*). Probably the clearest expression of the relationship between Forms and gods in a work bearing on the *Republic* occurs in the second half of the Greatest *Aporia* of the *Parmenides* (133a–134e), where we find an argument purporting to establish *inter alia* the impossibility that the gods could either know or rule over sensible particulars such as ourselves (on which, see McPherran 1999). This argument is founded on the account of Forms we find in the *Phaedo* and *Republic*, with the clear implication being that the Form-realm is also the heavenly home of gods who govern us as masters govern slaves and who apprehend all the Forms, including Knowledge itself (as opposed to the knowledge we possess; 134a–e). This brief glimpse of gods and Forms corresponds with the account of the gods offered first in the *Phaedo*, and then in the more complex portrait of the *Phaedrus*. In the course of the *Phaedo's* affinity argument for the soul's immortality (78b–84b), for example, we are told that our souls are most like the divine – hence, the gods – in being deathless, intelligible, and invisible beings that are inclined to govern mortal subjects (e.g., our bodies). When the philosophically-purified soul leaves its body, then, it joins good and wise gods – our masters (80d–81a). The sorts of activities they carry on together is left unclear, but since this section and others parallel the *Parmenides'* attribution of mastery to the gods (62c–63c, 84e–85b), we can expect that these gods are likewise able to rule wisely because of their apprehension of the Forms.

The *Phaedrus* also features souls and gods that are rulers and that know Forms, and by providing details of their relations in his outline of "the life of the gods" (248a1) Plato gives us a partial solution to the identity of the gods of the *Republic*. As part of his palinode (242b–257b), Socrates first offers proof that the self-moving souls of both gods and humans are immortal (245c–e) and then turns to a description of their natures (246a–248a). It is, however, too lengthy a task to describe accurately the soul's structure in a literal fashion: a god could do it, but not a mortal. It is, however, humanly possible to say what the soul resembles (*eoiken*) (246a3–6; cf. 247c3–6). Dismissing the common conception of the Olympian deities as composites of soul and body (246c5–d5), Socrates offers his famous simile, comparing every soul to "the natural union of a team of [two] winged horses and their charioteer" (246a6–7), whose ruling part is reason and whose horses correspond to the spirited and appetitive parts of the soul described in Book IV of the *Republic*.[31] Unlike the mixed team with which mortal drivers must contend, however, the souls of gods and *daimôns* have horses and charioteer-rulers that are entirely good. The most important of these gods are to be identified with the twelve traditional Olympians: their "great commander" is Zeus, who is then trailed by Hera, Poseidon, Demeter, Apollo, Artemis, Ares, Aphrodite, Hermes, Athena, and Hephaestus, while Hestia remains at home.[32] Being entirely good, these gods roam the roads of heaven, guiding souls, and then travel up to heaven's highest rim (247a–e).[33] From these heights each driver – each god's intelligence – is nourished and made happy by gazing upon the invisible, fully real objects of knowledge to which he or she is akin: Forms such as Justice and Beauty themselves; even Knowledge itself is here, "not the knowledge that is close to change and that becomes different as it knows the different things that we consider real down here," but "the knowledge of what really is what it is" (247d7–e2).

This account should recall both the *Parmenides'* characterization of the two kinds of knowledge – the Knowledge itself that ruling gods possess and the knowledge-among-us that we possess (cf. *Theaetetus* 146e) – and the *Republic's* declaration in L1 that the gods are the causes of good, as well as its allusion to the knowledge possessed by those guardians who are able to rule by virtue of the wisdom they have come to possess (428c–d) and whose intellects are nourished and made happy by their intercourse with the Forms (490a–b). These texts also possess parallel psychologies and eschatological myths, containing Olympian post-mortem rewards and punishments [*Phaedrus* 256a–c; *Rep.* 621c–d] and reincarnation into a variety of lives [*Phaedrus* 247c–249d; *Rep.* 614b–621d]).

In view of such parallels, it is reasonable to suppose that the deities sanctioned by the *Phaedrus* (or similar ones) would also be those of the *Republic*, and this seems especially true when we consider the conservative streak Plato displayed by putting Delphic Apollo in charge of the establishment of temples and sacrifices – hence, the installment of the specific deities the city will honor (427b–c) (and note that the *Phaedrus* similarly credits Delphi with the ability to offer sound guidance to both individuals and cities; 244a–b). Thus when Socrates acknowledges the Apollo of Delphi at 427a–b and Zeus at 583b and 391c, and defends the reputations of Hera, Ares, Aphrodite, Hephaestus, and Poseidon at 390c and 391c, he is affirming the existence of distinct deities with distinct functions. On this reading, it seems clear, the *Republic* can be cleared of the charge of complete heterodoxy (or atheism) that is sometimes leveled against it. Rather, it displays a methodological strategy that begins by placing the popular gods of Cephalus in the foreground (Book I), and then subsequent to the reformation of these gods and consequently their worship in Books II through IV, Plato uses the prestige of the traditional and stable core notion of "divinity" he has retained to introduce new divinities: the Forms. Using religious terminology that derives from the ecstatic side of Greek religion such as the Eleusinian Mysteries (see below) (while rejecting its cheap, mercantile side) he thereby makes a new form of worship primary, one that goes a full step beyond Socratic piety in its rigor: ascension to the Form-realm culminating in knowledge of the good (Books V, VI, VII).[34] As in the *Phaedrus*, Plato affirms that it is not possible to say what the gods truly are, but new stories that obey Laws L1 and L2 by offering images that resemble the truth – stories, say, of all-good, unchanging, truth-telling Olympians who ride their chariots to picnics featuring vistas of Forms – will unite the people of Kallipolis in a common piety. Stories such as these can initially serve to delight and mold children, and can then lend contiguous and familiar imaginative substance to both the rituals of adult life and the expert authority of the guardians.

What, then, is the relation of that superordinate Form, the Good itself (Books VI and VII), to these gods? It was a commonplace in antiquity that the good is God (cf., e.g., Sextus *Againat the Mathematicians* 11.70), a view still embraced in modernity (see, e.g., Adam 1965: 439–60).[35] If that were right, then we could postulate that the image of the Great Commander Zeus is one of Plato's ways of conceptualizing the good in order to make it a subject of honorific ritual. In fact, we are encouraged to think of the good as a god in several ways: the good is said to be (a) the *archê* – the cause of the being – of the Forms (509b6–8) and everything else (511b, 517b–c); (b) a ruler over (*basileuein*) the intelligible world in a way similar to the way the sun, a god, rules over the visible realm (509b–d); (c) analogous to the maker (*dêmiorgon*) of our senses (507d), the sun, one of the gods of heaven (508a–c [which is an offspring of the good; 508b; 506e–507a]). The characterization of the Good itself as a god can also explain Book X's odd and unique claim that the Form of Bed is created by the craftsman god, who is – in a sense – the creator of all things (596a–598c). Finally, if the good were not a god, then (i) the gods of the *Republic* would apparently be the offspring of a non-god (the good), or (ii) the good would be subordinate to these gods, or (iii) the gods would exist in independence from the good: but none of these possibilities seem to make sense in light of (a) through (c) (Adam 1965: 442). Against all this, however, is the characterization of the Good itself as being beyond all being in dignity and power (509b8–10): as such, it cannot be a mind, a *nous*, that knows anything; rather, it is that which makes knowledge possible (508b–509b). Thus, since it would seem that for Plato a necessary condition for something's being a god is that it be a mind/soul possessing intelligence, the good cannot be a god.

This long-standing dispute cannot be resolved here.[36] The right approach, however, would be to suppose that Plato's foremost concern in the *Republic* is ethical; hence, Plato intends for the good to function as both a formal and a final cause for all beings. Given that emphasis, he is willing to talk as though the good might be a god that we could call Great Commander Zeus (e.g., at 596a–598c), but without working out the problems of ascribing mental states to a being beyond being or explaining how the gods as knowers of Forms are the efficient causes of good events and things. But when his later concerns turn to cosmology, what he requires is the sort of anthropomorphic creator-deity that can serve as an ultimate efficient cause, and this is what we find in the demiurge of the *Timaeus* (37c–90d), *Philebus* (28c–30b), *Statesman* (269c–274e), and *Laws* (884d–889d) (cf. *Sophist* 265e–266e; *Cratylus* 389a; *Laws* 903c).[37]

Gods and Souls

Book X of the *Republic* can appear "gratuitous and clumsy . . . full of oddities," concluding with a "lame and messy" myth (of Er) whose "vulgarity seems to pull us right down to the level of Cephalus, where you take justice seriously when you start thinking about hell-fire" (Annas 1981: 335, 353, 349). Nevertheless, it makes contributions to our understanding of the cosmic activities of the *Republic*'s gods and the way in which the religion of Kallipolis contributes to its goal of producing just citizens and wise guardians – elements that Plato extends in his later reflections on the divine in works such as the *Timaeus*.[38]

The *Republic* ends with a consideration of the previously dismissed question of the rewards of justice by first proving the soul's immortality (608c–612a) and then arguing for the superiority of the just life in purely consequentialistic terms. First, Plato affirms Adeimantus' positive story (362d–363e) that the gods reward the just person and punish the unjust during the course of their lives (612a–614a), and then – just as Cephalus feared (330d–331a) – the gods do the same in the afterlife (614a–621a). In the world as it is, the *reputation* of being just – though often ill-accorded – correctly reaps the rewards that it does, but regardless of reputation, the gods always know who is just and who is not, always loving the former and hating the latter (612d–e; cf. 362e–363e). Hence, although it may appear that the truly just are neglected in favor of the seemingly just when they are visited by conventional evils such as poverty and disease, these must be understood to be only apparent evils: they are either beneficial punishments for the errors of a former life or they assist the recipient in some other fashion at some point in time. Besides such disguised benefits, however, the gods visit recognizable goods on the just person insofar as he or she resembles the gods by being good (612e–613b).

The myth of Er provides a last glimpse of the *Republic*'s gods as they dispense justice in the hereafter, but it is hard to know how to view this particular fiction in light of Plato's categorical denigration of all mimetic writing.[39] It is, however, both in theme and detail similar to Plato's other main eschatological myths that display a willingness to use pain and pleasure as inducements to virtuous behavior for those of us as yet unready to pursue virtue for its own sake (*Phaedo* 107c; *Gorgias* 523a–527e; *Phaedrus* 245c–257b): myths that are to be taken as true in their essentials (e.g., *Gorgias* 522b–523a, 526d–527c). Socrates also emphasizes the need to heed this myth's message (618b–d, 621b–d). Nevertheless, its complex portrait of the long-term rewards for striving after justice is often found to be depressing, not reassuring (e.g., Annas 1981: 350–3). For although there are ten-fold rewards for the just and ten-fold punishments for the unjust, there are also non-redeeming, everlasting tortures for those who, because of impiety and murder, have become morally incurable (615c–616b; cf. *Gorgias* 525b–526b). True to Law L1, however, Plato explicitly relieves the gods of all responsibility for the future suffering we will experience in our next incarnation by means of a lottery (617e, 619c). A soul's choice of a happy life of justice depends both on the random fall of the lots and that soul's ability to choose wisely, but it is unclear if the lottery is in reality determined by necessity, and we are then also told that a soul's degree of practical wisdom is constrained by its prior experiences, experiences that were in turn the result of prior ignorant choices. This means that those who have lived lives of justice – through habit and without philosophy – and who therefore arrive at the lottery after experiencing the rewards of heaven will, by having forgotten their earlier sufferings, make bad choices and suffer further (617d–621b). Finally, aside from the chancy work of the lottery, Plato has never adumbrated the many sources of evil mentioned in Book II, against which even the gods are powerless.[40] So although the last lines of the *Republic* encourage us to race after justice so that we may collect our Olympian rewards (621b–d), some will find Thrasymachean shortcuts a better gamble.

There is no sure way to determine how Plato meant for us to read this myth: perhaps all its details of colored whorls and lotteries are only entertaining bits of window-dressing, not to be taken as contributing to a philosophically coherent eschatology (cf. Annas 1981: 351–3). This is poetry, after all, and from a master poet who disdains poetry one may expect masterful fancies. On the other hand, it is possible to read Er's tale of reincarnation as alluding to the beneficial initiations of Eleusis, but now connected to the true initiation and conversion provided by philosophical dialectic (Morgan 1990: 150). There are also reasons to suppose that the display of whorls, sirens and necessity are symbolic of the metaphysical elements of the *Republic*'s middle books, and are thus meant to impress on each soul prior to its next choice of life and its drink from forgetfulness (620e–621c) the message of those books: that the happiest life is the life of justice and the good, and so ought to be chosen for that reason alone.[41]

The message that does come through loud and clear, however, is that no god or *daimôn* can be blamed for whatever fix we may happen to find ourselves in when we put down Plato's text. Moreover, by fixing the determinates and outcomes of our present choices in the lap of the gods of past choice (Lachesis) and future necessity (Atropos) – and whether Plato intends this effect or not – readers can find themselves inclined to recall the truly pious aspirations of philosophy developed over the preceding nine books. If so, they will perhaps find themselves encouraged and emboldened to dismiss the cheap motivations of carrot and stick that drive the vulgar many.[42] The end of the *Republic* can thus be read as returning us to the stern Socrates of Book I who urges us to choose the path of justice *simpliciter*, and damn the consequences (cf. *Crito* 48a–49e). To this, however, his pupil has now added in eight books of subsequent argument a more rigorous religious message that grounds that choice in a transcendental love for, and ascent and assimilation to, an unseen perfect justice apprehended by collegial, all-good gods. Thus it is that by pursuing the nature of just action in the here and now, Plato laid the groundwork for the flowering of western theology and mysticism.

Notes

1 Translation after Grube and Reeve 1992 (and hereafter). See Parker 1996: 170–5, on Bendis; Parker dates the installment of Bendis in Athens at 429; he puts the dramatic date of the *Republic* at 410. M. L. Morgan observes that "scholarly opinion suggests that the *Republic* was completed around 394–370" (1990: 102).

2 See Beckman 1979; Vlastos 1991: ch. 6; and McPherran 1996 on Socratic religion.

3 I shall avoid entering into such interpretive issues here, however.

4 The Socrates of Book I also contrasts sharply with the Socrates of the following books, who confronts no "strongly characterized interlocutors, and . . . delivers what is essentially a monologue" (Annas 1981: 16); he also bears an affinity to the historical teacher of Plato, at whose feet Plato encountered the new intellectualist piety he helped to forge; see, e.g., Vlastos 1991: ch. 6; McPherran 1996, ch. 2.

5 See, e.g., Zaidman and Pantel 1992: ch. 13; *Iliad* 4.40–434; Hesiod, fr. 174; Aeschylus, *Choephori* 314, *Agamemnon* 1560–4; Aristotle, *Nicomachean Ethics* 1132b21–7.

6 For examples of prayer, see *Iliad* 1.446–58; *Odyssey* 3.418–72; Hesiod, *Works and Days* 724–6, 465–8; and Aeschylus, *Seven Against Thebes* 252–60.

7 Gods are – by their very nature – perfectly knowledgeable, and thus, entirely wise (*Apology* 23a–b; *Phaedo* 63a–c, 80d–81a; *Hippias major* 289b; *Phaedrus* 246a–e, 278d); and since wisdom and virtue are mutually entailing, they are entirely good. Note that existing alongside the poetic conception of a divine double-standard morality, there was also a popular conviction that Zeus is just; thus, his interferences in human affairs are not capricious violations of our moral order, but contributions to a larger, coherent plan of events. See, e.g., Hesiod, *Works and Days* 256–5; Pi. . . . *Ol.* . . . 1.35; Aeschylus, *Suppliants* 359–64; Euripides, *Iphigenia among the Taurians* 391. For further discussion, see Lloyd-Jones 1971; Vlastos 1991: 162–5; McPherran 1996, chs. 2.2., 3.2.

8 Vlastos 1989: 235; McPherran 1996: chs. 2.2 and 4.2, 2000a, and 2003.

9 Note, too, that Xenophon portrays Socrates as "the most visible of men" in cult-service to the gods (*Memorabilia* 1.1.1–2, 1.2.64, 4.8.11; *Apology* 10–12). Socrates' last words at *Phaedo* 118a7–8 give powerful testimony to the idea that Socrates was so sensitive to the requirements of everyday piety that he could – even in his last moments – recall his debt to a relatively minor deity (Asclepius); Morrow 1996: 122.

10 Among other things, ritual behavior also helps to foster and maintain belief in the existence of gods, something that Socrates is clearly interested in promoting (*Memorabilia* 1.4.1–19, 4.3.1–17; Plato, *Apology* 21d–23c).

11 See Nails 2002: 84, on Cephalus.

12 For Euripides, see, e.g., *Bacchae* 216–20, and *Trojan Women* 1060–80; cf. Thucydides *Peloponnesian War* 2.8.2.

13 See Parker 1996: chs. 10 and 11; and Ostwald 1986: ch. 5, on fifth- and fourth-century clashes between intellectual reformers and Greek popular religion.

14 Plato also often mentions "the divine" and the other two primary forms of divinity: *daimôns* and heroes; on these see Burkert 1985: chs. 3.3.5 and 4.

15 Morgan 1990: 111–14, discusses the vulgarized Orphic and Eleusinian practitioners and texts to which Plato refers here and at 363a–d.

16 See Beck 1964 on the traditional education; see, e.g., Gill 1993; Halliwell 2002: ch. 3 for discussion of Plato's treatment of poetry.

17 Plato uses the figure of Euthyphro to warn against taking such figures as role models; *Euthyphro* 5d–6c.

18 Reiterated for emphasis at 379c2; Vlastos 1991: 163 n. 28.

19 Plato was later of the same mind in his *Laws*, e.g., 941b, 636c, 672b.

20 Yunis 1988: ch. 3. Texts such as Homer's *Iliad* did not have the status of a Bible, and there was no organized church or set of doctrines enforced by them.

21 The *Laws* also fails to list piety as a cardinal virtue (see, e.g., 965c–d). For detailed discussion of this issue, see McPherran 2000b.

22 Note Kahn 1976: 22: "the key to interpreting Plato's early work is to see that all roads lead to the *Republic*."

23 E.g., we are told nothing about enrollment into religious associations like the *phratry*, festivals, the selection of religious officials, and so on; on this, see Burkert 1985: ch. 2.6; Zaidman and Pantel 1992: part III.

24 Morgan (1990: 106) notes that this charge to the Delphic oracle is "completely normal." Plato assigns the same function to Delphi in his *Laws* (738b–d, 759a–e, 828a) and pays better attention to such details (e.g., 759a–760a, 771a–772d, 778c–d, 799a–803b, 828a–829e, 848c–e). These details are rather conventional, something we should expect, given that Plato's Athenian Stranger insists that his Cretan city will absorb and preserve unchanged the rites of the Magnesians (848d).

It is puzzling that after declaring these educational elements to be the most important, Plato assigns their formulation not to the semi-divine philosophers of Kallipolis but to the puzzling dispensations of an oracle. This choice reflects Plato's desire to build on the general respect his contemporaries had for the Delphic oracle, one clearly shared by Plato (see Dodds 1951: 222–3; Morrow 1993: 402–11). We may also hypothesize that the philosophers of Kallipolis will be so expert in the interpretation of oracles that the Pythia's pronouncements will be tantamount to direct instruction from the god Apollo.

25 On this and Plato's theory of *homoiôsis theôi* in general, see Sedley 1999.
McPherran (2000a) argues that Platonic prayer should be thought of as a kind of
virtue-training, theatrical portrayal of divinity.

26 Here we have an instance of the way Plato deliberately "pours . . . new wine into old
bottles" (Morrow 1993: 401) by calling these new rulers not *archons*, but *basileis* –
the name given to the "kings" whose official function was primarily religious – and
then making each one religious in the new sense of being a "*mystes*, a devotee of
ecstatic rites, a philosopher" (Morgan 1990: 145–6).

27 See Morgan 1990: chs. 3 and 4; 1992: 236–40. This gap is *the* central category of
Greek religion; Ostwald 1986: 287.

28 See Vlastos 1991: ch. 4 for an account of how contemporary achievements in mathematics contributed to Plato's epistemology and his theory of philosophical education
as involving the soul's "conversion" (*periagogê*; 518d, 521c) toward true being.
Pythagorean mathematics appears to have been a key influence, linking deductive proof
to certain knowledge, recollection, and the immortality of the rational soul; Morgan
1990: 101. See McPherran 1996: ch. 5.3, on Socratic versus Platonic religion.

29 It was still a commonly accepted notion in Socrates' day that immortality was a pre-
rogative of divinity (see, e.g., Guthrie 1950: 174), and Socrates – if not *convinced*
of this view – seems at least to have been restrained to a cautious agnosticism by his
own reflections on the matter (*Apology* 40c–41c).

30 E.g., Morgan unpublished. Plato's ascription of agency and mental states to his gods
(e.g., 560b, 612e–613a) make it clear that the Forms are not themselves gods (but
see *Timaeus* 37c).

31 Hackforth 1952: 72. Plato's appropriation of the immortal horses of the gods (the
hippoi athanatoi – offspring of the four wind-gods, *Iliad* 5.719–777; Quintus
Smyrnaeus 12.189) is typical of his entire approach to the myths of Greek religion:
he retains the traditional ambrosia and nectar as food and drink for the lower, horsy
parts of the soul (*Phaedrus* 247e), but has the philosophical Intellect feed on the
new, true ambrosia of the immortal Forms.

32 Hestia is replaced by Dionysus on the east frieze of the Parthenon.

33 Hackforth (1952: 71) holds that the claims that the soul cares for the inanimate
(*Phaedrus* 246b) and that Zeus orders and cares for all things (246e) "are noteworthy as being the earliest intimation of the central doctrine of Plato's theology . . .
common to the myth of the *Timaeus* and the rational exposition of *Laws* X." There
is only the briefest foreshadowing of the *Timaeus'* divine craftsman – Plato's recognition of the need for a demiurge to implant the Forms in matter – in Book X
(596a–598c).

34 Morgan 1992: 233. Morgan notes that the *Republic* does not use the "vocabulary
of ecstatic ritual as explicitly as the *Phaedo*," but that it does employ the ideas of the
conversion (*periagogê*) of the soul and non-discursive "gazing" at Forms, elements
adapted from the Eleusinian Mysteries (1992: 239, 244; cf. Morgan 1990: 105,
124).

35 The issue was raised as early as Thrasyllus; Benitez 1995: 114 n. 8.

36 For a review of the literature, see Doherty 1956.

37 This is the approach taken by Benitez 1995. He also argues that there are suggestions in the *Philebus* that Plato wishes to treat the good and the demiurge as fused

in a single entity. Plato continues to speak of plural gods in his *Timaeus* and *Laws*, but also introduces a cosmic mind and maker whose activities provide the structure and orderly motions of the cosmos. Some take this to show that his Olympians have become mere legal fictions (*Laws* 889e); e.g., Morrow suggests that Plato's plural gods are only "images" and "sensuous personifications" of the divine principle "revealed to philosophical intelligence . . . they are objects of worship, not forces in nature" (1933: 133–4). But although it is true that the relation between Plato's omniscient, omnipresent deity and the other gods is left entirely obscure, to make sense of what he actually says about plural gods I think it more charitable to credit him with understanding the maker-god to be a supreme deity overseeing a community of lesser deities in the manner of Xenophanes' "greatest one god" (DK 21 B23). Plato might also have elaborated on the not-uncommon view that understood the gods to be manifestations of a singular supreme spirit; Guthrie 1971: 155–6; Zaidman and Pantel 1992: 176.

38 Despite Book X's condemnation of *all* poetry as a debased form of painting (595a–608b), Plato retains hymns to the gods (607a; cf. *Laws* 801d–802a) – and the category of hymn is a broad one. We can also imagine that Plato has on hand the sort of defense of poetry that he later produces in the *Laws* that would allow for the readmission of other sorts of poetry (606e–608b).

39 See Morrison 1955 for detailed discussion of the myth. Morgan (1990: 152) notes that although the precise sources of the myth "are beyond our grasp. There are doubtless Orphic, Pythagorean, and traditional elements."

40 The role of chance here, though, suggests that Plato may have had his later *Timaeus* view of the causes of evil in mind, causes that he locates in the disorderly motions of matter (see Cherniss 1971); cf. *Phaedrus* 248c–d. The *Republic* does at least make clear that human evil is a consequence of our having souls that are maimed by their association "with the body and other evils" (611c1–2; cf. 611b–d, 353e; *Phd.* 78b–84b; *Theaetetus* 176a–b; *Laws* 896c–897c); e.g., not even the *Republic*'s rulers are infallible in their judgments of particulars, and so Kallipolis will fail as a result of the inability of the guardians to make infallibly good marriages (given their need to use perception; 546b–c). Such imperfection is, however, a necessary condition of human beings having been created in the first place, a creation that Plato clearly thought was a good thing, all things considered.

41 See Johnson 1999 for this reading.

42 Annas 1982 seems to come to this view of the effect of the myth, moderating her 1981: 349–53, assessment.

I am indebted to Jan Kaufman and Jennifer Reid for their helpful remarks on a previous version of this paper, and to Gerasimos Santas for the invitation to write it. My thanks as well to Michael Morgan for letting me have a copy of his unpublished paper.

References

Adam, J. (1965) [1908] *The Religious Teachers of Greece; being Gifford Lectures on Natural Religion delivered at Aberdeen*, Edinburgh: T. & T. Clark.

Annas, J. (1981) *An Introduction to Plato's* Republic, Oxford: Oxford University Press.
──(1982) "Plato's myths of judgment," *Phronesis* 27, pp. 119–43.
Beck, F. A. G. (1964) *Greek Education 430–350 B.C.*, London: Methuen.
Beckman, J. (1979) *The Religious Dimension of Socrates' Thought*, Waterloo: Wilfrid Laurier University Press.
Benitez, E. E. (1995) "The good or the demiurge: causation and the unity of good in Plato," *Apeiron* 28/2, pp. 113–40.
Burkert, W. (1985) *Greek Religion*, Cambridge, MA: Harvard University Press.
Cherniss, H. (1971) "The sources of evil according to Plato," in G. Vlastos (ed.) *Plato*, vol. 2, Garden City, NY: Anchor Books.
Dodds, E. R. (1951) *The Greeks and the Irrational*, Berkeley: University of California Press.
Doherty, K. F. (1956) "God and the good in Plato," *New Scholasticism* 30, pp. 441–60.
Gill, C. (1993) "Plato on falsehood – not fiction," in C. Gill and T. P. Wiseman (eds.) *Lies and Fiction in the Ancient World*, Austin: University of Texas Press.
Grube, G. M. A. (1968) [1935] *Plato's Thought*, Boston: Beacon Press.
Guthrie, W. K. C. (1950) *The Greeks and Their Gods*, Boston: Beacon Press.
──(1971) *Socrates*, Cambridge: Cambridge University Press.
Hackforth, R. (1952) Plato's *Phaedrus*, Cambridge: Cambridge University Press.
Halliwell, S. (2002) *The Aesthetics of Mimesis: Ancient Texts and Modern Problems*, Princeton, NJ: Princeton University Press.
Irwin, T. (1995) *Plato's Ethics*, Oxford: Oxford University Press.
Janaway, C. (1995) *Images of Excellence: Plato's Critique of the Arts*, Oxford: Oxford University Press.
Johnson, R. R. (1999) "Does Plato's myth of Er contribute to the argument of the *Republic?*," *Philosophy and Rhetoric* 32/1, pp. 1–13.
Kahn, C. (1976) "Plato on the unity of the virtues," in W. H. Werkmeister (ed.) *Facets of Plato's Philosophy*, Assen: Van Gorcum.
Lloyd-Jones, H. (1971) *The Justice of Zeus*, Berkeley: University of California Press.
McPherran, M. L. (1996) *The Religion of Socrates*, University Park, PA: Pennsylvania State University Press (paperback edn. 1999).
──(1999) "An argument 'Too Strange': *Parmenides* 134c4–e8," in M. L. McPherran (ed.) *Recognition, Remembrance, and Reality: New Essays on Plato's Epistemology and Metaphysics*, Apeiron suppl. vol. 32/4, pp. 55–71.
──(2000a) "Does piety pay? Socrates and Plato on prayer and sacrifice," in N. D. Smith and P. Woodruff (eds.) *Reason and Religion in Socratic Philosophy*, Oxford: Oxford University Press. Also in T. C. Brickhouse and N. D. Smith (eds.) (2002) *The Trial and Execution of Socrates: Sources and Controversies*, Oxford: Oxford University Press.
──(2000b) "Piety, justice, and the unity of virtue," *Journal of the History of Philosophy* 38/3, pp. 299–328.
──(2003) "The aporetic interlude and fifth *Elenchos* of Plato's *Euthyphro*," *Oxford Studies in Ancient Philosophy* 25, pp. 1–37.
Morgan, M. L. (1990) *Platonic Piety*, New Haven, CT: Yale University Press.
──(1992) "Plato and Greek religion," in R. Kraut (ed.) *The Cambridge Companion to Plato*, Cambridge: Cambridge University Press.

——(unpublished) "The gods of Plato's *Republic*."

Morrison, J. S. (1955) "Parmenides and Er," *The Journal of Hellenic Studies* 75, pp. 59–68.

Morrow, G. R. (1966) "Plato's gods," in K. Kolenda (ed.) *Insight and Vision: Essays in Honor of Radoslav Andrea Tsanoff*, San Antonio, TX: Principia Press of Trinity University.

——(1993) [1960] *Plato's Cretan City*, Princeton, NJ: Princeton University Press.

Nails, D. (2002) *The People of Plato: A Prosopography of Plato and Other Socratics*, Indianapolis: Hackett Publishing.

Ostwald, M. (1986) *From Popular Sovereignty to the Sovereignty of Law: Law, Society and Politics in Fifth Century Athens*, Berkeley: University of California Press.

Parker, R. (1996) *Athenian Religion: A History*, Oxford: Oxford University Press.

Plato (1992) *Republic*, trans. G. M. A. Grube and C. D. C. Reeve, Indianapolis: Hackett Publishing.

Sedley, D. (1999) "The ideal of godlikeness," in G. Fine (ed.) *Plato 2: Ethics, Politics, Religion, and the Soul*, Oxford: Oxford University Press.

Vernant, J.-P. (1980) *Myth and Society in Ancient Greece*, trans. J. L. Lloyd, Atlantic Highlands, NJ: Humanities Press.

Vlastos, G. (1989) "Socratic piety," in J. J. Cleary and D. C. Shartin (eds.) *Proceedings of the Boston Area Colloquium in Ancient Philosophy*, vol. 5, Lanham, MD: University Press of America.

Vlastos, G. (1991) *Socrates, Ironist and Moral Philosopher*, Ithaca, NY: Cornell University Press.

Yunis, H. (1988) *A New Creed: Fundamental Religious Belief in the Athenian Polis and Euripidean Drama*, Hypomnemata 91, Göttingen.

Zaidman, L. B., and P. S. Pantel (1992) *Religion in the Ancient Greek City*, trans. P. Cartledge, Cambridge: Cambridge University Press.

6

Plato on Learning to Love Beauty

Gabriel Richardson Lear

In the *Republic,* Adeimantus says that if Socrates wants to understand how to argue that justice is beneficial in itself, he must recognize how inadequate the poets' defense of justice has been. The problem is not only that they praise justice as good for its rewards. Just look, he says, at the rewards they give it. The "noble Hesiod and Homer" celebrate just people only by showing them as blessed with plenty of acorns and sheep and fertile land (363a–c). In effect, they depict just people as blissful rustics! Or, if the poets want something more dashing (*neanikôteron*), "they lead the just to Hades, seat them on couches, provide them with a symposium of pious people, crown them with wreaths, and make them spend all their time drinking – as if they thought drunkenness was the finest (*kalliston*) wage of virtue (363c–d)."[1] Surely these "fine wages" of justice can be had by the unjust too, and without having to endure all the pious people! And in fact, Adeimantus says, a "noisy throng of books" (364e) shows that the life of vice is easy, so long as you soothe the gods with prayers and sacrifices. They even go so far as to suggest that injustice is shameful and ugly (*aischron*) only by convention (364a). Given this education, he says, it is no wonder that clever young men, who can synthesize a general impression from all the sayings of poetry, opt for a life of vice disguised as virtue (365b ff.).

Adeimantus' complaint contains an important proposal: as he represents it, we begin to deliberate about which course of life is better, more beneficial, only after we have absorbed opinions about which way of life is fine (*kalon*). Indeed, he suggests that our judgment of the good is in some way or other shaped by an antecedent aesthetic sense. Socrates evidently agrees: musical-poetic education in the ideal city must be univocal in celebrating as fine the very behavior required of warriors for the good of the city as a whole. Indeed he declares that this education is complete not merely when the young guardians' develop good taste, but when they *love* the fine and the beautiful (403c). The love Socrates has in mind is erotic love, and in the first instance he is referring to the seemly passion the young guardians will feel for beautiful boys. But their education is intended to create in them a love of beauty wherever it appears, whether in poetry, paintings, and buildings or in the orderly movements of the heavenly bodies (401a–d; 529c–530b).[2] Socrates seems to think that a proper sense of and passion for beauty and the fine is a prerequisite for justice in the city. And since the city is an allegory of the soul, we can conclude that (some part or parts of) a person, too, must love beauty in order to be just. But why is this so?

It is sometimes suggested that *kalon*, which I have translated as "fine" and "beautiful," is ambiguous between aesthetic and moral senses. In the latter case, it would be more properly translated as "noble," with its connotations of dutifulness and rectitude. We might suppose that this is the sense of *kalon* relevant to childhood education. But Socrates' easy movement among mimetic arts, tools, furniture, people's bodies and souls, and indeed the Form of the Beautiful itself as all *kalon* suggests that the love he seeks to instill in the young guardians is not a specifically moral motivation. Moreover, Plato's own Theory of Forms should encourage us to look for what is common in the different uses of the word *kalon*. His mention of *eros* here and his argument in the *Symposium* that all these beauties are objects or offspring of love suggest that even when the object in question is an action or is only intelligible and not physical, appreciation of it as *kalon* carries something akin to the sensual delight captured by our word "beautiful." What Aristotle says of the virtuous person, in *Nicomachean Ethics*, seems to be equally the position of Plato's Socrates: "The decent person, insofar as he is decent, delights in virtuous actions and is pained by bad ones just as a musical person delights in fine and beautiful songs and is pained by worthless ones" (1170a8–11). Thus, however it may be that beauty is related to goodness in the *Republic*, we should not assume that the young guardians' love of beauty is anything like a Kantian respect for moral duty or that it is some other specially moral motivation.

But this makes Socrates' claim about the goal of musical-poetic education all the more curious. What is the significance, from the point of view of justice, in learning to love beauty? It is true that virtuous actions (and the ideal city, Kallipolis) are fine. Is his point that a person with a taste for beauty in general will also be attracted to acting justly, moderately, and with courage? If this is all he has in mind, then the guardians' love of fineness appears oddly tangential to proper moral motivation. It may reliably support virtuous motivation, but so too might other attitudes, as for example, fear of what it is like to be unjust. The nightmare of the tyrannical soul in Book IX is certainly miserable and if, in addition, we consider the consequences of injustice as presented in the myth of Er, we are likely to be all the more anxious to be good. If fear can have such a powerful effect and a well-trained sense of fear can steer us accurately, it isn't clear why moral education should focus on the beauty of virtue in particular.

Now Socrates seems to believe that a well-trained taste for beauty leads to moral knowledge and the rule of reason in the soul. A person with a proper musical education "will sense it acutely when something . . . hasn't been finely crafted or finely made by nature" (401e). Just as a child learns to distinguish the various letters and to identify them wherever they appear, so too musical youths will "know the different forms of moderation, courage, frankness, high-mindedness, and all their kindred, and their opposites too, which are moving around everywhere" (402c). The ability to pick out images of fine virtue and to distinguish them from vice does not amount to understanding why these judgments are true any more than a child's ability to pick out letters of the alphabet implies any understanding of what the words they spell mean. As Glaucon says later of the guardians' poetic education, "Its harmonies gave them a certain harmoniousness, not knowledge" (522a). Yet to a person who is good at recognizing courage when he sees it, the rational account of courage will have "the ring of truth" since it harmonizes with his sense of the way things seem to be. Thus "he will welcome the reason when it comes and recognize it easily because of its kinship with himself (402a).[3]

This idea has an air of plausibility. We can well imagine that a person who sees a passionate life of adventure as glorious will have a hard time believing in the goodness of a quiet life of civic duty. But it must also be granted that, for all we have seen so far, Plato's coupling of beauty and truth, aesthetic taste and knowledge, is a bit wishful. First, take the assumption that people more readily accept as true theories that *harmonize* with their sense of the beautiful. This is not obviously correct. The truth it not always pretty nor do poems that show us pretty things strike us as more likely to be true than those that show ugly ones. (Indeed, sometimes the very ugliness of an account of human nature lends it credibility.) Second, even if beautiful actions or people appear to be good (and this itself is debatable), there is no reason to think that an interest in beauty will necessarily lead to an interest in the truth of the matter. This is a point Socrates himself makes. Whereas it is essential to the desire for good things that we desire what really is good, when it comes to beauty our desire can be satisfied with what merely seems to be beautiful (505d). It is no accident that Socrates depicts the lovers of mere opinion (as opposed to knowledge) as people who study – indeed love and cleave to – beautiful things (476b, 479e).

So on the one hand, Socrates advocates a musical-poetic education whose goal is love of the fine and beautiful on the grounds that it prepares the soul to grasp moral knowledge. On the other hand, as we have just seen, he seems to think that love of beauty is entirely consistent with superficiality, even when a person's taste is good.

Yet Socrates is serious about the importance of beauty for virtue. For instance, he argues that philosophic natures are corrupted by spending time in theaters and other public gatherings where judgments of beauty and the fine are made (492b–c). He often expresses his despair for "the many" by reference to their mistaken or inappropriate understanding of beauty; they cannot "in any way tolerate the reality of the beautiful itself, as opposed to the many beautiful things, or the reality of each thing itself, as opposed to the corresponding many"

(493e–494a; cf. 479d, 557c, 602b). And finally, the very first sign of deterioration from aristocracy to timocracy is that the leaders "have less consideration for music and poetry than they ought" (546d). From there, every stage of the decline towards tyranny is accompanied by, and to some extent caused by, an ever-declining aesthetic taste. The same is true for the analogous decline in the individual soul.

Glaucon's challenge to Socrates to show the benefit of justice "in itself" determines the central line of argument of the *Republic* and is usually considered more serious than his brother's. But it is clear that Socrates shares Adeimantus' view that our sense of the fine and the beautiful, particularly as it is shaped by poetry, is crucial to whether or not we choose the just life as the best rather than as merely the best we can do. In this essay I will explore this subsidiary theme of the *Republic*. Why must we learn to love beauty in order to become good? Plato's account is extraordinarily rich, but broadly speaking it has two aspects: (1) as we saw, a proper sense of beauty aids the development of knowledge and (2) beauty gratifies a particular sort of desire in a way that is necessary for justice. But first, a few general remarks about Plato's conception of the *kalon* are in order.

Beauty and Goodness

According to Socrates, goodness is the standard or target of beauty (452e, 457b). He also says that the Good is "the cause of all that is correct and beautiful in anything" (517c) and suggests that knowledge of beauty depends on knowing what really is good (505b). Now in these passages he is speaking of genuine beauty, but we should notice that the connection between beauty and goodness seems to be part of the concept of beauty per se, regardless of whether one's sense of beauty is good or bad. For example, democratic cities claim that freedom is the finest thing they possess, but according to them freedom is also the greatest human and civic good (562b–c). Here the standard of what they take to be fine is their belief about what's good, even though their belief is (according to Socrates) false. Furthermore, the experience of beauty fills us with desire. And although this is not emphasized in the *Republic*, in the *Phaedrus* and *Symposium* it is central to the experience of beauty that it causes joy and delight (*Phaedrus* 251d; *Symposium* 206d). The fact that beautiful and fine things delight us as (appearing) perfect explains the very close connection between *to kalon* and praise (e.g. 492c). Praise, admiration, and honor are natural responses to seeing (either physically or intellectually) the excellence that beautiful things manifest.

We can be more specific about the sort of goodness that determines beauty, at least of a genuine sort. In the discussion of tragedy in Book X, Socrates says that "the virtue or excellence, the beauty and correctness of each manufactured item, living creature, and action is related to nothing but the use for which each is made or naturally adapted" (601d). That is to say, genuine beauty in things is derived from natural (or, in the case of artifacts, artificial) good or function. Appropriateness or "fit" is also a feature of aesthetic judgments (420c–d). So we might venture to say that, according to Plato, where a beautiful thing's good is its function, its beauty will lie in the way its parts are well suited in themselves and in proportion to each other – in the way they are ordered – to contribute to its proper work.[4]

Insofar as Socrates makes real or apparent usefulness the standard of the *kalon* and implies that delight in and desire for this constitutes aesthetic experience, readers are sometimes tempted to suppose that he is no longer talking about beauty, at least not in our sense.[5] However, we should notice that there are two sorts of pleasure we may take in the experience of seeing something as well suited to benefit us. The pleasure could be one of anticipating our future well-being. If this is what Socrates means by experiencing something as *kalon*, then he would not be talking about what we call beauty. But the pleasure in experiencing something as *kalon* could instead be one of wonder at how appropriately the various parts of the thing are ordered to its end. Such delight would not be selfless, exactly, since the beautiful thing's function (or apparent function) in this case is defined by reference to our benefit. But it would nevertheless be directed towards the beautiful object rather than to some future good condition of ourselves. Thus it is not obvious that when Socrates calls shoes or other artifacts *kalon* on the grounds that they are good at performing their function, he is referring to something other than what we would call their beauty. We are not strangers to this sort of beauty. The grace of Shaker furniture or the elegance of Mies van der Rohe skyscrapers is due in large part to the visibility of function.[6] So Socrates might well be inviting us to look at (or otherwise contemplate) the manifest functional excellence of certain artifacts and to take pleasure in the experience.

But although Socrates thinks of the experience of beauty as the experience of perfection, we must be careful not to conceive of this in too rational a way. Nothing in the *Republic* suggests that we must have a fixed understanding of what constitutes perfection for something in order to see it as beautiful, much less that we must see it as being like the ideal Form in which it participates. The experience of beauty as Socrates understands it seems to be more immediate than that. (Think again of the lovers of sights and sounds who rush around "studying" beauty. When Socrates says they behave as if their ears were under contract to listen to every chorus, he suggests that they are compelled by the many manifestations of beauty in body, color, and sound to keep all their attention on the immediate sensual experience. This is what makes them impatient with any serious discussion of beauty and unable to understand that there is some Form in virtue of which all beautiful things are beautiful (475d, 476b–c, 479e).) Thus the perception of beauty is not an inference from a judgment of perfection. Furthermore, it is possible to see something as beautiful without believing, all things considered, that it really is good. Not only does this accord with common sense, but Socrates himself seems to bear witness to it when he confesses his attraction to the charms of tragedy even while he bans it as harmful (607c).[7] (Here, we would say that tragedy *seems* beautiful though in truth it is not.) Thus if aesthetic experience involves the thought that the beautiful thing is perfect, that thought is not the sort that presupposes distinguishing the reality of perfection from its mere appearance. Beautiful things shine forth (either sensually or in thought) in their perfection (beauty is the most radiant Form, *Phaedrus* 250b, 250d); they seem to be ideal, worthy of praise, where "seem" has all its ambiguity.[8] That is to say, the seeming may be veridical or not, but it is not part of the experience itself to take a stand on which it is.

So perhaps we can adopt the following provisional definition of beauty as Plato conceives it in the *Republic*: a thing seems beautiful when it appears to be (in some respect) perfect; it is beautiful when its proper power or excellence shines forth for us to see, either with physical eyes and ears or with the eye of the soul. With this in mind, let us return to the question of how a musical-poetic training that culminates in love of beauty prepares the soul for knowledge.

Patterns of Beautiful Poetry

Socrates requires nurses in the ideal city to tell children only fine and beautiful stories (377b–c). It is taken for granted that the protagonists will be glorious gods and fine heroes. The point, rather, is that their behavior must follow certain prescribed patterns (*tupoi*). Since Socrates believes that a poem's pattern rightly determines virtually every other one of its aspects – its meter and the mode of its accompanying music (398d, 400d) – it seems fair to say that when a poem is beautiful that is so in virtue primarily of its pattern. He also claims that these poetic patterns imprint corresponding patterns on the soul of what the world is like and, in particular, how human beings figure in it (377b). Thus the principal cause of a poem's beauty, its pattern, is also the principal cause of its psychic power. Unfortunately, he never explains the mechanism by which the soul is molded or even what constitutes a *tupos*. He is clear that what he means by saying poetry can shape the soul is that it may instill beliefs (377b). But how does this happen?

One possibility is that since all speech is an image (*mimêma*) of belief (382b), children will tend to assume that the stories they hear are ones that, in some way or other, their nurses believe. And since the nurses have a natural authority with their charges, the children will tend to adopt these beliefs as their own before they have subjected them to rational examination. To this we can add that the children sing the poems themselves as well as listen to them. Thus, as they sing the same songs again and again they practice seeming to believe – producing an image of believing – the kinds of the thing the poems say. Over time, the appearance will become comfortable and, in effect, they will habituate themselves to believe, at least at some level, the myths they learn.[9]

I suspect that this is at least part of what Plato has in mind. But we should notice that Socrates does not invoke the idea that speech is an image of belief as part of his general rationale for censoring poetry. That idea comes up in the more specific criticism of poems that depict gods as lying, as giving a false image of what they know to be true. However, we find suggested a more complex picture of poetic influence if we concentrate on the fault Socrates finds with most poetry *before* he enumerates the acceptable patterns.

The "first and foremost" fault of most poems, Socrates says, is that they "give a bad image (*eikazéi kakôs*) of what the gods and heroes are like, the way a painter does whose picture is not at all like (*mêden eoikota*) the things he's trying to paint" (377e; cf. 484c–d). Notice that Socrates assumes here that all poets are in the business of making likenesses; this is what they do either well or badly. Given that likenesses are just the sort of thing poems are, he suggests that a good poem will be a good likeness. That is to say, it will be like reality, not in the sense of giving a literal image of the world (all children's stories are false in that sense, 382c–d), but in the sense of following a true pattern.[10] Now recall that, according to Plato, all beautiful things give an appearance of perfection. Their appearing as perfect is what their beauty consists in. If this is right, then stories that seem beautiful ought to be ones that seem to give an accurate image of what the world is like. And indeed in the *Laws*, the Athenian Stranger is quite explicit about making fidelity of image a criterion of beauty in poetry (667d, 668b).

Put so broadly, however, this standard of poetic beauty is too severe. It would imply, for example, that if the gods turn out to be disembodied, we must ban all stories that show goddesses putting on their veils or arming for battle or, in fact, any element of fantasy. Fortunately, Socrates does not require this degree of verisimilitude. A poem's inaccuracy is particularly bad, he says, when the falsehood is not beautifully told, thus suggesting that accuracy is only part of what makes a poem's pattern beautiful (377d).[11] A few lines later he says that "someone who tells the greatest falsehood about the most important things does not tell his falsehood beautifully" (377e). His point, I take it, is that while any inaccuracy is technically a demerit in poetic image-making, only inaccuracies about important things bear on its beauty. Of course this is vague, but it accords with common sense. Insofar as we ordinarily take truthfulness as an appropriate measure of poetic value at all, we do not think it is compromised by being false to trivial details. (Although too many inaccuracies of this sort will be grating.) Its truthfulness depends on what it shows as meaningful and valuable. So it is more precise to say that in the *Republic*, genuinely beautiful stories are ones that get it right about the most important things, at least in their pattern. The beauty of a poem follows from the accuracy of its pattern in this sense.[12]

This, I believe, is a crucial element in the mechanism by which poetry shapes the souls of the young. Children cannot easily tell whether a story is a literal

likeness or an allegorical one (378d); that capacity develops with age and instruction. But they do not need to be taught to hear a story as a likeness of some
sort or other. That's just the sort of thing it seems to be. So when they experience a poem as beautiful, it shines forth to them and delights them as a good
– that is to say, an accurate – image of the world. This does not mean, of course,
that the image really is accurate. Nor does it mean that, from a reasoned point
of view, they would believe it to be accurate – if, that is, they had a fully developed reasoned point of view from which to judge it.

Let us be clear that, according to Socrates, children – like adults – do make
aesthetic judgments about poems as a whole and not only about the people in
them (401e, 492b–493d). In this, he seems to be following common sense. At
least we can imagine a (well-brought-up) child deploring *the story* of a beautiful
princess who chooses the odious but rich villain over the honest commoner. That
just isn't the sort of thing beautiful princesses do. But we must not suppose that
a child compares the stories he hears to his already formulated vision of the
world. On the contrary, the stories are creating this vision. So a child's opinion
that a particular story is a good one does not take the form of a reasoned judgment that it is truthful. Instead, he is charmed by how excellent an image it
seems. Everything in it seems to harmonize, both with other parts of the story
and, perhaps, with other ideas he already has. Thus, a danger in poetry is not
only that authoritative figures are *telling* it, and so seeming to believe it in some
way or other, but that the poem itself seems to *prove* what the nurses say, since
the more beautifully made it is, the more perfect it seems as a mirror of reality.

This is precisely the problem Socrates returns to and elaborates in Book X,
though now he argues it is a problem for adults as well. Mimetic poetry is not
banned merely because it is "at a third remove from the truth." Nobody needs
to be convinced by Plato that poems and paintings are only images of tables and
couches (although they would need to be persuaded that these, in turn, copy a
paradigm). Rather the problem is that children and foolish adults think that, since
the poems and paintings are so beautiful, they must have something to teach of
the truth.[13] "We must consider tragedy and its leader, Homer. The reason is this:
We hear some people say . . . that if a good poet produces fine poetry, he must
have knowledge of the things he writes about, or else he wouldn't be able to
produce it at all" (598d–e). As it turns out, what Homer and the tragic poets
appear to be teaching is fundamentally false. Indeed it *must* be false since,
Socrates argues, it is virtually impossible to create mimetic images that are
both true and pleasing to the lower part of our soul (605d–e). (An image of
"the most important things" from the point of view of appetite would inevitably
distort the truth.[14]) Now insofar as it is beautiful, poetry does not present
itself as *being* a perfect image, but only as *seeming* so, with all the ambiguity
of "seems." But this is just its danger. For, since it is only an image, reason
relaxes its guard (606a–b). Nevertheless, experiencing it as beautiful amounts

to assenting, albeit not necessarily with reason, to its false message. Even if we know the appearance is false, Socrates worries that repeated exposure to its apparent beauty risks affecting our rational understanding. If beautiful poetry can overthrow an adult's rational judgment, just imagine its power on the mind of a child.

We can now see one reason why Plato thinks education in beautiful poetry leads the young guardians "unwittingly, from childhood on, to resemblance, friendship, and harmony with the beauty of reason" (401d). Recall that, according to Plato, the appearance of beauty is the appearance of perfection in some respect or other. Since all poetry, good or bad, is an image of the pattern of reality, judgments of beauty in poetry are naturally related to judgments of truth in a way that judgments of beauty in other things are not. A beautiful image seems accurate or truthful at some level or other. Now as we saw, Socrates does not suggest that love of beauty in itself instills anything beyond a superficial interest in the truth. The lovers of sights and sounds are mad for the theater and for praising art, but they are impatient with Socrates' questions. So the idea is not that love of beauty is sufficient for love of truth. Nor, indeed, it is even required, since every human being, no matter how depraved, will sometimes care about the truth of what is good for him. However the point is this: Where the love of beautiful art develops before the advent of rational understanding, one's sense of beauty or the fine will provide presuppositions for later deliberation. This, I take it, is the point of Adeimantus' description of the young man considering, on the basis of poetry, what course of life to follow. Beautiful things don't, as a rule, seem to be true, but beautiful poems do. Not because they show us beautiful things – tragedy shows us horrible things – but because *as images of reality* (in its most important features) they charm us as being perfect, distilling the essence of life. Thus love of *this* sort of beauty is a proto-rational activity. As Socrates says, music and poetry exercise that aspect of the child's nature that is "philosophic" (411e): not philosophic in the sense of having or seeking genuine understanding (it involves no more than recognizing and loving things with which one is already acquainted regardless of whether they are truly good, 376a–b), but philosophic in the sense of taking pleasure in having, or seeming to have, some cognitive grasp of our social and natural world. When the young guardians develop a love of genuinely beautiful poems, the patterns they exemplify will "sound true" to them. Indeed, each new properly crafted poem they hear will harmonize with and thereby deepen their sense of what sounds true until these beliefs are absorbed into their souls "like dye" (430a).

It is consistent with this account to think that aesthetic presuppositions can be overruled by reason. The situation would be analogous to the straight stick in water which looks bent to the eyes (602c). There is a difference, though: we do not much care about the shape of sticks, or at least not usually. But since we do care about the things poetry represents, we can suppose that a false sense of the fine will be a perpetual source of deliberative trouble.

Human Excellence and the Standard of Poetic Beauty

I have emphasized the status of poems as images in order to explain their power, but we should not downplay the importance of their subject. As we saw, a poem is beautiful not merely by being accurate, but by being accurate about the most important things. Socrates makes it clear that poetry grips children because of what it represents: glorious gods and fine heroes. If the young guardians experience a poetic character as beautiful, then he must strike them as perfect, as, for example, the embodiment of manhood or of the most blessed life. This is an image that must naturally be riveting to young people who are themselves trying to grow up to be happy men and women. That is to say, beautiful poetry about beautiful people has a tendency to direct our aspirations.

The question of human attraction to beauty is one to which we must return soon. But before that, notice that in Kallipolis poets must not show heroes with evaluative or aesthetic attitudes dictated by appetite or love of money (e.g., 386a–388d; 390a–b; e). As Socrates says later, genuinely "fine things are those that subordinate the beast-like parts of our nature to the human" (589c–d). Once he establishes what patterns truthfully represent the glorious hero, every other aspect of the poem's beauty falls into place. Since the words depict moderate and courageous men, the modes and rhythms in which they are sung must harmonize with the verbal image (398d–400d). So, for example, the story of a leader admonishing his men to endure cannot be sung to a licentious mode or rhythm since in themselves a licentious mode or rhythm express self-indulgence. Every aspect of the musical-poetic education will harmonize with the beautiful words, themselves images of a good person's character (401b–c, 400d).

That Socrates treats the glorious human being *himself* as the standard of poetic excellence lies behind one of the more perplexing poetic rules: the elimination of the mixed style of imitative poetry, the sort that involves the direct speech of a multitude of kinds of characters and, consequently, a multitude of modes and rhythms that suit them (397c).[15] The demand that rhythm and mode suit the words seems to be the plausible requirement that all aspects of a poetic work be internally harmonious. But it is hard to see how the rule about mimesis could be justified in a similar way. Consider a story in which a hero refuses to behave disgracefully in order to escape the violence of a tyrant. It seems as consistent with the rules of poetic content to show this scene in direct dialogue as it is to show it in pure narrative. But Socrates does not justify the rule about mimesis by anything internal to the poem. Rather, he argues that since it is unjust for the courageous, moderate people the guardians will become to act in a slavish or wanton way, they must not be permitted to imitate such behavior either. Since a mixed style of speech is not one the decent person would find appropriate to his own beauty and goodness (395b–c, 396b–d), that style has no place in a beautiful poem.

The idea that a poem is acceptable only if it is in every way suitable to the excellent person is surprising, but one that Socrates evidently believes: "Rhythm and mode must conform to the words . . . [And] what about the style and content of the words themselves? Don't they conform to the character of the soul?" (400d). The soul in question is the *speaker*'s, provided that he is *kalos k'agathos* (396b–c). Notice that although this criterion of poetic excellence is not the same as the accuracy criterion we discussed before, it is consistent with it. Beautiful poems are truthful images, and it is a bedrock of the decent person's personality to be literally – or where that is impossible, allegorically – truthful (382c–d, 389b–c). Thus accurate stories harmonize with the decent person's character and are ones he'd be happy to tell – provided, that is, that they are told in a style that conforms to his goodness. Socrates can make the good person the standard of poetic beauty without contradicting anything he said before about the importance of accuracy.

Still, it is notable that Socrates shifts towards making the beautiful human being *himself* the standard with which beautiful poetry harmonizes. Truthful poetic patterns are, Socrates insists, ones that reveal courageous, moderate, and pious people as fine. But now it seems that these patterns belong to well-made poetry because they are acceptable to the courageous, moderate person himself. They don't just express the truth, but the truth *as* he sees it, and in a musical-poetic style that strikes him as worthy of his dignity (399a–c, 399e). In fact, the beauty of the human soul extends beyond poetry as a standard for the beauty of every aspect of the social environment. It is the standard of physical beauty – a beautiful body harmonizes with a beautiful soul (402c–d, 403d ff.). It is, as we might expect, the standard for beauty in painting and embroidery, but it is also the standard for beauty in buildings and furniture (400e–401d).

It is not clear what Socrates has in mind here, since there is no obvious way to think of a couch, say, as an image of the virtuous person. I suspect, though, that the key is in Socrates' claim that the beauty and correctness of furniture and all other equipment depends on its use (601d). As this passage in Book X makes clear, the person who knows whether or not an artifact is beautiful and good is the person who knows how to use it (601d–e). But who truly knows, as opposed to merely having an opinion, how to use these products of craft? Socrates does not say so explicitly, but we conclude that the true user of artifacts is the virtuous person (cf. 495a). Good, and therefore beautiful, artifacts are useful to excellent human beings. The implication is that behind every experience of the beauty of functional objects is a conception, however inexplicit, of the ideal user. For we cannot delight in an object's appearance of functional goodness without at some level approving of the sort of person who would find that object useful. Socrates talks of tables and couches, but we can think of more contemporary examples too. For instance, whether or not a person cooks, he may well love to look at gleaming, stainless steel professional stoves and, at the edges of imagination, picture the gourmet home-cook he admires.[16] Beautiful furnishings express a conception of human beauty that emanates like ripples from a stone dropped in water. The consequence is that every beautiful aspect of the built environment subtly contributes to the child's developing sense of human excellence, "striking their eyes and ears like a breeze that brings health from a good place" (401c–d).

The same reasoning holds, I suspect, for making the fine person the standard of poetic beauty. After all, poetic image-making has a function, according to Socrates: it allows the rulers and others in authority, for the civic benefit, to say something of the truth about the past (and perhaps about other matters, too) they don't fully know (382c–d, 389b–c). Beautiful and good poetry is truthful in its pattern because it *is* an image of reality and this is what it is *for*. But, as for all functional objects, the ultimate arbiter of perfection is the excellent user. Thus, Socrates' shift to talking of good poetry as harmonizing with the excellent human soul is but one example of his principle that functional beauty is determined by – and expresses a conception of – the ideal user.

So, human beauty is paradigmatic according to Plato. This claim might appear to be at odds with his metaphysics, but it is not. From a metaphysical point of view, of course, the Form of the Beautiful is the standard of beauty everywhere. But this is a point of view we adopt only after our sense of beauty is fairly well entrenched. In the *Republic*, as well as in the *Phaedrus* and *Symposium*, the most fundamental experience of beauty, the one that most shapes our taste and thus the one with which every other experience of beauty resonates, is the pleasure we take in human beauty. (Compare, by contrast, a Romantic sensibility that treats uninhabited nature as paradigmatically beautiful.) It manifests Plato's optimism that, in his view, such an anthropocentric sense of beauty prepares one for the rule of reason and, ultimately, for the life of a philosopher. The world of Forms is *remote* from the human, but it is not *alien* to it. And so in the *Republic*, as well as in the *Symposium*, the first stage of education ends with seemly erotic love for beautiful boys.

Moral Psychology

At this point we are in a position to appreciate an unexpected fact: when Socrates says that musical-poetic education ends in love of the beautiful, he does not mean that it instills an interest in beauty that was not there before. On the contrary, the entire program of training assumes that a desire for beauty is innate. For without this innate interest, no moral cum aesthetic education could be effective. If children were not antecedently attracted to the fine, they would not pay any more attention to beautiful stories than to ugly ones. Nor would they be especially inclined to emulate beautiful people rather than ugly ones. We see that

Socrates assumes the innate power of beauty in the structure of his argument. He does not argue that gods and heroes are fine, but that these fine beings are beneficent, truthful, and moderate. In other words, the legislator's task as Socrates describes it is to give children an aesthetic taste for goodness, not to instill aesthetic interest in the first place. No doubt, poetic education strengthens the child's interest in the beautiful in addition to directing it towards things that are truly fine. But that is not to say that it creates an interest in the beautiful and the fine *ex nihilo*. So although Socrates does not make this point explicit, it is something he ought to believe, for his theory of musical-poetic education presupposes it. What is more, his assumption appears plausible. Beauty is naturally attractive. Nor do children need to be taught to care about praise. It is natural to them to want to be seen by their parents (or others who matter) as measuring up to some ideal. In other words, it is natural both to notice beauty in others and to desire to be (considered) beautiful oneself.

Given that Socrates must think, and in thinking it, be correct, that there is an innate desire for beauty, it is tempting to wonder where in the tripartite soul this desire resides. That is to say, is the love of beauty typical of appetite, spirit, or reason? We ought to exercise some caution here, for Socrates has not yet divided the soul when he legislates the musical-poetic education for the ideal city, nor has he associated parts of the city with parts of the soul. Furthermore, his myth in the *Phaedrus* shows the charioteer and both horses – that is to say, all aspects of the soul – as attracted to beauty (253d ff.). Nevertheless, I think it is fair to assume that love of beauty is not *characteristic* of appetitive desire. Music and poetry affect the spirited and philosophic aspects of the guardians' personality (376c–e, 411a–412a, 441e–442a); and the group of young people to whom this education is explicitly directed grow up to be the warrior and ruling classes of the city, classes associated with spirit and reason respectively. So although sexual appetite is typically directed towards beautiful bodies, the goal of this desire is not beauty per se, but the physical pleasure beautiful bodies can give.

If we take the education that ends in love of the beautiful as our cue, there is ample reason to suppose that the desire for beauty in question is spirited, not rational. For there is ample evidence that this training is especially directed at *thumos*. For instance, Socrates worries that

> if our young people listen to [traditional] stories without ridiculing them as not worth hearing, it's hardly likely that they'll consider the things described in them to be unworthy of mere human beings like themselves or that they'll rebuke themselves for doing or saying similar things when misfortune strikes. Instead, they'll feel neither shame nor restraint but groan and lament at even insignificant misfortunes. (388d)

The attitudes of ridicule, self-rebuke, and shame are typical of spirit as described at 439e–440d. In addition, even if some of the children grow up to be rulers, equivalent to reason in the soul, the content of the education is aimed in the first instance at making them brave and obedient to their rulers or, in other words, suitable as members of the warrior class in the city that corresponds to spirit in the soul.[17] Finally, it is interesting to notice that the timocratic man is a great lover of music and poetry, even though his taste is "a bit estranged from the Muses," suggesting that graceful rhythms and melodies appeal to the spiritedness that rules him (548e).

It is true that, as we have seen, beautiful poetry appeals to the "philosophic" aspect of the child's soul, the part interested in what seems-true. But it is difficult to identify this aspect with reason, the part distinguished by its concern for overall good since, as we saw, it is indifferent to the goodness of what it recognizes (376a–b).[18] So it is more precise to say that this "philosophic" aspect is a sort of proto-reason that is stretched and developed into reason proper by fine words (441e).

In claiming that musical-poetic education trains a spirited love of beauty, we need not deny that beauty is attractive to reason, too. For reason is the part of the soul that pursues goodness as such, whether it be for the soul or the city, and genuine beauty, according to Socrates, is good. Indeed metaphysically it is difficult to distinguish the Forms of the Good and the Beautiful. Furthermore, the education of the taste for beauty is intended to "harmonize the soul with the beauty of reason" (401d). Nevertheless, if we recall the more general remarks Socrates makes about beauty, it is implausible that the fine is the *proper* object of reason. For example, whereas no one is content to have what merely appears good once they are in the business of desiring good things, it is perfectly possible, insofar as one desires beauty, to be satisfied by what is only reputed to be or seems to be beautiful (505d). The pursuit of genuine good, the desire for the real as opposed to appearance, satisfaction in truth as opposed to mere reputation, these are all characteristic of the rational part of the soul as Socrates describes it. Now beauty is the appearing of goodness, so it will be attractive to the part of our soul that pursues good. Indeed, it may even be true that human reason relies on the beauty of good things to find them – their beauty reveals their value. But reason doesn't pursue beautiful things because they *manifest* goodness, but because they *are* good. The love of beauty per se would, on the other hand, love beautiful things not because they *are* good, but primarily because they *appear* good.

Spirit is precisely the part of the soul that loves appearing good. On the one hand, Socrates introduces the spirited part of the soul with the story of Leontius in order to show that the pain we feel at being caught associated with ugliness or badness is distinct from appetite (439e–440a). But on the other hand, he distinguishes this spirited pain from any affection of reason precisely by pointing to the contrast between concern for genuine benefit and concern for apparent glory (441b–c). In the scene Socrates refers to, Odysseus, disguised as

a beggar, sees his maids cavorting with the suitors who are eating up his property, trying to take his wife, and plotting to kill his son. His spirit is outraged
at the maids' contempt for him and longs for a revenge that will show everyone
in the household who he really is. In other words, his spirit wants to show forth
his greatness immediately regardless of whether immediate action is prudent. His
reason, however, calculates that revenge will be more effective if he endures this
shameful appearance for the time being and waits for a more favorable moment.
It is important to see that although Odysseus' reason aims at an eventual scenario that will satisfy his spirit's need for revenge, the immediate course of action
it prescribes is wily, but not fine.[19] Odysseus must await the right moment by
creating the impression of being contemptible to the suitors who insult his name
– this is the pain his spirit must endure. It is spirit, not reason, that longs to
manifest his kingliness – to be *kalon* – right away without regard for his long-
term good. Because the story shows reason evaluating and opposing spirited
pride, it establishes them as different parts of the soul.[20]

There are other reasons for thinking that spirit is especially attracted to the
fine and beautiful. Consider, for instance, that spirit is the champion of justice
from the point of view of anger. That is to say, it does not fight for justice as
something good in itself; rather, it hates being treated unjustly (440c). But as
Glaucon showed in his challenge to Socrates, the person who treats another
unjustly thinks he can get the better of him. This is what the honor-loving spirit
cannot abide: if he allows an injustice to go unpunished, his dignity will go
unseen and unrecognized. Thus, spirit fights injustice and fights it with beautiful actions that in themselves demonstrate his excellence: "it will endure hunger,
cold, and the like and keep on till it is victorious, not ceasing from noble (*gen-
naión*) actions until it either wins, dies, or calms down" (440c–d). (Surreptitious
revenge is the sign of a weak spirit.) To this we can add that spirit is described
as loving honor, victory, and praise, all of which are traditionally thought of as
kalon (see esp. 554e–555a).

Now although it seems in the *Republic* that spirit is the part of the soul that
characteristically loves beauty, it would be wrong to define it as the aesthetic part
of the soul. That is to say, I am not suggesting that Socrates introduces spirit
alongside reason's orientation to overall benefit and appetite's orientation to
immediate sensory pleasure in order to postulate an independent source of aesthetic motivation in the human soul. Socrates is clear that spirit by nature is the
part of us that loves to win (547e, 548c) and his thought seems to be that human
beings have a competitive desire to be seen as the best that springs neither from
appetite nor reason.[21] My point, rather, is to suggest that according to Plato love
of beauty is one of potentially many manifestations of human competitiveness
and desire for self-esteem.

Much depends here on the brilliance of beauty in Plato's account. When a
person is beautiful, his perfection (in some respect or other) is on display for all
to see.[22] Thus beauty can gratify the basic human desire to be recognized (by

actual or imagined others) as superior. And when we experience the beauty of another, we see him as in some way worthy of admiration. Of course there are other ways to satisfy thumoeidic desire, for instance brute physical domination. Socrates says this is typical of timocratic souls ruled by spirit (549a). And even if a person thinks that beauty is one way to win, he may not think it is the best way. For example, a person might think a fine act of generosity would make him look good, but that the stingy action will leave him with more money. This appears to be the conclusion of the oligarchic man who "is not willing to spend money for the sake of a fine reputation" (554e–555a). His spirit is dominated by appetite in this choice, but it is not denied altogether since at bottom his spirit does not "admire anything but wealth and wealthy people [and does not] have any ambition other than the accumulation of wealth" (553d; cf. 572c). In other words, although the oligarchic person's spirit feels the attractions of (an appetitive conception of) beauty, it more deeply desires being richer than everyone else. Or, finally, a person might prefer being feared to being admired. The tyrant epitomizes this condition as he terrorizes his city and soul, utterly shameless before the gaze of his parents or his own childhood attraction to what's fine and good (573b, 574b, 574d). So for all these reasons a person's spirited desire may not find gratification in beauty and the fine. Perhaps it is worth pointing out at this point yet another reason beauty may fail to satisfy spirited desire: it may be that one's beauty goes unrecognised because everyone else has bad taste. Something like this is, I believe, the predicament facing Glaucon and Adeimantus in democratic Athens.

But let us spend a moment longer with Socrates' tale of the genesis and life of the timocratic man – the person whose soul is ruled by spirit and dedicates his life to honor, to *being recognized* as good. It isn't immediately clear that the timocratic man is such a bad fellow. (Indeed Adeimantus jokes that he looks a lot like Glaucon! (548d).) But Socrates says that "as he grows older he loves money more and more because he shares in the money-lover's nature and isn't pure in his attitude to virtue, having been abandoned by the best of guardians . . . reason mixed with music and poetry" (549a–b). Why does Socrates believe the timocrat's compromise – and by implication the rule of spirit – is unstable? Recall that although his father nourishes his reason, presumably by emphasizing the value of justice, the society around him – his mother, the servants – drown out the father's voice with their praise of money (549d–e). The timocrat must eventually alter his conception of the honorable so that he can achieve the honor he desires. If society honors the rich, the lover of honor must become like a moneymaker. This is not to say that inevitably he will *be* a moneymaker, in the sense of being dominated by appetite. Rather, the point is that his spirit will gradually adopt an appetitive conception of victory. Since love of victory cannot of itself determine what constitutes victory, spirited desire is always susceptible to the conception of excellence held by an external judge.

Love of Beauty and Being Just

At first, when we were looking at the relationship between the beauty of poetry and the truth of its patterns, we saw that a correct conception of beauty could shape the course of rational deliberation. Or as we might say now, the development of reason depends on *thumos*. For when poetic images strike us as beautiful, they appear accurate in their depiction of the most important things. Thus a sense of beauty in poetry provides presuppositions from which practical reason deliberates. But now that we appreciate the malleability of spirit, we can see that in the virtuous person the relationship between reason and spirit goes the other way. For when spirit takes beauty and the fine as its paradigmatic source of gratification, it is open to the persuasion of reason. Recall that, according to Plato, to experience something as beautiful is to see it as appearing excellent. By choosing the words it speaks to spirit carefully, reason can make brilliant the excellence of right action. What democracy calls boorishness, reason can call self-mastery; what democracy calls freedom, reason can call anarchy; what sophists call simple-mindedness, reason can call being well-ordered (400e; 560d–e). A person's reason can keep presenting to his spirit an image of his right action that is beautiful and thus gratifying to the natural human urge for recognition, even when recognition comes from nowhere else. And in so doing, reason expresses its own love of truthfulness, for its persuasion of spirit makes the ethical world seem the way it really is.

The just person's love of beauty is, in the *Republic* at least, shot through with spiritedness. It delights in the beauty of the human being and everything that harmonizes with it. Thus it is not pure of the interests of the lower parts of the soul. This may strike contemporary readers as odd, reared as we have been on the dutifulness and disinterestedness of the moral agent. But Plato's point is that competitive desire is fundamental to us as human beings. It cannot be eliminated. Thus it is part of the job of a virtuous person, even after he has become good, to nourish this part of his soul in a way that supports the rule of reason. When being beautiful is what counts as victory for us, it will be hard to feel self-esteem when contemplating a course of action reason shows us is disgraceful. And if our spirited love of beauty in this sense is strong enough, then we can take pride in virtuous action even on those occasions it meets with public disdain.

Conclusion

Let us return to the dramatic origin of the *Republic*: Thrasymachus' praise of injustice and Glaucon's challenge. Although I cannot recount it here, there is ample evidence that Thrasymachus (like the money-loving timocrat) is dominated by a spirit corrupted by appetite. And indeed his defense of injustice as a virtue suits such a character. When he praises injustice as "stronger, freer, and more masterly than justice" he is praising the beauty of a rapacious power of taking whatever one happens to want (344c). Notice that Glaucon is spirited too, although by contrast with Thrasymachus he seems to have all the characteristics a good poetic education is designed to produce. (Socrates gives him credit for good musical taste (548e) and jokes that he is an undiscriminating lover of fine and beautiful boys (474d–e).) It is he, for instance, who scorns Socrates' first city as fit for pigs – surely a complaint of spirit.

Keeping in mind the spirited origins of the praise of injustice sheds light on a difficulty facing Socrates we might not, at first, have noticed. When Glaucon requires him to show that the just person is happy even on the rack, the problem is not only how anyone could endure such pain and be happy, for the rack is a scene of public humiliation. How could the just person have such a firm sense of the beauty of virtue and be so passionately committed to being beautiful that he could endure being a loser in the eyes of all the world? As Socrates says, Glaucon scrubs the just man and the unjust man like statues being prepared for a competition (361d), but statues are judged for their beauty. Who, after hearing Glaucon's challenge, is able to see the thoroughly just life as fine? It is Socrates' difficult task to give a theoretical argument in favor of justice – an argument which appeals to reason – that at the same time persuades the spirits of his challengers. It is, therefore, an important moment when Glaucon con-gratulates Socrates for, like a sculptor, creating ruling men who are altogether beautiful (540c).

We cannot now investigate exactly how Socrates achieves this result, but perhaps we are in a position to reconsider the beauty of Glaucon's unjust man. The tale of Gyges' ring is a fantasy of hiddenness; the unjust person wins hap-piness by cloaking himself in false appearances (361a, 362b). But notice that the story appeals to us in part by *showing* the power and cleverness true injustice must keep secret. This, I suggest, is a problem for Thrasymachus and other spirited advocates of injustice. Whatever other competitive rewards injustice may gain, it is doubtful that spirit can ever truly be satisfied by a way of life that requires one to appear, by one's own lights, stupid, simple-minded, and contemptible and to hide what one takes to be one's own excellence. But this is precisely what the extreme of injustice requires.

Notes

1 Translations of the *Republic* are from Grube, rev. Reeve (1992), with some slight alterations.
2 Physical stars are the most beautiful visible things (529c). Of course, pure astron-omy does not concern itself with these, but since the guardians are introduced to all the mathematical disciplines "in play" as children (537a) in order to see who freely

gravitates to them, it seems reasonable to suppose that the great beauty of the physical heavens is part of the attraction at this early stage.

3 Burnyeat (1999: 283 n. 51) suggests that the advent of reason in this passage is not a significant cognitive achievement on the grounds that being able to recognize letters does not take much talent. But in the analogy with learning to read, the possession of reason is equated with being a competent reader, an ability that goes beyond the ability to pick out letters. Just as knowing the alphabet is necessary but not sufficient for being a competent reader, so too the musical person's ability to recognize the Forms of courage and so forth is necessary, but not sufficient, for understanding the truth of his judgments. (It is interesting in this regard to notice that the musical guardians can recognize Forms of all the virtues save wisdom.)

4 Cf. *Rep.* 353a. Although in the *Republic* Socrates specifies functional perfection as the sort of perfection relevant for beauty, this is not always his view. In the *Phaedrus* Beauty is the Form most easily recollected (250b). This suggests that even where we experience a genuinely beautiful object – one whose beauty expresses functional excellence – our experience includes an intimation of non-functional perfection. In the *Philebus* Socrates distinguishes relative beauty from things that are beautiful in themselves (51c). Whatever this non-relational beauty is, it seems not to be connected to function. If Socrates in the *Republic* had examined the Form of the Beautiful (and not only beautiful things), he might well have said more about the relationship between beauty and non-functional perfection. Since he does not and since the argument of this paper does not rest on the notion of functional beauty in particular, I too will leave this issue aside.

5 Janaway 1995: 62. His chapter 3 is a useful discussion of this issue, although he assumes that an aesthetic sense of *kalon* must be divorced from any appreciation of benefit.

6 Think also of Hopkins's "Pied Beauty," which calls us to rejoice in the beauty of "áll trádes, their gear and tackle and trim."

7 Socrates never actually calls Homer's poetry beautiful, although he strongly suggests it at 601a–b and he says that other people find it so (598e). Furthermore, he recommends as an antidote to the pleasure of poetry that we chant to ourselves the mantra that what poetry says isn't really true (608a). As I will argue in the next section, poetry in particular strikes us as beautiful when it seems like the truth.

8 What I am suggesting, then, is that the experience of aesthetic pleasure is akin to other passions in the sense that all involve an evaluative belief, but one that need not be assented to by the rational part of the soul.

9 I have in mind here the sort of process Burnyeat (1980) attributes to Aristotle in which repetition creates pleasure that, in turn, inclines us to believe that the repeated activity is good.

10 We should not infer from Socrates' later claim that some (but not all) poetry is mimetic that some (but not all) poetry is a likeness. What is special about mimetic poetry as he uses that term in Book III is not that it makes likenesses, but that it makes the poet or speaker himself seem like the character his poem represents (393a–c). It is not entirely clear whether Socrates means the same thing by *mimesis* in Book X; be that as it may, he at least implicitly maintains a distinction between mimetic poetry and likeness-making poetry. Hymns escape the ban on mimesis (607a), but are full of representation (if surviving hymns are any indication).

11 Socrates' qualification might be interpreted as suggesting that the beauty of a poem is something independent of its accuracy, that one and the same false story can be either beautiful or ugly depending on the telling. However, we should remember that the whole point of introducing the accuracy criterion is to help pick out the beautiful stories (377b).

12 Thus the good painter is a potent metaphor for the good philosopher-king (484c–d, 500e–501c). Notice how in this simile the good painter/philosopher keeps looking at the heavenly model for guidance; he wants the image he paints to be an accurate representation of reality. I do not mean to suggest that accuracy is the only criterion of poetic beauty in the *Republic* (consider mode and rhythm), but it is the one Plato emphasizes.

13 This interpretation is inspired and supported by Burnyeat's reading of 598b–c (1999: 300–5). He argues that an adept painter who paints a carpenter may deceive children into thinking that *he* is a carpenter (rather than that the painting is a carpenter, as this passage is usually read), i.e. that he really understands what goes into being a carpenter. I would add that this is because the painting he creates is beautiful, i.e. seems good as an image, i.e. seems like reality. Likewise for tragedy, whether or not it really is a good likeness, it *seems* to be so and in that lies its beauty as a poem.

14 Halliwell (2000: ch. 3) connects the lower part of the soul to a tragic worldview.

15 I agree with Ferrari (1990:117) that the passage as a whole and 398a–b in particular show that the rejected style is one that involves mimesis of a variety of characters.

16 I am sure that my grandmother's aversion to deeply upholstered club chairs was a product of *her* mother's conviction that one shouldn't "wallow" on the furniture.

17 For this and many other arguments that the educational program of *Rep.* II–IV is aimed at *thumos* see Hobbs 2000: ch. 1.

18 Notice also that the young guardians' souls are called philosophic on analogy with the same trait in hunting dogs (376a), later associated later with spirit (440d). Hobbs 2000: 11.

19 The fact that reason has a spirited conception of the good does not imply that reason and spirit have the same *formal* object.

20 See Irwin for the argument that higher parts of the soul oppose lower kinds of motivation *as such* (1995: 207–9; 211–13).

21 Cooper 1984.

22 Hobbs may have something like this in mind, although unfortunately she does not explain in detail why spirit in particular should be moved by beauty. Instead, she argues that since *thumos* is attracted to visible *kala*, and those are akin to ethical *kala*, desire for one will lead to desire for the other (2000: 227–30).

References

Burnyeat, M. F. (1980) "Aristotle on learning to be good," in *Essays on Aristotle's Ethics*, ed. A. O. Rorty, Berkeley: University of California Press, pp. 69–92.

——(1999) *Culture and Society in Plato's* Republic, *The Tanner Lectures on Human Values* 20, pp. 217–324.

Cooper, J. (1984) "Plato's theory of human motivation," *History of Philosophy Quarterly* 1, pp. 3–21.

Ferrari, G. R. F. (1990) "Plato and poetry," in *The Cambridge History of Literary Criticism*, vol. 1, pp. 92–363.

Halliwell, S. (2002) *The Aesthetics of Mimesis: Ancient Texts and Modern Problems*, Princeton, NJ: Princeton University Press.

Hobbs, A. (2000) *Plato and the Hero: Courage, Manliness, and the Impersonal Good*, Cambridge: Cambridge University Press.

Irwin, T. (1995) *Plato's Ethics*, Oxford: Oxford University Press.

Janaway, C. (1995) *Images of Excellence: Plato's Critique of the Arts*, Oxford: Oxford University Press.

Plato (1992) *Republic*, trans. G. M. A. Grube, rev. C. D. C. Reeve, Indianapolis: Hackett Publishing.

7

Methods of Reasoning about Justice in Plato's *Republic*

Gerasimos Santas

How did Thrasymachus arrive at his account of what justice is? At first he simply announces it, but soon enough Plato tells us that it is the conclusion of an argument: "if one reasons rightly, it works out that the just is the same thing everywhere, the advantage of the stronger" (339a; Shorey trans., modified). Not as explicitly but clearly enough, we can see that Glaucon works up his contractarian account of justice by looking at the origin of justice (358c–e). Earlier, Polemarchus fetches the idea of justice as rendering each man his due – benefits to friends and harm to enemies – from the poet Simonides.

Thus in three cases Plato tells us how the speaker gets to his account of justice. But he does not tell us how Cephalus does it; Socrates seems to put words in his mouth. Most importantly, Plato does not tell us explicitly by what method his Socrates arrives at his account of social justice in Book IV. Presumably Plato is using some method for constructing his definition of social justice, though it is pretty apparent that his Socrates does not proceed as Thrasymachus or as Glaucon did, nor yet as Socrates did in Plato's earlier dialogues. In the *Republic* we have at least three different major theories of what justice is (Thrasymachus', Glaucon's, and Socrates'), arrived at by three apparently different methods of reasoning about justice. The significance of methods of reasoning about justice becomes evident: different methods might give us different results, as they actually do in the *Republic*, and then perhaps we can better understand, even gain some control over, the differences; on the other hand, if different methods gave us the same result, our confidence in that result would reasonably be greater. If we need confirmation for the significance of methods of reasoning about justice we can find some in John Rawls's *A Theory of Justice* (1971: ch. III, sect. 30). He points out that in the Original Position the parties would choose the principle of average utility over the classical principle of total utility; he notes that the supporters of the latter knew this, and then in remarkable discussion Rawls finds a different method and foundation for the principle of total utility: the device of the ideal observer and the application of the principle of maximizing an individual's overall good to society.

Of course Plato did not have the benefit of the history of ethics and political philosophy, which Rawls knew well. Plato was a pioneer. Moreover, he used an indirect and informal dialogue style, and whether from ignorance, uncertainty, or choice, he wrote in an "artfull chiaroscuro," an interplay of light and shadow, voice and silence. We must to be clear about what he explicitly says and try to light the shadows and voice the silences by what we hope are educated guesses.

The Empirical Method of Thrasymachus

When asked about the burdens of old age and the uses of wealth, with a foot in the grave and preoccupied with thoughts of death and the afterlife, the wealthy Cephalus naturally thinks of wealth as a means of restitution and clearing his conscience, if he has injured anyone in this life by lying or breaking a promise. Socrates puts these two rules in Cephalus' mouth as an account of justice and brings up counterexamples to dispute it. Though the conversation with the old man foreshadows many themes of the *Republic*, there is no method here of arriving at this account of justice, other than Cephalus' circumstances and experience.

Nor is there a method of reasoning about justice in Polemarchus' appeal to the poet Simonides, for the view that justice is rendering to each man his due (or what is appropriate to him), harm being due to enemies and benefit to friends. It is simply an appeal to authority. The poets invoke the muses for inspiration, and Polemarchus appeals to the poets for justice. Perhaps Polemarchus thinks that the poets' inspiration is a pipeline to the gods and his appeal is to divine authority. But it is still an appeal to authority, not a method of reasoning about justice. And in any case, Plato tries to disarm such an appeal in the *Euthyphro*, and confirms the disarming later in the *Republic* (378) when he characterizes the gods in terms of goodness rather than the reverse. By contrast, Plato explicitly portrays Thrasymachus as employing a certain method for arriving at his account of justice as the advantage of the stronger party:

> don't you know then, said he, that some cities are governed by tyrants, in others democracy rules, in others aristocracy? Assuredly. And is it not this that is strong and has the mastery in each – the ruling party? Certainly. And each form of government enacts the laws with a view to its own advantage, a democracy democratic laws and tyranny autocratic and the others likewise, and by so legislating they proclaim that the just for their subjects is that which is for their – the rulers' – advantage and the man who deviates from this law they chastise as a lawbreaker

and unjust. This then, my good sir, is what I understand as the identical principle of justice that obtains in all states, the advantage of the established government. This holds power, so that if one reasons correctly, it works out that the just is the same everywhere, the advantage of the stronger. (338e–339a)

Thrasymachus begins with an elucidation of the term "stronger" in his initial definition: the ruling party in each form of government, whether a tyranny, a democracy, or an aristocracy. Next, he asserts a big empirical generalization: that in each form of government the ruling party enacts laws to its own advantage; the laws may be different in different kinds of government but they all have this feature in common. He then brings in an assumption, another generalization or a postulate, that each form of government proclaims that justice consists in observing the laws it has enacted and (punishable) injustice in breaking these laws; again these laws may be different in different forms of government and so justice may be different in content in different forms of government; but all these laws have in common that they determine what justice is in each form. And finally, he concludes from these three premises that justice is everywhere the same, the advantage of the stronger.

This is a method for determining what justice is: on the assumption that in each society (or each form of government) the laws determine what justice in that society is, the method consists in an empirical investigation of the aims of the laws and the motives of legislators in each society, and then generalizing from the results to what is common (if anything) to the justice of all societies. On the same assumption, anyone can perform this investigation and find out what the result is; it is an investigation which nowadays may be done by an empirical political scientist doing comparative government.

Thrasymachus did not actually do the empirical research, he only announced its alleged results. But Aristotle apparently did such an empirical investigation of different constitutions and found that in some cases (we don't know how many or in what proportion of the total), Thrasymachus' result does indeed obtain (*Politics*, Book III, chs. 4, 5). But he disagreed with Thrasymachus' conclusion that all constitutions have this common feature of aiming at the advantage of the stronger or ruling party; and he certainly argued that none of these constitutions are just. Plato himself foreshadows Aristotle's conclusion in the *Laws* (IV. 714–15; III.697).

Socrates' first argument against Thrasymachus (339) confirms the crucial importance of the assumption that makes the empirical investigation possible: that justice in each society is determined by the laws of that society. Socrates points out that rulers or legislators might sometimes make a mistake in supposing that a particular law they enact would be to their own advantage, and in such a case acting in accordance with such a law would be both just (by the assumption in question) and also unjust (by the definition of justice as the advantage of the ruler). This is correct, and has a more general validity: so long as laws are thought of as means to some end, such empirical mistakes are possible, whether the end is the advantage of the ruler or the advantage of every citizen or the common interest. Thus the assumption would be incorrect even if we defined justice as what is to the common advantage or the advantage of every citizen; even in that case it would be incorrect to claim that the laws of a given society completely determine what is just in that society. The possibility of such mistakes shows that laws can be unjust.Socrates' second argument against Thrasymachus' account of justice (341–3) confirms that the method is an empirical investigation and the main premise an empirical generalization. Socrates argues that if ruling is an art or science (technê), we can compare it to other human arts (such as medicine and navigation, for example) and see whether in such cases the aim is the advantage of the practitioner (the stronger) or something else such as the interest of the subjects (the weaker) over whom the art is practiced (healing of the patient and safety of the passengers at sea). He concludes that just as in the case of medicine and navigation the aim of the art is not the advantage of the practitioners but that of the subjects over whom the arts are practiced, so in the case of ruling, contrary to Thrasymachus' generalization. Socrates' argument has the form of an analogy, which is the right kind of argument for testing Thrasymachus' empirical generalization, short of carrying out an actual investigation of different kinds of constitutions, as Aristotle did.

We see then that Plato has Thrasymachus use a method of investigating the nature of justice (what justice is), he has Socrates dispute the assumption which makes that method possible (that the laws of a society completely determine what justice is in that society), and he even has Socrates dispute the empirical result of the investigation even if the assumption is granted (by Thrasymachus' restriction of a ruler to one who makes no mistakes; 340). Seeing clearly the method by which Thrasymachus reached his result enables us to assess that result critically, by examining its basis, the premises,, and the reasoning by which the conclusion is reached. We can even tell how one premise, the empirical generalization, might be confirmed or shown to be false: by examining the legislative practices of each society or form of government. The dispute about the other premise is fruitful too: by treating laws as means to ends Socrates opens up some logical space between law and justice: we can't suppose that laws are always just, no matter what ends laws are supposed to serve. Our empirical political scientists can still do interesting empirical investigations of the justice embedded in each form of government, but it has to be on the weaker assumption, that what a society thinks justice is can be found in its constitution and laws, an assumption that leaves it open that a whole society might be mistaken and its justice is really injustice. Thrasymachus' super-conclusion, that justice is the interest of the ruling party, will never follow; but at most, that what is thought to be justice turns out everywhere to be the interest of the stronger party, a disturbing enough conclusion. By opening up some logical space between justice and law Plato was able to dispute the justice of some laws even if they are universally present in all societies, as, for example, the laws determining the inequality of women, which were universally present in Plato's world.

The Contractarian Method of Glaucon

The speeches of Glaucon and Adeimantus enrich the *Republic* remarkably. Social contract theories of justice had hardly been born when Plato wrote the book. In one short paragraph Aristotle attributes one to the sophist Lycophon (*Politics* III. 9, 1280) and its significance seems to escape him (For a recent account of ancient contractualism, see Keyt and Miller 2004). It took some twenty centuries for such theories to make a second significant appearance, but then they had a most fruitful run, from Hobbes to Rawls.

It is not easy to say how far Plato appreciated the theory he puts in the mouth of Glaucon. The brothers' speeches take up some eleven pages (357–68), but only two short paragraphs are devoted to the question of what justice is; the rest take up the second great issue about justice, whether one is better off or happier being just rather than unjust (and the vast majority of the philosophical schol-arship on these speeches is devoted to this second issue). It is an understatement to call Plato's contractarian account of what justice is elliptical. The reader can see that for herself if she compares it to chapter III of *A Theory of Justice*, which we can fairly say is a state of the art account of a contractarian theory of justice; on all the guesses we make below to fill Plato's gaps Rawls is quite explicit. A contractarian theory of justice claims that justice is the object and the product of a voluntary and presumably rational choice or agreement among human beings; and it usually supposes that before there is such an agreement there is no such thing as justice. Contractarian theories must have at least two main parts: the conditions under which the agreement or choice is made – usually called the circumstances of justice – and the content of the agreement (or the alternative chosen) that is reached voluntarily and rationally in the circumstances described. The conditions under which the agreement is made and the reasoning used to reach some agreement may be called the contractarian method. Glaucon's account of justice is contractarian and it is usually so taken. He tells us explic-itly that the first thing he is going to do is to give "the nature and origin of justice," and he starts with the origin:

> by nature, they say, to do injury is good for one, to suffer injury bad, but the bad of being injured exceeds the good obtained from injuring others. So that when men injure and are injured by one another and had a taste of both, those who lack the power to avoid one and do the other determine that it is in their interest to agree with one another neither to injure nor to be injured; and this is the beginning of legislation and covenants among men, and they name what the law commands the legal and the just, and that is the origin and the nature of justice. It is a

compromise between the best, which is to injure with impunity, and the worst, which is to be injured without the power to retaliate. (359, trans. Shorey)

Here we find the two main parts of a contractarian theory: a state of affairs in which men presumably had no justice (Glaucon seems to say at 358a that in that state men did do injustice to each other, but to avoid inconsistency we have to correct him, by supposing that he means harm or injury rather than injustice, or that men do what would be injustice), and were injuring and harming each other and suffering the consequences; and the compact which they reached: each agrees not to injure others in return for a similar agreement by others not to injure him. The first part gives us the circumstances in which justice originated or was created by agreement, and the second part gives us the content of this fundamental agreement. Though we can see here these two parts of a contractarian theory roughly and in outline, many pertinent questions are not answered in our texts, and we can only try to make educated guesses about answers Plato would have given.

In the state before justice, the state of nature as the moderns call it, what was the environment like? Since it seems that men found it necessary to injure and harm each other, presumably as a means to getting the things they wanted (and not for its own sake), we can infer that these things were not in abundance – that it was a state of moderate scarcity in the things men usually need and want. Perhaps it was a state represented by a zero-sum game: if we sum up all the transactions among men, voluntary or not, the gains and losses sum up to zero, and normally one man's gain is another man's loss. Some have suggested that it might even be a negative sum game (since Glaucon says that "the bad of being injured exceeds the good obtained by injuring others" [359]).And what were the human beings like in this state? Apparently they were self-seeking, whether completely or predominantly so: each seeks the things which presumably he thinks he needs or wants or regards as good for him; including apparently injuring or harming others, at least as a means to getting what he wants, and apparently in the expectation he will not be retaliated upon or that he can successfully repel retaliation or that he can come out ahead even with retaliation.

This for their circumstances and their motivation. But what of their capacities? Apparently they were also minimally rational: at least able to learn from their experience in the state of nature, and able to figure out effective means to their own ends and their overall good. Thus, moderate scarcity in the things they want, their self-seeking nature, and minimal rationality, seem the minimum assumptions necessary to account for the conflicts among them, and their agreement with each other.

And what do they agree on? What is the content of this first and fundamental agreement? Glaucon says, "neither to injure nor to suffer injury." Apparently this means at least that each agrees not to injure others (or to give up his freedom to do that) provided that others agree not to injure him (or others give up their freedom to injure him). Once they set up laws in accord with this fundamental original agreement, just conduct will be determined by such laws; and sanctions for disobeying them presumably can be expected to give to each the security of not being injured by others in return for the freedom each has given up.

Glaucon also tells us that the justice that comes about by this agreement is regarded as a compromise between "the best, to injure with impunity, and the worst, to be injured without the power to retaliate." Apparently this means that the parties to the agreement think that the best state of affairs for them is to have the freedom to do whatever they please including injuring others, together with the power to do so with impunity; and the worst state of affairs is to have the freedom but not to have any such power, not even the power to retaliate when injured.

This interpretation of Glaucon's account of the origin and nature of justice, though minimal, is still full of inferences from out texts. We inferred moderate scarcity, we inferred at least predominant psychological egoism, we suggested a zero-sum game. We inferred rationality about one's overall good. We amplified the content of the agreement. Further, we guess that the principle of equality later mentioned by Glaucon (359c) refers to the content of the agreement: giving up the same freedom equally in exchange for the same security equally. We softened the extreme emphasis on injuring or harming others: we described it as a necessary means to one's perceived good (not as something pursued for itself). And we amplified the best and worst states that the agreement forbids and avoids.

Even so, several important questions remain unanswered. What alternatives did men have to choose from? Only the state of nature and what they ended up agreeing on? Why so? The contractarian method is open on what the alternatives are in front of the choosing parties. Even within the limited philosophical space of the *Republic*, we can imagine different principles of justice, and different constitutions and forms of government the parties could have considered: Thrasymachus' principle of justice, Plato's own principle of social justice, as well as the one they actually agreed on. Or, more concretely, they could have considered a choice among democratic, oligarchic, timocratic, even tyrannical constitutions. And if they had all these alternatives, they might have to use more complex reasoning to make a choice, and perhaps take into account odds as well as outcomes.

Another important question left unanswered: was the agreement unanimous? Our texts do not say, though conceivably they imply that it was. The problem is that Glaucon says: "those who lack the power to do the one [injure or harm others] and avoid the other [being injured or harmed by them to an even greater extent] . . . agree with one another." This suggests that not everyone was in that situation of weakness: perhaps there were some who had the power to injure or harm others and get away with it. Did they agree? Why would they? We may have to suppose a two-stage agreement: first, those individually weak agree among themselves for the reasons given; once they band together, being perhaps a considerable majority, they are collectively stronger than the few individually strong men, and then the latter find themselves in the weak position and also come to agree for similar reasons.

This interpretation perhaps accounts well for some of the things that Plato has Glaucon say in the rest of the speech: Glaucon claims that anyone in the created city-state would behave unjustly if given the magic ring of Gyges (which makes one invisible); but he also implies that only few in the state would have the societal equivalents of the ring, the ability to act unjustly secretly and to cultivate the deception of a just reputation. In turn, this seems to serve well Plato's implied criticism of Glaucon's contractarian justice: in the city-state which would result from Glauconian agreements, the best and brightest individuals would be dissatisfied and tempted to try to escape the bounds of the agreed upon justice; they would represent the strong in the state of nature and the least benefited by the original agreement. Glaucon's just city might be highly unstable. A justice which tempted the best and the brightest under it to act unjustly leaves something to be desired. Finally, there is the question of what are the goods or the interests for the sake of which men fought in the state of nature, and for which the best and the brightest might be tempted to act unjustly in the resulting society. In Glaucon's thought-experiment, when just and unjust men are given magic rings, they equally go after power, property, wealth, and pleasure; they are portrayed as happy because they get these things, and more generally because they can do and have whatever they desire or please (they conduct themselves as equal to a god! [360c]). So presumably it is for the sake of these things that they fight in the state of nature, and for the sake of these – or at least to avoid their opposite evils – that they compromise and agree, given that they lack the powers of gods. Relative to these goods and their situation, their choices and agreements can be rational.

It is remarkable that some of the most prominent goods in Glaucon's initial tripartite classification of goods (in his opening remarks, 357–8) are conspicuously absent in the rest of his story: apparently nobody fights for knowledge in the state of nature or guides his life by it in society; nor does seeing or being healthy seem to play a role in significant choices. And the pleasures of men with magic rings are anything but harmless. A significant theory of good – either hedonism or the satisfaction of desire – seems to underlie Glaucon's story, together with some restrictive assumptions about what men take pleasure in or desire. It is a theory that Plato attacks in several places in the rest of the *Republic* (see, e.g., 421–2, 557–61, 575–87).

The Functional Method of Plato

Plato does not tell us by what method of reasoning he is trying to find out what justice is, in a new inquiry he has his Socrates start right after the speeches of

Glaucon and Adeimantus. If we track his actual investigation from that point (367) all the way to his two accounts of a just city-state and a just person (432, 442), we can plainly see that there is no trace of Thrasymachus' empirical method, nor of Glaucon's contractarian method. And far from appealing to the poets, as Polemarchus did, the poets are severely criticized and even ostracized for saying false or unwise things about gods and heroes. Nor is there a trace of a Socratic method we might extract from the earlier dialogues of definition: collecting some clear examples of just actions or just persons, generalizing from them, and testing the generalization by further examples and by consistency with other firmly held beliefs. (The contemporary analogue of this Socratic method so conceived is, I believe, Rawls' method of "considered judgments in reflective equilibrium", Rawls 1971: ch. I, sect. 9.)Yet we can hardly suppose that Plato reaches his specific results randomly or by sheer good fortune. And since he does display considerable sophistication about philosophical methods, not only in the views of Thrasymachus and Glaucon but earlier too in the Socratic dialogues and in the *Meno* and the *Gorgias*, we must at least make a search for his method. Can we discover a method from what he actually does between his starting point and his definitions?

Well, Plato has Socrates begin by dividing the question into two, what is a just city and what is a just person, and starts with a just city (368e. Apparently Plato takes these two cases, the justice of a city and of a person to be the primary or central applications, and it is commonly thought he takes the justice of a person to be in some sense prior to that of a city; he of course knows that justice has other important applications, for example, to laws and actions). He supposes that if they imagine a city coming into being they would see justice or injustice coming into being too. He suggests that the city comes into being because humans, being individually not self-sufficient, come together to render services to, and trade with, each other, "because each supposes this to be better for himself . . . let us create a city from the beginning in our speech . . . its real creator will be our needs" (369c). In rapid order Socrates (1) proceeds to list the economic needs for food, shelter, and clothing, (2) proposes a division of labor for producing these goods, (3) supposes that human beings are born with different abilities for different kinds of occupations (what I call the natural lottery assumption), and concludes that "more things are produced, and better and more easily when one man performs one task according to his nature, at the right moment, and at leisure from other occupations" (370c). It is noteworthy that in this passage Socrates does not claim that each person can practice only one kind of occupation, but only that one cannot practice *well* more than one, given that different inborn abilities and education and leisure and timing are necessary for doing such things well. See also 374, and again 394e: given that inborn ability, education, and time are required, "it is impossible that one can practice well many arts." In this last passage it is clear also that it is not minute division of labor that is at issue (as in Adam Smith's, *The Wealth of Nations*, chs. 1–3), but division into the arts and sciences. In successive passages Socrates expands the needs of citizens of his imaginary city, beyond provisioning themselves, to defending and governing themselves (373d–374e); tries to figure out what inborn abilities are best suited for which of these several social tasks (374e–376e); suggests a system for educating these several abilities (376e–415db); proposes institutions of property and family for the citizens whose inborn abilities and education suit them to defend and govern (415–27); and ends up by claiming that the city they have imagined, if they made no mistakes, is "completely good" (427e).

He immediately infers from the city's complete goodness, that it is "wise, brave, temperate, and just." Finally, he proceeds to give an account of each of these four virtues in the order just given, trying to catch in each case the particular good that each virtue contributes to the city. He ends up with the claim that the justice of the city is to be found in the principle of organization they started the city with: "For what we laid down in the beginning as a universal requirement when we were founding our city, this, I think, or some form of this, is justice . . . that each man must perform the one social service in the state for which his nature was best adapted" (433a). The universal requirement clearly refers to the conclusion he drew at 370c, which we quoted above.

Now why should Plato suppose that by following this procedure he would discover what justice in the city is? Indeed, why did he suppose that by following it he would discover what a completely good city is? And why did he think that he could infer from its complete goodness that the city had these virtues? I think we can find convincing answers to these questions in a procedure suggested by a theory Plato has Socrates expound and use at the end of the first book (352e ff.). The theory first gives an account of two kinds of functions: "the work (*ergon*) of a horse or anything else [is] that which one can do only with it or best with it"; and again, " when I asked whether that is not the work (*ergon*) of a thing which it only or it better than anything else can perform" (353a7). I call the first kind of functions exclusive and the second optimal; Socrates gives seeing as the exclusive function of eyes (since only with the eyes can we see), and hearing as the exclusive function of the ears (since we can hear only with the ears); and he gives pruning as an optimal function of a pruning knife, since, he says, "we can use a dirk to trim vine branches and a knife and many other instruments . . . but nothing so well as a pruning knife fashioned for that purpose" (353a). Second, the theory proposes that there is (an) appropriate virtue(s) for each thing that has a function, and characterizes the appropriate virtue(s) of a thing with a function as that by which it performs its function well, and its vice(s) that by which it performs it poorly (353bc). Next, Socrates claims that this theory applies to "all other things" (presumably to all things with functions), and immediately applies the theory to prove to Thrasymachus that a just man is happy and an unjust one unhappy (353d–354a). This immediate application proceeds by supposing that the soul has the exclusive functions of managing, ruling, and deliberating, and that justice is the virtue of the soul and injustice its vice; from the theory and these premises Socrates then concludes that the just soul will do these functions well, the unjust one badly, and that the soul that does these things well will live well, the unjust will live badly; and further that the soul that lives well is happy and the one that lives badly unhappy.

During this application Socrates adds to the theory: he says that a soul that has the virtues of a soul will be a good soul (and one that does not have them a bad soul), and that a good soul will perform its functions well, a bad one poorly (353e). Presumably, generalized versions of these two premises can be added to the theory: a thing of a certain kind (with functions) that has the virtues appropriate to that kind will be good of its kind; and a thing good of its kind will perform the functions of that kind well. Arguably, in this application he also needs the assumption that functioning well is good for the thing that functions well, perhaps its chief good; seeing well, for example, is the good of the eyes, and anything that contributes to seeing well is good for the eyes.

I think we can see from the examples that Socrates gives that the theory generalizes from practices, including evaluative practices, in medicine and the productive arts. The medicine of Plato's day had determined that the human body has a natural division of parts (especially organs, but also fluids, tissues, and bones; see the long discussion of the human body in the *Timaeus*, 72–9) and a natural division of labor matched (or assigned by the divine craftsman in Plato's view) to those parts; eyes and ears are natural parts of the human body and each has a task unique to it; we can understand the human eye by understanding what its function is and by finding out what qualities, such as structure and composition, enable it to perform that function well. Further, we evaluate the human eye by how well it performs that function, and we can think of the qualities that enable it to perform that function well as its virtues. It is then a truism that an eye that performs its function as well as possible is a completely good eye and that a completely good eye has all the virtues appropriate to eyes (i.e. the virtues relative to that function). The theory for human artifacts is the same, except that the account of function is different: any artifact can be used for many purposes, but usually it is the best instrument (better than others) for the purpose or use it was designed for (rather than other uses); and it is good of its kind and functions well when it has the virtues appropriate to its function. (For a critical discussion of the functional theory, see Santas 2001: 66–75. For discussions of function see Hull and Ruse 1998.)

This theory suggests a procedure for discovering the virtues of objects of a given kind, on the assumption that such objects have functions: (1) find out what the functions of such objects are; (2) determine (by observation, experiment, or even thought-experiment) cases where objects of such a kind perform their functions well and cases where they perform them poorly, and (3) finally find out the qualities which enable them to perform such functions well (and in the absence of which they perform poorly), and these are their virtues. (For similar procedures, consisting of several ordered steps, which Plato calls a *methodos* (method), see *Phaedrus* 270b–271c, *Sophist*, 243d–244, and *Republic* 532ff.).

And we can now see that this procedure accounts well for Socrates' major moves in trying to determine what justice in a city is. On the assumption that justice can be found in cities (as well as in individuals), first he tries to discover what the functions of such city-states are, and finds that they are to provision, to defend, and to govern themselves. Next he tries to organize an imaginary city-state so as to perform these functions as well as can be conceived of by himself and his interlocutors; this would be achieved by division of labor matched to a division of citizens by natural ability for these functions and by suitable education. Finally, Socrates appropriately claims that if they made no mistakes in the way they divided, structured, and educated their imaginary city (so as to perform its functions as well as possible), their city is indeed completely good. If it is completely good it has all the virtues appropriate to the city; and since justice is a virtue of city-states, their city will have justice; and now they can try to locate justice among the qualities that enable their city to perform its functions well and be a good city.

This procedure is by no means complete. If, for example, a thing has many functions and many virtues, it does not tell us how to differentiate among its several virtues. Socrates claims that both city and soul have several functions and several virtues; but which virtue accounts for the good performance of which function, so that the virtue can be characterized accordingly? We can see his hesitation in trying to define the virtues of the city; he lists them in a certain order, leaving justice for last, as what is left over after wisdom, courage, and temperance have been defined. He has an easy time with wisdom and courage, since it is clear to what functions each contributes (427–430), but struggles with temperance, which is a virtue of the whole rather than any one part of the city. (He goes first to temperance as it applies to individuals, and finally defines it as a city virtue by saying that it combines control of the best part over the worst and harmony among the parts, 430d–432e.) When it comes to justice, which also is a virtue of the whole city, he feels he has to find arguments that what he has defined is the virtue of justice. Assigning city functions to parts of the city optimally, that is, on the basis of what city function each city part can do best, may help the city perform all its functions better, but why is this justice (432b–434c)? Despite these problems, in his accounts of the city's virtues we can see that in each one of them Socrates tries to catch some quality of his imagined city which would account for performing some one or all its functions well or better. Beginning with the less controversial cases, knowledge of what is good for the city as a whole is said to account for the city being well governed; its courage for being well defended; while temperance would account for the good of harmonious relations among the parts of the city, especially on the question of who should govern the city; and justice accounts for the good of all three functions being performed better than they would be under any other political and economic structure (i.e. a timocratic, oligarchic, democratic, or tyrannical constitution).

Now there are some who think that the first book is a Socratic dialogue whose theories cannot be relied on to interpret the rest of the work. They think this applies to the theory of function and virtue of the first book, and cite Socrates' remark at the end as specific evidence that the theory of function (*ergon*) is abandoned there (perhaps Vlastos 1991; Burnyeat 2002).

I certainly disagree with this general view; I think the first book foreshadows many important themes in the rest of the work and is beautifully integrated with it; but this is beyond the scope of this essay. However, aside from this general dispute, I think we have convincing evidence that the theory of function and virtue of Book I is used to give an account of justice in the rest of the work.

To begin with, Socrates' remark, at the end of Book I, is not good evidence that he abandons the functional theory. He says that, like a glutton, he rushed to discuss whether justice is a virtue, and whether it is better than injustice, before finding out the first object of the inquiry, what justice is. "So that for me," he continues, "the present outcome of the discussion is that I know nothing; for if I don't know what justice is, I can hardly know whether it is a virtue or not, and whether its possessor is or is not happy" (354b–c). I think this remark can be understood if we suppose Socrates to be saying that his arguments against Thrasymachus on the benefits of justice are unsuccessful because Socrates had no account of what justice is: he argued that justice is a virtue without saying what justice is; and again he argued at the end of the first book, using the functional theory, that justice makes one happy, and injustice unhappy, without saying what justice is. We obviously cannot suppose that Socrates was arguing that justice *according to* Thrasymachus (i.e. the advantage of the rulers) is a virtue and that it makes its possessor happy, since Socrates does not think that this is what justice is. So, he is correct in complaining that in effect he has been arguing that justice, *whatever it is*, is a virtue and makes its possessor happy. But how on earth could anyone possibly show or know *that*? In any case, his remark is no reason to throw out *all* the premises in those two arguments but only reason to try again, this time taking into account the priority rule of giving an account of what justice is before proceeding to show that it makes one happy. And this is just what Socrates does in the rest of the work.

More important, we have good textual evidence for thinking that Socrates is using the functional theory in the rest of the work. He uses the term *ergon* (function, work) significantly several times when he discusses the origin of the city and states the principle of social justice for the first time. Thus when he first proposes division of labor he asks: "Shall each of these [the citizens] contribute his own work (*to outou ergon*) for the common use of all?" (369e). Next, he uses the term when he introduces the natural lottery assumption: "our several natures are not alike but different . . . one man is naturally fitted for one task, another for another (*allos ep allou ergou praxein*)" (370b). Again, he uses the term to point out that the various occupations require leisure from other things so that the work can be done at the right time (*ergou kairon*, 370b). Then he combines the two in his conclusion, the very first statement of the principle of Platonic social justice (*eis en kata phusin kai en kairo . . . pratte*, 370c). Again, when trading is found necessary for the city, Socrates says that those weakest in body and useless for any other function (*ergon*) will be traders. Looking back at the account of *ergon* (function) Socrates gave in the first book, we can see clearly that the concept of optimal function is being used here: citizens are to be assigned that *ergon* for which they are best suited by nature and (added later) appropriate education.

Next, when Socrates introduces the need for defending the city, he extends the scope of the principle of social justice (whose point is restated at 374b in terms of *ergon*: "to the end that the cobbler's *ergon* is well done") to the function of defending the city: "Then, I said, to the same degree that the task of the guardians (*ton phylakon ergon*) is the greatest of all, it would require more leisure than any other business and the greatest science and education. Does it not also require a nature adapted to that very pursuit?" (374e). It is clear in this passage again that the concept of optimal functions is being used.In Book III. 406c, *ergon* is used in a version of the principle of social justice attributed to Aesculapius: "he knew that in all well governed peoples there is a work assigned to each man (*ergon ti ekasto en polei*) in the city which he must perform."

In Book IV, we find *ergon* explicitly linked to the typical formula which Plato uses for city justice and soul justice in that book (namely, *to eautou ekaston prattein*): each person does his own. In replying to Adeimantus, Socrates says: "but these helpers and guardians are to be constrained and persuaded to do what will make them the best craftsmen in their own work (*tou eauton ergou*), and similarly with all the rest [of the citizens]" (421c). And a bit later, in the discussion of the unity of the city and of each citizen, Socrates says: "the other citizens too must be sent to the task for which their natures were fitted, one man to one work (*ergon*), in order that each of them fulfilling their own (*en to autou epitethevon ekastos*) may be not many men, but one, and so the entire city may come to be not a multiplicity but a unity." *Erga* (functions) is also used in the beginning of the final argument Socrates gives to show "that each doing his own" is what justice is: "A carpenter undertaking to do the work (*ta erga*) of a cobbler or a cobbler of a carpenter . . . or even the attempt but the same man to do both . . . would not greatly injure a city?" (434a–c). Thus the two kinds of injustice, practicing an art to which one is not best suited by nature and education, and practicing many arts, are described here in terms of *ergon*; this is clearly once again the notion of optimal function (these two cases of injustice explain the four types of unjust city and unjust individual in Book VIII).

Now one might grant that Plato uses the three-step functional procedure to discover justice in the city, but deny that the functional theory plays any role in the account of the virtues of the soul. And it is true that for discovering justice

in the individual soul Plato does not explicitly use this functional three-step procedure, but rather a shortcut made possible by his assumption that a just soul is
isomorphic (the same in form) to a just city; it enables him to deduce an account
of the just soul from his account of the just city and from an independent argument for his division of the soul (434–442). But the close analogy between the
tripartite city and the tripartite soul (by nature both have parts equal in number
and of the same kind, 441c) that the isomorphism demands, suggests strongly,
I think, that in his division of the soul Plato supposes that the human soul comes
with a natural division of parts (powers or faculties, not agents, in my view) and
psychic labors (functions) unique (exclusive) to each part; and further that the
human soul can be educated so that its parts are matched optimally to the psychic
functions of an individual to provide for, defend, and govern herself. The isomorphism itself, which is very demanding (psychic parts must correspond to city
parts and psychic functions to city functions), requires that the cryptic formula
of justice in Book IV, that in both cases of city and soul justice obtains when
"each [part] is doing its own" has to have the same interpretation. And if in the
case of the city it means that each part of the city must do that city function (of
the three main city functions) which it can do best (i.e. optimally), then it must
mean the same thing for the soul; a soul is just when each part of it is performing that psychic function (of the corresponding three main psychic functions) which it can do best (i.e., optimally); for example, reason must rule
because it can so better than spirit can rule (as it does rule in the timocratic
man), better than appetite can rule, and so on. The functional theory is in the
background here, as it is also in the analogy between justice in the soul and
health in the body, since bodily health was conceived in terms of bodily parts
and their functions. (For discussion of the isomorphism between just city and
just soul, see Santas 2001: 111–17; and for the virtue/health analogy, pp.
133–8.)

A third use of the functional theory, I think, can be found in Plato's defense
of justice. His explicit first defense of psychic justice by the health analogy at the
end of Book IV, presupposes, I believe, the idea of bodily health as an organism functioning well. But aside from this, and also aside from his defense of
justice in terms of his distinctions among pleasures in Book IX, I think he has
a more fundamental defense of both city and soul justice, which relies on the
idea that happiness obtains when city and soul are functioning well. The functional theory itself supposes that functioning well, the fundamental normative
idea in terms of which every other value in the theory is explained, is good for
the thing that so functions: functioning well physically is good for the body;
functioning well socially is good for the city; and functioning well psychologically is good for the psyche. If happiness is a good, indeed the chief and most
inclusive good, then functioning well will be at least part of it. I think we can
see some of this when Socrates is made to defend the city he has been constructing against Adeimantus' objection in the opening pages of Book IV, that

by depriving the guardians of property and wealth (and all the goods and enjoyments these enable us to have) Socrates is making the guardians unhappy. Socrates makes a reply in two parts. First, in obvious contrast to Thrasymachus, he says that they were trying to imagine a city so organized as to promote the happiness of the city as a whole, not just the happiness of the rulers; for, they thought, it is in such a city that they would find justice. Second, he challenges the conception of happiness Adeimantus' objection assumes, and suggests a functional conception of happiness: happiness will be found, at least in part (the other part being psychic, not social), in citizens being "the best craftsmen in their own function" (*aristoi dimiourgoi ton outon ergon*, 421c), and concludes that in a well ordered city "each class is to be left to the share of happiness that its nature comports." Similarly, given the isomorphism, happiness is also to be found in each part of the soul doing well what it can do best. Each part of the city or soul doing what it can do best is simply a restatement of (the formal part) of what justice is; so justice, together with the other virtues, to be sure, since they contribute to functioning well, contributes to happiness. This is a more fundamental defense of justice, because, on the assumption that functioning well is good for a thing, the good of justice is inherent in the very nature of Platonic justice.

Finally, in Book X we find some further uses of the functional theory. At 601d we are told: "There are some three arts concerned with everything, the user's art, the maker's and the imitator's. Yes. Now do not the excellence, the beauty, and the rightness of every implement, living thing, and action refer solely to the use for which each is made or by nature adapted? . . . the user is the one who knows most of it by experience, and he reports to the maker the good or bad effects in use of the thing he uses." Though *ergon* (function) is not used in this passage, notice the characterization of the use in question as "the use for which each is made or by nature adopted," which echoes the two-fold account of *ergon* in Book I. A bit later, at 602d–603b, we have a subdivision of psychic powers, between opining on the basis of the appearances of distance and shape and size, and contrary opining on the basis of measuring, counting, and weighing; the division is made on the basis of the principle of contrariety, and it is clear in the context that measuring, counting, and weighing are exclusive functions of reason. Because of these functions reason is said to be the best part of the soul; and because of these exclusive functions, ruling is said to be the function of reason: "And have not measuring and numbering and weighing proved the most gracious aids to prevent the domination of our soul of the apparently greater or less or more heavier, and to give the control to that which has reckoned and numbered or even weighed? Certainly. But this surely would be the function (*ergon*) of the part of the soul that reasons and calculates" (602d–e). In this whole passage, how well a thing functions is made a basis for evaluation, exclusive functions are used to individuate parts of the soul, and the exclusive functions of reason are used as a basis for assigning to it ruling as its optimal function.

The uses of the functional theory I have been detailing may fairly be called normative uses of the theory: to discover what justice is in city and soul, to show that justice is better for us, and even to hint at the nature of happiness. Arguably, Plato's account of exclusive function underlies his division of the soul and his accounts of the nature of each part. But this is beyond the scope of this essay. (For discussions of Plato's division of the soul and the nature of each part see, e.g., Irwin 1995: chs 11, 12; Price 1995; Santas 2001; Bobonich 2002.) We asked earlier why Plato thought that by following the procedure his Socrates actually does follow he would discover what justice is. We answered that he thought so because he had a very general theory, taken from medicine and the productive arts, which suggested a procedure for discovering the virtue(s) of anything with function(s). In turn, we can ask why he thought that this functional theory, whose logical home is the realm of natural organs and of artifacts, would be appropriate for discovering justice, a virtue whose domain is not natural organs and artifacts but cities-states and souls. A good answer to this question is not easy to find, but its outlines may be partly in the *Phaedo*, partly in the *Republic*, and partly in the *Timaeus*. In the latter we have the postulation of a cosmic teleology, according to which a non-envious and good divine craftsman created the existing physical universe to be as good as matter allows, using the Platonic Forms as paradigms or patterns. The physical universe is generally the best it can be, and that is why Plato suggests in the *Phaedo* that the best explanation of why things are as they are, on a cosmic scale at any rate, is that it is best for them to be that way. When in a particular case they are not the best, as in the case of a defective eye or a rusted pruning knife, the fault is to be found in the nature of body or matter. The physicians of the day had began to discover, Plato thought, the natural goodness of the body (i.e. health), in the natural divisions of the body, the functions the natural parts served, and the structures that enabled those parts and the whole body to function well; and this is to discover the ways in which the divine craftsman created the body so as to be as best as it can be. Similarly with the astronomers and the celestial part of the universe, while human craftsman, such as architects and shipbuilders tried to discover and create, perhaps by imitation of the structures of the physical universe, structures that would enable their objects to be as good as possible and perform their functions as well as possible. Similarly perhaps, Plato thinks of legislators and educators as trying to discover and enhance the structures in cities and souls, which would make such cities and souls the best they can be and perform their functions as well as possible.

The Significance of Methods

Plato has his speakers employ different methods of reasoning about justice and he has them reach different conceptions of justice. But he does not explicitly discuss the significance of using such different methods. Would anyone of his three main speakers, Thrasymachus, Glaucon, or Socrates, reach the result he did reach by using the others' methods? Given what Plato has actually written, we might suppose that his answer would be no. Different methods gave him different results; so why should we suppose that the three methods might give us the same result, or that Plato would think so?

These questions are not easy to answer, partly because the distinction between methods and substantive or empirical assumptions made in applying the methods might not be all that sharp. If our question includes differences in such assumptions, then it would not be too surprising if different methods gave us different results, though logically there might still be room for the same result, since the same conclusion can be validly deduced from different premises, something Plato was probably aware of from, say, the different existing proofs of the Pythagorean theorem.

In fact, Plato does seem to criticize the method Thrasymachus used, by criticizing the assumption that makes the empirical investigation of justice and its result possible: that justice is to be found in the laws of each society or form of government, and by investigating the laws and legislative practices of each society and generalizing from them, we can find out what justice is. But Plato correctly points out that by investigating the laws and practices of a given society, the most we can discover is what justice is thought to be in that society, a thought that might be mistaken. And thus the super-conclusion, that justice is the advantage of the stronger party, does not follow, even if it were universally true of all societies that the laws in each were made for the advantage of the rulers. Thus Plato implies not only that Thrasymachus' super-conclusion is false – a conclusion he attacks independently of method in his second argument by analogy – but also that the method is wrongheaded. And we can reasonably suppose that Plato thought one would not reach his (Socrates') conception of justice by using Thrasymachus' method, since most societies did not practice Plato's justice; nor Thrasymachus' result by using Plato's own method, since in fact Socrates reached a different result. However, Plato does not explicitly or implicitly criticize Glaucon's method for discovering the nature of justice by looking for a contractarian origin of justice. Nor does he consider the question whether his own conception of justice would be reached by using Glaucon's method. If we raise that question for him, very probably the answer is negative. We say very probably, at most, because what results are reached by Glaucon's method does depend on what material assumptions are made about men and their circumstances in the state of nature (e.g. moderate scarcity, degree of rationality, motivations, and conceptions of the human good), as well as procedural assumptions, such as unanimity, and the reasoning used to make a choice.

Conceivably, Plato thought that if we supply what he thought were true or reasonable assumptions, men in a state of nature would choose his principle of social justice over the state of nature. Certainly, his main thesis in the *Republic*, that men are better off or happier being Platonically just rather than unjust, might have led him to argue that in a state of nature individuals would rationally choose his principle of social justice over the state of nature, each on the basis of his or her happiness. He might also accept the procedural assumption of unanimity of agreement, since his social temperance implies agreement among all the citizens on who should rule and who should be ruled, and unanimity on his principle of social justice would produce temperance in addition to justice.

But would individuals rationally choose Plato's principle of social justice over the less restrictive and minimal principle Glaucon has them choose? In a state of nature, would they rationally agree to give up not only their freedom to harm others, but also the freedom to choose a career or occupation in society, the freedom to own property, or the freedom to choose a mate – all the freedoms lost in Plato's just society (at least for rulers and warriors)? Here the theory of human good embedded in Glaucon's theory of justice, in which the freedom to do as one pleases is thought to be a great good, stands in the way. If we could replace Glaucon's theory of the human good with Plato's own and attribute Plato's conception of human goods and happiness to men in a state of nature, such men might well choose Plato's principle of social justice over the state of nature (and include Glaucon's minimal agreement in their choice), each making the choice on the basis of his own good as Plato conceives it. But Plato's own theory of human good, with its radical downgrading of freedom and the goods and pleasures of ordinary men (e.g. 555–61, 582–7), seems hardly something that we can attribute to men in a state of nature; at least most men as we know them have something closer to Glaucon's conception of the human good than Plato's. All in all, it seems doubtful that Plato could claim that Glaucon's contractarian method would produce Socrates' result, at least if we make reasonably realistic assumptions about the state of nature and men's capacities, conceptions, and desires.

Finally, we can raise the question whether by using Glaucon's method one would reach Thrasymachus' result. This is one way to test the view of some scholars who think that Glaucon takes up Thrasymachus' cause not only on the question of the benefits of injustice but also on what justice is. Suppose then that in Glaucon's state of nature the warring parties have not only the two alternatives Glaucon gives them but also Thrasymachus' principle: their options are to stay in a state of nature, or to agree to give up equally the freedom to harm others in exchange for equal security of not being harmed by others, or to agree to the principle that justice is the advantage of the ruling party.

Now offhand it is not clear how agreeing to the third option would solve their problem in the state of nature, as it is clear that the second option would. But aside from that, there is an obvious question that each party would need to ask about the third option, In the ensuing society would I be a member of the ruling party or a subject? In a Thrasymachean society, clearly a member of the ruling party would be better off than a subject would be; justice would favor him. Whereas for a subject justice would be, as Thrasymachus says, "the other person's good," the other person being a member of the ruling party (343c); and this would be true for all three constitutions, aristocracy, democracy, tyranny, which Thrasymachus claims exemplify his justice. Now if a choosing party could not reasonably answer this question – either because of a veil of ignorance or because of too much uncertainty even without a veil – he could well reason that he would run the risk of being on the losing side of Thrasymachus' justice and perhaps be no better off than in a state of nature; whereas he would run no such risk by choosing Glaucon's compromise in which he would definitely be better off than in a state of nature. On the other hand, if he did know whether he would be member of the ruling party or be a subject, he would opt for Thrasymachus' principle in the former case and for Glaucon's in the latter. Thus unanimity on Thrasymachus' option would not be rationally possible; indeed probably only a minority would go for it. With these three options, behind a veil or under uncertainty, the rational choice would be Glaucon's justice; and with complete knowledge, there would be no unanimity on Thrasymachus' justice.

How far Plato considered this question – whether Thrasymachus' view on what justice is can be reached using the contractarian method – we can only conjecture. It is one of Plato's silences. But if we are correct in thinking that the answer is negative, we have one more reason not to attribute to Glaucon a defense of Thrasymachus on the nature of justice (what justice is). However, this gives us no reason for supposing that Glaucon does not provide a further defense of Thrasymachus on the benefits of injustice. On the contrary, our texts support the view that Thrasymachus and Glaucon have the same conception of the human good embedded in their different theories of what justice is; and they share the view that injustice is a greater good to the unjust man than justice in circumstances of secrecy and deception favorable to the unjust man. This in fact broadens the targets that Plato sets up for refutation in the rest of the *Republic*: not only in Thrasymachus' several systems of justice which would embody his fundamental principle (Thrasymachean aristocracy, oligarchy, or democracy), but also in the more egalitarian and seemingly fairer system of Glaucon, a citizen would be better off being unjust if he could place himself in such favorable circumstances. On the reasonable assumption that it would take very good intelligence and courage to place oneself in such circumstances and carry out significantly profitable acts of injustice, Plato would be suggesting that in such systems the brightest and best would be only too tempted to lead a secret life of injustice (secret in Glaucon's story, secret or successfully violent in Thrasymachus'). Perhaps Plato thought that only by going to extremes, in his radical proposals on the institutions of his just city, could justice overcome such temptations.

But this is may be too speculative. What we can say perhaps with more confidence is that Plato in fact used three different methods to answer the question, what justice is, and that he plausibly obtained three different results. The different results were obtained by using different substantive assumptions as well as different methods; and Plato apparently did not appreciate fully the power of the contractarian method, and he certainly did not use it as an analytic device to test the results reached by Thrasymachus or by his Socrates. But by including a diversity of methods as well as a diversity of accounts of justice in his discussion, Plato broadened and deepened both the accounts of justice he criticizes and the justice he defends.

Note

An earlier draft of this paper was read at the University of Arizona Plato Colloquium in February 2004. I am indebted to my commentator, Rachana Kamtekar, and to the audience for many helpful comments.

References

Bobonich, C. (2002) *Plato's Utopia Recast*, Oxford: Clarendon Press.

Burnyeat, M. F. (2002) Review of *Goodness and Justice*, *Times Literary Supplement*, June 14.

Hull, D., and M. Ruse (eds.) (1998) *The Philosophy of Biology*, Oxford: Oxford University Press.

Irwin, T. (1995) *Plato's Ethics*, Oxford: Oxford University Press.

Keyt, D., and F. Miller (2004) "Ancient political thought," in G. Gaus and C. Kukathas (eds.) *Handbook of Political Theory*, London: Sage.

Price, A. W. (1995) *Mental Conflict*, London: Routledge.

Rawls, J. (1971) *A Theory of Justice*, Cambridge, MA: Harvard University Press.

Santas, G. (2001) *Goodness and Justice: Plato, Aristotle, and the Moderns*, Oxford: Blackwell.

Smith, A. (1937) *The Wealth of Nations*, New York.

Vlastos, G. (1991) *Socrates, Ironist and Moral Philosopher*, Ithaca, NY: Cornell University Press.

8

The Analysis of the Soul in Plato's *Republic*

Hendrik Lorenz

I

In analyzing the soul into three parts, the *Republic* is offering both a theory of human motivation and a theory of the constitution of the embodied human soul. The theory of motivation demarcates a distinctively rational form of motivation as well as two non-rational forms. In doing so, it provides a framework that makes room for the possibility of motivational conflict between how a person thinks it best to act and such factors as desire for pleasure, aversion to pain, or an angry person's urge to inflict punishment or obtain retribution.[1] These and other such factors, the theory holds, can affect a person's behavior *directly* – without, that is to say, first changing how the person thinks it best to act.

The soul, for Plato, is not just a principle of psychological states and activities such as thoughts, desires, and emotions. It is not just something that in some way or other enters into explanations of psychological phenomena. For Plato, the soul is *itself* the subject of all psychological predicates: it is the soul itself that thinks, desires, and experiences emotions. The *Republic*'s theory of the constitution of the soul envisages it as a composite entity, composed of three parts with their own ways of acting and being acted on; each with its own concerns, its own distinctive way of desiring, and its own emotions.

Both theories are new, replacing and in fact contradicting earlier thoughts. So as to appreciate the significance of these new theoretical developments, we should begin with the thoughts from which they depart.

II

In the *Protagoras,* Socrates presents a curious picture of motivation, according to which it is a fact of human nature[2] that no one can hold a view about what it is best for him or her to do in the circumstances and, at the same time, act against it. Socrates is evidently aware of the fact that this picture differs sharply from ordinary opinion. According to the latter, he concedes at *Protagoras* 352d6–352e2,

> most people are unwilling to do what is best, even though they know what it is and are able to do it. And when I have asked them the reason for this, they say that those who act that way do so because they are overcome by pleasure or pain or are being ruled by one of the things I referred to just now.[3]

by which he means anger, sexual desire, and fear (352b7–8). Despite initial appearances, Socrates is not merely claiming that *knowledge* cannot be "dragged around like a slave" (cf. 352b–352c2). By this he means that if someone *knows* that it is, in the circumstances, best to do X, they cannot be prevented from doing X by any emotional state they may be in. In addition to that strong claim, however, the picture he presents includes an even stronger claim that no one can act against their own currently held view about what it is best for them to do in the circumstances, however inadequately that view may have been arrived at and however unstable it may be.[4]

According to the *Protagoras'* picture of motivation, it is a fact of human nature that people *always* try to maximize benefit and minimize harm. Thus knowing or even just believing that, in the circumstances, doing X is overall best – most beneficial, that is, or least harmful – is sufficient for being decisively motivated to do X. On the other hand, being motivated to perform an action that is, as a matter of fact, overall worse than some other course of action that one thinks is also available always reveals, and springs from, a false belief about how the relevant courses of action ought to be ranked in terms of benefit and harm. Socrates denies emphatically that a view about what it is best to do could, while it is still being maintained and endorsed, nevertheless become motivationally inert, or anyhow lose its ability to control the person's behavior, under the influence of an intense emotional state such as fear or sexual desire. The human soul, on the *Protagoras'* picture, is a remarkably simple thing. What a person is motivated to do is always controlled by whatever view they take about what it is best for them to do in the circumstances. As a result, all it takes to make sure that people always act in the way they should is to make sure that they always take the right view about how it is best for them to act.

It is perhaps worth noting that the *Protagoras'* picture does *not* deny the existence of emotions. Nor is it unable to allow them a role in the motivation of behavior. It can concede that anger, for instance, can thoroughly distort a person's judgment, so much so that it can actually get someone to believe that, say, taking revenge is what it is best for them to do in their circumstances. On the *Protagoras'* picture, though, no emotion can ever get a person to act against what they believe is best *as long as they maintain that belief.* This, I think, is a rather implausible view. As we will see, it is emphatically rejected by the *Republic*'s theory of motivation.

It is of no importance for our purposes whether or not Plato endorsed the *Protagoras*' picture of motivation when he wrote the dialogue. There is some reason to think that the *historical* Socrates subscribed to at least one of its claims: that knowing or properly understanding what it is best to do in the circumstances is sufficient for being decisively motivated to do it. Aristotle uses the *Protagoras*' memorable expression of knowledge being "dragged around like a slave" in attributing just this view to the historical Socrates.[5] This too need not concern us, though. What should be noted is just that Plato evidently considered this curiously simple picture of human motivation to be sufficiently plausible and worthy of attention – and perhaps also of critical scrutiny – to lay it out and argue for it in considerable detail.[6]

The soul, for Plato, is not only the origin and bearer of people's psychological states such as beliefs and desires. It survives the death of the person whom it temporarily ensouls; in fact it is immortal. In the *Phaedo*, Socrates attempts to underwrite its immortality by disassociating it from things that are composite and hence subject to decomposition. "Is not anything that is composite", he asks Cebes at *Phaedo* 78c1–4, "and a compound by nature liable to be taken apart into its component parts, and only that which is incomposite, if anything, is not liable to be taken apart?" Cebes is inclined to think – as are, according to Simmias, the majority of people – that "when a man dies his soul is dispersed and this is the end of its existence" (77b3–5; cf. 69e7–70b4). Socrates, by contrast, is arguing for the soul's immortality. In the context, his suggestion that only incomposite things are not subject to decomposition reveals his confidence that the soul is in fact incomposite, even though he does not seem to think that he has a decisive argument for this view. The *Republic*'s analysis of the soul into three parts shows it to be a composite thing; we will see that Plato is aware of the questions this raises for the soul's immortality.

III

We now turn to the *Republic*. The larger context of the analysis of the soul in *Republic* IV is the task, set at the beginning of Book II, to produce an adequate account of justice. While it is Socrates' primary task to say what it is for a person to be just, he proposes to begin by trying to discover what it is for a *city* to be just, expecting that the larger scale will facilitate the task of discovery. By the time he returns to justice in the individual person, he and his interlocutors have described what they take to be the best city they can think of. Such a city would, they are sure, possess justice as well as the other virtues. In fact, Socrates has already offered preliminary statements of what it is for a city to be just and to possess the other virtues. These statements are preliminary because he accepts the requirement that an adequate account of justice (etc.) in a city must be applicable to the individual person so as to reveal what it is for an individual to be just (etc.), and it remains to be seen whether the accounts so far offered can in fact meet that requirement. The best city contains three classes of citizens: rulers, the military, and businesspeople of various sorts. Justice in the city, according to Socrates' preliminary account, consists in each class adequately performing, and strictly limiting itself to, its own proper function. The analysis of the soul that follows right away is supposed to show that the soul contains three parts that correspond to the three classes of citizens in the best city (cf. 441c4–7). As a result, Socrates is in a position to apply to the individual soul his earlier account of justice as it applies to the city, and thus to confirm it as the correct account of the unitary feature that is justice. As we will see, it would be a mistake to think that Socrates' analysis is merely supposed to uncover three tendencies or capacities of the soul, so that what corresponds to each one of the three classes of citizens in the best city is simply some tendency or capacity of the soul. What Socrates wants to show is something stranger than that. He wants to show that it turns out on careful examination and reflection that the embodied human soul consists of three things, each one of which has, as it were, a mental life of its own, by which I mean that it has its own characteristic concerns and sensitivities and its own objects of pursuit and avoidance. Let us look at how he attempts to show this.

His argument is elaborate and careful. He begins with a question: when we are motivated to exert ourselves in some way or other – for example, in the process of learning, or when we are angry and seek retribution, or when we are hungry and want to have a meal – do these motivating conditions belong to a number of distinct parts of ourselves, or does every one of them belong to the soul as a whole (*Republic* 436a8–436b2)? In other words, is there only one desiring subject in every one of us, or are there more than one?[7] Now it is clear – Socrates claims and his interlocutor Glaucon agrees – that the same thing could not at the same time do or suffer opposites in the same respect and in relation to the same thing. Socrates immediately indicates that if cases of motivation come to light that involve opposition of the relevant kind, we will know that the individual person contains a plurality of items that serve as the subjects of the opposites in question (436b8–436c1). Before the matter can be decided, however, Socrates needs to make clear what kind of opposition reveals a plurality of subjects. He does this by considering two cases of simultaneous opposition. Only one of them is such as to reveal more subjects than one.

An objector might say that the same thing can in fact do opposites at the same time. Consider a man who stands still in one place but moves his arms and head – let us call him the playful man. This, one might think, is a case of the same thing being at the same time at rest and in motion. Socrates rejects this on the grounds that what one should say is not that the playful man is at rest and at the same time in motion, but rather that one part of him is at rest and another is in motion (436c11–436d1). This is exactly like the archer example that Socrates offers a little later:

> To say of the archer that his arms at the same time push the bow away and draw
> it towards him is not to speak well. We ought to say that one arm pushes it away
> and the other draws it towards him. (439b8–11)

Now, it is not *false* that the playful man is at the same time at rest and in motion,
nor is it *false* that the archer's arms at the same time push the bow away from
him and draw it towards him. There is, after all, a clear sense in which the playful
man is in motion just because his arms and his head are, and is at the same time
at rest just because the other parts of his body are. But to say (for instance) that
the man is in motion is to speak inaccurately. It is not to identify accurately what
it is that is in motion. The playful man is not in motion as a whole. Many, indeed
most, parts of his body are not in motion. If we want to be accurate in identifying the subjects of the predicates in question, as is sometimes appropriate, we
should say that the man's arms and head are in motion while the other parts
of his body are at rest. Let us say that the accurate identification of the subject
of a given predicate specifies the predicate's *proper subject*. What Socrates seems
to have in mind can then be put like this: the same thing cannot at the same
time be the proper subject of opposites (in the same respect, and in relation to
the same thing). The playful man is no counterexample to this: no part of him
is at the same time the proper subject of motion *and* rest. The second example
Socrates considers is a spinning top, which is *as a whole* at rest and in motion at
the same time (436d4–8). Socrates' analysis of the example is somewhat unclear,
but probably amounts to something like this.[8] It is true that a spinning top can
as a whole be at rest and in motion at the same time. In that case, though, it
is at rest in one respect and in motion in another. It is at rest in that it does not
incline; it is in motion in that it rotates. But inclination is motion in one respect
and rotation is motion in another. Since non-inclination and rotation are thus
not opposites in the same respect, one thing can at the same time be the proper
subject of non-inclination and rotation.

Socrates treats desire and aversion as opposites, and in fact as opposites in the
same respect.[9] The idea seems to be that desiring something is or involves some
sort of motion of the soul towards it, whereas being averse to something is or
involves a motion of the soul away from it.[10] Unfortunately, Socrates does not
provide even the vaguest of outlines as to how this might work in physical or
physiological terms. But once one accepts an idea along these lines – never mind
what the details of the mechanism involved might be – it does become reasonable to think that nothing could at the same time be the proper subject of a
desire for and an aversion to the same thing: for that would require that something could at the same time be the proper subject of motions *in opposite direc-
tions*. If it turns out, then, that people can at the same time desire and be averse
to the same thing, Socrates is in a position to conclude that the soul must contain
at least two things that can serve as the subjects of whatever the relevant motivating conditions may be.

It is easy enough to grant him what he needs at this stage: a simple case of being thirsty and intensely desiring to drink and at the same time being averse to drinking, say for reasons of health. Suppose his doctor has told the thirsty man that he must *absolutely* refrain from consuming any liquid today. Socrates can now pinpoint two distinct parts of the soul, one of which is the subject of the desire to drink, the other is the subject of the aversion to drinking. He characterizes the thirsty part as being called into play "through affections and diseases" (439d1–2), by which he presumably means imbalances of the body such as depletions, and as a "friend of certain replenishments and pleasures" (439d6–8). The subject of the aversion to drinking, by contrast, operates on the basis of reasoning (439c9–439d1). In this way, he introduces reason on the one hand and appetite, as it is usually called, on the other.

Since he thinks the soul contains a third part, he must distinguish a further part both from appetite and from reason. Being angry was mentioned as one of three kinds of motivating conditions right at the start of Socrates' analysis of the soul: the question was whether being angry belongs to the soul as a whole or specifically to some part of it (436a8–436b3). Moreover, anger has been associated with the character trait of "spiritedness" (435e4), and he has already said quite a few things about that trait. Members of the ideal city's military class must be spirited, so as to be courageous, fearless, and undefeatable (375a11–375b2). Spirited individuals may tend to treat others savagely without much discrimination, unless they receive the right kind of upbringing (375b9–10, with 410c8–375d2). Socrates also calls such characters "high-spirited" (375 C7), evoking a common Homeric heroic epithet. The character trait he has in mind will have been familiar enough to ancient readers. For our purposes, though, some commentary is needed. Being notable for being especially spirited is not simply a matter of being excessively prone to anger; in fact Socrates *contrasts* it with that (411b7–411c2).[11] It crucially involves an aspiration to distinguish oneself, typically through conspicuously bold and decisive action. Equally crucially, it involves an awareness of one's own worth and level of accomplishment. If things go well, spirited characters will take pride in who they are and what they have done, and will feel strongly that they deserve the respect and esteem of others.[12] This makes them acutely sensitive to (what they perceive as) slights and insults; hence the connection between spiritedness and anger. Something that will turn out to be important for our purposes is that it must be part of being spirited to have acquired a fairly settled and rather specific sense as to what kinds of behavior are respectable and worthy of esteem and what kinds are not. People no doubt acquire that sense in social interactions from their early childhood onwards. As Socrates is well aware, it may change profoundly from one generation to another.[13]

Given how unreflective and downright irrational anger can be, it is natural for Glaucon to suggest that it might belong to appetite (439e5). Socrates rejects this by reminding Glaucon of a well-known anecdote. Their contemporary

Leontius once came across some corpses of recently executed criminals. Leontius had an intense desire, Socrates reports at 439e7–440a3,

> to look at them but at the same time he was disgusted and turned away. For a time he struggled with himself and covered his face, but, finally, overpowered by desire, he pushed his eyes wide open and rushed towards the corpses, saying, "Look for yourselves, you evil wretches, take your fill of the beautiful sight!"

Socrates takes the anecdote to be evidence that anger sometimes "makes war" against the desires of appetite. Since it takes two parties to make war, anger and the desires in question must belong to two distinct subjects. There is reason to think that Leontius was a well-known necrophile,[14] and so the intense desire to see the corpses that famously overpowered him was probably sexual in nature. At the same time, Leontius struggles hard against that desire, and he gets angry at himself when in the end he gives in to it. Perhaps somewhat surprisingly, Socrates seems to think that it is Leontius' *anger* that does the war-making against the desires of his appetite (440a5–6). Does not Leontius' anger only come into play when his desires have already carried the day? As we have seen, Socrates has all along associated anger with the character trait of spiritedness – an association, one might add, that is extremely natural to speakers of ancient Greek – and through *that* with a person's sense of what kinds of behavior are respectable and worthy of esteem and what kinds are not. When Leontius gets angry at himself, this is presumably because he is keenly aware that he is doing something quite disrespectable: it is *shameful* for him to gape at the corpses, and he knows it. But being spirited to any extent at all is not just a matter of getting upset when someone (including oneself, as in this case) violates one's sense of what counts as respectable conduct. It is also to have settled dispositions to desire to act as that sense requires and to be strongly averse to behavior that offends it. It is thus quite natural for Socrates to attribute to Leontius' spirited part not only his anger, but also, implicitly, a strong aversion to corpse-gazing that puts up a valiant, though in the end unsuccessful, fight against intense sexual desire.

We can see, then, that Socrates' argument for the distinctness of spirit from appetite implicitly follows the pattern set by the preceding argument that distinguishes between appetite and reason. One part of Leontius' soul, his appetite, strongly impels him to go and take a good, close look at the corpses. At the same time, something else in his soul pulls him the other way and brings to bear an amount of force that temporarily suffices to counteract and arrest the initial impulse. What counteracts Leontius' appetitive impulse, and then gets upset as that impulse prevails, is spirit, the part of the soul responsible not only for anger, but also for the complex character trait of spiritedness and all that goes along with it. In counteracting appetite, Leontius' spirit must bear a strong aversion to taking a look at the corpses. Socrates takes himself to have shown, then, that appetite and spirit must be two distinct parts of the soul, able to serve as the proper subjects of simultaneous, but opposite, psychic motions in relation to the same thing.

It remains to show that spirit is distinct from reason. This is especially pertinent in that, at least in well-brought-up and properly habituated individuals like Glaucon (440b4-8, with 441a2–3), spirit tends to ally itself with reason in such psychological conflicts as may arise between the dictates of reason and the desires of appetite. Perhaps it is simply an aspect of reason? After two preliminary, and inconclusive, arguments – to the effect that children and non-human animals manifest spirit but not reason – Socrates offers another argument from motivational conflict. By the beginning of book 20 of the *Odyssey*, Odysseus has returned to his palace on Ithaca. He is pretending to be a penniless migrant while he is working out an effective plot against his wife's numerous suitors. On one occasion he sees his maidservants giggle and laugh as they leave the house to spend another night with the suitors, with whom they have been sleeping for some time. He is so outraged by their shamelessness that he is sorely tempted to punish them right away, in fact by killing every one of them. He manages to stop himself, though, controlling his anger, in order not to lift his incognito prematurely. In Homer's words,

> He struck his chest and spoke to his heart:
> "Endure, my heart, you've suffered more shameful things than this."
> (*Odyssey* 20. 17–18)

According to Socrates' interpretation, Homer is depicting how Odysseus' reason, having "reasoned about better and worse," rebukes the irrationally angry part of his soul, his spirit. Socrates seems to think it is clear from the fact that reason *rebukes* spirit that they are distinct items (441b7–441c2). What he does not say in so many words, though he plainly assumes it, is that Odysseus' reason also counteracts spirit's intense desire to inflict punishment on the women there and then. In light of that, it seems reasonable, and perhaps best, to see reason's rebuke of spirit as an expression of its firm – and, in the end, victorious – aversion to the object of spirit's intense desire. We can then interpret this argument, too, as following the pattern set by the argument that distinguishes between reason and appetite. Spirit is shown to be distinct from reason by the fact that reason and spirit can at the same time do or suffer opposites in the same respect and in relation to the same thing, as when someone's spirit bears a desire to do something or other and their reason at the same time bears an aversion to doing just that.

IV

Socrates' argument for tripartition is meant to bring to light the three parts that compose the embodied human soul. Socrates subsequently applies the theory of the tripartite soul in his accounts of justice and the other virtues in Book IV; in his comparative discussion of the various forms of psychic and political constitutions in Books VIII and IX; and also in his critique of mimetic poetry in Book X. Those applications add a good deal of detail to the rather bare initial descriptions of the three parts of the soul.

Let us begin with a characterization of reason. A striking fact that should be noted right away is that Socrates takes reason to be capable of generating, and indeed of being the bearer of, desires and aversions of its own. These, as we have seen, can conflict with desires and aversions generated by other parts of the soul. At least some of reason's desires and aversions rest on reasoning. The thirsty man's aversion to drinking is said to arise from reasoning (439c9–439d1), and Odysseus' impulse right away to punish the maidservants is stopped in its tracks by "that which reasons about better and worse" (441c1–2). Part of the idea is presumably that reason is so constituted as to be naturally inclined to respond to the varied circumstances of life by forming more or less reflective beliefs, often supported by reasoning, about what it is best for the person to do in the relevant set of circumstances. The reasoning that enters into such belief-formation will often be informal reasoning about how to achieve or secure some good. Socrates offers an example at 604c5–604d2. As any tolerably intelligent person knows, giving oneself up to grief in a situation of bereavement prevents one from doing what is most urgently called for, which is to deliberate with a view to arranging one's affairs "in whatever way reason determines to be best." One must therefore make it one's habit to put grief and lamentation behind oneself as quickly as possible when one's life is visited by serious losses and other disasters. Thinking along these lines, a man who has lost his son may form the belief that it is best for him not now to grieve and lament, and his reason may on that basis form a suitable aversion.

It is obvious that for reason to be in a position to form views about what it is best to do in some set of circumstances, it must already have all sorts of beliefs or insights, crucially including ones about which things are worth pursuing. The thirsty man's reason, for example, seems to regard health as very much worthy of pursuit. As is well known, the *Republic* includes an ambitious educational program which is designed to foster in suitable students a comprehensive understanding of reality, ultimately in light of knowledge of the Form of the Good.[15] Such understanding will enable its possessor, among other things, reliably to recognize the variety of things that are good and worth pursuing, and it will also ensure their proper appreciation. It is clear, however, that Socrates does not limit desires of reason to people who have benefited from the *Republic*'s extensive educational program. The sort of psychological conflict that Socrates relies on in showing the distinctness of reason from appetite – that a thirsty person is at the same time averse to drinking – is supposed to occur, as Glaucon says, "to many people, and frequently" (439c4).[16] But even in the favorable conditions of Socrates' ideal city, only a small elite of outstandingly talented individuals would be eligible for, and could appropriately benefit from, the *Republic*'s educational program. Socrates, moreover, takes Odysseus, who certainly did not receive advanced theoretical training, to reason about better and worse and to form a suitable desire of reason that confronts his anger. It should be clear, then, that Socrates credits even the imperfectly developed rational parts of unphilosophical souls with the ability to generate and sustain their own desires, however flawed and inadequate their beliefs and efforts at reasoning may be.

Reason's performing its proper function, however, is plainly not just a matter of generating desires and aversions on the basis of practical beliefs and bits of reasoning "about better and worse," *however flawed and inadequate they may be*. Reason's function turns out to be complex, including both practical and theoretical aspects. In his accounts of the virtues in Book IV, Socrates emphasizes the practical aspect: it is appropriate for reason to rule over the other parts of the soul, being wise and exercising forethought on behalf of the whole soul (441e4–5). The wise person's reason, he adds a little later, has knowledge of "what is advantageous for each part and for the whole soul, which is the community of all three parts" (442c6–8). In the context of Book IV, it is not yet clear what is involved in, and required for, reason's knowledge about matters of advantage, nor is it clear what it is for reason to rule over the other parts of the soul. It is much later, in Book VII, that Socrates indicates that knowledge of any good in fact requires knowing the Form of the Good (534b8–534c5), so that it turns out that both wisdom and justice are limited to appropriately trained philosophers.[17] Just on the basis of what Socrates says in Book IV, one might think that reason's function, as he conceives of it, is to direct and coordinate intelligently and efficiently the person's pursuit of the various things that the other two parts of the soul desire. Even when reason conflicts with another part of the soul – as when a thirsty man is unwilling to drink because his doctor has told him not to – it may seem that reason is simply protecting the other parts' long-term best interest by resisting short-sighted, irrational impulses. It is of course true that Socrates' account of wisdom presupposes that reason, like the other parts of the soul, has its own good. But reason's good, for all we know in Book IV, could simply be to achieve, and maintain itself in, a condition in which it can effectively coordinate the concerns and objectives of the other two parts. Reason's *rule* might then consist simply in making sure that the person in question is never prevented by irrational impulses from obtaining, and making intelligent use of, whatever resources are required for optimally satisfying their appetitive and spirited desires.

It becomes clear in subsequent books of the *Republic*, however, that Socrates does *not* conceive of reason's rule simply as a matter of reason ensuring that the long-term interests of the non-rational parts are served in an intelligent and effective manner. To begin with, it turns out that he thinks reason has an object of pursuit all of its own, which in no way depends on the concerns and desires of the non-rational parts. "It is clear to everyone", he claims at 581b5–6, "that the part with which we learn is always wholly straining to know where the truth lies." Reason's desire to know where the truth lies manifests itself at first in rather humble ways, as when it applies measurement and arithmetic so as to figure out whether two things that *look* to be differently large in fact *are* that way (602c7–602e2). After the central books of the *Republic*, however, it is also clear that, in its developed and mature form, that desire to know the truth is the desire to achieve and maintain a comprehensive understanding of reality, which includes prominently, and indeed requires, knowing the Form of the Good. Reason desires knowledge for its own sake, in a way that does not depend on any practical benefits that may, and typically will, result from it. This is what I have referred to as the theoretical aspect of reason, as Socrates conceives of it. Its practical aspect is closely related to this theoretical aspect. Reason's desire to know the truth will, among other things, yield views and insights to the effect that something or other is of value, for instance, in that it is advantageous for a person, or for some part of their soul. Reason, moreover, will not simply take things to be advantageous. It will also generate desires to perform at least those actions it takes to be advantageous all things considered. As Socrates says, it is appropriate for reason to exercise forethought on behalf of the whole soul. As one can easily see already in Book IV, this will crucially involve motivating the person to act as reason dictates, and it may occasionally require counteracting an irrational impulse deriving from appetite or spirit.

As we have seen, reason has its own special object of desire, knowing the truth. Thus exercising forethought on behalf of the whole soul will involve attaching value, not only to the objects of appetitive and spirited desire, but also to the special object of rational desire. Moreover, Socrates takes it that for each one of the parts of the soul, there is a characteristic form of psychic rule (580d7–8). Souls, and people, can thus be ruled, not only by reason, but also by appetite and spirit. One example of a person ruled by appetite is the oligarchic character, who is supposed to correspond to a city ruled under an oligarchic constitution. This is a person who, according to Socrates,

> establishes his appetitive and money-making part on the throne, setting it up as a great king within himself, adorning it with golden tiaras and collars and girding it with Persian swords . . . He makes reason and spirit sit on the ground beneath appetite, one on either side, reducing them to slaves. He won't allow the first to reason about or examine anything except how a little money can be made into great wealth. And he won't allow the second to value or admire anything but wealth and wealthy people or to have any ambition other than the acquisition of wealth or what might contribute to getting it. (553b4–553d7)

Socrates' attribution to appetite of a desire for and love of money requires, and will in a bit receive, some comment. For now we should note that the passage strongly suggests that the rule of appetite is a matter of appetite's imposing its own object of desire – in this case, wealth – on the other parts of the soul. In the course of a complex and gradual psychological process that Socrates describes with considerable care (553a6–553c4), the developing oligarch comes to be disposed so that the higher parts of his soul – reason and spirit – value and desire only what his appetite values and desires: wealth. Now there is no reason to think that the full-fledged oligarch's reason and spirit have been wholly incapacitated or rendered inert, while his appetite is solely responsible for all his psychic activities. On the contrary, what Socrates says clearly suggests that the oligarch's reason tries to identify money-making opportunities, presumably because it believes – just as the oligarchic city does – that wealth is the overarching good (cf. 555b8–10). If and when his reason figures out an unusually lucrative opportunity, it will no doubt generate a desire to pursue it, and that desire may well conflict with, and on occasion get the better of, a simultaneous appetitive desire for short-term gratification of some sort or other. Similarly, the oligarch's spirit values and admires wealth, and so we may safely assume that it too will in suitable circumstances generate specific desires to pursue money-making opportunities as well as specific aversions to courses of actions that involve significant financial losses (cf. 590b6–9).[18]

Socrates' analysis of the oligarch and some related passages[19] suggest, then, that for a given soul-part to rule in a person is for an object of desire characteristic of it to be the person's dominant object of pursuit, which will normally involve that it is embraced by the rational part of the person's soul as the dominant good.[20] If this is along the right lines, it has a number of implications for the rule of reason, as Socrates conceives of it, two of which may be worth spelling out. First, people who take objects of appetitive or spirited desire to be the good and cultivate their reason so as to direct and coordinate efficiently the pursuit of the relevant objects of desire in fact turn out on Socrates' view to be ones whose reason is *enslaved*, as is the case with the oligarch. Secondly, there is a crucial difference between reason's rule and the rule of the other two parts of the soul. Under the rule of both appetite and spirit, reason accepts as the good, and pursues as an object of desire, something that is alien to it and its natural and proper concerns – for instance, "to be as wealthy as possible" (555b10). Under the rule of reason, by contrast, no part of the soul is attached to objects of desire that are inappropriate to it; rather, each part is, within reasonable limits, free to pursue its own proper objects of desire. This chimes in well with, and goes at least some way towards justifying, Socrates' evident belief that the different forms of psychic rule are not on a par: for a soul to be ruled by reason is for it to be ordered as it should be (441e4–5), while the other two forms of rule are forms of psychic disorder.

What the rule of reason seems to come to, in its mature, perfected form, is that the person in question makes achieving or maintaining a systematic, principled understanding of reality their dominant object of pursuit, and that their reason embraces such understanding as the dominant good. This is a concern that springs directly from love of understanding and of the intelligible items it depends on. However, that concern naturally engenders and sustains further concerns, including practical ones, in that it brings with it accurate and well-grounded views about what, for instance, is advantageous for a person and for each part of their soul. Given a well-developed reason, such views will go hand in hand with a proper appreciation of the goods they concern, and will generate or involve suitable desires and aversions.

Appetite is initially introduced as the part of the soul that is responsible for desires for "pleasures to do with nutrition, reproduction, and what is akin to these things" (436a8–436b1). Socrates also associates it with unbalanced bodily conditions (439d1–2), and calls it a friend, not only of pleasures, but also of certain replenishments (439d6–8). This suggests that the desires of appetite are responses of the soul to unbalanced bodily conditions such as dehydration, and that they are desires for suitable processes which restore the body to its properly balanced condition. What must be added to that picture, though, is that appetites are desires for *pleasures*. Undergoing the restorative processes that many appetites are desires for normally involves being pleasantly affected in some way or other. In desiring some restorative process or other, appetite will be focused on the pleasant affections that are normally involved in undergoing the process in question. Thus Socrates can say both that what a thirsty person's appetite desires is *to drink* (439a9–439b5), and that what appetite desires are the *pleasures* to do with nutrition, reproduction, and the like (436a8–436b1). Appetite does in suitable circumstances desire to drink, but in so doing it is focused on the pleasant affections that are normally involved in drinking when one's organism is dehydrated.

Seeing the connection between appetite and pleasure is in fact crucial for making sense of the way Socrates goes on to expand appetite's repertoire beyond the recurrent bodily desires for food, drink, sex, and the like, to include desires for such things as making a profit, dabbling in politics, and even doing a bit of philosophy, if a suitable occasion presents itself (561c6–561d5).[21] Already in Book IV, Socrates makes clear that appetite naturally takes a strong interest in, and in fact is insatiable about, money (442a4–442b3). "We called it the appetitive part", Socrates recapitulates in Book IX, "because of the intensity of its appetites for food, drink, sex, and all the things associated with them." He then adds that

> we also called it the money-loving part, because it is most of all through money that such appetites are fulfilled. . . . Then, if we said that its pleasure and love are for profit, wouldn't that best determine its central feature for the purposes of our argument and ensure that we are clear about what we mean when we speak of this part of the soul, and wouldn't we be right to call it money-loving and profit-loving? (580d11–581a7)[22]

It is sometimes claimed that Socrates is here crediting appetite with the capacity for means-end reasoning.[23] Socrates is *not* saying, however, that appetite desires money *as a means to* satisfying its desires for food, drink, sex, and the like. He says that appetite naturally takes pleasure in, and loves, *making a profit*. This suggests rather strongly, in fact, that he takes appetite to desire money for its own sake: simply because it loves having it and, in particular, because it loves getting more of it (cf. 581c8–581d3). Socrates is, of course, meaning to explain why it is that appetite is money-loving by appealing to the fact that desires for food, drink, sex, and the like are most of all fulfilled through money. It is both possible and plausible, though, to interpret what he says as an explanation of why it is that appetite normally comes to be so disposed as to take pleasure in, and love, the activity of money-making *itself*. The idea might well be something like this. As a person comes to be steeped in practices of using money to fulfill desires for food, drink, and the like, the appetitive part of their soul gradually acquires a *taste* for money-making. This is because making money, for the person in question, comes to involve being pleasantly affected in all sorts of ways. For instance, it increasingly tends to be accompanied by agreeable memories of delightful things purchased and enjoyed in the past, or by gratifying thoughts of prospective feasts, fine wines, and the like. In this way, the very activity of money-making comes to be shot through with pleasure. It is by focusing on, and being strongly attracted to, the pleasures involved in money-making that appetite becomes attached to it. As I hope it is clear, an explanation along these lines does not require crediting appetite with the capacity for means–end reasoning. Moreover, it makes appetite's love of profit continuous with its desires for the pleasures of food, drink, sex, and the like. Whatever it is that appetite desires to do, it is always focused on the pleasure involved in the very act of doing the thing in question.

We finally turn to spirit. As we have seen already, spirit is not only the source of anger. It is also associated with the character trait of "spiritedness," and through that with a person's sense of what kinds of actions are respectable and worthy of esteem and what kinds are not. Leontius' spirit is, as we saw, not only the source of his anger with himself as he fails to control his desire to look at the corpses. It is also the part of his soul that counteracts his appetite, being averse to appetite's object of desire, no doubt because it regards it as thoroughly disrespectable. One aspect of spirit that has not yet received the emphasis it deserves is its competitive streak. Spirit, Socrates says in Book IX,

> it is always wholly dedicated to the pursuit of dominance, victory, and esteem. . . .
> Then wouldn't it be appropriate for us to call it victory-loving and honor-loving?
> (581a9–581b3)

Spirit's central contribution to a person's mental life is the desire to distinguish oneself, typically of course by outdoing and outshining others, and to earn admiration and esteem by doing so. Nevertheless, spirit is not necessarily a socially disruptive force, constantly getting people to challenge others in a bid to establish dominance or achieve victory over them. Indeed it seems to be capable of *admiring* and *honoring* other people who are, or are taken to be, doing outstandingly well. Socrates says that the oligarch will not allow his spirit "to admire and honor anything but wealth and wealthy people" (553d4–5), and so we may assume that this is something that spirit can do. Presumably a well-adjusted spirit, which the oligarch's of course is not, will admire and honor those who genuinely deserve admiration and honor. Subordinating oneself to superiors, moreover, is something that comes remarkably easily to characters who are ruled by spirit. The timocratic character is someone who "surrenders the rule over himself to the middle part – the victory-loving and spirited part – and becomes a proud and honor-loving man" (550b5–7).

Socrates describes him as a person who is

> harsh to his slaves rather than merely looking down on them as an adequately educated person does. He'd be gentle to free people and *very obedient to rulers*, being himself a lover of ruling and a lover of honor. (549a1–4)

Socrates clearly sees no tension between the timocrat's love of ruling others and his willing obedience to those who rule him. There is no indication at all that the spirited part of the timocrat's soul resists or resents his subordination to his superiors. It very much looks as if spirit's competitive streak and love of victory are, or anyhow can come to be, tempered by a rather nuanced appreciation of whom it is and whom it is not appropriate to challenge, and of when it is and when it is not appropriate to make a bid to establish dominance or achieve victory.[24]

V

In the last book of the *Republic*, Socrates turns to the immortality of the soul, and to its life after its separation from the body. In that context, he finds the tripartite theory problematic. "We must not think", he says,

> that the soul in its truest nature is full of multicolored variety and unlikeness or that it differs with itself. . . . It isn't easy for a composite of many parts to be everlasting if it isn't composed in the finest way, yet this is how the soul now appeared to us. (611b1–7)

We will recall Socrates' suggestion in the *Phaedo* that anything that is composite is "by nature liable to be taken apart into its component parts, and only that which is incomposite, if anything, is not liable to be taken apart" (78c1–4). In making that remark, Socrates is taking issue with the view, expressed by his interlocutor Cebes, that the soul is destroyed at about the time of death by being dispersed. Socrates clearly accepts that all composite objects are at least in principle subject to decomposition. (He also accepts, I take it, that were a soul to be "taken apart," it would cease to exist. This of course is an assumption implicit in Cebes' picture.) Now it is possible for something to be in principle subject to decomposition, but never in fact to be taken apart, either for some reason or by sheer good luck. Socrates obviously does not want to say that souls are never in fact destroyed simply by sheer good luck on a massive scale. If he did think that the soul is a composite, we would expect him to be concerned to offer an explanation why our souls, though they are in principle subject to decomposition, nevertheless will not be taken apart. The *Phaedo* contains no indication at all that he feels any such concern. The best explanation for this, I suggest, is that the Socrates of the *Phaedo* sees *no* reason to think that the soul is a composite, and at the same time takes it that there are a number of admittedly inconclusive, but nonetheless significant, considerations in favor of thinking the opposite, such as the ones contained in the affinity argument (78c6–79e5).

The Socrates of the *Republic*, by contrast, accepts that the soul, or anyhow the embodied human soul, *is* a composite. He takes himself to have shown that it is composed of three parts, each of which can by itself act and be acted on. Each of them can initiate large-scale bodily motion, presumably by itself engaging in some kind of motion; and each of them can counteract other parts, presumably by engaging in some kind of motion in the opposite direction. If the soul is indeed a composite, however, it is in principle subject to decomposition. It should be clear that this raises serious questions about its immortality. Might the soul ever be taken apart? If not, why not, given that it is, as a composite, the sort of thing that is in principle subject to decomposition? If yes, could it perhaps *survive* being taken apart? What Socrates says at *Republic* 611b1–7 leaves open, and indeed draws attention to, the possibility that a composite *can* be everlasting if it is composed in a suitably fine way. Fineness of composition might be a reason why something that in principle is subject to decomposition will not, in fact, be taken apart. There is, moreover, an alternative way of preserving the immortality of the soul in light of the tripartite theory. This is to accept that the soul will be taken apart at the time of death, but to say that it survives its decomposition. It may, after all, not be essential to the soul to be a composite of reason, spirit, and appetite. It may be that in essence the soul is nothing but reason. For reason to be separated at death from spirit and appetite might be a bit like having a tumor removed.

The *Republic* does not decide between these options. In *Republic* X, Socrates confirms the tripartite theory as offering an adequate account of what the soul's "condition is and what parts it has *when it is immersed in human life*" (612a5–6). However, to see what it is "in truth" or "in its true nature," we must realize, Socrates says, what it would become if it followed its love of wisdom

as a whole, and if the resulting effort lifted it out of the sea in which it now dwells, and if the many stones and shells (those which have grown all over it in a wild, earthy, and stony profusion because it feasts at those so-called happy feastings on earth) were hammered off it. Then we'd see what its true nature is, and we'd be able to determine whether it has many parts or just one and whether or in what manner it is put together. (611e1–612a5)

Socrates is comparing the embodied soul to the sea god Glaucus, whose body is covered with "shells, seaweeds, and stones that have attached themselves to him, so that he looks more like a wild animal than his natural self" (611d4–6).

According to the picture Socrates is offering, stones and shells attach themselves to the soul during its embodied existence. To grasp the soul's true nature, he says, we must think what it would be like if three conditions were met: if it followed its love of wisdom as a whole; if that effort lifted it out of the sea in which it now dwells; and if the accretions of embodied life were removed from it. The sea presumably stands for embodied life and the cares and concerns it brings with it. What do the soul's accretions, those "many stones and shells," stand for? They might represent the *desires* of appetite and spirit that are characteristic of embodied life, resulting in disorderly conditions of the soul that include the various vices. They might also stand for appetite and spirit *themselves*. In either case, the soul could, after their removal, follow its love of wisdom as a whole, without division: either because appetite and spirit can no longer conflict with reason, or because they have been removed from the soul altogether. In the former case, the soul would be a composite even in its true nature. But it would not, in its true nature, be liable to division and conflict. And so one might think that, were one to see the soul in its true nature, one would realize that its mode of composition is in fact very fine, certainly fine enough not to endanger its immortality.

Notes

1 Current work in psychology vividly illustrates the importance of such "passionate" motivational factors, which interact with "rational" impulses that spring from cost-benefit calculations. See, for instance, de Quervain et al. 2004 and Knutson 2004. Much current work in psychology is aiming to supersede a narrowly rational picture of human motivation; such work stands to what Knutson calls the "rational model of economic man" (2004: 1247) much as the *Republic*'s theory does to the *Protagoras*' intellectualism.

2 Note *Protagoras* 358c7–358d1.

3 Here and in what follows, translations from Plato are based on Cooper 1997, but they often include slight modifications.

4 This becomes clear at *Protagoras* 358b7–358d2.

5 *Nicomachean Ethics* 7.2, 1145b23–4; cf. 7.3, 1147b16–7. Aristotle is fairly consistent in distinguishing between Plato's character Socrates and the historical Socrates by using the definite article in the former case but not in the latter. For discussion of this point, see Ross 1924: xxxix–xli. In *Nicomachean Ethics* 7.2–3, Socrates' name occurs three times, every time *without* the definite article.

6 See also *Meno* 77b6–78b2.

7 My exposition simplifies the argument – or at least its presentation – somewhat, though not, I think, illegitimately. At 436a8–436b2, Socrates does not yet explicitly attribute motivating conditions to the soul or to parts of it. Rather he speaks of "us" having the relevant motivating conditions in virtue of the soul as a whole or in virtue of different things in us. It becomes quite clear in a short while, though, that what he means by this is that *we* have the relevant motivating conditions because of the fact that *something or other in us* does, either the soul as a whole or some part of it. Already at 436b8–436c1 Socrates assumes that *the soul* does or undergoes things, for instance, that it desires and is averse to things, and on that basis raises the question whether it does or undergoes opposites at the same time, in the same respect, and in relation to the same thing. If the answer is yes, as Socrates thinks and will argue that it is, it will follow that the soul contains a plurality of desiring subjects.

8 For detailed discussion, see Bobonich 2002: 227–35.

9 Qualification in terms of different respects does occur in Socrates' analysis of a spinning top, but not in his analysis of the playful man or the archer. Socrates evidently applies the first kind of analysis to the thirsty man's desire/aversion conflict, distinguishing between subjects of desire and aversion rather than between respects in which the thirsty man desires to drink and is averse to drinking. Indeed Socrates' argument *requires* that desire and aversion are opposites in the same respect. Otherwise, the simultaneous presence in a person's soul of a desire for and an aversion to the same thing would fail to establish two distinct psychological subjects, as it would be susceptible to the alternative kind of analysis, according to which the soul as a whole can desire something and at the same time be averse to it, as long as it desires in one respect and is averse in another.

10 Note 439b1, 439b3, 439b4, 439d1. We might compare Aristotle's criticism that Plato, like others among the "predecessors," thought that for the soul to impart motion to the animal, it must itself engage in motion (*De anima* 1.2, 403b29–31; 1.3, 406b26–8; cf. *Timaeus* 89e3–90a2; *Phaedrus* 245c5–246a2; *Laws* 895e10–896b1). For arguments for the view that the *Timaeus'* soul-motions should be taken literally, see Sedley 1997 and Johansen 2000.

11 Being quick-tempered and prone to anger, he says in that text, is a consequence of an upbringing that fails to foster appropriately a person's spirited tendencies through vigorous (and no doubt competitive) athletic pursuits.

12 Cf. 550b5. A person who surrenders himself to his victory-loving and spirited part comes to be proud and honor-loving.

13 The oligarchic character, for instance, finds being wealthy respectable and worthy of esteem (553d4–5). His father, the timocrat, takes pride in his accomplishments on the battlefield, in athletic contests, and in hunting (549a4–7).

14 In a contemporary comedy by Theopompus, he was apparently portrayed as being smitten with the *corpse-like* complexion of the proverbially skinny Leotrophides. See Kock 1880: 739.

15 The program is presented in Book VII of the *Republic*. For a detailed discussion of its rationale, see Burnyeat 2000.

16 Note also 441a7–441b1: even small children "are full of spirit right from birth, while as far as reasoning is concerned, some never seem to get a share of it, whereas the majority do so at some later stage."

17 Given that wisdom requires knowing the form of the good, it follows right away that it is limited to philosophers. Justice consists in each part of the soul performing its proper function, and for reason to be in a position to perform its proper function it must be wise (441e4–5).

18 Incidentally, once it is seen that *all* the parts of the oligarch's soul are lovers of wealth, it becomes clear that the kind of psychological conflict that is characteristic of the oligarch (described at 554c11–554e1) may well be, not (as is sometimes thought) a conflict within the appetitive part of his soul, but in fact a conflict between short-sighted appetitive desires on the one hand and desires of reason as well as, perhaps, of spirit on the other. For discussion concerning this point, see Lorenz 2004: 102–10.

19 See, for instance, 550a4–550b7 and 581b12–581c4.

20 As Gerasimos Santas has pointed out to me, one might wonder how (if at all) this applies to the democratic character. I am inclined to think that it does not and is not supposed to. The democrat momentarily surrenders rule over himself "to whichever desire comes along, as if it were chosen by lot" (561b3–5). What he plainly lacks, though, is a *dominant* object of pursuit, something in subordination to which his life's various concerns and projects are organized and ordered. (As Socrates says, there is no order in his life: 561d5–6.) Socrates never says that the democrat is ruled by some part or other of his soul. The idea might well be that the momentary rule of "whichever desire comes along" is not in fact a genuine case of rule at all, because it does not involve one desire controlling another. The democrat simply satisfies any desire that arises precisely until it is fully satisfied and then turns to something else. A picture along those lines is suggested by the fact that Socrates speaks of democracy as an *anarchic* constitution: one, that is, which involves no rule at all. What the democratic city defines as the good, moreover, is what *it* calls freedom (562b9–12), which in reality is anarchy (560e5), the absence of rule.

21 For a persuasive defense of the view that the democrat's desires to dabble in politics and philosophy are *appetites*, see Cooper 1984. Scott (2000) offers an alternative account.

22 The passage expresses some embarrassment about how best and least misleadingly to refer to the soul's lowest part. For the sake of simplicity, I have been following convention in calling the lowest part appetite or the appetitive part, and in calling its desires appetites. It should be noted, however, that this use of language, conventional though it is, does obscure the source of Socrates' embarrassment at this point in the dialogue. The Greek word that Socrates uses to refer to appetites is the very same word he uses to refer to the desires of the other two parts of the soul (580d7–8). Thus "appetitive part" or, as one might alternatively translate, "desiderative part" is *not*, as he indicates at 580d11–580e1, a designation that is uniquely applicable to the lowest part: the other two parts too have desires, after all, and thus are also desiderative. "Money-loving part" and "profit-loving part," by contrast, are designations that apply uniquely to the lowest part: in a naturally ordered soul, only the lowest part loves money and profit.

23 For instance, by Bobonich (2002: 244). As Bobonich himself points out, though, attributing the capacity for means-end reasoning to parts of the soul other than reason will undermine the tripartite theory in that it will lead to further partitions (pp. 248–54).

24 We might compare Socrates' remarkable claim, at 440c1–5, that the nobler a person
    A is, the less he will be inclined to feel anger at some other person B inflicting various
    sorts of pain on him, if A thinks that he has wronged B, and that B is *justly* inflict-
    ing pain on him.

References

Bobonich, C. (2002) *Plato's Utopia Recast: His Later Ethics and Politics*, Oxford:
    Clarendon Press.

Burnyeat, M. (2000) "Plato on why mathematics is good for the soul," in T. Smiley (ed.)
    Mathematics and Necessity: Proceedings of the British Academy 103, pp. 1–81.

Cooper, J. M. (1984) "Plato's theory of human motivation," *History of Philosophy Quar-
    terly* 1, pp. 3–21; repr. (1999) in J. M. Cooper, *Reason and Emotion: Essays on Ancient
    Moral Psychology and Ethical Theory*, Princeton, NJ: Princeton University Press.

——(ed.) (1997) *Plato: Complete Works*, Indianapolis: Hackett Publishing.

de Quervain, D. J.-F. et al. (2004) "The neural basis of altruistic punishment," *Science*
    305, pp. 1254–8.

Johansen, T. (2000) "Body, soul, and tripartition in Plato's *Timaeus*," *Oxford Studies in
    Ancient Philosophy* 19, pp. 87–111.

Knutson, B. (2004) "Sweet revenge?," *Science* 305, pp. 1246–7.

Kock, T. (1880) *Comicorum Atticorum Fragmenta*, vol. 1, Leipzig: Teubner.

Lorenz, H. (2004) "Desire and reason in Plato's *Republic*," *Oxford Studies in Ancient
    Philosophy* 27, pp. 83–116.

Ross, W. D. (1924) *Aristotle:* Metaphysics, vol. 1, Oxford: Clarendon Press.

Scott, D. (2000) "Plato's critique of the democratic character," *Phronesis* 45, pp. 19–37.

Sedley, D. (1997) "Becoming like god in the *Timaeus* and in Aristotle," in T. Calvo and
    L. Brisson (eds.) *Interpreting the* Timaeus-Critias: *Proceedings of the IV Symposium
    Platonicum*, Sankt Augustin, Germany, pp. 327–39.

9

The Divided Soul and the Desire for Good in Plato's *Republic*

Mariana Anagnostopoulos

Then we do not wish to slaughter or banish from the cities or seize property thus simply, but if these things are beneficial, we wish to do them, while if they are harmful we do not wish [to do] them. For we wish good things, as you say, but we do not wish things that are neither good nor bad, nor bad things.

Gorgias 468c

"Let no one then," said I, "disconcert us when off our guard with the objection that everybody desires not drink but good drink and not food but good food, because (the argument will run) all men desire good, and so, if thirst is desire, it would be of good drink or of good whatsoever it is; and so similarly of other desires."

Republic 438a[1]

Among the many and ingenious arguments presented by the character Socrates in Plato's dialogues are two apparently incompatible accounts of desire. One of these is the argument establishing the tripartition of the soul in Book IV of the *Republic*. The Socrates who declares the soul to be composite, and thus some desires to be non-rational, admits to having in mind an opponent with the contrary view that all desire is for the good. That view may be found in Plato's *Gorgias*, *Meno*, and *Protagoras*, championed by a character Socrates who, whether representing Plato's early view, Socrates' actual view, or both, takes great pains to convince his incredulous interlocutors that the true nature of desire is such as to align every human with the *truly*, not merely the *apparently*, good.[2] Thus the wrenching apart of rational and appetitive motivations in the partitioning of the soul at *Republic* IV appears to be an attempt by Plato to meet the challenge of his mentor Socrates – to show that, knowing the better, one can nevertheless desire, and do, the worse. Close attention to Plato's early dialogues reveals Socrates' attachment to the "paradoxical" denial of this view; his insistence that knowledge may *not* be overcome by passion has provoked much disbelief and, in turn, countless scholarly attempts (including that of Aristotle) to reveal its incoherence. The present discussion will aim to bring into focus Plato's supposed rejection of Socrates' account of desire. Two matters fundamental to this rejection will frame the inquiry. One concerns the precise relationship between the Socratic view of desire, according to which all desire is for the good, and Plato's apparent rejection of this view in favor of the multifaceted account of desire affirmed by his partitioning of the soul in the *Republic*. A second point of concern is Plato's own understanding of the motivational power of the desire for good, which appears, in light of his remark at *Republic* 505e, to be universal and overarching, just as Socrates supposed it to be: "[The good is] that, then, which every soul pursues and for its sake does all that it does, with an intuition of its reality, but yet baffled and unable to apprehend its nature adequately . . ."

A preliminary point of connection between the two issues is the fact that Plato sets his own view *against* the view that all desire is for the good. A reasonable interpretation of Plato's view of the composite nature of the soul must retain this opposition. This can be accomplished by supposing the "parts" of the soul to be *agents* within the soul, and consequently attributing to Plato the view that some actions aim at the satisfaction of appetite, with no regard whatever for the agent's overall good. Despite the textual support for this view, it is challenged by Plato's contention that every action aims at the good, with which it is plainly incompatible.

Matters are complicated further by a dispute as to just what Socrates means when he asserts that no one desires bad things, or that no one errs willingly. Interpretations of these views differ radically in the degree to which they retain the controversial aspects of Socrates' assertions – some, that is, attempt to show that Socrates had nothing as unusual in mind as his words in Plato's early dialogues suggest. By "no one desires bad things," it is argued, Socrates meant to express the commonsense view that no one wants anything *believing it to be* worse for him, or *under the description* "thing that is bad for me."[3] Still others insist that Socrates really did mean to deny that desire is for bad things, and to assert that desire is for truly good things only.[4] We may make our way back to Plato's *Republic* by considering a key statement of that masterpiece: "when it comes to the good nobody is content with the possession of the appearance but all men seek the reality, and the semblance satisfies nobody here" (505d). How Socratic this seems; yet it seems just as clear that Plato rejected Socrates' conception of the object of desire.

Our difficulty is coming into view: if Socrates, as presented in Plato's early work, means to affirm that every object pursued is desired under the aspect "good for me," Plato might oppose him by asserting that some objects are desired under descriptions having nothing whatsoever to do with the agent's overall good – but only with the agent's immediate pleasure, for example. If, on the other hand, Socrates affirms that desire is for true goods only, Plato need not reject the view that every action *aims at the good*. Instead, Plato can oppose Socrates by main-taining the possibility that desires be misdirected by false conceptions of that good. In addition, if the most coherent, textually consistent reading of Socrates suggests a genuine denial of weak-willed actions, Plato may counter this view by appeal to a more complex psychological apparatus than Socrates had envisioned, one that explains just how non-rational forces may derail a soul in search of that elusive treasure whose nature only reason may apprehend.[5]

I hope to show that Plato retains some aspects of the Socratic view of the good, and that the key difference between the views is not what it is often sup-posed to be. Two elements of Plato's view shape his rejection of Socrates' view that, while many things may be "thought best" for oneself, only what is truly good is desired (*Gorgias* 466–8 and *Republic* 438a). First, Plato recognizes the diversity of desires in the soul; the simplest of these are purely appetitive, and present a psychic motivation distinct from the universal desire for the good. Most desires, however, are complex, requiring input from the soul's reasoning element. Thus, conceptions enter the picture; what begins as a simple urge develops into a desire for the specific object conceived to be potentially satisfying. The subse-quent exercise of reason in initiating action also integrates desires into the agent's view of her overall good, with the result that complex executive desires aim toward true goods *or* apparent goods. On this reading, Plato introduces into his analysis of ordinary action elements Socrates would find wholly unacceptable. Plato, however, does hold that all desire is for the true good, in the completely virtuous soul governed by its optimally functioning rational element. This is not so much a claim about desire itself, as was Socrates' claim that all desire is for the good, but part of a description of the best soul, which description also seems to characterize the *natural* condition of *any* soul, in Plato's account. Thus, Plato associates the pursuit of *true* good with every soul's *actions*, though not with every *desire* of every soul.

Plato's Argument for the Tripartition of the Soul

Plato must address the nature of desire if he is successfully to complete his for-mulation of the odd analogy between the just city and the just soul that frames a significant portion of the *Republic*. By a principle of isomorphism, rooted in a deep concern with definition, Plato asserts that things properly *called* "just" must *be* just by way of the same essential features; thus just cities and just souls will be similar in structure and arrangement, two aspects of cities and souls relevant to justice. Because the city has been found to have three parts, the proper arrangement of which constitutes justice, Plato next undertakes to discern "whether the soul really contains these three forms (*eidē*) in itself or not."[6] While it is no doubt easier for Socrates' interlocutors to understand the soul via a model of the city, the assumption that the two entities are analogous in structure and composition does not constitute an argument that the soul has three parts, nor is it so construed by Plato.[7] Plato needs, and thus begins, an independent argument to reveal the parts of the soul, if it has any. Let us make our way to Plato's partition of the soul via his striking description of someone under the influence of desire:

> Will you not say, for example, that the soul of one who desires either strives for that which he desires or draws towards its embrace what it wishes to accrue to it; or again, in so far as it wills that anything be presented to it, nods assent to itself thereon as if someone put the question, striving towards its attainment? (437c)

Rather than their differences, here Plato emphasizes the interplay between appetite and reason in the soul, and hints at the involvement of *activities of reason* in any movement to acquire. Such a movement indicates to Plato the presence of an acceptance or agreement, which, even if short of a full *decision*, constitutes a cognitive activity; this it must be, if it is like an answer to a question! However, can appetites "nod assent" to a question posed? Plato's subsequent argument, in my view, reveals that he did not think so. To clarify the question, we must note that there are both simple and complex (or "qualified") desires in appetite. I understand Plato to hold that *simple* appetites are not an independent source of the *movement to acquire*, which is something "the soul" is doing in the above passage, as a response to the desire found within it. So what kind of desire is this, if not a simple one? Appetites *qualified* are motivating, but these involve reason's specification of some object. Before turning to the argument, I would like to note several difficulties it raises.

While Plato takes his discussion of opposite tendencies in the soul to be exceptionally helpful to his aim in Book IV, the kind of "parts" it implies the soul to have is not immediately clear. First, Plato sets for himself the goal of finding in the soul conflict between opposites; but if these belong to distinct parts, one of which is cognitive and the other not, how can they conflict? A possibility is that reason and appetite each engage in cognition and desire. This is one prevailing interpretation of Plato's tripartition; it construes the parts as agents, rejecting the alternative that only the person, or soul as a whole, is capable of agency.[8]

Our interpretation of Plato on psychic parts must not damage the consistency of his larger argument, some facets of which are the assumption of similarity in structure of city and soul, the definition of justice as proper correspondence of part to function, and the perplexing universality of desire for good. The strength of Plato's conclusions about the composition of the soul is tested when the nature of the supposed parts is considered further. Are the conflicting elements different mental attitudes, or might they be different persons within each person? If Plato is saying no more than that each soul experiences different tendencies or motivations,[9] he does not succeed in proving much in the transition from the premise establishing conflict in the soul to the conclusion establishing parts, or indeed saying much in his guiding principle that the presence of certain types of conflict implies the presence of parts, as Irwin notes.[10] Were "parts" equivalent to tendencies, the principle of opposites would reveal no more than that opposing tendencies are different tendencies; surely Plato holds a more substantial view. However, if Plato establishes the presence of distinct agent-parts of the soul, his argument is threatened in a different way; it becomes susceptible to the problem of infinite divisibility, as it would then stand to reason that the principle of opposites may be applied to further divide each agent.[11]

The question whether the soul's parts are agents requires us to determine the precise nature of appetite (does it contain only simple appetites?) and reason (does it have desires?). But let us first follow Plato in his attention to activities of the psyche:

> The matter begins to be difficult when you ask whether we do all these things with the same thing or whether there are three things and we do one thing with one and one with another – learn with one part of ourselves, feel anger with another, and with yet a third desire the pleasures of nutrition and generation and their kind, or whether it is with the entire soul that we function in each case when we once begin . . . (436a–b)

In the clause here translated "when we once begin," Plato is pointing to the impulse toward something, using the same term he uses in explaining that the thirsty soul's "impulse" is toward simple drink (*epi touto orma*) (439b). Thirst is the starting point, and source of, a movement to acquire some particular drink, but does not, on its own, drive that movement to completion. Plato's attention to basic activities is worth noting, especially with reference to desire: the soul's seeking of pleasure in generation and nutrition is commonly thought to be instinctive and bodily.[12] Simple desires are players in the precise conflict Plato believes will reveal the soul to be multi-part, rather than simply complicated. Not any conflict will serve to establish *clearly* the presence of two parts. Conflicts of the most familiar kind – one desires a second sweet, yet one resists in adherence to precepts of health, for example – involve desires with evaluative aspects, or judgments in the service of desires. What will cut through a multilayered product of desire *and* cognition to reveal forces which are not properly attributable to the *person*, but to some part thereof? Simple desires accomplish this goal; Plato's remarks at 439a9–439b5, well into his argument, reveal the core conflict in the individual soul:

> The soul of the thirsty then, *in so far as it thirsts*, wishes nothing else than to drink, and yearns for this and its impulse is towards this . . . Then if anything draws it back *when thirsty* it must be something different in it from that which thirsts and drives it *like a beast* to drink. (439a–b, my emphasis)

We know Plato conceives the soul that is driven to drink yet restrained from drinking to be experiencing conflict of a simple kind, but why must Plato make precisely this kind of conflict the focus of his attention, if he intends to divide the soul? A soul in this condition *must* have multiple parts, Plato reasons, if it is to conform to his Principle of Opposites, which is an initial premise in his argument for psychic partitioning:[13]

> It is obvious that the same thing will never do or suffer opposites in the same respect in relation to the same thing and at the same time. (436b)[14]

Plato next explains the relevant application of the principle, noting the path of his inquiry: "if ever we find these [opposites] in the functions of the mind, we shall know that it was not the same thing functioning but a plurality" (436c).[15] Rather than rejecting one phenomenon that troubled Socrates, Plato divides the soul.

To consider the soul, "in so far as it thirsts," is to abstract from the ordinary case of thirsting for a specific (kind or instance of) drink. Plato, in Santas's words, "strips objects of appetite," really in an attempt to strip *appetite*, down to that which identifies it as thirst. Santas's derivation of basic thirst by abstraction reconstructs Plato's initial discussion of simple desires. But from what does Plato abstract? He begins by identifying classes, noting that "endeavor after a thing" is opposed to rejection of the thing, as is "embracing" to "repelling" (437b). Here he may have in mind general tendencies, or particular cases of conflict over a specific object. If we start with an ordinary (learned) desire for a specific kind of drink, then remove all "qualifications" from the object and the desire, we reach the simple, pure desire and object.[16] With the class of desires in mind, Plato asks whether "the most conspicuous members of that class are what we call thirst and hunger," thus explicitly sifting out a subsection of the relevant class (437d). There are, of course, other members of the class, examples of which are given immediately ("thirst for much," or "for hot drink or cold" (437d–e)[17]) and later in Plato's analysis of unjust souls. This allows Plato to specify one kind of motivation, and distinguish it from another, but nowhere commits him to the belief that pure appetite is capable of motivating action. Notice that Plato abstracts *from a desire*; it is clear that *this desire* is the motivating one, not the kernel that is "simple."

What draws the thirsty soul back is countering the soul's *thirst* ("when thirsty"), *not* the complex desire which the soul feels *toward a particular object*. Simple thirst, Plato explains, is not for any such object: it "wishes nothing else than to drink." What drives "like a beast" is driving in an unreasoned way, without direction specifiable in belief-terms.[18] Thus Plato avoids the charge of confusion over what psychic conflict reveals about multiple sources of elements in conflict; he is not simply missing the fact that humans experience many different kinds of conflict. Nor is he so easily subject to the criticism that his method implies specialized parts of the soul for each different kind of conflict. Were he to take a familiar case of conflict as his model, Plato would burden himself with the extra task of first distinguishing evaluative elements of the desire from appetitive ones. In fact, it is *our* focus on familiar cases that may lead us to misunderstand the degree to which Plato was aware of countless possibilities of conflict and indeed fully intended to *ignore* those cases, in favor of one typifying the *core conflict* in (many) instances of psychic turmoil.

Let us return to the particular conflict Plato finds so revealing: sometimes souls, while thirsty, do not want to drink (*dipsontas ouk ethlein piein*) (439c). *Both* of these forces are described in desire-terms (thirsting and not wanting).[19] When Plato seeks their sources, he distinguishes forces issuing from "passions and diseases" from those deriving from reasoning; because the two sources are distinct in activity and effects, they deserve different names, the "rational" (*to logistikon*) and the "non-rational and appetitive" (*to alogiston te kai epithumêtikon*). Plato's relating of the appetitive element to diseases serves to confirm that he has in mind physiological urges as sources of the soul's drive toward drink. The "pull" opposing drinking arises "out of reasoning" (*ek logismou*), a source distinct from that of the simple appetites.[20]

In pointing to two sources from which psychic forces derive, Plato does not imply that what arises from either is wholly constituted by its origin. I do not think it a stretch to say that reason's input changes simple appetites into complex ones, and existing appetites affect reason's conception of what is good for the agent to pursue. Thus Plato's analysis of simple desires should not be taken to capture fully the character of appetite as a multifarious entity. This has the important implication that Plato's analysis of the soul's conflict over drink does not reflect just *any* kind of psychic opposition. If it were intended to do so, it would surely be open to Price's objection that "the fallacy is that, though thirst exhausts the soul *qua* thirsty, it does not exhaust the soul *qua* appetitive, for thirst is not the only appetite."[21] Thirst and hunger are "the most conspicuous" but they are not the *only* desires within the class, as Plato makes clear in his discussion of relative terms at 438b–439b. The *identification* of appetite, via truly and purely appetitive forces, precedes the full analysis of desires "belonging to" that part of the soul.[22] Plato could only accomplish his stated aim, in my view, if he focused on the kind of conflict that pits a simple appetitive need against a reasoned proclivity toward restraint. The conflict he envisages allows Plato to retain the possibility of substantive psychic conflict, and thereby reject Socrates' view of the soul as an entity seeking always and only its own *true* good.[23] This aim is clear in Plato's caution at 438a:

> "Let no one then," said I, "disconcert us when off our guard with the objection that everybody desires not drink but good drink and not food but good food, because (the argument will run) all men desire good, and so, if thirst is desire, it would be of good drink or of good whatsoever it is; and so similarly of other desires." "Why," he said, "there perhaps would seem to be something in that objection."[24]

The basis for the objector's claim that good drink and good food (never just drink or just food) must be the objects of desire is the theory that all desire is for the good. This is not fully reflected in Socrates' statement that "all men desire the good" (*pantes gar ara tôn agathôn epithumousin*), as this desire for good could be one among many. The view Plato has in mind is clear, however, from his reference to its implications: his objector can derive the conclusion that anything that is a desire must be for the good only from the view that all desire is for the good.[25]

We must next consider complex appetites, and the executive force they assert. Plato suggests that the difference between simple and non-simple desires is that the latter are qualified: what *attaches to* thirst *renders* it a desire for a particular kind (or instance) of drink. Thus the other desires in the class, if they are not simple desires, are built upon the simple ones. If what attaches to thirst modifies its general nature in the way Plato describes, it can only do so via cognition about specific means to fulfilling the desire; this, appetite itself (characterized by simple desires), cannot supply; if there are no simple desires for cold drink there are surely none for Coca-Cola, much less Coca-Cola in a glass bottle. It follows that reason must become aware of the properties of such objects, and make desire "aware" of them *as means to satisfying thirst*, thus contributing to the production of a new desire (perhaps eventually detached from its foundation in thirst) that nevertheless "belongs to" appetite, though not "natural" to it (see 439a).

Noting Plato's use of the term *epithumia* for the general class of desires *and* for the specific part of the soul distinguished from reason and spirit, we may further focus our attention on the desires that deserve the name of the psychic part appetite.[26] Their basic origin and character (as *bodily*) is given by the fact that they spring from something not capable of calculation. For example, an "appetitive" desire to eat springs from hunger rather than from a calculation that eating now would be productive of health for me. Desires for food, however, rarely, if ever, appear in a mature soul in this simple form; they usually attach to some particular edible object. Are these desires also "appetitive"? Rather than proceeding directly from the recognition that dandelion greens are beneficial to my health, for example, a "craving" for the vegetables has its source elsewhere, in a need to satisfy hunger or remedy some deficiency. To say that the desire for dandelion greens is appetitive, however, is not to say that it is purely bodily, that it is a simple urge. Plato does not need to say this to retain the distinctions he envisages. Instead, Plato uses simple desires to isolate parts of the soul, all the while recognizing the complex desires *built upon* the simple ones by the addition of a qualifying feature.[27]

How does appetite come to be attached to something? It is only reasonable to suppose that it is via a belief that it is pleasant. But can appetite have this belief itself? Is appetite equipped with the cognitive faculties, such as, for example, the memory of the last time a sweet was pleasant, or the processing of the perception that this is a sweet into a belief that this sweet would now be pleasant? It would seem that only the person as a whole experiences such processes and phenomena; the multiple *kinds* of experiences of sweets do suggest different elements of the soul are at play, but not necessarily that they are acting, or experiencing, in isolation (instead the person experiences through *integrated* parts). Santas, working from a recognition of the importance of the function argument (in *Republic* I) to Plato's subsequent theory, maintains that "calculating is the exclusive function of reason."[28] Learning and experience bring the psychic elements together into individual and distinctly personal human mental events. It is not, then, that reason learns to desire, or appetite to calculate; no more could the ear adopt the natural function of the eye. Instead, the functions of different parts – whether bodily or psychic – come together in the individual's activities. Seeing is the exclusive function of the eyes, but an ordinary act of seeing, or, more aptly, perceiving, involves more than the work of the eyes. Even isolating the purely bodily part of this perceptual event is difficult; hence, the common phenomenon in which multiple witnesses to an event provide as many versions of the event witnessed.

I therefore disagree with Cooper's suggestion that the calculation involved in the formation of myriad "appetitive" desires is not properly an exercise of reason, as Plato construes it.[29] "Reason" is not an alternative name for the exclusive faculty with which the human grasps the forms, nor does it specify a part of the human responsible only for managing the soul. Instead, it is identified by Plato in precise contrast to the part of the soul that cannot calculate, and is thus called "arational" (*alogiston*) at 439d. It is consistent with this distinction to suppose that, in addition to calculating and promoting what is good for the soul as a whole, reason specifies which objects may successfully fulfill a desire of appetite. Cooper claims that simple desires, which are purely bodily, "have a direct motivating influence on action, as the fact of conflict to which Plato appeals very clearly indicates."[30] Penner is wholly convincing in his argument about the extreme limitations of any such influence; action could not proceed directly from a simple desire.[31] Reason's critical role is apparent in the fact that any immediate precursor to action must direct it toward some *particular* object; it is not possible for simple appetites to confer a specificity that they themselves lack. A model of action relying on simple executive appetites would imply that one could be in the process of seeking a drink, yet "have in mind" no kind of drink, neither cold, sparkling, fruity, etc. It does not seem possible to describe such an action, but neither does Plato's account of the soul require him to do so. It must be, then, that simple appetitive forces *originate* independently of reasoning, but that they do not remain simple and simultaneously function as motives to action.

In explaining the requirements for the proper use of external goods, Rowe notes that these are desired, not by reason, but by the arational parts of the soul. Reason, he explains, must guide their proper use, if they are to be good for the agent at all.[32] Though reason itself is oriented toward the finest exercise of its contemplative capacities, it must also sort out the soul's dealings with the world of experience. It is not in appetite to determine which way and to what extent to seek or use external goods. This is obviously the sphere of reason's exercise, and an activity that constitutes but a small part of reason's directing the individual as a whole toward flourishing, the understanding of which is linked to an apprehension of the form of the good.

A more serious objection arises at this point, however. Penner rejects Plato's account of the soul as a flawed attempt to refute Socrates on *akrasia*, precisely on the point of simple desires. Penner rightly argues that simple desires cannot move a soul to acquire something specific; thus, no simple desires can be "executive" desires. However, Plato requires simple executive desires for his case of conflict in the soul, to stand in opposition to the rational desire to avoid drinking, which must be executive, Penner claims: "Reason's (initially indefinite) desire for whatever is best in this situation, *becomes* reason's desire that one *not* drink in this situation."[33] The objection is this: Plato requires simple desires to establish a non-rational part of the soul, yet no conflict can occur between a simple desire (which is general in scope) and a rational executive desire, which is the only kind of rational desire that *could* forbid the soul from drinking.

I see a way out of this dilemma for Plato, in his statement that thirst is a simple desire to drink. Does he not conceive of the opposing desire in a similar way – as a general desire to avoid drinking? It is obvious that *most* cases of psychic conflict involve two executive desires, but Plato's aim in this passage seems to be to identify the power that constitutes the core of each element in the conflict. Strange as it sounds, the desire that opposes the desire to drink is not the desire to avoid *this* drink, but the desire to avoid drink *in general*; this is clear in Plato's claim that the thirsty soul does not want to drink (*dipsontas ouk ethelein piein*, 439c).

One might respond by asking, if Plato's thought-experiment sees no equivalent in actual souls, how it is intended to characterize those souls and the conflicts they endure? And thus Irwin objects: "Facts about rulers qua rulers and doctors qua doctors do not show that there are any actual rulers who do not make mistakes or doctors who do not make money. Similarly, facts about thirst as such do not show that any of our actual desires is a desire for drink as opposed to drink qua good."[34] This is true, but does Plato *intend* to show that our actual desires are simple? His example is ordinary: seeking and avoiding. However, his discussion of thirst is an abstraction from the example, not a description of the example.[35] He seeks only to grasp more clearly the *root* of the conflict. Penner and Irwin both insist that Plato's division of the soul requires the existence of executive simple desires. However, we see that simple desires exist only as a core element of ordinary executive desires, forming a basis for the formation of something more complex, which *translates* instinctual need into a movement to acquire a particular *thing*. In becoming complex, that is, the simple desire becomes focused in a particular direction, yet remains something we can ascribe to appetite.[36] Plato reminds us of this core, or origin, of (some of) our wants, without suggesting that a desire for berry tart is purely appetitive in nature. Thus,

Plato *does* need to show that there are actual executive desires for something other than good(s), but he can do this without supposing that the same desires are simple.

Psychic Justice and the Composite Soul

A question that arises in connection to the specification of the nature of appetite and reason is whether the parts of the soul are independent agents. They are not, if I am correct about Plato's understanding of the desires within appetite. It has, however, been argued that the partitioning of the soul, together with Plato's characterization of unjust souls, establishes the presence of distinct agents within the soul. Bobonich offers one such argument, stating the two main theses of the partitioning argument to be, "(1) the person is a compound of distinct agent-like parts that are themselves the proper or ultimate subjects of beliefs, desires, and other psychological states and activities, and (2) these parts have different characteristic beliefs, desires, goal, and abilities."[37] As each part is an agent, ordinary psychological attributes are found in *each* part, rather than divided among the parts; on this view, appetite has beliefs and goals, and makes decisions that it must defend to the other parts. A key piece of textual evidence for this view occurs in close proximity to the initial partitioning. Necessary for the just arrangement of the soul is reason's possession of "the knowledge of what is beneficial for each [part] and for the whole, the community composed of the three" (*olô tô koinô sfôn autôn triôn ontô*, 442c). If taken literally, this reference to the community within the soul is not only incredible, it is flatly incompatible with Plato's earlier characterizations of appetite (only the core desires of which are simply appetitive) and reason, whose function it is "to rule, being wise and exercising forethought in behalf of the entire soul" (441d).

Taking into consideration the context in which this reference occurs, however, we see Plato drawing to a close his two-tiered investigation of the virtues by returning to and substantiating the driving assumption of isomorphism: "Then does not the necessity of our former postulate immediately follow, that as and whereby the city was wise so and thereby is the individual wise?" Glaucon answers in the affirmative, and agrees that the same is true for the other virtues (441c–d). I take this and other such references to be exaggerated, revealing not a conception of psychic parts as agents, but simply Plato's becoming carried away in a lively modeling of corresponding exemplars of virtue. In fact, Plato's belief that concordance of the rational and spirited parts will be accomplished through teaching the first (with words) and soothing the second (with harmonies) better aligns with the view I attribute to him, namely that spirit and appetite do not themselves reason.[38] I take the supposed unity *of belief* at 442d[39] to be an imaginative way of rendering a different kind of unity altogether. The just soul is a complex entity in which each element plays a particular role in bringing about the good of the whole. Plato's analogy between justice and health, which serves to cement his definition and to preface his answer to the question whether justice or injustice is more profitable, also indicates that the soul, for Plato, is a complex of parts, not a small community (444c–e). This analogy is not a loose one: justice is the soul's version of health, and its nature becomes clearer in light of an understanding of the latter. The elements of the body need not *agree to* anything for their proper functioning to constitute the body's well-being. In a healthy and just individual, each bodily and psychic element performs in such a way as to contribute to total flourishing, without necessarily being cognizant of this end.

The aim, after all, of seeking for oneself the condition with which Plato identifies justice is that one may make of oneself "one unit, one man instead of many" (443e). We must take the reference to "many men" to be merely illustrative, or else take "one man" in this way. For Plato cannot believe both that each soul is essentially composed of three subjects and that the proper condition of the soul is to be "one," unless what is one is a community, rather than a man. I do not believe there is sufficient evidence to privilege Plato's talk of multiple subjects within, when the heart of his argument establishing the composite nature of the soul tells otherwise.

An alternative way to reject the view that the soul is composed of smaller agents is via Plato's beliefs concerning the immortality of the soul. Shields does not take *Republic* IV to establish "essentially distinct parts," and focuses his study on the contrast between the individual soul as an embodied entity and as an immortal entity. The term "sullied," often used to refer to a soul's viciousness, is used by Shields to show that mere *embodiment* is damaging to the soul's true nature.[40] The thesis that appetite is an independent agent within the soul is incompatible with a conception of the soul as immortal, as this immortality does not seem to Plato to extend to those essentially bodily human activities. Kenny explains that the tripartite, or embodied, soul is but a brutish approximation of the "far lovelier" soul in its *true* and *immortal* form.[41]

This problem has a parallel in the case of the city. Placing Plato's early discussion of the ideal city alongside his claims late in the *Republic*, we see that it is the non-ideal city that is partitioned into ruling, defending, and provisioning elements. The clearest example of the way in which the just city of Book IV is imperfect is the presence of the Auxiliary class, which is absent from Plato's early depiction of the "true" and "healthy" city (372e). Plato identifies the city's parts according to needs of the city; the need for defense presupposes less-than-ideal internal and foreign relations. Absent the luxuries Glaucon thinks belong in the fine city (372d), there is little need for "a whole army that will march forth and fight it out with assailants in defense of all [the] wealth and the luxuries" (374a). The same may be said for the soul; finding itself in a body, it must stand guard against appetites from within and temptations from without. Plato's fundamental point concerning justice must be that, whatever parts develop in an ordinary, embodied human life, with its likely share of less than harmonious relationships and experiences, they must develop and remain in concordance with reason as ruler and guide. Thus, even if the soul is naturally *simple*, Plato's Book IV definition succeeds in capturing the essence of justice in the principle that each part of the soul must do its own proper work.

Another avenue presents itself; Aristotle's answer to one apparent conflict within his *Nicomachean Ethics* may illuminate several of Plato's claims in the *Republic*. Whereas the highest and best activity for a human soul is contemplation, this is suitable to it only insofar as it is intellectual; the happiest life for a human in the embodied, and thus partly animal, state is one of virtuous *activity*. When specifying the function particular to the human being, Plato ignores and Aristotle puts aside the activities that fall under the control of appetite. When a whole person perfects the human function, the requisite flourishing of each element of that person is possible only insofar as it is directed by the rational element. This view, taken together with Plato's claims about the immortality of the soul, bring into greater focus the nature and role of the parts of the soul. It does not seem to be definitive of the human soul that it has precisely these three parts, if to be truly human is to be wholly rational, and reason alone survives the transition of death intact.

The Problem of Unjust Souls

If we doubt that the parts of the soul are agents within the soul, and therefore hope to show that Plato believed *every* soul's actions to be directed toward a conception of the good, we must not ignore Books VIII and IX. In his dramatic account of the changes the soul undergoes in its descent toward the worst possible condition – psychic tyranny – Plato speaks as if reason, spirit, and appetite are independent agents battling for power. Even before he partitions the soul, Plato criticizes that psychic arrangement whereby "the better part . . . is dominated by the multitude of the worse" (*hotan . . . kratêthê hupo plêthous tou heironos smikroteron to beltion on*, 431a). When Plato makes clear what this domination entails, he reveals the depth of the contrast between the best and worst soul, and concludes his inquiry into the question whether justice is preferable to injustice. Let us see how Plato's analysis of the four-stage downfall and ruin of a good soul highlights the powers and activities of the parts in conflict.

Annas, in her discussion of the complexity of the changes involved in psychic deterioration, rejects one model of the shifts in power it involves: the responsibility for such shifts lies in the *person*, she claims, not the parts of the person. Following key examples of Plato's attribution of agency to the whole soul rather than to one of its parts, Annas concludes that "no account of the progress from virtue to vice can be produced just by citing dominance of one or another part of the soul; the progress looks more like a person making a series of increasingly catastrophic decisions as to which kinds of motivation to prefer."[42] This is indeed where the weight of the evidence lies. The young man whose soul becomes timocratic learns from the comments and admonitions of those at home and in the city that ambition pays; thus, rejecting his father's contrary teachings, he "comes to a compromise and turns over the government in his soul to the intermediate principle of ambition and his spirit" (550b). Similarly, one whose soul is becoming oligarchic "will . . . establish on that throne the principle of appetite and avarice, and set it up as the great king in his soul . . . he will force the rational and high-spirited principles to crouch lowly to right and left as slaves, and will allow the one to calculate and consider nothing but the ways of making more money from a little" (553c–d).[43]

I therefore find entirely persuasive Price's argument that *souls do things*, by means of their parts, or aspects. "Mental parts should not be taken to be subjects of mental activities," he argues, "for a subject of an activity cannot also be the aspect of another subject in respect of which this subject performs it."[44] Plato's analysis of the unjust souls "ruled by appetite" is not incompatible with the earlier analysis of that part of the psyche, for the appetites of the unjust do not flourish on their own; they do not discover new and various means of gratification via secret digressions from the path set out by the wise member of the psychic community, but develop, *in the person as a whole*, when particular combinations of circumstances and urges result in the rational matching of object to desire. Plato *does* speak of a secret expansion of appetites, which then "seize the citadel of the . . . soul" in the democratic person (560b). But we know that the path to this condition is not simple and direct, nor is it a path traveled by one "part" of the soul in isolation, nor does appetite, as one of three *agents*, drag the other two toward its own licentious activities and aims. To say that reason becomes displaced, as Plato does, is not to say that it is simply knocked out of place, according to some plan that appetite constructs by its own devices. The problem is instead reason's failure to "stand guard," or, in other words, to choose correctly a plan of life. The person, moving toward new objects determined to satisfy desires, comes to acquire new beliefs regarding the way and degree to which pleasure, for example, may be attained. In a democratic soul, these are "false and braggart words and opinions," which have come to be in part because of the young man's associations with others who are unjust (560c and 572c). The tyrannical person is the one who, "*by nature or by habits or by both*," becomes fixated on one of the appetites, and eventually one of these in particular; it is thus that "appetite" comes to "rule" the soul (573c). Just what is this rule? Plato tells us, in terms of the interplay between desires and *opinions* in the soul: "the opinions accounted just, will be overmastered by the opinions newly emancipated and released, which, serving as bodyguards of the ruling passion, will prevail in alliance with it" (574d–e). Thus, unjust lives are led by appetite in the sense that reasoning powers are never developed correctly, or they are so degraded as to be almost entirely focused on the attainment of what are falsely believed to be the greatest pleasures. The whole soul has turned toward the satisfaction of its lesser elements, *hence* their continuing growth. It is not surprising that new and varied appetites would come to have greater strength than their possessor might realize, but they can do this without literally conspiring against reason.

Plato's presentation of the demise of the soul is interspersed with his account of the decline of the city; the resulting picture is vivid and forceful. It is, however, also exaggerated. As in earlier comparisons of the city and soul, Plato's use of language of agreement, discord, or power-struggles between the parts of the soul is an extension of the way he specifies the possible relationships between the parts of the city. He overdoes the parallel, in such a way that obscures his own convictions about psychic turmoil and harmony. As Santas explains, Plato's "anthropomorphic language . . . for parts of the soul may reflect *not* the thought that parts of the soul are little persons, as is often supposed. It may reflect the opposite thought, that citizens are like parts of the soul, in the sense that the good of citizens bears to the good of the whole city the same relation as the good of parts of a person bears to the whole person."[45] When Plato does explicitly speak of multiplicity within the person, he does so hesitantly, to express a condition of deep psychic turmoil, as in his description of the oligarchic person who is "not really one, but in some sort a double man" (554d). Plato's discomfort with this and similar expressions would be truly strange if it were his considered view that there are three agents in each soul.

Desire for the Good

The desires of appetite have formed the focus of the preceding analysis; it is important to examine their connection to the soul's rational desires. In calling one part of the soul "rational," Plato only hints at his view of the tremendous potential human reason holds. Plato's eventual turn to the epistemological and metaphysical explanations of the good soul contribute to a more complete, precise account of the differences between rational and non-rational desires. What connection is there between the complex desires of appetite and conceptions of the good? We find out in Plato's setting apart of philosophers from "doxophilists,"[46] or opinion-lovers, who believe good things to be many, and eschew all talk either of the singular form Goodness – which infuses with goodness all other good things – or of the possibilities for cognitive ascent toward knowledge (479–80). It is with reason that the soul must traverse the stages represented in Plato's Divided Line, which reveals two worlds, the physical and the intellectual, each divided into two segments representing rational faculties and their objects. That types of human cognition differ in their relationship to truth explains why a soul limited to the lower levels is mired in a world of appearances. The beliefs that shape one's appetitive desires (giving them content), and thus one's ordinary pursuits, are relegated to the lower, physical world, the furthest from truth. In contrast to knowledge, the highest faculty, belief concerns that which is ever-changing, and that toward which any soul excessively captivated by the "so-called pleasures" of the body is oriented (583–4). Plato explains that, to the shifting nature of the objects constituting this realm there corresponds an equally unstable faculty, through which it is "impossible to conceive firmly" (479c). If one disregards knowledge in favor of opinion, one will seek, and desire, the countless beautiful things in preference to the one "beautiful itself."

Thus the faculty with which reason attends to its task of determining and promoting the good of the soul is critical to the character of the soul's resulting desires. With this new theoretical framework, we may understand the truly just soul to be one in which reason's specification of appropriate objects of desire will align completely with reason's *knowledge* about the good itself, and the good of the soul. We also see that aspects of Plato's account of knowledge preclude the attainment of justice by anyone other than the philosopher; only the philosopher ascends toward knowledge of the Good, whose understanding brings into view the good for the soul and city.[47] One who has no knowledge of the Good will not be equipped to rule her own soul in such a way as to promote its flourishing.[48]

On this view, attachment to the Good is not a feature of all desire as such, for the reason that desire is more complex than Socrates supposed it to be. It is, however, a feature of rational desire that it *aims at* goodness, and in turn a feature of the philosopher's desire that its object is the true good. Cooper describes the relationship between reason and desire in the just soul as follows: "appetite, restrained and moderated by reason and aspiration, drives [one] on toward pleasures of eating, drinking, sex and other bodily gratifications when and as, and only when and as, reason approves."[49] Noting that *simple* appetites push the soul even without reason's approval, we may say that, in the just soul, no appetites ever drive the soul *into action* without reason's approval. But what is this approval? Certainly, an appetite cannot conclude in action without reason's *involvement*, but the nature of reason's positive endorsement depends on the role of reason in the soul. In the philosopher's soul, the endorsement of an action occurs in light of full knowledge about its goodness, whereas in the soul of one who refuses to look past the many captivating things within reach, reason is operating imperfectly.

What, then, will we make of Plato's aforementioned contention that the soul does *all that it does* for the sake of the good? One way to reconcile this very Socratic claim with Plato's account of unjust souls is to suppose that reason's input into the formation of executive desires also serves to link them to the soul's search for the good; that is, reason's decisions occur in light of a conception of the good. Plato indicates as much when he asks, "is not the transition from oligarchy to democracy effected in some such way as this – by the insatiate greed for that which it sets before itself as the good, the attainment of the greatest possible wealth?" (555b; see also 562b). Plato seems to hold that, for action to occur, the object of action must be integrated into the agent's conception of the good, even in an unjust soul. Cooper takes reason's desire to know to be one of the essential elements of human psychology. A person who does not have this desire has "no mind at all, and so [is] not a human being after all," he explains.[50] In the epistemology of the *Republic*, this quest is inseparable from the quest for knowledge *of the good*, and for its manifestation in one's life.

While reconciling several of Plato's key claims, this view seems to weaken significantly the degree to which Plato rejects Socrates' view. Rowe, reading *Republic* 505d–e, finds that, "it is axiomatic for Plato, as for the historical Socrates, that all our actions aim at the good, where 'good' means good for us as individuals."[51] In the *Gorgias*, for example, Socrates asks,

> Thus it is in pursuit of the good that we walk, when we walk, conceiving it to be better; or on the contrary, stand, when we stand, for the sake of the same thing, the good: is it not so? . . . And so we put a man to death, if we do put him to death, or expel him or deprive him of his property, because we think it better for us to do this than not? . . . So it is for the sake of the good that the doers of all these things do them? (468b1–8)

In one respect, the distinction is far narrower than ordinarily supposed; Plato specifies the ultimate goal of action to be the good in his early and middle work, though his understanding of the good is greatly underdeveloped in the former. In the *Gorgias*, Plato's specification of the wider goal of *action* is followed by a restrictive analysis of the objects of *desire*. Socrates' aim is to show Polus that, while many actions are pursued, only *truly* good actions are desired. This is why, contrary to popular opinion, tyrants and orators really do nothing that they wish to do![52]

It is usually assumed that, in the *Republic*, Plato is rejecting the claim that all desire is for what appears good, which is in turn assumed to be Socrates' view. But taking Socrates to believe that desire takes as its exclusive object is what is *truly* good will change the nature of the opposition. If this analysis is correct, what we find at *Republic* 505 should not be so surprising: all intentional action aims at one's conception of one's good. Plato does not need to affirm that there can be intentional action toward another motive in order to disagree with Socrates; instead, he needs to show that in all the ordinary cases that seem to involve reason's failing to specify the best course of action, one nevertheless *desires* the course of action taken.[53] Plato acknowledges that some do desire truly bad things, but maintains the overarching and universal desire for good. What Socrates denies and Plato comes to accept is that executive desires stemming from appetitive sources take as their objects things falsely considered to be good. Flourishing is not only a matter of being in the right cognitive state, but of conforming one's entire psyche to the structure and organization optimally conducive to human well-being. Habit and education bring one into this proper form, so that the lesser parts of the soul are molded by, and fall in line with, reason's directives. What Socrates attributed to any soul, Plato attributes to "the whole soul," but, recognizing the danger implicit in the process by which beliefs shape and direct appetites, not to every complex desire of every soul.[54]

Plato seems squarely to disagree with Socrates' identification of the object of desire with the truly good. But the healthy soul – also the happiest soul – desires and experiences the truest pleasures. These remain the objects of every soul's desire, in the sense identified. Some souls become blemished, and learn ways that distance them from the truest satisfaction. Plato cannot admit that they fail to desire what they pursue – in this he abandons the Socratic position by allowing false "conceptions" of the good to form part of the explanatory mechanism offered in the *Republic*. Plato's theory can be judged an improvement over Socrates' for good reasons: it posits and explains psychological entities that seem, on reflection of oneself and others, to influence, guide, or subvert virtuous action. While every soul pursues the good, Plato's affirmation of complexity in desire leads him to see the failures of unjust souls as more than cognitive errors. This is due to two aspects of Plato's view: the basic source of "appetitive" motivation is identified in precise *contrast to* that which links one to the good. In addition, the individuals who fail to discern that which is truly good consequently grasp at mere appearances. As Plato understands desire in the *Republic*, their error is in cognition *and* in appetite, as desires for those objects mistakenly thought to be good develop and flourish.

Notes

1   Shorey's (1937) translation of Plato's *Republic* is given throughout, unless otherwise noted.

2   This is the developmental conception of Plato's thought; taken in a certain rough order, Plato's works reflect an initial agreement with, and then a questioning and eventual rejection of, many of the views of the historical Socrates. Annas is especially critical of the assumption that Plato's own views may reliably and consistently be found in the words of the character Socrates (1999: 24–6, 119). Bobonich, endorsing the developmental view, traces Plato's thought away from an initial denial of *akrasia*, toward the partitioning thesis, then finally away from partitioning to a "new more unitary understanding of the nature of the soul" (2002: 219).

3   See Vlastos 1991: 150–3 and Santas 1979: 186ff. According to Taylor, "provided that the agent has a conception of what is overall best for the agent, or (equivalently) what is maximally productive of *eudaimonia* (for the agent), that conception is sufficient to motivate action with a view to its own realization" (1998: 58).

4   I endorse this view, following Penner and Rowe (Penner 1991, Penner and Rowe 1994).

5   These problems constitute a maze of interpretive difficulties, many of which have received careful scrutiny; I will refer to a limited number of the numerous analyses that illuminate aspects of Plato's work.

6 Plato prefaces the division of the soul argument with a note as to its insufficiency, declaring, "We shall never apprehend this matter accurately from such methods as we are now employing." His longer, more accurate method proceeds by way of the relevant forms, including that of Justice, to which Plato does not link his initial definition of justice in Book IV.

7 See Santas 2001: 153, and Cooper 1999: 188.

8 This difficulty appears in a different way in Plato's definition of temperance as (in part) an agreement between the three parts that reason should rule. Is this agreement *rational agreement* or harmony of function?

9 In this case, the term "parts" (*merē*) to which Plato was not particularly attached, would be a misleading way to speak of distinct psychic phenomena.

10 Irwin 1995: 203.

11 Plato's assumption of isomorphism seems to require the view that the soul contains three agents, as the city contains three classes. It may seem that the identity of virtues of the city and soul becomes tenuous in the absence of agent-parts. I do not think this is so; while the ruling class may be broken down into constituent philosophers (their knowledge of the Form Good and their social wisdom suits them to ruling), the reasoning part of the soul is the smallest unit serving to explain the character of an individual and of the social class she inhabits. It is neither part of, nor conducive to, Plato's account to suppose that reason, spirit, or appetite must themselves be arranged properly, with their desires and beliefs in proper alignment. Reason is *part of the individual*, not an individual itself.

12 Though Plato, unlike Aristotle, does not explicitly consider these activities as candidates for the human function, the particular activities he does name are all intellectual ones: "management, rule, deliberation, and the like" (353d).

13 This principle is understood in different ways, as the law of non-contradiction (Shorey 1937: 382; Adam 1963: 246–7; Vlastos 1965: 71) and as a weaker principle of contraries or opposites (Robinson 1971; Irwin 1995: 204; Price 1995: 40–1).

14 See Stalley 1975 for a discussion of the meaning of the clause, "in the same respect in relation to the same thing."

15 Plato's earlier remark that the expression "master of oneself" is awkward reflects a similar concern. The strangeness of the term resides in its placing one entity in two roles, each relative to a weaker or stronger entity. One and the same person (*ho autos*) cannot be the stronger and the weaker relative to himself. Behind Plato's concern is a fear that the concept of self-mastery is inconsistent with the principle of opposites; thus he finds the term to be appropriate if there are two entities present, one of which controls, the other of which is controlled. Plato's reference to a single person suggests a negative answer to the question whether the "elements" are themselves agents. The same is suggested by Plato's belief that the worse element intensifies through the habituation of "bad breeding" (431a).

16 Santas 2001: 131.

17 These are more complex, as they are combinations of simple desires, but they are not the "learned" desires by which the soul fixates on particular kinds of drink, and is thus driven to the point of action.

18 The fact that many "beasts" seem to have beliefs aside, Plato clearly intends this analogy to reveal the instinctual nature of thirst. Shorey calls this kind of desire "animal appetite" (1937: 395).

19   Bobonich takes this to establish "distinct subjects which have the relevant complete contraries, that is, each part has one of the conflicting desires" (2002: 224). He does not find the problem of further divisions worrisome, if the parts are not *complete* smaller versions of the whole. But the parts seem complete enough to bring out precisely the conflicts Plato envisioned as requiring a partition; it is hard to see how an entity with beliefs, desires, and decisions will avoid the phenomenon of inner conflict. The difficulty is acute in the case of the soul in the worst stages of a development toward psychic tyranny. How must we construe the battle leading up to the emergence of one desire as primary? Do many unique voices within appetite make themselves heard? How exactly does one persevere and win?

20   In Irwin's analysis of the conflict, the opposition is most likely between a desire and a rational opposition to acting on appetite as such, and not between a desire and an aversion to that desire. The aim and consistency of Plato's argument, he explains, require that the "unwilling" issue from a rational desire for the good. Thus, what reason opposes is the soul's "acting without regard for the good" (1995: 208). Because simple appetites are not the sort of thing that *could* produce action, as Penner shows, I argue below that reason does not oppose simple desires as such (as they do not threaten the soul's pursuit of good) but only their development and fulfillment when it would be positively *bad* for the soul. See Penner 1990, and also Smith 2001: 118–20, on aversion vs. lack of desire.

21   Price 1995: 49.

22   See Robinson 1971: 41ff. on the difference between the meaning of "thirst" and the way thirst occurs in the soul.

23   Price argues that Plato can affirm psychic conflict without denying that the good is the aim of all desires (1995: 50).

24   The view here posing the threat to the unfolding argument is explicitly presented, and (more or less) defended, at *Gorgias* 468a, *Meno* 77c, and *Symposium* 204e. Adam does not recognize a difference between this and other views of desire in Plato's works, but claims that "Here, as always, Socrates would of course concede that all men desire the good; but we need the λογιστικόν [*logistikon*] in each act of desire to specify what the good really is" (1963: 251). This may be true, but Socrates and Plato characterize almost every other aspect of the relationship between reason and desire differently. For example, Socrates does not say simply that the good is a universal object of desire, but that *only* good things are objects of desire. As Irwin puts it, "In the Socratic view, no desire conforms to the description of 'thirst qua thirst'" (1995: 207). Plato, on the other hand, insists that precisely this kind of desire is *not* for the good.

25   An important distinction is noted in Adam's argument that Plato's objector is guilty of an equivocation, which, once removed, leaves him with no significant objection at all. The problem is supposedly in the very claim that drink, as a desire, is always of *good* drink, as this is true if "good" is taken as *apparently* good, but false if taken as "in reality good" (1963: 250). However, while we may not agree that desire is *only* for the *truly* good, this is precisely what Plato's early dialogues reveal Socrates to think. This is why Plato must be wary of the Socratic objection to his specification of thirst; *as Plato understood him*, the "opponent" would deny that thirst (or any desire) is simple in that it involves no impulse toward the good.

26   Irwin comments that Plato may want to distinguish rational from non-rational types of desire – appetite (*epithumia*) from wish (*boulêsis*), for example. Plato is so incon-

sistent in the *Republic* as to make this task very difficult. Cooper and Irwin point out the surprising fact that Plato's choice of term when he claims, at 580d5, that each part of the soul has desires (*epithumiai*) is identical to that reflected in his differentiation of the appetitive part (*to epithumêtikon*) from the rational part (Cooper 1999: 190; Irwin 1995: 205–8, and 381 nn. 14, 18).

27 Plato's discussion of Leontius (439e–440a) is inadequate to this task and does not replicate for spirit the argument distinguishing appetite from reason, as it stops short of completing the abstraction to a simple case of conflict.

28 Santas 2001: 123. At 353a, Plato refers to two kinds of function: the job for which a thing is the only tool, and the job for which a thing is the best tool. Santas (2001: 69) calls these "exclusive" and "optimal" functions.

29 Cooper 1999: 196–7. Bobonich argues that each part has its own reasoning abilities (2002: 220, 235–47).

30 Cooper 1999: 197.

31 Price (1995: 50) calls this fact "incredible" if it is true of *every* appetite; but it is not true of complex appetites.

32 Rowe 1984: 89–90. I take this to be the second way in which reason influences "appetitive" desires; the first is reason's input into their formation.

33 Penner 1990: 54–8.

34 Irwin 1995: 207.

35 Smith's examples of psychic conflicts involve desires more complex than the ones Plato has in mind (Smith 2001: 120). Plato would abstract from Smith's case of a man battling the desire to drink "the water he sees in front of him," to the purely appetitive desire simply *to drink*.

36 Looking to the young – as Plato does to show that spirit is distinct from reason at 441a – we see that young children are also full of appetite (as they are "chock-full of rage and high spirit") but it is a feature of young creatures to be *incapable* of seeking objects to ease the frustration of desire, for lack of the cognitive layers which give a complex desire character *and* make it satisfiable.

37 Bobonich 2002: 217.

38 That is, habit, not instruction, will cause the desires of spirit and appetite to "take only those pleasures which reason approves," and thereby seek "the pleasures that are proper to them and their own" (586d). On this view, a soul that wants less fitting pleasures is one in which complex desires develop with reason's input, but not its guidance.

39 Plato says that the parts are "at one in the belief [*homodoxôsi*] that reason ought to rule."

40 Shields 2001: 141–3.

41 Kenny 1969: 249. See also Smith 2001: 128.

42 Annas 1998: 129.

43 It is striking that, though appetite is supposedly ruler of the soul, the oligarchic *man* is described at 554a as restricting which appetites he will satisfy, restraining some while allowing others satisfaction.

44 Price concludes that "if the parts are not subjects, they are not agents either, though their contents are causes of actions" (1995: 54).

45 Santas 2001: 152.

46 Shorey's (1937) take on Plato's word φιλοδόξος [*filodoxos*] at 480a.
47 Vlastos calls " 'psychic harmony' . . . the condition in which the soul is healthy, beautiful, and in the ontologically correct, hierarchic, inner order" (1969: 2). In *this* soul, it is hardly conceivable how anything appetitive could overturn or overrun judgment.
48 Cross and Woozley defend this view (1964: 269), as do Cooper (1997: 20, 29 n. 8), and Bobonich (2002: 51ff.).
49 Cooper 1997: 18.
50 Cooper 1999: 190.
51 Rowe 1984: 87.
52 Gorgias 466d. See also *Republic* 577–8 on the misery of the tyrannical soul.
53 I disagree with Taylor's claim that, in the *Republic*, "Plato no longer accepts . . . the strong thesis that every intentional action is aimed at the realisation of the agent's conception of his or her overall good" (1998: 67).
54 Plato uses this phrase at 577d–e to illuminate his developed analysis of the tyrant's unhappiness: "the tyrannized soul – to speak of the soul as a whole . . . will least of all do what it wishes, but being always perforce driven and drawn by the gadfly of desire it will be full of confusion and repentance."

I would like to express my gratitude to Jerry Santas, for all I have learned from him about Plato's *Republic,* and for reading and providing helpful suggestions for improving the present paper.

References and further reading

Adam, J. (1963) *The* Republic *of Plato,* Cambridge: Cambridge University Press.
Annas, J. (1981) *An Introduction to Plato's* Republic, Oxford: Clarendon Press.
——(1999) *Platonic Ethics, Old and New*, Ithaca, NY: Cornell University Press.
Bobonich, C. (2002) *Plato's Utopia Recast*, Oxford: Clarendon Press.
Cooper, J. M. (1997) "The psychology of justice in Plato," in R. Kraut (ed.) *Plato's* Republic: *Critical Essays*, Lanham, MD: Rowman and Littlefield.
——(1999) "Plato's theory of human motivation," in G. Fine (ed.) *Plato 2*, Oxford: Oxford University Press.
Cross, R. C., and A. D. Woozley (1964) *Plato's* Republic, London: Macmillan.
Irwin, T. (1977) *Plato's Moral Theory,* Oxford: Oxford University Press.
——(1995) *Plato's Ethics*, Oxford: Oxford University Press.
Kenny, A. (1969) "Mental health in Plato's *Republic*," *Proceedings of the British Academy* 55, pp. 229–53.
Penner, T. (1990) "Plato and Davidson: parts of the soul and weakness of will," in D. Copp (ed.) *Canadian Journal of Philosophy*, suppl. vol. 16, pp. 35–74.
——(1991) "Desire and power in Socrates: the argument of *Gorgias* 466a–468e that orators and tyrants have no power in the city," *Aperion* 24/3, pp. 147–202.
Penner, T., and C. J. Rowe (1994) "The desire for good: is the *Meno* consistent with the *Gorgias*?," *Phronesis* 39/1, pp. 1–25.
Price, A. (1995) *Mental Conflict*, London: Routledge.
Robinson, R. (1971) "Plato's separation of reason from desire," *Phronesis* 16, pp. 38–48.

Rowe, C. J. (1984) *Plato*, New York: St Martin's Press.

Santas, G. (1979) *Socrates*, London: Routledge and Kegan Paul.

——(2001) *Goodness and Justice*, Oxford: Blackwell.

Shields, C. (2001) "Simple souls," in E. Wagner (ed.) *Essays on Plato's Psychology*, New York: Lexington Books.

Shorey, P. (trans. and ed.) (1937) *Plato:* The Republic, Loeb Classical Library, Cambridge, MA: Harvard University Press.

Smith, N. (2001) "Plato's analogy of soul and state," in E. Wagner (ed.) *Essays on Plato's Psychology*, New York: Lexington Books.

Stalley, R. F. (1975) "Plato's argument for the division of the reasoning and appetitive elements within the soul," *Phronesis* 20, pp. 110–28.

Taylor, C. C. W. (1998) "Platonic ethics," in S. Everson (ed.) *Ethics*, Cambridge: Cambridge University Press.

Vlastos, G. (1965) *Platonic Studies*, Princeton, NJ: Princeton University Press.

——(1969) "Justice and psychic harmony in the *Republic*," *Journal of Philosophy* 66, pp. 505–21.

——(1991) *Socrates, Ironist and Moral Philosopher*, Ithaca, NY: Cornell University Press.

Woods, M. (1987) "Plato's division of the soul," *Proceedings of the British Academy* 73, pp. 23–47.

10

Plato and the Ship of State

David Keyt

In political activity ... men sail a boundless and bottomless sea: there is neither harbour for shelter nor floor for anchorage, neither starting-place nor appointed destination.
Michael Oakeshott

Introduction

In the sixth book of the *Republic* Plato uses the famous Ship of State simile to explain why philosophers are not honored in cities. He claims that a philosopher in a Greek city is like a skilled but disrespected steersman aboard a ship that has been hijacked by its unruly crew and whose helm has been placed in the hands of a sailor who does not know how to steer. Though Plato's use of this simile regularly earns a footnote in books on political philosophy, it has not received the attention accorded the central similes in the *Republic*: the Sun, Line, and Cave. Indeed, to my knowledge, it has never been fully analyzed in the light of what can be gleaned about ancient ships and seafaring. One reason for the neglect may be a failure to recognize just how potent an emblem of Plato's political philosophy the Ship of State is. For if Plato regards a ship with an unruly crew as a good image of the Greek cities with which he was familiar and of Athens in particular, then by extension he must regard a ship with an orderly crew and a competent steersman as a good image of his ideal city. There are thus two parts to the Ship of State simile, which are related to each other as the two parts of the Cave simile. In both similes the alien and the abnormal symbolize ordinary life, and the normal and the everyday symbolize a higher realm. As the strange firelight region within the Cave symbolizes the sensible realm of ordinary objects (and their images), a hijacked ship symbolizes actual historical cities; and as the familiar sunlit region outside the Cave symbolizes the intelligible realm of Platonic Forms, a free and competently managed ship symbolizes an ideal city. I hope to show that there is also another similarity between the two similes, that just as an exploration of the Cave draws the explorer deep inside Plato's epistemology and metaphysics, so a voyage on his Ship of State carries the voyager to the far reaches of his political philosophy. But before settling in for the cruise the voyager may want to explore the ship and meet the others on board.

Let's begin with the passage itself:

Conceive this sort of thing happening either on many ships or on one. The shipowner (*naukléron*) is bigger and stronger than everyone else on the ship, but he is hard of hearing and likewise a bit shortsighted, and his knowledge of seafaring is just as limited. The sailors engage in faction (*stasiazontas*) with one another about the steering (*tês kubernêseôs*) [of the ship], each one thinking that he ought to steer (*kubernan*), though he has never learned the art (*tên technên*) and cannot point out his teacher or a time when he learned. What is more, they claim it is not teachable, and are even ready to cut to pieces anyone who says that it is teachable. They are always crowded around the shipowner begging and doing everything so that he will turn the helm (*pêdalion*) over to them. Sometimes, if they do not persuade him but others are more successful, they either kill the others or throw them off the ship, and then, after binding the noble shipowner (*ton gennaion naukléron*) hand and foot with mandragora or strong drink or in some other way, they rule (*arxein*) the ship, using up what's in it, and, drinking and feasting, sail as such men might be expected [to sail]. Besides this, they praise the man who is clever at lending a hand in persuading or forcing the shipowner to let them rule and say that he is skilled in seamanship (*nautikon*) and in steering (*kubernêtikon*) and knows about ships, while the man not like this they condemn as useless. They don't understand that the true steersman (*tou alêthinou kubernêtou*) must pay attention to year and seasons and sky and stars and winds and all that belongs to his art, if he is to be really qualified to rule (*archikos*) a ship. How he shall steer (*kubernêsei*), whether people wish him to or not – the art and study of this and, at the same time, steersmanship (*tên kubernêtikên*), they think it impossible to acquire. When such things happen on board ships, do you not suppose that the man truly skilled in steering (*ton hôs alêthôs kubernêtikon*) would in fact be called a sky-gazer and an idle babbler (*meteôroskopon te kai adoleschên*) and useless to them by the voyagers (*tôn plôtêrôn*) in ships managed in this way?

Definitely, said Adeimantus.

Well, said I, I think you do not need for the image to be closely examined to see that it resembles the disposition in cities towards the true philosophers, but understand what I mean. (VI.488a7–489a6)

The Ship and Those on Board

The ship Plato envisages is a sailing vessel. Such a ship would have been steered, not with a rudder hinged to its stern, an invention of the twelfth century AD

(Casson 1994: 152), but with a pair of large steering oars (*pêdalia*) one on each quarter. It would have been a merchantman rather than a passenger ship. There were no passenger ships in antiquity (p. 124); people who traveled by sea were passengers on merchantmen.

Who exactly is aboard Plato's ship? Plato mentions "sailors" (*nautai*), "voyagers" (*plôtêres*), a "shipowner" (*nauklêros*), and a true and a false "steersman" (*kubernêtês*). The quotation marks signal that the English nouns are only rough renditions of the Greek; none of the Greek terms has an exact English equivalent. The *nautai* on Plato's ship are clearly sailors, though the word is occasionally also applied to passengers (*Epistle* VII.347a2; Sophocles, *Philoctetes* 901). The *nauklêros*, in spite of the customary translation of his name, was not necessarily the ship's owner; he might only have use of the ship under a charter, which could be for a given period of time or in perpetuity (Casson 1971: 315 n. 67) – a nicety that we shall henceforth ignore. In Plato shipowners are usually mentioned together with merchants (*emporoi*) (*Protagoras* 319d3; *Politicus* 290a1; *Laws* VIII.831e6, 842d3), their chief clients. A shipowner makes his living by transporting a merchant and his goods from one port to another, if he is not a merchant himself transporting his own goods (Xenophon, *Oeconomicus* 8.12; *Hellenica* 5.1.21.10). As the owner or charterer of his ship he hires the steersman (Xenophon, *Memorabilia* 2.6.38) and determines who and what comes aboard (*Epistle* VII.329e2–3, 346e7–347a3; Thucydides I.137.2). The shipowner and steersman would no doubt discuss route and weather conditions together. In the vivid account of Saint Paul's voyage as a prisoner to Rome, for example, the shipowner and steersman are pictured as jointly counseling, while safely in harbor, the leg of the voyage that was to end in shipwreck at Malta (Acts 27: 11). Once under way a ship was apparently under the command of its steersman. In the *Memorabilia* (3.9.11) Socrates remarks, at any rate, that "on a ship the man who knows [i.e. the steersman] rules, and the shipowner and all the others on the ship obey the man who knows."

The words on the stem *kubern* – *kubernan, kubernêsis, kubernêtês, kubernêtikos* – are a problem for translators. In the *Complete Works of Plato* (1997) edited by Cooper and Hutchinson, for example, the noun *kubernêtês* is variously rendered "steersman,"[1] "captain,"[2] "helmsman,"[3] and "navigator."[4] The phrase *hê kubernêtikê* (sc. *technê*) for the art of the *kubernêtês*, is variously rendered as "steersmanship,"[5] "helmsmanship,"[6] "helmsman's skill,"[7] "pilot's art,"[8] "art of sailing,"[9] "navigation,"[10] "nautical expertise,"[11] and "expertise that captain's have."[12] A reader with no Greek or no Greek text in front of him will reasonably think that Plato in these various passages is referring to different things; a reader who is following the Greek will wonder whether the translators are trying to resolve an ambiguity. We need to ask whether *kubernêtês* and *hê kubernêtikê* are ambiguous (or generic) terms. Were there three different officers on a typical Greek merchantman with three distinct skills, a captain, a helmsman, and a navigator, each of whom was called *kubernêtês*, or "steersman"?

The answer is "No": the steersman was captain, helmsman, and navigator all rolled into one. In vase paintings we see him sitting at the stern facing the bow with his hands on the tillers and shouting commands to his crew (Casson 1994: figs 57, 85; see also *Critias* 109c2–4). This is clearly how Plato pictures him. That Plato's steersman is a helmsman, that he has his hands on the tillers, is evident from a passage in the *Politicus*, where Plato writes of the steersman of the universe letting go of the handle (*oiax*) of the steering oars (*pêdalia*) (272e4; see also *First Alcibiades* 117e9–117d2, *Hippias minor* 374e4–5, *Clitophon* 408b1–3); that he is a captain is evident from a passage in the first book of the *Republic*, where a steersman strictly speaking is said to be a ruler of sailors (*nautôn archôn*) (*Rep*. I.341c9–341d3; see also 342d9–342e4 and *First Alcibiades* 125c6–11, 125d10–13); and that he is a navigator is evident from the Ship of State passage, for it can only be as a navigator that the steersman needs to know the stars (*Rep*. VI.488d6, 488e4).

In the *Republic* steersmanship (*hê kubernêtikê*) is called an art, or *technê* (I.341d2–3; II.360e7–8; VI.488b4–5, 488d4–7); but when Plato classifies the types of knowledge in the *Philebus* (55c4–59d9), it is not ranked so high. In the classification of the *Philebus* steersmanship falls within the lower of the two types of handicraft (*cheirotechnikê*), along with music, medicine, agriculture, and (military) strategy (55d5–56b2; see also [*Epinomis*] 975e1–976b1). This lower kind of handicraft, which is not given a name, is characterized by conjecture, the exercise of the senses on the basis of experience and routine (*empeiria kai tribê*), the use of guesswork, and the absence of even the most elementary use of mathematics such as in counting, measuring, or weighing. Socrates expresses confidence that steersmanship fits this characterization (*Philebus* 56b1–2); and of the three aspects of steersmanship – steering, commanding, and navigating – only the third might seem, from the false perspective of modern navigation, to involve something higher. The effective use of the tillers is clearly a matter of experience and routine. (For the operation of the tillers on a reconstructed trireme see Morrison and Coates 1986: 219–20.) And for any but a natural born leader of men the ability to command sailors owes much to experience. As for navigating, Plato's statement that the steersman "must pay attention to year and seasons and sky and stars and winds" (*Rep*. VI.488d5–7) gives an indication of what navigation involved in the fourth century BC. The ancient mariner had no compass. When he was out of sight of land, he had to study the sky and stars – the sun and the north star in particular – in order to determine the direction in which to steer. He needed to study the winds and pay attention to the seasons since in the Aegean the winds vary greatly with the season. (On the winds see [Aristotle], *Meteorologica* II.4–6 and *Problemata* XXVI.) Lacking instruments and charts, he had no way of using even the most elementary mathematics. Indeed, in the *Memorabilia* (4.7.4–5) Xenophon has Socrates distinguish the practical astronomy of the steersman from the theoretical and mathematical astronomy of the natural philosopher who is interested in the orbits of the planets, their periods of revolution, and their distance from the earth. (On ancient navigation see Bass 1972: 78.) In both the *Gorgias* and the *Laws* Plato distinguishes experience and routine from art on the ground that art, unlike experience and routine, rests on a rational principle (*logos*) and can give the reason (*aitia*) for its procedures (*Gorgias* 465a2–5; *Laws* IX.857c8, XI.938a3–4); and in the *Philebus* he is careful to say that the lower kinds of handicraft are "said to be" arts (56c4) and that "many people call them arts" (55e7–56a1), implying by these words that steersmanship is not an art strictly speaking.

The word *plôtêres* ("voyagers") which occurs nowhere else in Plato's dialogues, refers to anybody on board – steersman, shipowner, sailor, or passenger (Aristotle, *Politics* III.4.1276b20–4, 6.1279a3–4, 13.1284a22–5; VI.6.1320b33–9; VII.2.1324b31; Aristophanes, *Ecclesiazusae* 1087) – and thus allows for the presence of passengers as well as seamen on Plato's ship. Passengers would not be unusual. One such would be a merchant traveling with his goods, but there could be others as well. In the *Gorgias* Socrates mentions the modest fare required to transport a man himself, his children, goods, and womenfolk – in short, a man and his household – from Aegina, Egypt, or the Black Sea to Athens (511d6–511e3). In his commentary on the *Gorgias*, E. R. Dodds, citing *Laws* II.650a3–4 as a parallel passage, suggests that Plato uses the plural *gunaikas* ("womenfolk") rather than the singular *gunaika* ("wife") to indicate that the man's wife is accompanied by her female slaves (1959: 347). If we envisage such a family, including its slaves, as passengers on Plato's ship, it will carry representatives of the entire population of a Greek city, not just of its male citizens. (There were 276 souls aboard the ship carrying Paul to Rome [Acts 27: 37].)

The Unruly Ship

Socrates interprets his simile only in part. He tells us that the ship symbolizes a city, or *polis*, that the true steersman symbolizes the true philosopher, and that the sailors symbolize "our current political rulers" (*Rep.* VI.489a4–6, 489c4–7). He does not tell us explicitly what the shipowner symbolizes; but his description of the shipowner as bigger and stronger than everyone else on board but hard of hearing, shortsighted, and lacking in intelligence (VI.488a8–488b3) is of a piece with his description a few pages later of the big, strong, temperamental animal, to which the many (*hoi polloi*) "when they are gathered together in a body" (*hotan hathroisthôsin*) is likened (VI.493a6–493c8). The sort of gathering to which Socrates is referring is indicated a few lines earlier when he speaks of "many (*polloi*) sitting together in a body (*hathrooi*) in assemblies or in lawcourts or theaters or encampments or some other public gathering of the mass" (VI.492b5–7). The many (*hoi polloi*) are the *dêmos* (see *Laws* III.684c1–3; Aristotle, *Politics* IV.1292a11–13), defined later in the *Republic* as workers with few possessions and described, in words echoing the description of the shipowner, as "the largest and most powerful class in a democracy when it is gathered together in a body (*hotanper hathroisthê(i)*)" (VIII.565a1–3). Since the majority rules in the assembly and since the workers are the majority in a democratic assembly, the *dêmos* speaks for a democratic assembly and in consequence is sometimes identified with it (*Gorgias* 451b7, 500c5, 515d6) or with the citizenry as a whole, rich as well as poor (*Politicus* 298c3, 289e6, 299a1). Thus, the word *dêmos* has both a broad and a narrow sense. In the narrow sense the *dêmos* is the class of workers; in the broad sense it is the citizenry as a whole or the assembly of all citizens. The shipowner symbolizes the body through which politicians seek power. In a Greek city this body was the assembly; and in a Greek democracy it was the *dêmos* (= the assembly of all citizens), which was dominated by the *dēmos* (= the workers). Since the *dêmos* is a font of political power only when sitting as an assembly, the shipowner symbolizes the *dêmos* in the broad sense of the term. His limited knowledge of seafaring symbolizes its limited knowledge of statesmanship (*Politicus* 300e7–9); his deafness and shortsightedness symbolize its ignorance (*Rep.* IX.575c7) and lack of foresight, perceptual limitations symbolizing intellectual limitations as in the Sun and the Cave (VI.508c4–508d10, VII.514a1–517c5, 532a1–532d1). If this interpretation of the shipowner is correct, Plato's target in the Ship of State analogy is Greek democracy in general and Athenian democracy in particular. For it is only in a democracy that the *dêmos* and the assembly are identified, and the foremost democracy in the Greek world was the one inhabited by Plato and Socrates and in whose port the conversation of the *Republic* takes place.

That the shipowner symbolizes the *dêmos*, identified with the assembly of all citizens, is corroborated by a comment of Aristotle's in the *Rhetoric*. In explaining the difference between metaphors and similes, he says that in the *Republic* Plato takes the *dêmos* to be like a strong but shortsighted shipowner (*Rhetoric* III.4.1406b34–6). Aristotle usually thinks of the *dêmos* as consisting of those who must work for a living, and contrasts the *dêmos* with the notables (*hoi gnôrimoi*), the men of wealth and privilege (*Politics* IV.1298b20–1; V.4.1304a25–7, 30; V.6.1305b16–17; V.7.1307a29–33; V.10.1310b12–14; V.11.1313b18). But on occasion he identifies the *dêmos*, not with the workers, but with the assembly of all citizens including the notables (see *Politics* III.1.1275b7; III.11.1282a27–9, 1282a34–9); and this is presumably what he is doing in his comment in the *Rhetoric*.

What on first reading seems to be a weakness of the simile, the likening of a group of men to a single man, turns out on further reflection to be one of its strengths. For Socrates thinks that when people gather together in a body, the body has properties of its own distinct from the properties of the individuals composing it. He claims, for example, that the *dêmos* "when it is gathered together in a body" is powerful, implying by the qualifying phrase that the power of the *dêmos* dissipates when the gathering breaks up. It is natural, then, for him to liken such a body to a single large individual.

Plato's ship will not be a good image of a Greek city unless it carries counterparts of a city's entire population including its women, children, aliens, and slaves. This may be the reason, as I suggested above, that a reference to voyagers is slipped in at the very end of the simile; for his ship will carry counterparts of no one except adult male citizens if the only ones on board are the shipowner, the steersman, and the sailors.

Since the sailors are trying to persuade the shipowner to turn the helm over to them and since the shipowner symbolizes the assembly, the helm (*pêdalion*) must symbolize a lever of power, an office, that is put into someone's hands through an action of the assembly. Though most offices at Athens were filled by sortition, a few were filled by a vote of the assembly. Of these the most important in the fifth century was the generalship, the office through which the great Athenian statesmen, Themistocles, Cimon, and Pericles, exercised their power and steered the city in the direction they wished it to go. Insofar as the helm is the image of any particular office this office must be the generalship.

The sailors on board Plato's unruly ship, whom Plato identifies with "our current political rulers" (VI.489a4–6, 489c4–7), represent ambitious men, unenlightened by philosophy, who seek political power through their rhetorical skills, the arena for the exercise of these skills being the assembly, the council, and the lawcourts (see *Gorgias* 452d5–452e4). Their claim that steersmanship is unteachable mirrors the view underlying Athenian political practices that political art (*politikê technê*) is unteachable (*Protagoras* 319a3–320b5); their idea that the man who is clever in persuading or forcing the shipowner to let them rule is skilled in steering is analogous to the idea of Gorgias that the art of persuasion is the master art (*Philebus* 58a7–58b2; *Gorgias* 452d1–453a7); and their condemnation of the true steersman as useless is the counterpart of the complaint apparently widespread in contemporary Athens that philosophers are useless (*Rep.* VI.487c4–487d5; *Gorgias* 484c4–486d1). The simile of the unruly ship is thus among other things an expression of a favorite Platonic theme: the conflict of philosophy and rhetoric (*Gorgias* 500a7–500d4).

Plato uses the politically charged word *stasiazein*, "to form a faction" or "to engage in faction," to describe the sailors' activity (thus reversing image and original, symbol and object symbolized; the nautical is supposed to symbolize the political, but the political has here intruded itself into the nautical). Although Plato characterizes faction (*stasis*) as the domestic equivalent of foreign war (*Rep.* V.470b4–9), he does not intend for the sailors' rivalry to represent full-scale civil war such as that at Corcyra during the Peloponnesian War (Thucydides 3.69–85). Killing rival sailors or throwing them overboard represents the judicial murder or banishment of political rivals through the instrumentality of the popular law courts (compare *Rep.* VIII.565e3–566a4).

The victors in this factional struggle bind "the noble shipowner hand and foot with mandragora or strong drink or in some other way" (VI.488c4–5). The epithet "noble" (*gennaios*) is ironical, as often in Plato ("noble sophistry": *Sophist*

231b8; "noble tyranny": *Rep.* VIII.544c6). Mandragora is a narcotic (Aristotle, *De somno et vigilia* 2.456b28–30). James Adam takes it and the strong drink to symbolize pleasure: "False rulers," he writes, "dull the senses of the Demos by the opiate of Pleasure" (1902, vol. II: 10 n. 19). But this does not seem right, for on this interpretation symbol and object symbolized are different sorts of thing. Mandragora and strong drink are not, like pleasure, psychological states but substances that alter a psychological state. The analogue of these substances should also be something that alters a psychological state, not the psychological state itself. Since the sailors symbolize orators, the drugs they use to befuddle the shipowner should symbolize the things orators use to befuddle the *dêmos*, namely, words, emotive words in particular, whose power is aptly described by the rhetorician Gorgias in his *Encomium of Helen*. "Some words cause pain," Gorgias writes, "others joy, some strike fear, others stir those who hear them to boldness, some by evil persuasion drug and bewitch the soul" (Gorgias, *Helen* 14).

The victorious sailors spend their time drinking and feasting rather then performing their nautical functions. The incompatibility of drinking and feasting with wisdom and virtue and the pursuit of one's vocation is a constant theme in Plato. At the end of the *Crito* the Laws tell Socrates that if he goes to Thessaly as suggested by Crito (45c2–4), he will be forced to spend his time feasting rather than conversing about justice and the rest of virtue (53d1–54b1); and in the *Seventh Letter*, assuming its authenticity, Plato expresses his disgust with the drinking and feasting he observed on his first visit to Italy and Sicily and claims that such drinking and feasting is incompatible with a well-run city and with wisdom, temperance, or any other part of virtue (*Epistle* VII.326b5–326d6). In the *Republic* Socrates asserts that the farmers and potters in this ideal city will not be zealous farmers and potters if they are allowed to spend their time drinking and feasting (IV.420d5–421a2), refers to the "leaden weights, which becoming attached to foods and similar pleasures and gluttonies bend the vision of the soul downwards" (VII.519a1–3), and associates always feasting with inexperience of reason and virtue (IX.586a1–2).

The political analogue of the sailors' drinking and feasting can be inferred from a famous passage in the *Gorgias* where feasting is used as an elaborate metaphor: "You praise men," Socrates says to Callicles, "who have entertained these people and feasted them with what they had an appetite for. And people say that these men have made the city great; but that it is swollen and festering within because of those early leaders [i.e. Themistocles, Cimon, and Pericles], they don't perceive. For without regard to temperance and justice they have filled the city full of harbors and dockyards and walls and tribute and similar nonsense" (518e2–519a4). E. R. Dodds refers to this passage as Socrates' "magnificent dismissal of all the glories of Periclean Athens as so much trash" (1959: 365) – a bit of an overstatement since, as Dodds himself acknowledges (p. 33), Socrates' list of works does not include such glories as the Parthenon. The list focuses, not on art and architecture, but on projects that increased the wealth of Athens and along with it the wealth of many Athenian citizens. The reason for this focus is that wealth facilitates the satisfaction of the appetites for food, drink, and sex (*Rep.* IX.580e2–581a1). The drinking and feasting of the sailors symbolizes, then, not drinking and feasting itself, but the pursuit of projects that generate the wealth needed for drinking and feasting.

The true steersman, Plato says, must "pay attention to year and seasons and sky and stars and winds and all that belongs to his art" (*Rep.* VI.488d5–7; see also VII.527d2–4). He is a sky-gazer, not just a star-gazer, since, as befits a steersman as distinct from an astronomer, he gazes at things in the sky (*ta meteóra*), not just stars (Guthrie 1975: 431 n. 3). Though Socrates does not spell it out when he interprets the Ship of State simile, gazing at things in the sky symbolizes apprehending the Forms. This is made explicit when the imagery of sky and stars recurs in the allegory of the Cave (VII.514a–518b). The released prisoner, when he emerges from the cave, is blinded by the light and first looks at shadows, then at images of men and other things in water, then at the things themselves; when he turns to the sky, he looks at the stars and the moon at night before attempting to glimpse the sun; finally he is able to see the sun and to infer that it is the cause of the seasons and the years (VII.516a5–516c2). As Socrates explains, the physical journey of the released prisoner from the cave to the upper region corresponds to the intellectual journey of the soul from the sensible to the intelligible realm; the objects in the upper region correspond to Forms; and the sun corresponds to the Form of the Good (VII.517a8–517c5, 532a1–532d1). The image of sky and stars and wind links the Ship of State with the Sun and the Cave and thus with the central metaphysical ideas of the *Republic*.

The Ship of State differs from the Sun and the Cave in one important respect. In depicting the Sun and the Cave Plato is attempting to illuminate his Theory of Forms, not arguing for it: that the generation (*genesis*) of sensible objects is due to the sun (VI.509b2–4) provides no grounds for thinking that the being (*ousia*) of intelligible objects is due to the Form of the Good (VI.509b6–10). The Ship of State, on the other hand, is argumentative as well as illustrative; it is not only an analogy but also an argument from analogy. One argument that is implicit in the simile, for example, is that just as a shipowner should not surrender the helm of his ship to a person who is ignorant of steersmanship, so the citizenry should not surrender the leadership of their city to a person who is ignorant of statesmanship (see Xenophon, *Memorabilia* 1.2.9).

The voyagers on the unruly ship call the true steersman a "sky-gazer and idle babbler" (*meteóroskopos te kai adoleschés*) (*Rep.* VI.488e4–489a1). These, or their close cousins, are the epithets popularly associated with Socrates during his lifetime. In Aristophanes' lampoon of Socrates in the *Clouds*, Socrates is referred to as a "sky-sophist" (*meteórosophistés*) (line 360) and his teaching as "idle babble" (*adoleschia*) (line 1480). In Xenophon's *Oeconomicus* Socrates mentions his reputation as a person expected to babble (*adoleschein*) (XI.3), and in Xenophon's *Symposium* he is called "a thinker on things in the sky" (*tôn meteôrôn phrontistês*) (VI.6). In Plato's dialogues the disposition of contemporary Athenians to attach the two epithets to Socrates is mentioned or alluded to repeatedly. In the *Apology* Socrates refers to his reputation as "a thinker about things in the sky" (*ta meteôra phrontistês*) (18b7); in the *Phaedo* he says that no one listening, not even a comic poet, would say that he was babbling (*adoleschô*) (70d10–70c1); and in the *Theaetetus* he calls himself a "babbler" (*adoleschês*) (195b10, 195c1–2). In the *Politicus* the epithets are associated with Socrates indirectly. On the paranoid ship of the *Politicus* there is a law allowing the true steersman, this time called a "sky-prattler, a babbling sophist" (*meteôrologos, adoleschês sophistês*) (299b7–8), to be indicted for corrupting the young and encouraging them in steersmanship (299b8–299c1). This is a clear allusion to the later and earlier charges against Socrates (Campbell 1867: 153); for corrupting the young was part of the indictment of Meletus (*Apology* 24b8–24c1), while teaching others about things in the heavens, the analogue of encouraging people in steersmanship, was among the "first" charges, going back at least a quarter of a century to the production of the *Clouds* (*Apology* 19b4–19c2).

That the voyagers on the unruly ship apply the same epithets to the true steersman as Socrates' countrymen applied to *him* suggests that Plato intends his readers to identify the two, that he takes Socrates to be a prime example of what the true steersman stands for: a true philosopher. By this identification, argued for at length by W. K. C. Guthrie, the message of the simile is that true philosophers such as Socrates are useless in cities because they are regarded as sky-gazers and idle babblers rather than as the philosopher-statesmen they are (Guthrie 1969: 364, 374; 1975: 431, 499). If Plato intends to cast Socrates in the role of true philosopher, he has good reason to indicate this indirectly through symbols rather than by a direct statement. A direct statement would have to be put into the mouth of Socrates or one of his interlocutors. But it would be boastful and tasteless for Socrates to make such a claim himself (see *Charmides* 158d4–5), and his interlocutors lack the ability to recognize a true philosopher.

There is a problem, however, in casting Socrates in such a role: it is inconsistent with his portrayal in the *Republic*. By the theory of the *Republic* a true philosopher must have knowledge of the Form of the Good (VII.540a4–540c2), and Socrates disclaims such knowledge. When asked to give an account of the good, he demurs, denying knowledge of it – "Do you think it is right," he asks, "to speak about things one does not know as if one knew?" – and offers instead a story of an offspring of the good (VI.506b2–506e5). Like Moses (Deut. 32: 48–52), Socrates views but never enters the Promised Land (contrary to Kahn 1996: 100). Plato's concept of a philosopher has become so lofty that his chief spokesman no longer qualifies. The true philosophers of the *Republic* are in fact not philosophers at all, as Diotima explains the concept in the *Symposium*. Repeating a lesson he says he learned from Diotima (*Symposium* 201e3–7),

Socrates claims that one desires, or loves, not what one has, but what one lacks (199e6–200b3). From this premise Diotima in her speech infers that no one who is wise, who is *sophos*, is a lover of wisdom, a *philosophos*. The gods in particular, being wise, are not lovers of wisdom. A lover of wisdom is one who is not wise but desires to become wise, the prime example for Diotima being that intermediary between gods and men, the daimon Eros, the symbol of Socrates himself (*Symposium* 203e4–204b5; see also *Lysis* 218a2–218b1 and *Phaedrus* 278d3–6). There are thus two concepts of philosophy in Plato: the love of wisdom of the *Symposium*, which we might dub "daimonic" philosophy, and the wisdom of the *Republic* that comes with knowledge of the good, which we might call "godlike" philosophy. The philosopher-kings of Plato's ideal city are godlike philosophers and are even called wise (*sophoi*) (*Rep.* VIII.546a8, 547e1). Socrates, who denies that he is wise (*Apology* 21d2–7, 38c3–4; *Theaetetus* 150c8–150d1), is consistently portrayed in the *Republic* and in the other dialogues in which he appears as a daimonic, never as a godlike, philosopher. Consequently, if the true philosopher symbolized by the true steersman is a godlike philosopher and if his epithets nevertheless allude to Socrates, the moral of the simile must be that godlike philosophers would be as useless in cities as the daimonic philosopher Socrates was in Athens since, like Socrates, they would be regarded as sky-gazers and idle babblers rather than as the philosopher-statesmen they are. It is true that in the *Gorgias* Socrates claims to be a true statesman (521d6–8); but his explanation of this claim makes it clear that he is not claiming to be a true statesman in the sense of the *Republic*. His claim is only to have a correct system of values (Gorgias 521d8–521e1; see also *Apology* 29d7–30b4, and Dodds 1959: 355).

Having been plied with drink or drugs, the shipowner forgets that his goal is to make money by transporting goods and passengers from one port to another and acquiesces in the folly of the unruly sailors, if he does not actively share in it (for the goal of the shipowner see *Gorgias* 467d1–5 and Aristotle, *Nicomachean Ethics* VIII.9.1160a14–16). Their folly is to consume the ship's cargo in drinking and feasting and "to sail as such men might be expected to sail" (*Rep.* VI.488c4–7). How might they be expected to sail? The sailors seem to vie for the helm simply to enjoy steering, not because they are intent on sailing somewhere; and since they do not know how to steer, the fate of the ship when the winds shift or a storm comes up or night falls is easily imagined. The folly in which the intoxicated shipowner acquiesces or shares is costing him his livelihood and may cost him his life. Though it may seem good to him at the moment, it is not really good for him.

This distinction between what seems good and what is good, between the apparent and the real good, plays a central role in Plato's argument against Athenian democracy and for philosopher-kings. The untrained and unqualified steersman is an image of an uneducated (*apaideutos*) ruler. What seems good to the citizenry while they are under the influence of the intoxicating words of such a man – in the Athenian assembly, for example – is not their real good. Such rulers are bound to fail, Socrates says, because "they do not have one single mark at which they aim in doing everything that they do in private and in public life" (*Rep.* VII.519c3–5), implying that there is one single mark at which the true statesman aims. This mark, Socrates maintains, is the Form of the Good (VI.505d11–509b10), knowledge of which is attained only by true philosophers after a long and rigorous education (VII.519c8–10, 534b8–534c5, 540a4–9). Furthermore, as Socrates points out, "no one is content to possess things that only seem good (*ta dokounta agatha*), but they seek things that are really good (*ta onta agatha*)" (VI.505d5–10). If we suppose that a person who seeks an end also seeks the means to that end, it follows that people really seek to be ruled by philosopher-kings.

We are now in a position to evaluate a well-known criticism of Plato's simile. In a famous article Renford Bambrough claims that Plato in this simile "takes the crucial step in the wrong direction when he draws a parallel between a governor's choice of a policy and a navigator's setting of a course." He thinks that "Plato represents a question about what is to be done (as an end) as if it were very like a question about what is to be done (as a means) in order to achieve some given or agreed end" (1956: 105). Michael Walzer rejects Plato's analogy for the same reason. "[W]e entrust ourselves to the navigator," he says, "only after we have decided where we want to go; and that, rather than the setting of a particular course, is the decision that best illuminates the exercise of power" (1983: 286). The criticism is that Plato confounds questions about ultimate objectives with questions about how such objectives are to be reached. Plato's analogy between ship and state breaks down, so it is argued, because a steersman deals with the latter sort of question – how to reach a given destination – whereas a ruler deals with the former sort; what the destination is to be. Plato's true statesman, Bambrough claims, "is like a navigator who is not content to accept the fares of his passengers or the fee of his master, and then to conduct them where they wish to go, but who insists on going beyond his professional scope by prescribing the route and the destination as well as the course by which the route can best be traversed and the destination most suitably reached" (1956: 105). By formulating his criticism in terms of the image itself, Bambrough provides an easy test of its cogency. We need only ask whether Plato's true steersman is like Bambrough's imperious navigator. That he is not should be clear. Plato's true steersman, were he to win the helm of the unruly ship, would sail, not for a destination of his own choosing, but for the very one the shipowner wishes to reach. The shipowner will not reach it without him, for in his state of intoxication he appears to have forgotten his destination and the profit to be made by transporting cargo to it. The only one aboard who has not forgotten is the true steersman. This is a perfect image of Athenian democracy and of the true philosopher as Plato conceives them. Leading lives focused on bodily gratification, the citizens of Athens, Plato believes, are unaware of their real good. The only one who knows it and knows how to reach it is the true philosopher, whom they spurn. The image of the unruly ship may be a hostile political cartoon of Athenian democracy, but the political philosophy it encapsulates does not confuse ends and means. The issue turns rather on Plato's notion that what people really seek is their real good. In nautical terms the issue is whether a shipowner should prefer a steersman who will stay the course and sober him up should he get drunk over one who will plot a circular course and join the festivities should the shipowner in a state of intoxication decide to sail in circles and to consume his cargo in eating and drinking.

The Normal Ship

Just as Plato takes his unruly ship to be an image of Athenian democracy so he takes a normal merchant ship, steered and captained by a competent, or "true," steersman, to be an image of an ideal city, referred to once as "the beautiful city" (*hê kallipolis*) (VII.527c2). On a normal ship the steersman's authority derives from his knowledge of steersmanship; he does not need and does not use a book of rules, since his own knowledge of seafaring is superior to anything that can be learned from such a rule-book (*Politicus* 296e4–297a2); and he rules, insofar as he is a steersman,[13] not in his own interest, but in that of his ship and his sailors (*Rep.* I.342e2–4). Similarly, the authority of the rulers of Plato's ideal city is based on their knowledge of the political art (*Politicus* 297a3–5, 300c9–300d2); they rule without law (*Politicus* 293c5–294a4; *Laws* IX.875c3–875d2); and they rule, insofar as they are rulers, not in their own interest, but in that of their subjects (*Rep.* I.342e6–11, 345d5–345e2; *Laws* IX.875a5–875b1). This is as far as Plato develops the analogy. Further details he leaves for his reader to supply from his description and interpretation of the unruly ship. We may infer that the owner of a well-run ship is not under the influence of intoxicants, that he has not forgotten that his goal is to make a profit by transporting goods from one port to another, and that his sailors stick to their own jobs and do not try to supplant the steersman. Since the workers of Kallipolis are referred to collectively as a *dêmos* (*Rep.* V.463a1–463b3), the shipowner can remain a symbol of the *dêmos* if the word is taken in its narrow, rather than its broad, sense. The sailors can no longer represent "our current political rulers" (VI.489a4–6, 489c4–7); but, as subordinates of the steersman, they are good analogues of Plato's auxiliaries. On one interpretation, then, the steersman, sailors, and shipowner on a normal ship correlate precisely with the rulers, warriors, and workers of Kallipolis.

The sobriety of a shipowner may be due merely to the absence of intoxicants on his ship, but it may also be due to his temperance. The absence of intoxicating substances symbolizes the absence of the intoxicating words of demagogues in Kallipolis. The temperance of the shipowner, if his sobriety is due to temperance, would symbolize the virtue of the *dêmos*.

But do the workers of Kallipolis have any virtues? Some scholars think not. John Cooper claims that "Plato consistently restricts justice, as a virtue of individuals, to those who possess within themselves *knowledge* of what it is best to do and be" (1997: 20, emphasis his). Since in Plato's view only philosophers have such knowledge, workers cannot on Cooper's interpretation be just. Jonathan Lear makes a similar claim. He says that "Plato does not believe the appetitive person [i.e. a worker] has the *virtue* of temperance" (1997: 75, emphasis his). Both claims are demonstratively false. Though the workers of Kallipolis do not have *true* virtue, with wisdom (*alêthês aretê, meta phronêseôs*) (*Phaedo* 69b3; see also *Theaetetus* 176c5; *Symposium* 212a5–6; *Rep.* VIII.554e5), they do have virtue of an inferior grade, called "demotic" virtue (*dêmotikê aretê*: literally, virtue of the *dêmos*), which comes from habituation without philosophy and reason.

We meet a person with such virtue in the final pages of the *Republic*. In the myth of Er the first discarnate soul to choose the life it is to enter in the next cycle of reincarnation foolishly chooses the greatest tyranny. "He was one of those who had come from heaven," Socrates explains, "having lived under an orderly constitution during his former life and having participated in virtue by habituation without philosophy" (X.619c6–619d1). In the *Phaedo*, again in a story of transmigration, this inferior grade of virtue (which in this dialogue earns its possessor reincarnation as a social insect) is defined in almost exactly the same words, given a name, and particularized as temperance and justice. Of the discarnate souls that do not love wisdom the happiest, Socrates claims, are "those who have practiced demotic and political virtue (*tên dêmotikên kaì politikên aretên*), which they call temperance and justice, and which comes from habituation and practice without philosophy and reason" (*Phaedo* 82a11–82b3).

Demotic virtue is referred to by name only once in the *Republic*, when Socrates describes a philosopher who uses the Forms of temperance and justice as a craftsman uses a model to shape the characters of men. "If a necessity should be laid on [a philosopher who has seen the Forms] to practice putting into the characters of men both individually and collectively (*kai idia(i) kaì dêmosia(i)*) what he sees there and not to mold himself alone, do you think," Socrates asks, "he will be a bad craftsman of temperance and justice and of the whole of demotic virtue (*dêmotikês aretês*)?" (VI.500d4–8). The two words on the stem *dêmo-* indicate that the men whose characters are being molded are members of the *dêmos* rather than future warriors or rulers, a conclusion buttressed by the fact that the specific virtues mentioned – temperance and justice – are precisely the ones a philosopher-ruler would want to cultivate in the *dêmos*.

Those who have acquired the demotic virtues of temperance and justice have escaped from the slavery of uncontrolled appetite (for which see IX.577c1–577e3). In the allegory of the Cave, which is among other things an allegory about justice (VII.517d4–517e2), they are symbolized by the people who have been released from their bonds (*desmoi*) and been turned towards the fire (VII.515c4–515d8). This has sometimes been doubted, most notably by Terence Irwin (1995: 276), on the ground that the lower classes of Kallipolis to whom the philosopher returns when he is sent back into the cave after apprehending the Form of the Good are referred to by the word *desmôtas* ("prisoners," VII.519d5), a word that has so far been used only of those in bonds (VII.514b4, 515a4, 516e9). But this point is not decisive. For between the earlier and the later occurrences of the word the cave has been called a prison (*desmôtêrion*, 517b2), and *desmôtês* can refer to someone in prison (*en desmôtêriô(i)*) as easily as to someone in bonds (*en desmois*). Those who possess demotic virtue, though unbound, are still of course in prison.

Let us turn now to the relation of the shipowner to the steersman. The goal of steersmanship is safety while sailing (*sôtêria en tô(i) plein*) (I.346a8). Since their safety is in the steersman's hands, the shipowner and everyone else on board a normal ship willingly obey him (see Xenophon, *Memorabilia* 3.9.11). The relation of *dêmos* to ruler in Kallipolis is supposed to be similar. We are told that whereas in many cities the *dêmos* calls the rulers masters (*despotai*) and the rulers in turn call them slaves (*douloi*), in Kallipolis the *dêmos* calls the rulers saviors (*sôtêres*) and auxiliaries (V.463a1–463b9). The question that must be answered at once is whether the *dêmos* calls its rulers saviors rather than masters in spite of being slaves. For that is what a notorious passage in Book IX seems to imply. In this passage Socrates says that servile employment and handicraft (*banausia kai cheirotechnia*) earn reproach "when someone is weak by nature in his best part, so that it is not able to rule the beasts within him" (IX.590c2–5). Such a person needs, he says, to be ruled by the sort of thing that rules the best man and to be a slave (*doulos*) of the man who has within himself a divine ruler: "it is better for everyone to be ruled by a divine and wise ruler, preferably having his own within himself, but failing that imposed from outside, in order that as far as possible we may all be alike and friends, steered (*kubernômenoi*) by the same [steersman]" (IX.590c8–590d6). Socrates is sometimes interpreted as saying that the rational part of those who are suited by nature to be workers is too weak to rule their appetites and that workers should therefore be slaves of those in whom reason rules. Citing the passage before us Irwin, for example, writes:

> Plato argues that the best thing is to be ruled by one's own reason and wisdom, but if this is not possible, the next-best thing is to be ruled by someone else's reason and wisdom; this second condition is the one Plato intends for the lower classes in the ideal city (*R.* 590c2–d6). [Plato] neither says nor implies that the wisdom and reason of the ruler guides the subject through the subject's own reason and wisdom; this is not surprising, since he never suggests that the members of the lower classes are ruled by their own rational parts. (1995: 351, transposing "best" and "next-best" to correct an obvious typographical error)

Irwin does not take the further step and claim that the lower classes of Kallipolis are slaves of their rulers; but this step, not a very great step given the mention of slavery by Socrates himself, is taken by Gregory Vlastos and by W. L. Newman in his great commentary on Aristotle's *Politics*. For Vlastos the relation of ruler to worker in Plato's ideal city is "idealized slavery" (1995: 92); for Newman it is literal slavery (1887: 109–10).

The interpretation of all three scholars goes far beyond the text. To begin with, Socrates makes no claim about the lower classes in general. The *dêmos* includes farmers as well as artisans (*banausoi*) and handicraftsmen (*cheirotechnai*) (*Rep*. IV.420e1–421a2; Aristotle, *Politics* IV.3.1289b32–3, IV.4.1291b17–28, VI.7.1321a5–6); and it seems unlikely that Plato means to count them as handicraftsmen or include them by synecdoche, since Socrates is explaining the social stigma attached to servile employment and handicraft, and in ancient Greece little attached to farming, probably because farmers owned land and served as hoplites (Aristotle, *Politics* IV.6.1292b25–6, VI.4.1318b9–12, IV.4.1291a30–1). (For the social stigma attached to the crafts see *Rep*. VI.495c8–495e8; Xenophon, *Oeconomicus* IV.2–3; and Aristotle, *Politics* VIII.2.1337b8–15.) Furthermore, Socrates does not even claim that artisans and handicraftsmen usually have weak rational parts. He does not say that servile employment and handicraft earn reproach *because* the artisan or handicraftsman has a weak rational part; he says he earns reproach *when* (*hotan*) he has a weak rational part. (One might wonder, too, whether Plato, so acutely conscious of good taste and good manners, not to mention filial piety, would put such a claim into the mouth of a son of a midwife [*Theaetetus* 149a1–2] and a stonemason [Guthrie 1969: 378, n. 2].) And, finally, Socrates does not exclude the possibility of strengthening a person's rational part relative to his appetites by habituation and practice (on this point see Kraut 1973: 216–18). Indeed, this possibility is exactly what the immediately following passage on the government of children seems to envisage. Children are not allowed to be free, Socrates says, "until we establish a constitution in them as in a city and, by fostering their best [part] by means of the like [part] in us, establish as a surrogate a similar guardian and ruler in the child – only then do we set it free" (*Rep*. IX.590e2–591a3). These children are not said to be children only of the upper classes. Moreover, it is difficult to understand what demotic virtue could be if it is not the sort of internal constitution to which Socrates refers (for which see also IX.591e1). It seems reasonable to conclude, then, that the passage under discussion makes no claim about the mental endowment of the lower classes, implies nothing about the free or slave status of the workers of Kallipolis, and does not conflict with the earlier characterization of the relation of the rulers to the *dêmos* in the ideal city as non-despotic. The workers become slaves of their rulers only upon the downfall of the ideal city and the rise of timocracy (VIII.547c1–3).

In believing that their rulers are not their masters the workers of Kallipolis are not deceived. But in calling their rulers "saviors" the workers are expressing an evaluation of their rulers that goes beyond their belief that their rulers are not despots: one who is not a master need not be a savior. That the workers' evaluation is correct may, for the sake of argument, be conceded. But the question arises, even given this concession, whether they have a rational basis for believing that their rulers are their saviors or whether, as a result of indoctrination, they are simply mouthing the rulers' own self-evaluation. If they do not have a rational basis, there is an important disanalogy between ship and city. For a shipowner, after a few voyages in various types of weather, will be able to make his own evaluation of his steersman's skill in commanding the crew, plying the steering oars, and navigating from one port to the next; he will not be dependent upon his steersman's own self-evaluation. Before we can answer this question about the workers, however, we need to know the content of their evaluation. What are the rulers saviors of? We are told in the *Republic* only that they are saviors of their city and of its constitution and laws (IV.425e3–4, V.465d8, VI.502d1–2), and the workers probably have something more concrete in mind than this.

We find a detailed list of the goods associated with statesmanship in the *Euthydemus:*

Then the other works, which someone might say belong to statesmanship – these perhaps would be many, such as making the citizens wealthy and free and factionless – all these appeared neither bad nor good; but [statesmanship] had to make [the citizens] wise and give them a share of knowledge, if this was to be the [art] that benefited them and made them happy. (292b4–292c1)

According to this passage the five goods at which statesmen aim are wealth, freedom, domestic tranquility, wisdom, and happiness. The corresponding evils from which statesmen are supposed to save their subjects are thus foreign domination, faction (*stasis*), poverty, folly, and wretchedness. The one other such list of the goals of statesmanship in the dialogues, the thrice-reiterated triad of freedom, friendship, and intelligence (*Laws* III.693b3–5, 693d7–693e1, 701d7–9), is a subset of the list of five – friendship, or *philia*, the opposite of faction (*First Alcibiades* 126c1–3; *Rep.* I.351d4–6, IV.442c10–442d1), being the same thing as absence of faction. The first three items of the list of five, it is claimed, are goods (and hence legitimate goals of statesmanship) only when they are under the control of wisdom (*Euthydemus* 281d2–281e1), which is sought in its turn as the source of happiness (282a1–7, 282c8–282d2, 292e4–5). The primary aim, the final end, of statesmanship is thus happiness, even though Plato omits it from the list of three and sometimes says that statesmanship has a single aim: virtue (*Laws* XII.963a2–963b3; see also *Gorgias* 502d10–503b3, 513e5–7, 515b8–515c3). (For happiness as the goal of statesmanship see, among other places, *Rep.* IV.419a1–421c6, V.465e4–466a6, VI.500e2–4, VII.519e1–3, 541a4–6; *Politicus* 301d4–6, 311b7–311c6; *Laws* III.683b3–4, 697a10–697b2, IV.710b4–7, 718b3–5, V.742d7–742e1, VI.781b4–6, XII.945d1–4.) When the lower classes in Kallipolis call their rulers saviors, what they principally have in mind, then, is that their rulers are saviors of their happiness.

But are they in a position to recognize a savior of happiness? Wealth, freedom, and domestic tranquility – saviors of these are not difficult to recognize. Saviors of happiness are more problematic. For Plato believes that there is true and false, genuine and illusory, happiness (*Rep.* V.466b7–8; see also III.406c7, IV.420a6, IX.591d8, and *Sophist* 230e3); and if the lower classes are unable to distinguish the two, they will be incapable of evaluating the success of their rulers in giving them what they really want, which is true happiness. To see the problem we must briefly examine Plato's conception of happiness. Plato thinks that happiness consists in the possession and use of good things (*Euthydemus* 280b5–6; *Symposium* 202c10–11, 205a1; *First Alcibiades* 116b7; *Laws* I.631b3–6) where the good things are reason, temperance, justice, bravery, health, beauty, strength, and wealth (*Laws* I.631b6–631d2; see also *Euthydemus* 279a1–279c4). He thinks that some of these goods are by nature better than others, that there is a natural hierarchy of goods with reason at the head and the other goods following in the order of the list above (*Laws* I.631d1–2, IX.870b5); and he thinks that true happiness consists, not only in possessing good things, but in ranking them according to the natural hierarchy. Most people, Plato believes, rank the various goods according to a popular hierarchy that is almost the reverse of the natural hierarchy (*Apology* 29d7–30b4; *Rep.* II.364a1–364b2, VIII.550e1–8; *Laws* II.661a4–661b4). Subscribing to the popular hierarchy, they have a mistaken conception of happiness and falsely believe that a ruler who pursues the goods at the foot of the natural hierarchy at the expense of those at its head, who makes his city wealthy and powerful by ignoring justice and temperance, is a true statesmen (*Gorgias* 518e2–519a7; *Laws* V.742d2–7). Their mistaken conception of happiness blinds them to true statesmanship and renders them incapable of recognizing a savior of genuine happiness.

Are the workers of Kallipolis similarly blind? Do they, like the citizens of Athens, rank wealth over virtue? Not on the interpretation I have been offering. Such a belief would be inconsistent with their demotic virtue. The person who is demotically temperate has been habituated to believe that reason should rule, rather than merely serve, the appetites (*Rep.* IV.442c10–442d1); and to believe this is to rank temperance above wealth (see *Laws* II.653a5–653c4), the means by which the appetites are satisfied (*Rep.* IX.580e5–581a1). In the allegory of the Cave those with demotic virtue correspond to the unbound prisoners who are compelled to turn their heads toward the fire (VII.515c4–515d4). The turning around symbolizes, among other things, the reorientation of their system of values.[14]

It seems, then, that the lower classes in Kallipolis have as firm a basis for evaluating their rulers as a shipowner has for evaluating his steersman. A shipowner need not know how to steer or how to choose a steersman to recognize that his life has been saved by his steersman's skill. Similarly, the lower classes in Kallipolis need not know how to rule or how to choose a ruler to recognize that their happiness is due to their rulers' skill. Their belief that their rulers are the saviors of their happiness is an inference from a correct conception of happiness and true beliefs about the effectiveness of their rulers in fostering the things that constitute true happiness such as justice and temperance. Although their conception of happiness, being a part of their demotic virtue, is implanted in their souls by habituation (X.606a8, 619c7), their true beliefs about their rulers' effectiveness is a matter of their own experience. Thus, when they call their rulers their saviors, they are not simply mouthing their rulers' own self-evaluation.[15]

The *dêmos* of Kallipolis obeys its rulers willingly just as the shipowner on a normal ship obeys the steersman willingly. To this extent Kallipolis is like a normal ship. But on a normal ship the steersman works for the shipowner and can be discharged by him at his pleasure or at the end of their contract; if he refused to relinquish his job at the behest of the shipowner, the shipowner could have him removed from his ship by force. Should the *dêmos* in Kallipolis tire of its rulers, however, it is powerless to replace them. The analogy of ship and city breaks down at this crucial point. The authority of the rulers of Kallipolis stems from their knowledge rather than from those they govern (for the authority of knowledge see *Laws* III.690b8–690c3); but the simile implies the reverse, that their authority should derive from the *dêmos*, that they should be elected by it and serve at its pleasure or for a fixed term, an idea that Plato accepts only for his second-best city of the *Laws* (VI.751a1–768e3). Kallipolis resembles, not a merchantman carrying its owner, but a naval vessel with a brilliant and charismatic captain, who is willingly obeyed by his crew, though not selected by or answerable to it.

This should be a matter of concern for the *dêmos* of Kallipolis. For the authority its rulers exercise over it, like the authority of a naval captain over his crew, includes the authority to enforce authority by the use of force. So little is said in the *Republic* about the use of force within the borders of Kallipolis that a reader might form the impression that it is entirely absent. But several remarks made in passing indicate that it is always in reserve (V.465a8–10, VII.519e4); and the warriors are explicitly given the task, not only of defending the city against external aggressors, but of enforcing the laws against internal transgressors (III.415d8–415e3). Since the authority of the rulers to use force stems from their knowledge, not from the *dêmos*, one would expect the *dêmos* to fare poorly when knowledge falters, an expectation born out by Plato's account of constitutional decline. For when aristocracy changes into timocracy owing to a fatal miscalculation by the rulers of the ideal city, and the rulership passes from philosophers to warriors, the *dêmos* is immediately enslaved (VIII.547b7–547c4).

Choosing a Steersman

The owner of the unruly ship does a bad job of choosing a steersman. How does Plato think a steersman should be chosen? He never says, though we get a clue from Aristotle. In the *Politics* Aristotle examines an argument that addresses this very question and that seems to be Platonic. According to this argument the election and audit of officials should not be in the hands of the mass because "choosing correctly is a job for those who know: for example, choosing a geometer is a job for those proficient in geometry, and choosing a steersman is a job for those who are good at steering" (*Politics* III.11.1282a7–14). Although Plato never expresses the idea quite so clearly and succinctly, he says something similar at *Charmides* 171a3–171c10 using a physician rather than a steersman or a geometer as his example; so perhaps it is not too bold to refer to the idea as the Platonic maxim. Aristotle introduces the maxim only to question it, and to question it, surprisingly enough, on Platonic grounds. In the tenth book of the *Republic* Plato claims that the user is a better judge of a product than its maker, that a flute-player knows whether a given flute is good or bad whereas a flute-maker has at most a correct belief about its quality (X.601d1–602a2). In the same vein Aristotle notes that "a steersman is a better judge of a steering oar than a carpenter" (*Politics* III.11.1282a17–23; see Plato, *Cratylus* 390d1–2) and implies, contrary to the Platonic maxim, that a shipowner in turn is a better judge of a steersman than other steersmen. In defense of the maxim a Platonist would reply that a steersman is neither a maker nor a counterpart of a maker. He is not even a counterpart because (according to *Republic* X) user is to maker as knowledge is to correct belief, and it is not the case that a shipowner knows, whereas a steersman has at most correct beliefs, about sailing.

Let us turn, then, to the use of the Platonic maxim in choosing a philosopher-king. One notices right off that the fact that normal merchantmen exist and ideal cities do not leads to a problem in the use of the maxim in choosing philosopher-kings that does not arise when steersmen choose steersmen. Steersmanship is a skill that is passed down from one generation to another, and younger steersmen can be chosen by older steersmen in accordance with the Platonic maxim. Similarly, once the ideal city has been founded and is up and running, new philosopher-kings can to be chosen by their predecessors, by other philosopher-kings, in accordance with the Platonic maxim (VII.519c8–521b11; VIII.546d3–4). But since Kallipolis does not yet exist, Plato faces the problem of its foundation and of the initial philosopher-king. Where does he come from and how is it founded? Well, Plato imagines that someone who is in line to inherit a kingship is born with a philosophic nature – a golden soul – and through luck receives a good education and becomes a philosopher; in due course he inherits the kingship, declares himself a philosopher-king, and proceeds to found Kallipolis by, among other things, deporting everyone over 10 years old (VI.502a5–502b6, VII.540e5–541a1). As this envisaged deportation indicates, the claim to be a philosopher as well as a king is for Plato a substantive claim with revolutionary consequences. So we must ask, Who validated the claim of the initial king to be a philosopher?

The question arises not because of any self-doubt on the part of the king himself. To be a true philosopher one must apprehend the Form of the Good, and it would seem impossible to apprehend the Form of the Good without knowing that one has apprehended it. Thus, worry over whether or not one is a true philosopher would seem to be incompatible with being a true philosopher. But the initial philosopher-king cannot carry out his revolution all by himself; he will need supporters. Let us suppose that the newly enthroned philosopher-king orders one of his rational and conscientious lieutenants, who, like Socrates (*Crito* 49a4–49b8), wishes to treat no one unjustly, to aid in the deportation of everyone over 10. Let us also suppose that the family is a basic institution under the old regime and that, consequently, separating children from their parents is regarded under it as the height of injustice. Our Socratic lieutenant, balanced between the old and the new regimes and their different conceptions of justice, will be in a quandary. Should he disobey the king and refuse to participate in an action that, from the standpoint of the old regime, is a gross injustice? Or should he believe the new king when he tells him that the revolution will inaugurate an ideal society and a higher standard of justice? The answer to these questions will depend upon whether the king's claim to be a true philosopher can be validated. How is this to be done?

There are only three possibilities. The lieutenant can rely on his own judgment, the king's self-evaluation, or the evaluation of a third party. Realizing that a powerful man to whom everyone defers easily develops an inflated opinion of his own ability, our Socratic lieutenant will be skeptical of the king's self-evaluation. The self-deception of those in positions of power is of course a major theme in the dialogues from the *Apology* to the *Laws*. In the *Apology* Socrates relates how in attempting to understand the oracle's declaration that no one is wiser than he, he sought out a politician with a reputation for wisdom, engaged him in conversation, and discovered that he did not know what he thought he knew (*Apology* 21b1–22a6); and in the *Republic* he remarks, in reference to those who are deceived by the praise of the many into thinking that they are true statesmen, that it is impossible for a man who does not know how to measure not to believe he is six feet tall when many others who also do not know how assure him that he is (IV.426d4–426e3). Our Socratic lieutenant will fear that the king suffers from such twofold ignorance and, in the words of the Athenian Stranger, "is gripped not only by ignorance but also by a [false] belief in his own wisdom, believing that he has complete knowledge of things about which he knows nothing" (*Laws* IX.863c4–6).

Not trusting the king's self-evaluation, our lieutenant might decide to consult a third party. Faithful to the Platonic maxim, he seeks a true philosopher. But are there any to be found? If the lieutenant lives in the fifth century BC, he would surely consider Socrates. But if the argument earlier in this paper is correct, Socrates is not a true philosopher. The lieutenant needs someone philosophically superior to Socrates. The only philosopher who is presented in the dialogues as even an equal of Socrates is Parmenides. Though Parmenides is reported to have made laws for the citizens of Elea (Diogenes Laertius IX.23), his credentials as an expert on statesmanship are otherwise unknown. Our lieutenant may be hard pressed to find a qualified consultant if he lives in the fifth century. If he lives in the fourth century, he might consider a visit to Plato's Academy and a chat with Plato or Aristotle. But Aristotle can be ruled out at once. He is certainly not a true philosopher in the sense of the *Republic*; not only has he not apprehended the Form of the Good, he does not even believe it exists (*Eudemion Ethics* I.8.1218a33–4, *Nicomachean Ethics* I.6). So our lieutenant is left with Plato himself. It would be presumptuous to deny that Plato is a true philosopher. Conceding his philosophical credentials, the lieutenant might still not trust his judgment given the failure of his political adventures in Syracuse. (The Platonic maxim gives a necessary, not a sufficient, condition of correct choice.) In the end, it seems, our lieutenant must rely on his own judgment.

His situation resembles that of Socrates in some of the shorter Socratic dialogues. Though the lieutenant is not a possessor of wisdom, we may imagine that, like Socrates, he is a lover of wisdom. His encounter with a king who wishes to enlist him in a revolutionary project involving activities that are unjust from the standpoint of received morality resembles Socrates' encounter with Euthyphro, whose prosecution of his own father for homicide seems impious from such a standpoint (*Euthyphro* 3e4–5a2). And his need to ascertain whether or not the king is a true philosopher, and hence wiser than he, resembles Socrates' quest for a solution of the riddle about no one being wiser than Socrates (*Apology* 20c4–23c1). This suggests a procedure for getting the lieutenant out of his quandary: the Socratic elenchus. If the king can give an account of justice that survives the sort of scrutiny given the ideas of Cephalus, Polemarchus, and Thrasymachus in *Republic* I, the lieutenant might have grounds for accepting his claim to be a true philosopher and for joining his revolution.

Conclusion

I hope the forgoing discussion has established the following points. First, the Ship of State complements the Sun, Line, and Cave, and stands in as important a relation to Plato's political philosophy as the three other similes stand to his metaphysics and epistemology. Second, the multi-skilled ancient Greek steersman, who was captain, helmsman, and navigator rolled into one, is a fitting symbol of a ruler in whom political power and philosophy coalesce. Third, a merchantman, if its owner is taken to be a symbol of the *dêmos*, is a good image of Greek democracy. Fourth, a hijacked merchantman is a bitter political cartoon that brilliantly captures Plato's jaundiced view of Athenian democracy. Fifth, the very feature that makes a merchantman a good image of democracy, namely, that the shipowner hires and fires the steersman, makes it a bad image of aristocracy. Consequently, sixth, the Ship of State provides no analogical support for Plato's ideal city.

Other subsidiary points are the following. Seventh, the true steersman of the simile does not stand for Socrates. Eighth, the intoxicated shipowner symbolizes a *dêmos* that is morally inferior to the *dêmos* of Kallipolis. Ninth, that merchant-men exist whereas ideal cities do not is an important disanalogy that raises the problem of the initial philosopher-king. In discussing this problem I maintained that a king who declares himself a true philosopher should be met with skepticism when he attempts to rally support for his revolution among rational men and women, and I suggested that such prospective recruits might want to test their revolutionary king's declaration by subjecting him to a Socratic elenchus. If this rather speculative suggestion is correct, the tenth and final point is that the Ship of State raises a problem the solution of which entails that the constructive, "Platonic," philosophy of the second through the tenth books of the *Republic* presupposes, rather than supersedes, the elenctic, "Socratic" philosophy of Book I.

Notes

1   The usual, but not invariable, rendition of C. J. Rowe and Trevor J. Saunders in their translations of the *Politicus* and the *Laws* respectively.
2   One of the changes in C. D. C Reeve's revision of G. M. A. Grube's translation of the *Republic*.
3   Anthony Kenny at *Second Alcibiades* 147a8.
4   Mark Joyal at *Eryxias* 394e6.
5   Rowe at *Politicus* 299b3.
6   Donald J. Zeyl at *Gorgias* 511d1.
7   Nicholas Smith at *Theages* 123b7 and d11.
8   Rosamond Kent Sprague at *Charmides* 174c6.
9   Richard D. McKirahan, Jr. at [*Epinomis*] 976b1.
10 Dorothea Frede at *Philebus* 56b1, Paul Woodruff at *Ion* 537c6, and Reeve at *Rep.* 346a7 and 346b2.
11 David Gallop at *Sisyphus* 389c8.
12 Saunders at *Laws* 961e4.
13 This restriction and the similar one in the next sentence are necessary because the steersman is himself one of the sailors and the rulers are themselves members of the citizen body. Thus, in ruling in the interest of the ruled, they also rule incidentally (*kata sumbebékos*), as Aristotle would put it (*Politics* III.6.1278b30–1279a8), in their own interest.
14 The interpretation of the Cave in Malcolm 1962 and 1981 seems to me to be basically correct.
15 The interpretation offered above, that the warriors and workers of Kallipolis have true beliefs about the hierarchy of goods and lead happy lives, is surprisingly contentious. C. C. W. Taylor maintains that "only the guardians, and to a lesser degree the auxiliaries [warriors], are capable of *eudaimonia* [happiness]" (1997: 40), and Christopher Bobonich goes one step further and argues that happiness is beyond the reach even of the auxiliaries (2002:, 51–8, 81). But when Socrates emphatically asserts that the guardians are truly happy (V.465d–466c5), he expressly brings the

auxiliaries within the scope of his assertion (466a8); and it is difficult to see how the whole city can be happy (IV.420b4–8, 420c1–4) – how Kallipolis can be a city of happy people (V.458e1) – if the workers are not happy.

I am indebted to Debra Nails, Rachana Kamtekar, David Reeve, Angela Smith, Nicholas D. Smith, and my wife Christine Keyt for helpful comments on earlier versions of this paper.

References

Adam, J. (1902) *The* Republic *of Plato, edited with Critical Notes, Commentary and Appendices*, 2 vols., Cambridge: Cambridge University Press.

Bambrough, R. (1956) "Plato's political analogies," in P. Laslett (ed.) *Philosophy, Politics and Society*, Oxford: Macmillan.

Bass, G. F. (ed.) (1972) *A History of Seafaring*, London: Thames and Hudson.

Bobonich, C. (2002) *Plato's Utopia Recast: His Later Ethics and Politics*, Oxford: Oxford University Press.

Campbell, L. (1867) *The* Sophistes *and* Politicus *of Plato*, Oxford: Clarendon Press.

Casson, L. (1971) *Ships and Seamanship in the Ancient World*, Princeton, NJ: Princeton University Press.

——(1994) *Ships and Seafaring in Ancient Times*, Austin: University of Texas Press.

Cooper, J. M. (1997) "The psychology of justice in Plato," in R. Kraut (ed.) *Plato's* Republic: *Critical Essays*, Lanham, MD: Rowman and Littlefield.

Cooper, J. M., and D. S. Hutchinson (eds.) (1997) *Complete Works of Plato*, Indianapolis: Hackett Publishing.

Dodds, E. R. (1959) *Plato's Gorgias, a Revised Text with Introduction and Commentary*, Oxford: Clarendon Press.

Guthrie, W. K. C. (1969) *A History of Greek Philosophy*, vol. IV: *Plato, the Man and His Dialogues: Earlier Period*, Cambridge: Cambridge University Press.

——(1975) *A History of Greek Philosophy*, vol. III: *The Fifth-Century Enlightenment*, Cambridge: Cambridge University Press.

Irwin, T. (1995) *Plato's Ethics*, Oxford: Oxford University Press.

Kahn, C. (1996) *Plato and the Socratic Dialogue*, Cambridge: Cambridge University Press.

Kraut, R. (1973) "Reason and justice in Plato's *Republic*," in E. N. Lee, A. P. D. Mourelatos, and R. M. Rorty (eds.) *Exegesis and Argument, Phronesis Supplement*, Assen: Van Gorcum.

Lear, J. (1997) "Inside and outside the *Republic*," in R. Kraut (ed.) *Plato's* Republic: *Critical Essays*, Lanham, MD: Rowman and Littlefield.

Malcolm, J. (1962) "The Line and the Cave," *Phronesis* 7, pp. 38–45.

——(1981) "The Cave revisited," *Classical Quarterly* NS 31, pp. 60–8.

Morrison, J. S., and J. F. Coates (1986) *The Athenian Trireme*, Cambridge: Cambridge University Press.

Newman, W. L. (1887) *The* Politics *of Aristotle*, vol. I, Oxford: Clarendon Press.

Oakeshott, M. (1991) *Rationalism in Politics and Other Essays*, Indianapolis: Liberty Fund.

Taylor, C. C. W. (1997) "Plato's totalitarianism," in R. Kraut (ed.) *Plato's* Republic: *Critical Essays*, Lanham, MD: Rowman and Littlefield.

Vlastos, G. (1995) "The theory of social justice in the *polis* in Plato's *Republic*," in *Studies in Greek Philosophy*, vol. II: *Socrates, Plato, and Their Tradition*, Princeton, NJ: Princeton University Press.

Walzer, M. (1983) *Spheres of Justice*, New York: Basic Books.

11

Knowledge, Recollection, and the Forms in *Republic* VII

Michael T. Ferejohn

I

Not only Platonic epistemology, but also more generally epistemology itself as a distinct field of study, can plausibly be viewed as an outgrowth of a rather pragmatically motivated type of investigation often conducted by the character of Socrates in Plato's earlier dialogues.[1] Notoriously, Socrates' conversations in these works are centered almost exclusively on the practical issues of identifying, embracing, and promulgating the best possible, i.e., the most virtuous, form of human life. The immediate problem he faces, however, is that he perceives no shortage of people in Athens who profess themselves, or are reputed among others, to possess sufficient expertise to speak authoritatively on such matters. One of Socrates' chief concerns, then, is to figure out how to distinguish effectively between the genuine expert in ethical matters – the authentically wise person whose advice should be followed – and various false claimants to this position.

In approaching this task, Socrates quite naturally proceeds by attempting to formulate necessary conditions, or *tests*, for the possession of genuine expertise. In the first instance he is principally concerned with distinguishing between genuine experts and mere pretenders in ethical matters. However, it appears that he sees this distinction as applying to other fields as well, since in some passages he clearly takes up the more general issue of what conditions a genuine expert would have to satisfy in any field whatsoever.[2]

As it happens, these early Platonic texts record hardly any visible progress in this endeavor. Socrates evidently can do little more than insist that a genuine expert would be able to adequately defend and explain not just the views he espouses, but his entire manner of life,[3] in the rough and tumble of Socratic elenctic interrogation. But this test of "elenctic survival," the ability to avoid being caught up in contradictions or other sorts of "incongruencies" is essentially negative in character, and in any case is too dependent upon the competence of whoever happens to be conducting the interrogation. However, as Plato moves through this earlier stage, into the *Meno*, and towards his middle period, the topic undergoes two important transformations. In the first place, the issue is now "depersonalized". Whereas in the *Euthyphro* or the *Ion* it seems to be important in itself for Socrates to show that his interlocutor is either a fraud or a fool (depending on whether he is merely deceiving others, or himself as well, in professing wisdom), in other settings he poses the issue of testing expertise in a more impersonal manner, by asking what conditions *anyone* would have to satisfy to be counted a genuine expert. Often he does this by resorting to the use of the first person plural. For example, at *Laches* 186a–b he includes himself (along with his two principal interlocutors) among those who must be tested for expertise in the matter of identifying and imparting courage, even though he himself never claims to have any expertise whatsoever in this field.

The second, equally significant, transformation of this Socratic "proto-epistemology" occurs in the *Meno* itself. In such dialogues as the *Ion* and *Laches* Socrates had been exploring the issue of what chronic characteristics an alleged expert must possess in order to be certified as genuine, where the idea seems to be that once certified, the expert's deliverances could generally be counted as authoritative.[4] By contrast, in the last part of the *Meno* Socrates appears to be more narrowly focused on the question of what conditions must obtain in order for a person to be said to possess knowledge – as opposed to mere true belief – *on a given occasion*. This "episodic" perspective is especially evident at 97a–d. There, recalling Meno's earlier agreement that virtue – considered as a chronic psychological condition – should be classified as "a sort of wisdom" (88d), and therefore as a kind of knowledge, Socrates then brings in the additional datum that virtue, whatever it is, must be *useful*. He then challenges his own earlier identification of virtue with a species of knowledge by pointing out that if you were simply interested in getting from one place to another, it would not make any difference, from a purely *practical* point of view, whether you consulted someone who really *knew* the way to the desired destination or someone who merely had an ill-founded opinion on the subject that happened to be true.

This Platonic movement from the chronic to the episodic perspectives on knowledge, however, is both incomplete and temporary. For even in the *Meno* passage just discussed, after arguing that there is no *practical* difference between knowledge and mere true belief (again, considered episodically), Socrates immediately goes on to make a *conceptual* distinction between the two by invoking the image of the self-moving statues of Daedalus. He likens them to mere true belief the grounds that, insofar as they are not "fastened" (*dedemena*) they are worth little because they do not "remain" (*paramenei*) but instead tend to "run away" (*apodidraskei*). On the other hand, he continues, genuine knowledge would be analogous to such a statue that *was* "fastened," and would therefore have a much greater value.

In a moment we will need to consider what exactly is this metaphorical "tying up" that is supposed to transform true belief into knowledge. However, the important point to notice immediately is that by making the distinction between cognitive items that "remain" and others that "run away" in order to characterize the superior reliability of knowledge over belief, Plato has quietly reverted to thinking in terms of chronic conditions of the knowing subject rather than identifying the conditions under which someone holding a given true belief *on a particular occasion* can be classified as a case of knowledge. What's more, as we shall see, when he returns in the middle books of the *Republic* to this task of making a conceptual distinction between knowledge and mere true belief, he again does so by identifying a certain standing condition of the knowing subject (namely, familiarity with the Forms) that is achieved by means of a long and difficult educational process.

Nonetheless, this temporary engagement in the *Meno* with the episodic conception of knowledge does provide Plato with an opportunity to formulate for the first time what has since become the "traditional" conception of knowledge as the possession of true belief together with the right sort of justification. In the passage immediately following his introduction of the automatic statues, he makes the following intriguing remark concerning the epistemological analogue to the "fastening" of the statues.

> [Mere] true beliefs are not worth much until one fastens them with *accounts of causes* [*aitias logismô*] But this process, dear Meno, is recollection [*anamnêsis*], as we have agreed in our previous discussion. (98a)

I characterize this remark as intriguing, not as especially illuminating. For even though it certainly brings to mind much recent discussion concerning the nature of knowledge and its difference from true belief, Plato himself does nothing in the *Meno*, or anywhere else in his early works, to make clear exactly what he means in this passage by an "account of the cause."[5] So even though Plato here puts his finger on what eventually turned out to be an insight of signal importance in the history of epistemology, that the ability to explain *why* a proposition is true is a necessary condition for knowing that it is, he evidently lacks the theoretical resources at this point to say what exactly this condition amounts to because he had not yet thought through the issue of what constitutes an adequate explanation.

Somewhat paradoxically, one thinker who apparently was deeply influenced by Plato's suggestion of *Meno* 98a was his own best student in the Academy. For even though Aristotle himself shows little interest in mathematical research, in his *Analytics* he nonetheless develops and refines this Platonic insight by bringing together observed features of contemporary geometrical method with a theory of deduction of his own invention to develop a "foundationalist" conception of epistemic justification, or what he calls "demonstration" (*apodeixis*), as a truth-preserving (and hence, necessity-preserving) sequence of syllogistic inferences grounded exclusively upon the appropriate sort of "first principles" (*archai*).[6] It is thus something of an historical curiosity that his teacher, who evidently *was* an avid and accomplished geometer, looks in an entirely different direction when he himself returns to the issue of distinguishing knowledge and belief in the *Republic*. That direction is the metaphysics of Forms.

II

Plato is rightly regarded as a highly systematic philosopher, and the *Republic* is rightly regarded as one of his most systematic works. This is because the dialogue touches on topics in nearly every area of philosophy, yet it remains from beginning to end a work in ethics. More specifically, the work presents us with a sustained attempt to do two things: (1) elucidate the nature of justice as a condition of the human soul and (2) demonstrate that justice, so understood, is beneficial to its possessor.

This is certainly not to deny that other philosophical topics have genuine independent interest for Plato, but his treatments of them are always eventually brought to bear on this central concern with ethics. The example of this most familiar to general readers of the *Republic* is perhaps in the area of the political theory, where Plato's extensive theorizing on the characteristics of the best form of political state is undertaken for the sake of identifying the nature of justice in a human soul. However, the point applies equally to more technical and esoteric parts of philosophy as well. For although the *Republic* can undoubtedly stand on its own as a classical sourcebook in both epistemology and metaphysics, Plato's forays into these areas are never undertaken simply for their own sake. Rather, the metaphysical doctrines of the dialogue are specifically designed to provide an ontological underpinning for the epistemology, and inasmuch as Plato's foremost epistemological concern in the work is with knowledge of objective *value*, his work in both of these areas is ultimately done in the service of his central ethical project. Plato's subordination of metaphysics to epistemology will be our chief concern here.

Some features of Plato's metaphysically-based epistemology are relatively easy to discern and also relatively unproblematic, in particular those pertaining to the highest reaches in the field of epistemic states posited by the theory. Plato's ethics and political theory both require the real possibility of an exceptionally reliable human capacity to make correct ethical judgments, which can then be utilized in the proper sort of governance of a well-functioning political state or a well-developed ethical person. Plato's pivotal idea is that if such ethical judgments are not to be "fleeting" in the manner of Daedalus' statues[7] they must have as their objects entities with natures that are sufficiently fixed, stable, and determinate. Now since Plato believes both that such knowledge is possible, and that the sensible world is utterly lacking in this sort of entity, he is led to postulate the existence of such stable entities "elsewhere": in a place "separated" from the world presented by the senses.[8] It thus appears that Plato's best-known philosophical invention, the Theory of Forms, was designed specifically for this epistemological purpose. In *Republic* VI and VII, he deploys two complementary expository devices, the Divided Line diagram, and the allegory of the Cave, to describe an epistemic ascent, made possible by the long and arduous educational process mentioned earlier, culminating in a condition wherein one enjoys direct acquaintance with the Forms, the highest sort of knowledge. First, near the end of Book VI he invites his interlocutor, Glaucon, to imagine a diagram of a line that is first bisected into unequal segments, each of which is then also bisected unequally in the same proportions. Socrates asserts that this diagram may be taken to represent a fourfold classification of hierarchically ordered sorts of cognition, each with its appropriate type of object. The initial, major division in the diagram is meant to represent the distinction between knowledge (*epistêmê*), which has as its proper objects intelligible entities (*noêta*), and opinion (*doxa*), which has as its objects visible things (*horata*), and the unequal proportions are intended to represent different degrees of "clarity" (*saphêneia*), which has now evidently replaced the *Meno's* criterion of "being fastened" (*dedemenon*) as what distinguishes knowledge from lesser types of true belief.

The purpose of the diagram, however, is not simply to classify these kinds of cognition, but also to indicate how it might be possible to move from the lower to the higher states it represents. Socrates begins his exposition by focusing on the lower two sections, which together comprise the realm of opinion. Here he trades on the fact that Glaucon is already conversant with the distinction within the sensible realm between such two-dimensional entities as shadows, reflections, etc., which he refers to collectively as "images" (*eikones*), and the three-dimensional physical objects of which such things are representations. On this basis, Socrates then introduces the two higher sections of the line, with which Glaucon is not familiar, by means of a simple analogy: "as the opinable is to the knowable so is the likeness to that of which it is a likeness" (510a).

The point of the analogy is evidently that by fixing on the relation between a "likeness" and what it represents as it applies within the visible realm, one can gain at least a glimmering of the central tenet of Plato's theory, namely that the entire visible realm itself is but a collection of likenesses of a higher order of "intelligible" entities.

At the beginning of *Republic* VII, Socrates then goes on to offer a second and more dramatic presentation of the same theory. He describes an imaginary situation in which a number of people are imprisoned within a subterranean cavern. They are shackled in a sitting position so that their entire field of vision is limited to the cavern wall in front of them. Above and behind them (and therefore outside their sight), stands a low wall, and beyond that a walkway across which carved likenesses of various sorts of natural objects are conveyed back and forth in such a manner that they, but not their bearers, protrude over the top of the wall, "in the style of the puppeteers" (514b).[9] Finally, at the rear of the cavern is a fire that projects shadows of these artifacts upon the front wall, so that these shadows are the only "entities" ever perceived by the prisoners. At 515a Glaucon immediately remarks upon the strangeness of the image, where-upon Socrates replies that they are "like us" (*homoious hêmin*). We shall return to this later.

With the initial elements of the allegory in place, Socrates first garners Glaucon's agreement that these prisoners would naturally believe that these shadows were the only real (and therefore the most real) entities (515b–c), and then introduces a new phase of the allegory. He now asks Glaucon to imagine that for some unspecified reason one of the prisoners is released from his bonds, compelled to stand, look about, and see the situation in the cave as it really is, and then dragged forcefully up a steep and difficult ascent out of the cave and into the world above. After some initial period of habituation, he comes to appre-hend first reflections of men and other things, then those things themselves, after that the stars and the moon, and finally the sun itself.[10] Socrates and Glaucon then agree that during this sequence of revelations the protagonist would first come to understand that the shadows that he had regarded as the most real things were in fact merely representations of things that are *more* real, namely the artifacts conveyed along the wall, and eventually that these things themselves were but representations of even greater realities, namely the "men and other things" residing in the upper realm (515d–e). Now insofar as the division between the cave and the upper realm in this story no doubt corresponds to the main distinction between the realms of opinion and knowledge in the Divided Line diagram, we can plausibly regard the allegory as reinforcing the Divided Line passage in depicting an epistemic ascent from mere opinion of sensible things to knowledge of intelligible realities, which are, of course, the Forms.

III

While the epistemological function of the Forms is relatively clear in the case of the highest sort of cognition introduced by these passages in the *Republic*,[11] it is not nearly so obvious what role, if any, they play in the occurrence of lower-level cognitive states within Plato's overall epistemology. Perhaps most conspic-uously, there is the question of whether, in holding that the Forms are eminently suitable objects of knowledge, Plato means thereby to deny that there can be knowledge of sensible objects as well.[12] This restriction certainly seems to be sug-gested by the most straightforward and natural reading of an argument given at the end of *Republic* V (at 477–9), which seems to rely on a principle that different capacities (*dunameis*) (including epistemic capacities such as knowledge and belief) must have different sorts of objects. On the other hand, if one keeps in mind my earlier observation that the epistemology of the *Republic* is subordinated to its paramount ethical concerns, this interpretation becomes problematic. For if Plato's ultimate purpose in positing the Forms is so that he can argue that knowledge of them can be *applied* to make highly reliable ethical judgments, then since these judgments presumably pertain to issues and circumstances in the sensible world, someone who had come to know the Forms should consequently have a much more reliable basis for judging things *in the sensible world* than someone who had never made the ascent. Indeed, Plato seems to suggest as much at *Republic* 520c, where Socrates remarks that when the prisoner who had been released later returned to cave he would be able to discern the shadows therein "immeasurably better" (*muriô beltion*) than those who had remained shackled. Now if Plato still maintains in the *Republic*, as he had in the *Meno*, that what distinguishes knowledge from mere true belief is a higher degree of reliability, it is hard to imagine why he would deny that such application of Form-knowledge to the sensible world is itself a type of knowledge.[13]

IV

This issue of ascertaining what role the Forms play in judgments concerning sensible things *after* one has completed the epistemic ascent of *Republic* VI and VII has been much discussed in the recent literature, and I shall not have more to say about it here. Instead, I want to focus on yet another question about the epistemological function of the Forms that has received much less attention, namely whether the Forms figure in any way at all in judgments concerning sensible things formed by people who have *not* made the ascent described in *Republic* VI and VII (and in almost all cases, never will). Here there can be no question about whether such imperfect judgments might qualify as knowledge; they clearly should be classified as cases of mere opinion, even if they turned out to be true. But on the other hand, the simple fact that none of these beliefs rises to the exceptionally high level of reliability required for knowledge in Plato's system doesn't by itself entail that he regards them all as *equally* defective. He could still believe it possible to rank them as better and worse according to their accuracy, reasonableness, or other some positive epistemic value. If he does, it may be because he thinks the superiority of some of these beliefs over others is connected in some way with the existence of the Forms.

David Bostock has offered perhaps the clearest articulation of the view that the Forms are involved in pre-philosophical cognition, in his book on Plato's *Phaedo*.[14] In discussing an argument for the Forms advanced by Socrates at *Phaedo* 74–6, Bostock suggests that Plato works with a two-level theory of knowledge. On the one hand, there is the fully conscious knowledge of the Forms represented by the top section of the Divided Line diagram and the upper world in the Cave allegory. This, according to Bostock, is "proper philosophic knowledge of [Forms]," which "involves the ability to give an account."[15] As I suggested above, virtually no interpreter disagrees with this. However, Bostock argues further that Plato also recognizes a lower grade of knowledge as well: "ordinary humdrum knowledge which *everyone* has, simply as a result of being reminded: there is no special limitation to philosophers in this claim."[16]

Bostock's phrase "being reminded" here explicitly links the issue of whether the Forms have any epistemic role to play in pre-philosophical cognition with another component of Plato's metaphysically-based epistemology that has so far remained in the background, the doctrine of "recollection" (*anamnêsis*). This doctrine first appears in the *Meno*[17] as a reaction to a Meno's complaint at 80d that Socrates' attempt to learn the nature of virtue, indeed attempting to learn anything at all, is a futile enterprise. Conceiving of inquiry as an attempt to find something, namely the answer to the question one is pursuing, Meno argues that either we already know what we are seeking, in which case our search cannot discover it (and no learning occurs), or we do not know what we are seeking, in which case we will not recognize it even if we happen to come upon it (so that, again, no learning occurs).

Socrates first agrees at 80d–e that this is indeed a formidable epistemological quandary, and then proceeds to respond to it obliquely by means of a well-known pedagogical experiment. He commandeers one of Meno's young household slaves, determines that the boy has had no previous mathematical training what-soever, then presents him with a moderately difficult geometrical problem. The boy first impetuously makes a couple of uneducated guesses, which Socrates quickly refutes. He then presents the boy with a diagram of the problem and leads him through a series of questions about it, and at the end of which the boy is able to give the correct answer to Socrates' initial question. Socrates then declares that since he himself did nothing except pose questions to the boy, he could not have given him the answer,[18] and concludes that the answer must have been "within" the boy even before the experiment began, and that his own ques-tioning simply caused him to remember an answer he already possessed.

Bostock's view is that Plato in fact recognizes two grades of recollection of the Forms. On the one hand, there is the fully explicit and complete sort of rec-ollection that is achieved by a long and arduous educational process described in *Republic* VI and VII. This is reserved to philosophers alone. But on the other hand, according to Bostock, Plato also believes that virtually all humans are capable of understanding language "only because they once beheld the [F]orms and can (dimly recollect) them."[19]

This latter claim of Bostock's, that Plato recognizes a lower and "dimmer" grade of recollection of the Forms available to virtually everyone, has since been challenged by a number of writers. One of these, Dominic Scott, conducts a careful examination of every passage where Plato mentions the doctrine of recollection and concludes, unlike Bostock, that taken together they are most plausibly interpreted as implying that Platonic recollection is not undergone by people generally, but only by a very few as the result of the kind of intense philosophical training described in the middle parts of the *Republic*.[20]

As a technical philological matter, it seems that Scott holds the high ground. It does indeed appear that in all three dialogues that explicitly mention recollection (the *Meno*, *Phaedo* and *Phaedrus*), Plato consistently reserves his technical expression *anamnêsis* for the process of coming to a fully conscious acquaintance with the Forms,[21] and is not willing to extend and dilute its use to "ordinary humdrum knowledge" as Bostock suggests. At the same time, however, Scott evidently believes that his resolution of this scholarly question about Platonic terminological patterns also closes the deeper and more philosophical question mentioned above, namely whether the Forms are involved in any way in pre-philosophical cognition.[22] Scott's conflation of these two questions is evident from the following characterization of the difference between his own position and Bostock's:

> Consider the status of [pre-philosophical] opinions that arise with perception. [On Bostock's interpretation] these represent the results of partial recollection and the movement from them to the final goal [sc. philosophical knowledge] is in some sense continuous. They are starting points to be built upon, parts of an overall picture that has to be filled in. On [my interpretation], however, things are very different. . . . [these opinions] are messages to deceive us and are to be scraped away. We discard them, not build on them. There is a radical discontinuity as we become aware of the deception.[23]

Scott here represents Bostock as holding that Plato believes low-level (dim or partial) recollection of Forms to be involved in the formation of (at least some) pre-philosophical opinions concerning sensible things, whereas, as we saw, Scott himself argues that Platonic recollection only comes into play in the course of advanced philosophical training. However, Scott suggests further that the two lines of interpretation take fundamentally different positions on Plato's view of the relationship between pre-philosophical opinions about the sensible realm, and knowledge of the Forms gained through (full) recollection.

According to Scott's own view, the relationship is purely contrastive: pre-philosophical opinions are utterly false and deceptive, and contain nothing of truth whatsoever within them. As one achieves philosophical enlightenment, they are simply to be discarded, or as Scott puts it, "scraped away." The "scraping away" metaphor is part of an analogy Scott uses to present his view. He alludes to an anecdote in Herodotus about a certain Demaratus, a Greek spy who deceived the Persians by inscribing a warning of impending invasion on a wooden tablet, then covering the tablet with wax, which he left blank. Scott introduces a slight alteration to the story, imagining that rather than leaving the wax surface blank, Demaratus had inscribed upon it another message completely unrelated to the one below. On this version, says Scott, "[We] would now have two messages, one obvious but unreliable, the other true but completely hidden away from view."[24] This, according to Scott, is analogous to the relation between pre-philosophical opinion and philosophical knowledge of Forms in Platonic epistemology, and he consequently labels his interpretation "Demaratian."

By contrast, Scott calls Bostock's interpretation "Kantian" on the grounds that it treats (partial or dim) recollection of the Forms as necessary for the acquisition of general concepts (i.e., the mastery of general terms), which in turn is taken to be necessary to make any sense at all of what otherwise would be an unintelligible onslaught of sensory impressions. On this "Kantian" interpretation, according to Scott, Plato sees pre-philosophical opinions not as something to be discarded, but "built upon," as "parts of an overall picture that has to be filled in."[25]

But clearly there are two separable theses at issue here. One is an epistemological thesis (K1) that, according to Plato, the acquisition of general concepts (and the mastery of general terms) achieved by people generally would not be possible had they not previously "beheld the Forms."[26] The other is a philological thesis (K2) that Plato sometimes employs the term "recollect" to describe whatever residual epistemic effects of this past acquaintance with the Forms makes such everyday achievement possible. Scott correctly reports that Bostock believes that both theses are true, and Scott himself plainly thinks they are both false. My contention here is that although Scott succeeds in refuting K2, he does nothing whatever to undermine K1. Moreover, in what follows I will endeavor to provide textual support for K1.

Before we proceed further a couple of preliminary clarifications are required. The first has to do with a superficial difference in the language Scott and Bostock use to present their respective views. Bostock claims that past acquaintance with the Forms is necessary for the basic human ability of "understanding language,"[27] which can be glossed as the basic competency to apply general terms more or less correctly.[28] On the other hand, unlike Bostock, Scott contends that the formation of "pre-philosophical opinions" about sensible things does not require any past acquaintance with the Forms. Scott does not specify exactly which "pre-philosophical" opinions he has in mind here, but we can plausibly bring these two positions into alignment by supposing that at least some of these opinions involve the application of general concepts to particular sensible objects, as for instance when someone judges that a certain pair of sticks is equal, or that a particular act is an instance of some virtue.

The second issue needing clarification has to do with the proper scope of Bostock's claim about the worth of these "pre-philosophical" opinions. Now, of course, Plato could not possibly hold that *all* pre-philosophical opinions have epistemic value, since it will be obvious to anyone (not least Plato) that the majority of them are false and misguided, and should simply be discarded. But if this is the interpretation Scott contrasts with his own, he is targeting a straw man. The strongest thesis Bostock *needs* to defend is that Plato thinks that at least *some* pre-philosophical opinions concerning the sensible world are true, even if most of them are mistaken, and that it is possible to rank these opinions according to their accuracy or reasonableness, even if none of them meets the exceptionally high standards for genuine knowledge required by his theory. For if this were the case, it would provide some reason to suspect that past acquaintance with the Forms is in some way involved in at least the most accurate of these opinions.

V

Our proving ground for these two opposing positions regarding K1 will be *Republic* VII, and more specifically Plato's description of the initial predicament of the prisoners in the cave. Admittedly, this would not be appropriate if we were concerned here with K2, since recollection is never mentioned in this passage, or for that matter anywhere else in the *Republic*. However, this consideration is irrelevant now that we have separated the two theses and are concerned only with the question of whether some residual effect of past acquaintance with Forms is involved in pre-philosophical cognition. On the other hand, what *is* crucially relevant for our purposes is Socrates' passing remark mentioned earlier that the prisoners in this situation are "like us" (*homoious hêmin*). For they are portrayed as engaged enthusiastically in issuing various opinions about the things displayed before them, and this can plausibly be taken to represent the "pre-philosophical opinions" with which K1 is concerned.

Let us then examine the places where Plato speaks most directly about the relative value of the opinions formed by prisoners in their original unenlightened condition. The passages of greatest importance occur at the point in the allegory immediately after the prisoner who had been released is made to return to the cave and rejoin his erstwhile peers. As he does, he finds them engaged in making judgments about their environs, including some judgments that involve "naming the things they see" (*onomazein haper horôen*) (515b), which presumably is supposed to represent the classification of objects of experience under the appropriate general concepts. Later on, at 516c–d, these same prisoners are described as engaged in a sort of competition, according "honors and praises"[29] to one another, and giving prizes to those who were "most acute" (*oxutata*) at "discerning" (*kathorônt*) what was being presented to them (*ta parionta*).

Clearly, Plato wants his audience to take away from these passages the idea that all of these contestants are in a state of relative ignorance, especially when compared to his enlightened protagonist. For he has Socrates declare at 520c that the returning prisoner will first experience a brief period of confusion, but then be able to discern the shadows "immeasurably better" (*muriô beltion*) than the others.[30] However, it is crucial for our purposes to determine exactly what sort of mistake is being ascribed to these benighted souls. As it happens, the only belief they hold that Socrates explicitly declares to be false is the *metaphysical* thesis that the shadows they apprehend are the most real entities there are. But clearly the competition Socrates describes at 516c–d does not consist simply of repetitions of the single assertion-type, "Nothing can be more real than *that*!" Rather, the contestants are described as forming judgments about various patterns and interrelations that hold among the shadows they experience. Moreover, a close look at Socrates' characterization of the details of the contest gives the clear impression that winning is not just a matter of making the luckiest guess. To the contrary, according to Socrates' account the winner is described as having certain superior cognitive abilities: "[The prizes are given to the one who is] the most acute (*oxutata*) at discerning [the shadows] as [the artifacts] are carried by."

Again, this does not mean that Plato would regard even the very best among the subterranean contestants as any match for the philosopher-protagonist of the allegory. But it does suggest that he does not put all pre-philosophical opinions on a par, but instead believes that they can be ranked objectively according to their accuracy, plausibility, or other epistemic value. This is not at all what one would expect on Scott's "Demaratian" interpretation of pre-philosophical cognition.

VI

So far I have argued that Cave passage in *Republic* VII provides substantial evidence that Plato allows a considerable range in epistemic value among pre-philosophical opinions. In terms of the allegory, some unenlightened prisoners are naturally more adept than others at forming true beliefs and making accurate predictions about their shared, limited experience. The question now is whether the truth of such opinions that are true, and the epistemic superiority of some of them over others, is in some way due to the fact that their possessors had once known the Forms (whether or not they ever "recollect" this past acquaintance). One initially plausible line of thought is that some pre-philosophical opinions are more accurate than others because they have a comparatively greater basis in the way things really are. But since the ways things *really* are, according to Plato, is that sensible things are mere representations of the Forms, there is some reason to suspect that past acquaintance with the Forms might be involved in some way in the formation of the superior opinions.

But for the present this is only a suspicion. For Plato's recognition that pre-philosophical opinions vary in epistemic value by itself doesn't automatically implicate the Forms in pre-philosophical cognition. This is because there are at least two possible explanations for this difference in pre-philosophical cognitive abilities. One possible explanation is suggested by the strikingly "Humean" over-tones in the final part of Socrates' description at 516d of the "winning contestant":

> [He will be] the best able to remember such items that are prior [*protera*], poste-rior [*hustera*], and concomitant [*hama*] among them, and consequently, the most successful at guessing the future.

With its references to discerning and remembering which experiences are "prior, posterior, and concomitant" with respect to others, and to "guessing the future," this passage certainly gives the impression that Plato supposes that there are salient patterns and regularities inherent within the body of experience presented to the prisoners,[31] and that even without philosophical training some of them are just "naturally" better than others at detecting these patterns and extrapo-lating from them to make better predictions about subsequent experience. The key feature of this "Humean" interpretation is that the detectable patterns and regularities in question are *wholly contained* within the experiences themselves, so that no further source information is required to render the experiences under-standable and predictable. A scientific analogue to this would be a researcher who was able to detect and predict various correlations within a given body of observational data without having any inkling of the causal mechanisms respon-sible for producing those regularities. On this account, sense-experience, though limited in perspective, is also inherently intelligible inasmuch as it contains salient patterns and regularities, and differences in epistemic quality among pre-philo-sophical opinions are explained by native differences in the ability to detect, remember, and extrapolate from these patterns.

There is, however, another possible explanation to be considered. On this alternative account, we might think of sense-experience as analogous to a ciphered message that, when considered in isolation, presents no significant pat-terns or regularities. To all appearances, it is simply a randomly ordered sequence of symbols. In other words, it is such that even if a perfectly astute observer examined it for any length of time, and from however many perspectives, it would still simply not be possible to make any sense of it. The reason for this, of course, is that the key to its intelligibility does not lie within the message itself, but in something altogether external to it, namely the cipher-book. This is essentially the situation with sense-experience according to the alternative explanation we are considering. By itself it is inherently chaotic and disordered, and simply presents no detectable patterns or regularities. On the other hand, if one possesses further information about which sensible objects are representa-tions of which Forms, then it does become possible to make good sense of it. The source of this further information, according to K1, is ultimately the pre-natal acquaintance with the Forms.

It may be instructive to put this in terms of Plato's own allegory. Imagine, for the sake of simplicity, that the items conveyed along the walkway are not statuettes of humans and other animals (as in the original), but simple geometrical objects, that one of these is, say, a cylinder, and that the "appearances" of this particular object are quite regular – for example, that it is the object of every tenth "presentation." Now imagine further that our cylinder is presented in a wide variety of attitudes relative to the axis of the fire and wall. Sometimes it is displayed on end, sometimes sideways, etc., so that on one occasion its shadow might be circular, on another rectangular, and so forth. Finally, again for the sake of simplicity, let us suppose that none of the other objects presented is capable of projecting shadows like any of those cast by the cylinder.

Plainly, in this scenario, someone whose informational resources were limited to examination of the shadows alone would not have a basis on which to make what, *ex hypothesi*, is the correct judgment that there is a "natural" classification including every tenth presentation and nothing else. On the other hand, someone who had additional information about how the shadows were actually caused, and more specifically about the range of shadows that could be cast by each kind of object, *would* be able to make this judgment, and on the basis of that to make at least one moderately accurate prediction about future projections (namely that every tenth shadow will fall within a certain range of shapes).

How then are we to decide between these two very different explanations of the difference among pre-philosophical cognition? The "Humean" account is the one most naturally suggested by the language of *Republic* 516c–d, but it is not absolutely required by it. For Plato never says exactly what allows some prisoners to perform better in these competitions than others. In particular, he never specifies whether their advantage consists in their simply being congenitally more adept than others at pattern-recognition, or in possessing additional information that the others do not. And in any case, there are two other considerations that weigh heavily in favor of the alternative, "cipher-book" interpretation.

One of these, which is essentially philosophical in character, is that the "Humean" account would undermine part of Plato's rationale for positing the Forms in the first place. For if, as the Humean account requires, he believed that sense-experience is a self-contained informational system, and that relative proficiencies in making sense of it is due simply to innate differences in the skill of pattern-recognition, then he has no *principled* way of excluding the possibility that someone might naturally be *so* adept at that skill that his performance in guessing the future would approach that of the philosopher – even granting the latter's superior perspective. For after all, on that account, all of the information necessary to make correct judgments and predictions are available for public inspection.[32] Granted, our hypothetical *idiot savant* would not be privy to the *metaphysical* truth that the objects of his experience and beliefs are not the most real entities. But it is not clear why this ignorance should impede his ability to make accurate judgments and predictions if they are confined to the sensible realm. This point is especially telling in view of that fact, noted above, that Plato's ultimate purpose in designing his metaphysically-based epistemology is to ground the theoretical possibility of unerring ethical and political judgments, since presumably such judgments will pertain to the sensible realm.

The second consideration in favor of the "cipher-book" analogy is textual. When Socrates first introduces the prisoners at 515a–b he describes them as engaged in "naming the things they see" (*onomazein haper horôen*). As it happens, in *Republic* VII Plato doesn't bother to take up the question of what such "naming" might involve. However, there is a key passage in the *Phaedo* that bears directly on this topic. At 100c he officially introduces the Forms into discussion by means of a well-known metaphysical principle that has become known as "One-Over-Many": "If there is anything beautiful besides the Form of Beauty, it so because it participates in [that Form]."

Notice that this principle by itself has no epistemological content. It simply states the conditions under which a sensible thing falls within a certain "natural" classification, quite independently of whether anyone knows, or even *could* know, that it does. As such, it is not to be confused with another principle stated in general form just a few lines later. "the Forms exist, and . . . the other things that participate in them get their names from them" (102b).

Unlike One-Over-Many, this principle, which I shall call "Eponymy," does have an epistemological component, because it speaks to the question of how it is possible for people generally to apply the correct common name to a given "natural class" of sensible things. Part of this obviously has to do with the things themselves, that they all participate in a single Form, and that they therefore, so to speak, form a "nameworthy" grouping. This is essentially the force of One-Over-Many. However, Eponymy also concerns a certain human achievement. Things don't simply "get" their names in a vacuum; they are *named* by competent language-users. And according to Eponymy, they are not named arbitrarily, but for a principled reason: because of their common participation in respective Forms. But in order to accomplish this, it would seem that language-users must in some way or other have epistemic access to the facts about participation in Forms. In other words, if some group of sensibles participated in a single Form, but people generally were entirely oblivious to that fact, then Eponymy would seem to entail that they would not be capable the applying the common term associated with that Form.[33] Now since Plato's description of the unenlightened prisoners in *Republic* VII indicates that he thinks people generally do have the ability to name things with tolerable success, we have reason to believe he thinks they also have such epistemic access. And the most likely explanation of *how* they could have this is the one given by K1, that it is a residual effect of prenatal acquaintance with the Forms.

VII

In defending K1 I have been arguing for the involvement of prenatal acquaintance with the Forms in one particular type of pre-philosophical cognition, that which underlies the basic human capacity to classify and assign names to the objects of sense-experience. However, I have been careful to qualify my descriptions of this capacity with such phrases as "more or less accurately" so as not to overstate Plato's estimation of its value. In the Cave allegory, the unenlightened prisoners can apply names with sufficient accuracy to qualify them as competent language-users. Yet since the returning prisoner is described as immeasurably better (*muriô beltion*) than they are at judging things in the cave, it would seem that their level of performance must also allow room for significant improvement. What we need to determine, then, is the respect in which a Platonic philosopher will be better than competent language-users generally in applying names to the objects of sense-experience. I will close by briefly addressing this issue by relating it to an epistemological problem that arises in connection with the Socrates' method of inquiry in Plato's earlier dialogues.

At *Euthyphro* 4e, a skeptical Socrates wonders whether his interlocutor knows piety so "exactly" (*akribôs*) that he can confidently prosecute his own father for murder on a decidedly questionable set of facts. After Euthyphro brashly answers in the affirmative, Socrates implores him to say "what piety is" – to give the definition of piety – so that Socrates himself can use what Euthyphro says as a "standard" (*paradeigma*) to determine which acts are holy and which not (5c–d, 6d). To be sure, Socrates doesn't say outright here that having the definition is *necessary* to make such determinations, but the incredulous tone of his earlier question strongly suggests that he believes that it is. The problem this presents is that Socrates seems perfectly willing in numerous passages throughout the early dialogues to rely on his and his interlocutors' pre-theoretic judgments about the application of the virtue-terms in order to *test* various proposed definitions.[34] This has given rise to the charge that Socrates is involved in a vicious epistemic circularity of believing both (1) that one cannot know what are instances of a virtue without knowing the definition and also (2) that one cannot come to know the definition of a virtue without already knowing what are instances of it.[35]

One proposal for extricating Socrates from this difficulty turns on ascribing to him a tacit distinction between "hard" and "easy" cases.[36] On this line of defense, the examples Socrates uses to test proposed definitions are confined to "easy," or "clear-cut" cases, examples that no reasonable person would dispute. On the other hand, it is argued, he reasonably believes that with a correct definition in hand, he will have the sort of "exact" knowledge needed to effectively adjudicate *all* cases, including the "hard" or controversial ones.

I am not so much concerned here with whether this constitutes a successful exoneration of Socratic method in the early dialogues. I introduce it here because I believe its distinction between hard and easy cases offers us a plausible way of understanding the difference between pre-philosophical opinion and the genuine philosophical knowledge in *Republic* VII. As Plato's cave-bound prisoners classify and assign names to the objects they experience, they do so in a manner accurate enough to justify describing them as competent users of their shared language. On the present proposal, however, their competence in classification is restricted to unproblematic and uncontroversial cases. This is essentially the condition in which Socrates finds his interlocutors in the early dialogues. By contrast, in describing his philosophical protagonist in *Republic* VII as "immeasurably better" than the others, Plato means to attribute to him the sort of "exact knowledge" that Socrates had demanded of Euthyphro, the sort that would allow the correct application of names with unerring precision in all possible cases, including the "hard" ones.

Now it might seem that on this interpretation the distance between pre-philosophical opinion and philosophical wisdom is too small. That is, it might be objected that if pre-philosophical opinion provides enough accuracy in naming to make its possessors competent language-users, it cannot be all that inferior to knowledge gained through philosophical training. In other words, it may be wondered why Plato should quibble over a few percentage points in accuracy, especially given the high costs involved in making up the difference.

This way of thinking is engendered by the illusion that "accuracy" in naming is always to be understood in purely quantitative terms. However, this illusion can be dispelled if we recall the key point made earlier: that all of Plato's diverse philosophical work in the *Republic* is ultimately subordinated to his central ethical project. In the present context, this means that in *Republic* VII Plato is not thinking about the application of just any general term, but more particularly of such *ethical* terms as "just," "courageous," and the like. This is crucial. For in the case of ethical terms, "accuracy" consists not in the percentage of correct applications, but in one's ability to advance beyond applying the term "more or less correctly" to applying it appropriately even to the most unclear or complex cases. Now it is arguably the essential purpose of ethical *theory* to furnish the conceptual means to accomplish this difficult advance, and within the system of the *Republic*, the acquisition of ethical theory is tantamount to coming to know the Forms.

Notes

1   I take no position here on whether the philosophical projects of these early works are those of the historical Socrates, or are instead innovations of Plato himself in his early period.

2   See for example his interrogation of a renowned rhapsodist through much of the *Ion*.

3   See *Laches* 187e–188c together with *Gorgias* 495d–e.

4   This perspective is reflected in Socrates' ironic suggestion at *Laches* 186a–187b that the process of certifying ethical experts might be accomplished by a comparison of professional resumés.

5   This naturally prompts the further question of whether Plato is *ever* able to complete the thought of *Meno* 98a. In the final section of the *Theaetetus*, which is generally agreed to be a late work, Plato does consider three possible ways of conceiving

of the sort of "account" (*logos*) that could transform mere true belief into knowledge. There are, however, two formidable reasons to resist seeing this as an amplification of his remark at *Meno* 98a. To begin with, the *Theaetetus* ends inconclusively, with Plato indicating serious problems with all three of the possibilities entertained. More importantly, it is not at all clear how any of the three sorts of "accounts" considered, even if it were genuinely Platonic, could plausibly be regarded as "causal."

6   See Ferejohn 1991 and also McKirahan 1992.

7   Notice that there seems to be some slippage here between a cognitive state *itself* being fixed and stable in the *Meno*, and a cognitive state having an *object* with a fixed and stable nature in the *Republic*.

8   It is not clear whether Plato's reasons for thinking that sensibles are not suitable objects of knowledge stem from the fact that they are constantly changing their properties through time, or from what seems to be a very different consideration (which has been called the "compresence of opposites") that any predicate that applies to them can also be shown, with equal plausibility, not to apply. On this, see Irwin 1977b.

9   One key piece of information missing from Socrates' story is how it is determined which objects are conveyed along the walkway, and in what order they are conveyed.

10 In *Republic* VI, prior to presenting the diagram of the Line, Socrates employs yet another expository device, a simile in which the sun is likened to the Form of the Good, which occupies a privileged position in Platonic philosophy. On this see Santas 1999: 247–74.

11 This is not to deny that there are serious problems in understanding many aspects of the theory of knowledge presented in *Republic* VI–VII. One issue in particular that has exercised scholars greatly is interpreting the final transition in the Divided Line passage wherein one is supposed to advance from one sort of knowledge (*dianoia*), which Plato describes as the soul proceeding from assumptions (*hupothesis*) to a final conclusion (*teleutên*), to another, higher sort of knowledge (*nous*), in which one somehow is supposed to proceed from assumptions to a first principle (*archên*).

12 The affirmative answer to this question is defended, on different grounds, in Vlastos 1999: 64–92, and Armstrong 1973, and has more recently been challenged in Fine 1999: 215–46.

13 Largely on the basis of this sort of consideration, but for other reasons as well. Gail Fine (1999) rejects the usual interpretation of *Republic* 477–9, according to which all relevant occurrences of the verb "to be" are existential and Plato is intending to establish the *metaphysical* thesis that knowledge and belief have different sorts of *objects*. On Fine's alternative interpretation, the verb is used "veridically" and Plato is arguing for the *epistemological* conclusion that *propositions* that are known must be true, whereas those that are merely believed can be either true or false.

14 Bostock 1986, esp. 66–72.

15 Ibid.: 68.

16 Later on, while discussing the *Phaedrus*, Bostock connects this low-level, "ordinary humdrum knowledge" with the general human "ability to understand language" (1986: 70), i.e., with mastering the use of general terms. I shall return to this connection later.

17 The doctrine also appears in the *Phaedo*, and later in the *Phaedrus*, but is curiously absent from the *Republic*. Nevertheless, I will suggest below that certain elements of the doctrine are implicit in Books VI and VII of that work.

18 Whether Socrates had been providing the boy with substantive information about the problem and its solution by posing leading questions is a separate issue.

19 Bostock 1986: 72.

20 D. Scott 1999: 93–124.

21 This is not to say that recollection only occurs at the *termination* of this process. Even in the *Meno* Socrates is willing to allow that the slave-boy has begun to recollect, while also denying that he yet *knows* the answer (cf. 84a with 85c).

22 In similar fashion, Scott summarily dismisses the contention in Bedu-Addo 1991: 27–60, that pre-philosophical knowledge of Forms operates "subconsciously" on the extraneous philological grounds that Plato never *mentions* the subconscious (Scott 1999: 106 n. 11). In fact, Socrates' diagnosis of the slave-boy in the *Meno*, as possessing the answer even while sincerely denying that he does, commits Plato to the existence of subconscious cognitive states, whether or not he has a general term under which to classify them.

23 Scott 1999: 97.

24 Ibid.: 94.

25 Ibid.: 97.

26 Bostock 1986: 72.

27 Ibid.: 71.

28 The qualification here is crucial, and will be taken up in my closing remarks in Section VII below.

29 Evidently these are meant to stand for social esteem and political advancement.

30 Plato also notes a radical difference in the motivational structures of the protagonist and the other prisoners, since the former is described repeatedly as having no interest in the "honors, praises, and prizes" mentioned at 516c–d.

31 Again (see note 9), Plato never bothers to say what accounts for these regularities. Within the allegory itself, the agency of the bearers of the carved objects may just be a literary device, but the real question is what – other than the Forms – could possibly underlie the patterns and regularities presented by perceptual experience.

32 I don't mean to suggest that this would entirely vitiate the theoretical function of the Forms. It might be argued that they also provide a metaphysical basis for objective values in Plato's system, and that correct ethical judgement requires knowledge of this basis. If Plato observed an "is/ought" distinction, he might then believe that even complete "factual" knowledge of the sensible realm could not bring ethical knowledge in its train.

33 Which particular sounds or written marks are employed in the naming process in a given language is of course a separate issue (with which Plato is concerned through much of the *Cratylus*).

34 See for example Socrates' use of examples at *Laches* 191d–e and *Republic* I. 331c–d.

35 The original attribution of this so-called "Socratic fallacy" is found in P. Geach 1966. On different defenses against Geach's charge, see, e.g., Santas 1972: 17–41; Irwin 1977a: 37–101.

36 See Nehamas 1986.

References

Armstrong, D. M. (1973) *Belief, Truth, and Knowledge*, London: Cambridge University Press.

Bedu-Addo, J. (1991) "Sense-experience and the argument for recollection in Plato's *Phaedo*," *Phronesis* 36, pp. 27–60.

Bostock, D. (1986) *Plato's* Phaedo, Oxford: Oxford University Press.

Ferejohn, M. T. (1991) *Origins of Aristotelian Science*, New Haven, CT: Yale University Press.

Fine, G. "Knowledge and belief in *Republic* 5–7," in G. Fine (ed.) *Plato I: Metaphysics and Epistemology*, Oxford: Oxford University Press.

Geach, P. (1966) "Plato's *Euthyphro*: an analysis and commentary," *The Monist* 50, pp. 369–82.

Irwin, T. (1977a) *Plato's Moral Theory*, Oxford: Oxford University Press.

——(1977b) "The Heracleitianism of Plato," *Philosophical Quarterly* 27, pp. 1–13.

McKirahan, R. (1992) *Principles and Proofs*, Princeton, NJ: Princeton University Press.

Nehamas, A. (1986) "Socrates' intellectualism," *Proceedings of the Boston Area Colloquium in Ancient Philosophy* 2, Lanham, MD: University Press of America, pp. 275–316.

Santas, G. (1972) "The Socratic fallacy," *Journal of the History of Philosophy* 10, pp. 17–41.

——(1999) "The Form of the Good in Plato's *Republic*," in G. Fine (ed.) *Plato I: Metaphysics and Epistemology*, Oxford: Oxford University Press.

Scott, D. (1999) "Platonic recollection," in G. Fine (ed.) *Plato I: Metaphysics and Epistemology*, Oxford: Oxford University Press.

Vlastos, G. (1999) "Socrates' disavowal of knowledge," in G. Fine (ed.) *Plato I: Metaphysics and Epistemology*, Oxford: Oxford University Press.

12

The Forms in
the *Republic*

Terry Penner

1 On What the Forms Are:
the Present State of the Question

What are those supposedly eternal, unchanging, and somehow perfect entities that Plato refers to using such expressions as "Justice itself," "the just itself" and even sometimes simply "justice"? More to the point for readers of the *Republic*, what is the Form of the Good, without which none of the other Forms would be knowable or even exist, and which is "beyond being" (508b–509b)? Is it the Form of *benefit* in general, so that for a person to seek to partake in it is to seek benefit *for* someone (oneself, one's city, or perhaps others)? Or is it the Form of Good-*as-such*: the Form of good without qualification and entirely without relation to oneself or to any particular person or persons? In the latter case, for a person to seek to partake in it is to seek not some personal good (of oneself, one's city, or others) but what is good *as such*: what is, so to speak, *impersonally* good. A slight tweaking of the latter notion, it has been suggested (n.3 below) would give us the Form of what is good-for-its-own-sake, which would bring us to the Form of what is *morally* good.

The *Republic* does not contain anything that looks like a full-dress exposition of a "Theory of Forms." This has not stopped legions of otherwise very impressive interpreters of Plato – some of them, beginning with Aristotle himself, outstanding philosophers in their own right – from telling us, in considerable detail, what the "Theory of Forms" is, and diagnosing its many supposed errors and confusions. For some, (1) the Forms are no more than universals or attributes of the sort picked out by predicates such as "just" and corresponding abstract nouns such as "justice." For others, (2) the Forms are more like *ideal objects, paradigms*, or *models*. Here the Forms are not attributes so much as objects *pos-*

sessing those attributes (and to an ideal and perfect degree). For Aristotle, (3) the Forms were actually a bit of both: the product, he thought, of a metaphysical confusion wherein Plato construed universals or attributes (*such*-es) as if they were objects – substances, things (*this*-es).

In (2) and (3), we begin to see the view emerging of a certain metaphysical excess to the Forms. Such views tend to gain credence from such Platonic images as we find in the Divided Line and the Cave, where interpreters have all too easily supposed that (4) we have, corresponding to the four types (or faculties) of cognition singled out there, four different sorts of objects, ranked in accordance with their *degree of reality*, only the highest objects being fully real – the objects of knowledge, i.e., the Forms.

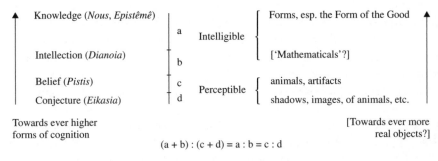

$$(a + b) : (c + d) = a : b = c : d$$

Diagram of the Divided Line

This separating of the Forms from less real objects, especially the physical objects of the perceptible world, if taken far enough, could lead to the following (positivist) worry: "You send the guardians off to the isles of the blest, as it were, to study the ultimate realities in another world. How does that help them rule in *this* world – the perceptible world – given that all they have been studying is objects of quite a different (and higher) degree of reality?"

Finally, in modern times, philosophers following in the footsteps of the impressive formalist/logicist tradition of Frege, Russell, and Hilbert, bequeathed to modern analytical philosophy a fundamentally linguistic method, in which what *people* are saying by means of their sentences – and what things they are referring to (intend to refer to) by means of their words – can only be handled in terms of what their *sentences* say (what "propositions" they express) and what their *words* refer to. The sentences of interest are then embedded in relatively short, and self-standing, strict (and formalizable) "deductions" in order to see what conclusions are "entailed."[1] This "formalist/logicism" amongst interpreters, combined with the careful linguistic attention to single words, phrases, and sentences which came both from linguistic philosophy and from a long tradition of important work in classical philology, led to very minute, apparently rigorous – and allegedly metaphysically neutral – logical analyses of the arguments of Plato and Aristotle. Especially in the Wittgensteinian era, in which Plato was suspected of being rather confused and primitive from a philosophical point of view (by contrast with the more sensible-looking and down-to-earth Aristotle), it became all too easy to seize on individual sentences or phrases in the text which, plugged into strict logical formulations of Plato's arguments, appeared to commit Plato to some very confused and indeed preposterous theses. Thus some interpreters took it that (5) Plato was committed to Universal Literal Self-Predication.

ULSP: For any Form, *F*-ness, that Form is itself the one perfect instance of *F*-ness (except possibly for some other Forms), while all perceptible instances of *F*-ness are at best imperfectly *F* things.

Those who attribute ULSP to Plato naturally find confirmation for their interpretation in the way it coheres with the accounts (2), (3), and (4) above. "Self-Predication" makes Plato an utter fool metaphysically. How could largeness be itself a large object? (A HUGE object, one would have to suppose.) Yet the most "rigorous" literal analysis of particular sentences seems to show Plato's sentences saying just this in certain cases. ("Look, he says it right here," interpreters say, lifting a single sentence, or even a few sentences from their contexts and formulating them as propositions to be plugged into formalizable "entailments."[2]) True, some found this preposterous thesis to have compensations in interpreting, say, Plato's ethics. For consider: Won't the Form of Beauty at *Symposium* 210e–211a win hands down the "beauty contest" with beautiful perceptible objects (Vlastos 1954 in Allen 1965: 231)? Doesn't Plato say here that the Form is not – as the perceptible beautifuls are – beautiful in one way, ugly in others; beautiful at one time, ugly at another; beautiful in relation to one thing, ugly in relation to another; beautiful here ugly there? So isn't the Form of the Beautiful *itself* a beautiful object, an object that is beautiful *non-relationally* and *without qualification*? Hence, won't the Form of the Good, which we are to *imitate*, be perfectly good? And won't it be *non-relationally* good – not good *for* anyone or anything? Thus a Form of the Good that is non-relationally good in this way might seem to give *me* a good to realize in my life that is not just *my* good, but instead something like a *moral* good. ("Wouldn't it be appalling," moral philosophers since Prichard have asked, "if Plato were to be promoting self-interest as a way of life?") Self-Predication here gives such moralists a new way out of this perennially felt difficulty.[3]

Space limits any attempt to develop here the *philosophical* case against the assumptions employed in such unfavorable accounts of the Forms, especially those underlying the Aristotelian and self-predicationist accounts of the Forms in (3) and (5). But I note here my opposition to formalist/logicist methods. In my view, what is at issue in the dialogues is not what the *sentences* of the interlocutors say, let alone "entail," as fitted into relatively brief formalizable deductions, but rather what the *interlocutors* are saying by means of these sentences. What *people* are saying I take to involve crucially what they intend their words to refer to. For me, such matters as what interlocutors are referring to (what they intend to single out) cannot be determined simply from semantic, linguistic, and logical analyses of the interlocutor's *words* and *sentences*. Only far closer attention to the larger human context of individual arguments, and indeed to the project of the *Republic* as a whole, will sufficiently clarify what *interlocutors* are talking about and saying. (The present article is, I hope, itself a manifestation of this alternative approach.)

2 Sketch of the View to be Offered Here

I shall argue here that, in partial agreement with (1), Forms *are* universals or attributes. They are not, however, just any universals or attributes, but rather certain fundamental attributes only: those that are the objects of the sciences or expertises:[4]

health in the science of medicine,
food in the expertise of farming,
[safe and efficient] transport [by sea] in the science of navigation,
the nature of the shoe in the craft of shoemaking,
number and figure in arithmetic and geometry.
and, most importantly (and especially clearly in Socratic passages)
the good of the individual in the science of the good (= virtue: see n. 4)
together with
the good of the citizens in the science of politics.

The easiest way for a modern reader to understand what Plato is up to here in the case of these "objects of the sciences" is in terms of the idea of the universe as having an underlying structure, already there prior to our thought and language, involving eternal and unchanging laws of nature, in terms of which all change in the perceptible universe takes place. For simplicity's sake, suppose we think of laws of nature as Humean constant conjunctions (of pairs of attributes). Then these attributes too will have to be eternal and unchanging, existing antecedently to our thought and language. I shall call these attributes "real natures."[5] Thus, while rejecting utterly the accounts of Forms in (3), (4), and (5) above, I find in this laws-of-nature account an explanation of why treating Forms as universals or attributes, if still incomplete, is not entirely mistaken. Similarly, the account of Forms as paradigms in (2), if incomplete, is also not entirely mistaken.

On this view, the fundamental place of the Forms in Plato's ontology implies the fundamental place of the sciences in Platonic epistemology, ethics, and political philosophy.

3 Plan of this Discussion of the Forms

I take it that Plato, like the great tragedians, has a purpose for every word and sentence his characters use, a purpose to be grasped only in terms of the way in which *what characters are saying* figures into the project of the work as a whole. Mining the dialogues for nuggets of brief formalizable analytical arguments, in my view, deprives us almost entirely of context,[6] distracting us from the way in which Plato uses *what his characters are saying* and *how they say it* in advancing his larger argumentative project. Accordingly, I proceed by looking at the four principal groups of passages on the Forms in the *Republic*, trying to see what the Forms will *have* to be if they are to function as what the character Socrates intends to be referring to in the argumentative context of the *Republic* as a whole. The four groups of passages, in ascending order of complexity and difficulty, are:

A: V.472b–e (the Form of Justice as a model we *look to* in devising this ideal city that is itself the model of the just person that we look to in order to see what justice and injustice are) with 454a–456c (on finding the right Forms for deciding whether the nature of women is as adapted to the science of ruling as the nature of men).

B: X.596a–602b (the Forms as they show up in the claim that mimetic [representational] pursuits, such as tragedy and painting, are "at the third remove from reality").

C: V.475e–480b with VI.484b–485b, 486d–e, 490a–b, 4293e–494a, 500b–502d (eternal, unchangeable Forms as objects of knowledge, contrasted with perceptible things which are merely objects of opinion [or perception: 507b, 509d–510a]: the whole range of Forms constituting the object of study for the true philosopher).

D: VI.502c–VII.541b (the Form of the Good as the *megiston mathêma* ["the greatest thing to be learned"]: the Sun; the Divided Line; the Cave; and dialectic and the theory of the sciences).

I shall look at these in succession. But if we are to see the arguments here in context, we must begin with an account of the general project of the *Republic* as a whole.

4 The *Republic*'s Project as a Whole

The central aim of the *Republic* is to answer the question so beautifully set up in Book I, whether the just person is happier than the completely unjust person. Books II–IV are devoted to that question, and to the prior question *what justice is*. Actually Plato takes up most of Books II–IV in answering not the main question but the prior question. He does so using an analogy he constructs between a certain (rather artificial) ideally just city (Kallipolis) constructed in our imagination,[7] and the just individual. This analogy yields, first, an account of *what justice is*, arguing that justice is a certain identical *constitution*[8] present both in the just individual and in Kallipolis. As the justice of Kallipolis consists in each of its three classes "doing its own" (i.e., fulfilling its function)[9] and not interfering with others doing *their* own; so too, justice in an individual consists in each of the three parts of the individual's soul – the rational, spirited, and appetitive parts – doing their own, and not interfering with the other parts doing their own. Here justice is – astonishingly! – not a matter of the individual's *external* behavior towards other citizens (say, within Kallipolis), but rather a matter of the *internal constitution* of the soul (no matter of what city the individual is a citizen).[10] Plato is saying that justice is a certain *well-adjustment of the parts of the soul to each other*. He then argues – with mind-boggling brevity (444e–445b) – that, given this account of *what justice is*,[11] it is clear that the just person *will* be happier than the (completely) unjust person. Thus the argument seems to be complete by the end of Book IV, excepting only an addendum that takes up the second half of Book X. This suggests that the remaining five and a half books are nothing but a ragbag of digressions – utopian-political, metaphysical, sociological, and aesthetic – from this supposed main issue of the happiness of the just and unjust individuals. This suggestion may make us wonder whether we have perhaps misconstrued the project of the *Republic*.

We have not. To begin with Books VIII–IX, they are *not* digressions – merely a completion of the argument of IV.444a–445e (n. 11) by looking at the constitution of the soul in each of four different kinds of unjust individuals, each such constitution being identical with the constitution of one of the four corresponding constructed cities. There is no departure here from the idea of using the city/soul analogy to answer the main question about the happiness of the just.[12] So these books are not a digression, but rather what we would have regarded as a very long footnote (or an appendix) to the treatment of the ideal city and the just soul: material that fits better as footnote or appendix than it would if it interrupted the flow of Book IV by being inserted at 445b. Hence Plato cleverly has Glaucon and Adeimantus interrupt with questions about the possibility of realizing the ideal city (449b ff.).

This still leaves three and a half books. I grant immediately that Book V – at least the parts concerning communism of wives, children, and property, and the equality of women – *is* a political digression. What analogues are there here to what goes on within the individual soul, what considerations bearing on the greater happiness of just individuals?[13] But what of the rest of Book V, Books VI–VII, and the first half of Book X? Do they not also concern the plainly political question (472b ff.) whether the ideal city could ever be realized, and how it should be realized, with discussion of the Theory of Forms as a digression (on higher education and the place of tragedy in Kallipolis) within that political digression?

To suppose this is to misconstrue Plato's project in the *Republic*. The material on the Forms is not a digression. Its primary point – largely missed by earlier

interpreters (and certainly by my earlier self) – is rather to address the inadequacy Book IV notes. This inadequacy arises when Socrates finally applies the
long account of justice in the ideal city (368e–434c) to justice in the individual
soul (434d–435c), by arguing that the justice of the ideal city is identical with
that of the soul – *because the soul, like the ideal city has three parts*, a ruling, intellectual part, a spirited part, and an appetitive part. To address the inadequacy in
question, we must take a "longer road" (435d, 504a–506e: see 435c–d within
the context 434d–435c for the change, finally, from the ideal city to the just
individual). But what *is* this "longer road"? It turns out to reside in the "greatest thing to be learned," which itself turns out to be the Idea or Form of the
Good (503e–504a, 505a, 519c). Once more, the flow of Book IV would be best
maintained by the ancient equivalent of a long footnote or appendix, or even
the equivalent of an entire new chapter supplying the essential content explicitly
promised in the preceding chapter. Plato's equivalent to these literary devices
turns out to be having the Form of the Good show up in a digression on higher
education within a political digression. What the Book IV account of justice and
the parts of the soul lacks, I claim, is an account of *the knowledge of the good*
which it is the function of the rational part of a completely just soul to acquire
in order to rule all three parts – the good in question being the *good* (*advantage, benefit*: 442c with 339b, *Meno* 87e) *of the parts of the soul, both separately
and together* (441e, 442c, with 441b–c, 427c ff., esp. 428c–d). This connection
between

A: the Form of the Good (to which "the longer road" leads), and
B: the function of the rational part to look to the advantage of the parts of
   the soul taken separately and as a whole

shows us why what Plato presents as a digression in Books VI and VII is in fact
central not only, as it obviously is, to the *Republic* as a whole, but also to the
project of Books II–IV.[14]

Let us turn now to our passages.

5 The First Group of Passages on
the Forms (V.472b–e with 454a–456c)

As already noted, Book V is devoted to a series of apparent utopian-political
digressions: on the equality of women, on the communism of women and children, and on the "philosopher-rulers." It is in the digression concerning the need
for philosopher-rulers if the ideal city is to be realized (471e ff.) where the
expression "Justice itself" shows up first – front and center at V.472b–c. Here
Socrates says: Remember our main aim: to discover whether the just person is
happier than the completely unjust person by inquiring into *what justice is*

(472b4) in the ideal city. This project, Socrates implies, will lead us to look at the just person as either "like *the just itself* in every respect" or "as like it as possible." Does the talk of the person being *like* the Form suggest that the Form is itself perfectly just (Self-Predication)? Let us look at some of this passage more closely. (Crucial references to the Forms are underlined.):

> **472b7** If we discover <u>what justice is</u> (*hoion* it is),[15] and the just man, are we to demand that the just man shall differ from it in no respect, but shall be in every way like (*toiouton hoion*) <u>what justice **c1** is</u> (*hoion* justice is)]? Or will it suffice us if (he approximate to) <u>it</u> as nearly as possible and <u>partake of it</u> more than others? . . . **c4** It was for the sake of a <u>pattern</u> [*paradeigma*], then, that we were inquiring into <u>justice itself and what it is</u> (*hoion* it is), and likewise into the perfectly just man **c7** were he to come-to-be,[16] and what he would be like (*hoios* he would be) in coming-to-be – inquiring also into injustice **c8** and the most unjust man – so that looking to <u>them</u> and how they would appear to us with respect to happiness or the reverse, we would necessarily agree, even about ourselves, that whoever is most like (*homoiotatos*) <u>them</u> will have the allotment of happiness and unhappiness **d1** most like (*homoiotatên*) theirs. Our purpose then was not to show that these things could come-to-be . . . **d4** Do you think, then, that he would be any the less a good painter, who, after portraying a <u>pattern</u> (*hoion*) [of such a sort as] the most beautiful man would be, and omitting no touch required for the perfection of the picture, should not be able to prove that it is actually possible **d7** for such a man (*toiouton andra*) to come-to-be? . . . (translation adapted rather extensively from Shorey)

The first thing that must strike us here, besides the reference (out of the blue almost) to "Justice itself" and its appearance, at dead center of the project of determining how justice stands to happiness, is the talk of "patterns" and the discovery of such patterns. Quite as striking is a certain superficial confusion as to what the pattern is here: Is it Justice itself, or *the perfectly just man* which the painter aims to depict? The phrase "if he should come-to-be" added to "the perfectly just man" even suggests Plato is treating interchangeably the painter's ideal man and a painter's ideal city[17] – another superficial confusion. (What is the man who strives to be just supposed to be *like*? The Form? The ideal man? Or the ideal city?)

It is such apparent confusions, and such talk of "imitating," that leads some to find Self-Predication here. The Form would be an abstract object that, for example, itself *behaves in a perfectly just fashion*! (The man who strives to be just is to imitate precisely this behavior in the Form.) Isn't Plato, then, confusing universals or attributes with certain ideal and perfect instances ("patterns") of those universals or properties?[18]

Not if we try to see the passage as a whole and in its wider context. What we have here is the purely verbal product of compression of style, and the desire to speak at once of (a) the Form, (b) the perfectly just person the painter tries to depict, and (c) actual persons, and perhaps even (d) the perfectly just city which the *Republic* is depicting. Let us disentangle several important points about the Forms that emerge fairly clearly if we do not rush to judgments of confusion. First, how the Form Justice itself functions in this passage is as the answer to the question "What is justice?" (472b4, 472b7, with 472b9–472c1). Second, "what justice is" is used interchangeably with "What Justice itself is" (472b4, 472b7, with 472c4–5; also n. 18 above). Isn't Plato's intention then, third, that one take this Form, Justice itself, which one is trying to discover, as a pattern (an abstract pattern telling us what justice is), by *looking to which* a painter may depict the perfectly just man. It is this perfectly just man the painter depicts, and which, like the ideal city Plato depicts, *partakes in* this Form, or *has perfectly*, this attribute of justice, so that actual just men (imperfectly just men) will partake in that Form (or have that attribute) to the greatest extent possible. None of these points require the claim that the Form of Justice is a being who acts perfectly justly, except as a misunderstanding of certain elisions in Plato's manner of speaking. The point is merely that the Form tells us what justice is, and we look to that account of what justice is in trying to embody justice in ourselves or in a city. Let us ask what *Plato* is saying, not what certain *sentences* (proof-texts) say, looked at in isolation.

Consider now this notion of *looking to*[19] a Form in order to embody that Form as perfectly as possible in the world of things that come-to-be. The notion is clearly what is at stake in the *Cratylus*, where we see that the carpenter, when trying to replace a broken shuttle, looks not to the broken shuttle, but to that Form – the shuttle itself (389b), the *nature* (389c) *of the shuttle* – which he looked to in making even the shuttle that is now broken, embodying that (antecedently existing real) nature in his work. That shuttle itself – the shuttle by nature (389c–d) whose Form one embodies in the material (390e) – is the natural implement for the task of weaving. The suggestion here is that there is an expertise or science of shuttle-making, to the object of which expertise (namely, the real nature of the shuttle, the shuttle itself), the carpenter looks. As

A: the carpenter, if the shuttles he makes are to be good instruments for weaving, looks to the real nature, or Form, of the Shuttle (which is not, however, some abstract object which is itself a super-good instrument for weaving but rather that, by knowing which, we know what a shuttle is)

so

B: the just person, if the life he strives to live is to be a just life, looks to the real nature, or Form, of Justice (which is not, however, some abstract object which itself behaves in a super-just way but rather that, by knowing which we know what behaving justly is).

No tincture of Self-Predication. Indeed, neither *Cratylus* 389b–390e nor *Republic* 472b–e come within a million miles of suggesting any such thing as that the *Form* of the shuttle might be a good instrument for weaving. (Any more than a modern might suggest that one might live in the *blueprints* for a building which the builder looks to.)

It is true that some commentators have seen just this self-predicationist suggestion in Plato's remarks a little lower down in the *Republic*, at 500b–c, to the effect that the true philosopher whose thoughts are directed to *the things that are* will try to be *like* these *eternal, organized, and unchangeable entities*. This is read as saying that the human becomes intrinsically good (that is, organized, unified, and harmonious) by imitating these eternal entities that are themselves, quite literally, intrinsically good (that is, organized, unified, and harmonious).[20] Thus the Form of the Good would itself be an intrinsic good, and (as suggested by 500c) the Form of Justice would itself be just – the kind of thing that would behave purely and perfectly justly. (This exhibits the self-predicationist view of imitating the Forms: the Forms themselves have the very attributes we wish to have.) Each Form is the perfect exemplification of itself (and indeed the only such perfect exemplification, except perhaps for certain other Forms).

But the suggestion founders on the fact that when Socrates speaks here of the Forms to be imitated, he says not only that they do not *adikein* (*do* injustice) but also that they do not *adikeisthai* (*suffer* injustice). Was it any part of Plato's intention to suggest that in striving to be like these entities, we should strive not only to avoid *doing* injustice, but also to avoid *suffering* injustice? Surely not. At most, the passage is suggesting something like the view that communing with the peace of the changeless world of thought (in which injustice isn't even *suffered*) will help one avoid the doing of injustice (compare 480b–c, 486d). The talk of *imitating* the Form of Justice simply says that one should *look to* the Form of Justice (which tells us what justice is) in order to embody justice in oneself (500c–e) in the way in which, as noted above, the shuttle-maker looks to the Form of the Shuttle (no super-shuttle, but that which tells him what the shuttle is) in order to make shuttles.

Thus, 470b–d and 500b–c give us no reason to attribute the silly view of Self-Predication to Plato. To sum up, 470b–d, viewed within its argumentative context, tells us simply that

> F1:   The Forms are the general properties or structures which it is the business of an appropriate science or expertise to study, and which the appropriate expert will look to, using them as patterns, in attempting to embody the Form (to the extent possible) in things that come-to-be.

This picture of the Forms is amply confirmed in the earlier discussion of the equality of women. Should the apparently differing natures of men and women lead us to assign ruling to men and not to women? That is only to be settled by "dividing nature according to Forms" (454a). And here we find that it makes no sense to treat those who *bear* children differently from those who *beget* children with respect to who should be allowed to qualify in the expertise of ruling – any more than it would to make sense to treat hirsute and bald men differently with respect to who should be allowed to be a shoemaker. The Forms that have to be divided correctly here are the real natures of *man, woman, ruling, baldness, shoemaking,* and so forth which it is the business of the appropriate sciences or expertises to study – just as we find in (F1). We are not talking about Forms that beget and bear children.

Let us see whether this general conclusion from Book V is supported by the treatment of the Forms and the expertise of carpentry in Book X.

6   The Second Group of Passages (X.596a–602b)

In Book X, the Forms turn out to be central to the discussion of the shortcomings of drama for purposes of the good of the ideal city (and so also, by implication, for the good of the individual). Like the *Cratylus* passage, the Forms turn up (596c–598d) in consideration of what a carpenter looks to in making particular beds, chairs, wooden flutes, and so forth. Unlike the *Cratylus* passage, however, this time we also find more troublingly metaphysical-looking things said about the Forms, apparently connecting them with suspect talk of *perfection* and *greater reality*. Socrates says here, in connection with the Form of the Bed, that the carpenter doesn't make *what a bed is*, but merely *a* bed. He doesn't make *what is* (or *being*) but merely what is *like* what is, which is <u>not</u> *what is*. The product or work (*ergon*) of the carpenter is not *what perfectly is*, indeed, it is "somewhat obscure with respect to truth." In connection, then, with what a representational artist like a dramatist or a painter produces, we find the following analogy deployed, concerning "the three beds": As

the painter stands to a painting of a bed,

so

the carpenter stands to the bed he manufactures,

and so

God stands to the Form of the Bed (God as the real maker of the really real bed: 597c–d).

What God makes – "what the bed is," the thing itself which is "one in nature," whose Form both the carpenter's and the painter's bed possess – is made by God because he doesn't want just to make *a* bed, one of many physical beds. From this analogy, Plato tells us that we can see that the painter resides at "the third remove from reality" (*alêtheia*: truth). (And the carpenter, who presumably *looks to* what the bed is, comes in second, while only one with knowledge of the Forms comes in first.[21]) Such is the alarmingly obscure account of why tragedians are at the "third remove from reality" and must be excluded from Kallipolis.

This odd language has given interpreters all sorts of trouble, and spawned all sort of theories about what the Forms are – theories of the kind "logicist" and self-predicationist interpreters will pounce on. Nonetheless, Plato's main purpose in introducing the Form of the Bed here emerges clearly enough. And, indeed, were it not for this handful of odd-looking locutions, we should surely suppose that what the passage says is not much more than that the Form is simply an attribute or universal – *being a bed*, the real nature of the bed – that is the object of the science of carpentry (or bed-manufacturing), and which the carpenter "looks to" in order to embody that attribute or universal in the carpenter's material.

What then are we to make of the talk of these three kinds of objects that appear to be divided by their differing degrees of "reality" or "truth," the Form being "perfect," perceptible beds being "obscure," and paintings being "at the third remove from reality [or truth]"? Why is one any less real than the other? Surely if each *exists* it is real enough? (We return to "degrees of reality" in section 9 below.)

Have we any assurance that the main point of 596c–598d is no more than I have suggested in the paragraph before last? We do. For when, in a doublet of this passage at 600e–602b, Socrates turns to explaining again the point of the earlier passage, he gives the following variant of the triad *painting/artifact/Form*: that the painter imitates not the physical flute the carpenter makes, but the *appearance* of the physical flute; while the flute-maker does not have knowledge of whether the flutes he makes are good or bad; rather, the *user* of the flute has that knowledge. What this means is that now we have, interchangeably with the first triad of makers: *painter/carpenter/God*, a second triad: *painter/flute-maker/flute-player*. It is the *flute-player* (!) – the expert at realizing the function of the flute – who knows *what the flute is*. This is because he or she knows the *end* of the flute – what the flute is *for* (n. 4 above). What is crucial here about the Form of the Flute is that it tells us *what a flute is* and thereby gives us *the function of a flute as used by an expert flute-player*: to know *what a flute is* is to have that abstract conception of what a flute is that one can convey to a flute-maker who is making flutes. The knowledge of the Form of the Flute is thus, surprisingly enough, *the knowledge possessed by any and every expert flute-player*. In the absence of other passages, why should we suppose there is any more point to this apparent talk of degrees of reality or truth than there is to the idea of alternative conceptions of *what a flute is* (in ascending order of merit: painter, maker, user)? What we have here is that

> F2: The Form of certain groups of perceptible particulars is the general property or kind or abstract structure the expert maker of such objects has to *look to* in order to embody it in its material, perhaps informed by one who knows the good that is to be achieved by using such objects. Once more the Forms are the objects of sciences or expertises; but knowing the Forms requires also knowing the good it is the function of objects

of that kind to achieve. One who tries to understand what the flute is, using solely existing physical flutes (some perhaps even a broken or damaged flute – compare the shuttle above) is further from the truth (or from reality). Yet further from the truth (or from reality) will be one who tries to understand what the flute is using solely *paintings* of flutes.

Why need the content of 595c–598a be more than this? Notice, incidentally, how "truer" (closer to the truth, closer to how things are) seems more appropriate here than "more real." *Equally real things* (painting, beds, and the real nature of the bed) may nevertheless be closer to or further from the *truth* than each other about *what a bed is*. (A similar thought will occur to us when we come to the Line and the Cave below: see (F5) with the concluding remarks of section 9 below.)

Notice that goods of the sciences, like the sciences themselves, may be hierarchically arranged (*Euthydemus* 289c–292c, *Cratylus* 388c–d with 390a–d, *Statesman* 304b–305e). To know *what beds are* one needs to know what sleep (the good of beds) is, and to know what sleep is, one needs to know what human life (the good of sleep) is, and to know this one needs to know what the human good (the good of human life) is, and to know this one will have to know what the good quite generally is. This indeed explains the extraordinary suggestion at 508b–509b (section 1, paragraph 1 above) that the Form of the Good is the cause of our knowledge of all the other Forms. By the same argument, the *nature of the bed* will not exist unless there is such a thing as *what a bed* is, hence also such a thing as *what sleep is*, and so forth, as above, till we come to *what the good is*. So we also have an explanation of why Plato says that Form of the Good is the cause of the *existence* of the other Forms.[22]

What remains over as puzzling, nevertheless, is this talk of *being* in Book X, and of the *things that are* in the passage 500b which we have looked at above. *This* oddness could reinforce insistence on the oddness of Self-Predication. Let us see how this idea shows up in Plato's further elaboration in our third group of passages, which are rather more explicit about such odd contrasts as that between *being* and *coming-to-be*.

7 The Third Group of Passages on the Forms (V.475e–480b, VI.484b–485b, 486d–e, 490a–b, 493e–494a, 500b–502d)

What is it for the Form of Beauty to *be* or exist? It is for beauty to be *one* (476a, 479a, 507b, 524b–c, 596a). But what is it for beauty to be one? Well, what would it be for beauty to be many? It would be for beauty never to be *anything but many* – that is, for there to be no saying something truly of beauty that isn't

the same as saying that same thing of beautiful things (that is, beautiful perceptible things). One could not even say that beauty and ugliness are *opposites*, since
there would then have to be *two* opposites, and beauty would again be one! But
there is no way for beautiful perceptibles not to be *many* perceptible beautifuls.

This sets us up for Plato's big contrast at V.476c–480b between those who
believe in the Forms and those who do not. Here, Plato contrasts the true
philosopher with the "lover of sights and sounds" (the "sight-lover"), with
respect to what the objects are of their different approaches to *what is*. The sight-
lovers are described as "dreamers" (476c–d, compare 520c, 533b), while the true
philosophers, the believers in the Forms, are described as "awake."

So, what is this dreaming? It is *not believing in beauty itself* (the nature of
the beautiful), but only in beautiful perceptibles (color, shapes, sounds),
thinking that beautiful perceptibles aren't merely *like* beauty itself, but actually
are beauty itself (476d). This characterization is confirmed in the identification of being "awake" with thinking the beautiful itself *is something*, and being
able to see that it *is not* the things that partake in it, and that they *are not* it
(47c–d).[23]

But how are we to understand this? Socrates tells us that the dreamers (a)
believe that beauty itself does not exist, and yet (b) affirm that *what it is*, is the
many beautiful perceptibles. But then if beautiful perceptibles exist – as
the dreamers will surely suppose – then, *contrary* to (a), it will turn out that the
beautiful itself *does* exist. How are we to avoid this apparent contradiction: that
beauty itself both (b) exists and (a) does not exist? There appears to be only one
way to understand this: by supposing that what the dreamers actually think is
that *all there is* to the so-called beautiful itself is the many beautiful perceptibles.
For the dreamers, then, there exists no beautiful itself *in addition to* the many
beautiful perceptibles themselves.

What dreaming is, in this treatment, is the affirmation of what modern
philosophers of science call a "destructive reducing identity." (Compare: *All there
is to "possession by devils" is behavior in epileptic seizures.*) If "nominalism" stands
for the reductionist view that all there is to *beauty, equality, the square, and the
like,* is the many particular beautiful (equal, square) perceptible objects, then the
dreamers are what modern philosophers call "nominalists." These nominalists
give us a particular account, one Plato thinks false, of the answer to the question "What is beauty?" The true philosophers, the believers in Forms, by contrast, are anti-nominalists. They deny such identities, affirming that there exists,
in addition to the many beautiful perceptible objects, some further object: not
a visible object, presumably, in the way all the beautiful perceptibles are, but an
abstract object. Given what we have said already about the objects of the sciences, Plato will take these abstract objects to exist antecedently to our thought
and language. They are not objects *created* by us,[24] but objects already there
awaiting our *discovery* of them. (Opposites, if thought of as each one, are abstract
objects.[25]) This constitutes an answer to the question "What is beauty?" which

is altogether different from the nominalist answer. This new answer resides in the apprehension of certain abstract objects as already there awaiting discovery by the sciences.

But why does Plato contrast beautiful perceptible objects with the Forms as being merely "opinable," "objects of opinion" (477a ff.) rather than as "knowable," as constantly changeable (484b ff.) rather than eternal, and indeed as not even *being*, but rather as merely "between *being* and *not being*" (477a–479c)? Why does he regard them as being mere "becomers," things that merely *come-to-be* (508d, 518c–d, 519b, 525a ff., 534a)? Here we need to remember that within this passage (475e ff.) Socrates identifies what opinion and knowledge are with *dreaming* and *being awake* respectively, *not* with knowing certain propositions. But now the dispute between "dreamers" and those who are "awake" is over what beauty itself is to be identified with, over whether to affirm or deny the (destructive reducing) nominalist account of what beauty is; and if the nominalist account is false, then there is more to beauty than simply the many beautiful perceptibles (with the "something more" spelled out as above). Hence the talk of knowing is not talk of *knowing that some proposition or propositions are true*, but rather of knowing something that arguably cannot be encapsulated in some mere proposition or plurality of propositions – that is, knowing the Form by looking to which alone we may come to understand what beauty is.[26] *This* is the knowledge in question in this passage.

Why then does the passage say that there can be no knowledge of perceptible beautifuls? It does not. What it says – whatever may be further true about the possibility or impossibility of various forms of *knowledge that* (if there is such a thing) about beautiful perceptibles – is rather that there is no understanding of what beauty is which is identifiable with encountering beautiful perceptibles. From all this, I conclude that

> F3: to say that Forms such as Beauty itself and Justice itself alone have *being* is to say such things as that the Form of Beauty tells us what [perceptible] beautiful things *are*. What beauty *is*, is not reducible to perceptible beautiful things. What is more, what beauty *is* gives perceptible things such beauty as they have, as the Form of the Flute gives flutes such identity as they have. (A bit of wood is a flute only so long as it partakes of the Form of the Flute.[27])

Other passages fill in the detail of this a bit. VI.484b–485b says that perceptible things (which are many) are constantly changing and that Forms (each of which "is one": 493e) are models that the politician with knowledge will *look to* in order to embody them in the world of coming-to-be. In addition, the Form of Justice, in the world of *being*, is *what justice is* (486d–e, 490a–b, n. 15 above, nn. 28, 29 below). And at 500b–502d, discussed above (section 5), Socrates also notes that the just person will imitate the Form of Justice (without the slightest suggestion of Self-Predication).

Let us see now whether the picture of the Forms in (F1)–(F3) is fulfilled by what we see in the main part of Books VI and VII.

8 The Fourth Group of Passages (VI.502c–VII.541b: Sun, Line, and Cave) as Describing the "Longer Road": Plato's Identification of *The Good* with *The Form of the Good*

To see how the images of Sun, Line, and Cave work within the project of the *Republic* as a whole, we need now to elaborate on our claim in section 4 that the main purpose of the long section on the Forms, and especially the Form of the Good, was to address the inadequacy in Book IV's parts-of-the-soul account of the virtues in an individual. This claim links the "longer road" and our long section on the Forms not with utopian politics, but with the parts of soul (*individual* souls) and the virtues *of individuals*.

What is this "greatest thing to be learned"? What could be greater, Glaucon asks (504d), than the virtues Justice, Wisdom, Temperance, and Courage accounted for in terms of the parts of the soul at 435d–444e? The answer is:

> **505a2** . . . you have often heard that the greatest thing to be learned is the Idea of the Good by reference to which just things and all the rest become useful and beneficial. And now I am almost sure you know that *this* is what I am going to speak of and that I am going to say further that we have no adequate knowledge of it. And **a6** if we do not know [this], then, even if without this we should know all other things never so well, **a7** you know that it would avail us nothing, just as no possession either is of any avail **b1** without the good. Or do you think there is any profit in possessing anything if it is not good, or in understanding all things else **b3** without the good while understanding and knowing nothing that is fair and good? (trans. adapted from Shorey, my underlining)

Here the Idea or Form of the Good is plainly identified with the good.[28,29]

Now, we have seen (section 4) that the function of the rational part – and what it is for the rational part to "do its own" – requires it to secure *the knowledge (science) of the good* which it is to employ in securing the good (advantage, benefit) of the three parts separately and together. This connects the Form of the Good with the parts-of-the-soul account of the virtues, the announced inadequacy of Book IV being just the incompleteness of failing to specify *what that good is*, that is, what the Form of the Good is.

Does our picture of the Form of the Good so far stand up in the rest of Books VI–VII? The relevant passages are (again with my underlining):

A: The argument that neither pleasure nor knowledge is <u>the good</u> (n. 28 above).

B: *The simile of the Sun.* Socrates can't say what <u>the Form of the Good</u> is, but he can propose an image of it. As the Sun stands to the existence of, and our perception of, the realm of *coming-to-be*, i.e., the perceptible realm; so <u>the Form of the Good</u> stands to the existence of, and our knowledge of, the realm of *being* and truth, i.e., the intelligible realm.

C: *The analogy of the Divided Line.* The diagram of the Divided Line, above, shows Plato's representation of both (d) perceptible images, reflections, and shadows, and (c) the perceptible originals of those images as *visibles*; and of both (b) certain objects of geometry and (a) a certain *un*-hypothetical first principle of everything (511b–d, 533c with 532a–b) which *is* <u>the Form of the Good</u> (517b–d, 532b) as *intelligibles*.[30]

D: *The allegory of the Cave.* Certain initially chained and immobilized prisoners in the cave of this allegory are taken on an adventure-in-seeing, through a series of attempted identifications of what is *there* to be seen, from

(d) black shapes moving on a rock, to

(c) statues moved in front of a fire which cast shadows on the rock, to

(b) the animals outside the cave which the statues are statues *of*, to

(a) the heavenly bodies and indeed the Sun itself that nurtures these animals.

The Sun allegorizes <u>the Form of the Good</u> (517b–c, 532a, 532c), as the other heavenly bodies probably allegorize the real natures (Forms) embodied in each of the kinds of animals.

E. The question what studies to prescribe to a trainee "guardian" in order to turn the eye of the soul from the realm of *coming-to-be* to the realm of *being*. (The study of numbers, of lines and figures, of solids, of ratios in the theory of celestial movements, and of ratios in the theory of harmonics.) The point (532a, 532c, 533a, 533c, 534c, 540a–b) is to find <u>the good itself</u>, <u>what is best</u>, <u>the Form of the Good</u>. Indeed in each of these five discussions, the ultimate aim is to come to know <u>the Form of the Good</u>.

The "longer road" (A)–(E) is extremely absorbing at epistemological, metaphysical, educational, and political levels, thus tempting the supposition that the passages are merely parts of a digression, the question of the "longer road" having been dropped. But, as always with Plato, we have to stay focused. The "longer road" appears only in VI–VII because Plato needed a stretch of dialogue long enough to introduce the proper further discussion of the good which it is the function of the rational part of the soul to aim at. (Transparency of exposition would hardly have been served by interpolating most of Books VI and VII, let alone all of Books VIII and IX as well, into the text of Book IV, at, say, IV.442d and 444a respectively.)

On self-predicationist interpretation of these passages, the Form of the Good is literally the best thing there is, indeed impersonally best (not best for me or for you, or for the ideal city, or for anyone at all). It is then argued that this is close enough to the *moral* good. Against this, the present interpretation has shown how, if my rational part looks to the Form of the Good, it does so to bring about *my* good – not some impersonal, *moral* good – just as, in the ideal city, the guardians aim to bring about the *city's* good, not some impersonal good. (Similarly, if the shoemaker looks to the Form of the Shoe, he does so not to make *general* shoes, let alone *moral* shoes, but the particular shoes *he* will soon be selling. Whatever modern moralists brought up with Christian notions of self-lessness may think, for Plato, as for Socrates, the good is to seek one's own good. (This does not identify the good with selfishness [caring for no one but your-self] since both Socrates and Plato also held that harming others inevitably results in harm to oneself. Caring for others *is* caring for oneself.)

It will turn out, in fact, that there is considerable continuity here with the Socratic approach to ethics. For it turns out to be as difficult to answer the question "What is the good?" in the *Republic* – and hence (by n. 26) any other "What is it?" question as it is to answer the question "What is virtue?" in the earlier dialogues, where Socrates himself does not know the answer to any such questions, in spite of being the wisest person there is.

I conclude that

F4:   the Form of the Good just *is* the good we all desire:[31] the real nature or attribute which is the object of the science of the good.

There are two elements to the interpretation we get from (F1)–(F4): (a) anti-reductionism, and (b) the theory of sciences as having objects that exist antecedently to our thought and language.[32] Plausible as I think this interpretation position is, some may feel that the famous images of the Sun, Line, and Cave passages undermine this with some sort of really odd metaphysical theory of degrees of reality. I turn now to showing that Sun, Line, and Cave give us no more than the anti-reductionism about the objects of the sciences that we have found so far.

9 The Anti-reductionism of the Sun, Line, and Cave about the Real Natures of Things that Structure the Universe

The Sun passage begins as if it is going to cohere straightforwardly with our earlier passages concerning the dreamers as "nominalists" (section 7), since it refers explicitly to just the passage about the dreamers:

[Let me remind] you of what has been said here before [475e ff.] and often on other occasions . . . We say many beautiful [things] and many good [things], each of them, *are*, and we mark them off [from each other] [*diorizomen*] in our speech . . . And again we speak of a beautiful itself and a good itself, and so with all the things that we then posited as many, we turn about and posit each as a single Idea in each case, it being one, and we say that it is what *is* in each case . . . [The many beautiful perceptible things] we say are to be seen, not thought, while the Ideas are to be thought and not seen. (507a–b, adapted from Shorey)

The talk of beauty being one and not many, and of its being knowable and not merely perceivable gets us the same anti-nominalist view that we uncovered in discussing the dreamers. True, Socrates also makes here the at first sight aston-ishing claim (508e–509b) that

A: the Form of Good is the cause both of our knowledge of, and of the being of all the other Forms, and that it is not *being*, but surpasses *being*, or is "beyond *being*."

But we have already shown in section 6, second last paragraph, that there is an entirely innocent interpretation of (A). Still, that interpretation, like any inter-pretation, could still be undermined from elsewhere. For example, what of the metaphysically arresting suggestion that

B: the Divided Line and the Cave are to be understood in terms of four kinds of cognition, and, correspondingly, four kinds of objects, each of a different degree of reality)?

For (B) would give us something rather metaphysically extreme by comparison with the anti-reductionist account above of the objects of the sciences. On this view, each kind of cognition is as adequate as it can be for its corresponding object; and since the higher kinds of object are successively "more real" as one cognitively ascends (in the Line or in the Cave), the higher faculty also yields a superior cognition, purely by virtue of its object being more real.

But there is a flaw in the Degrees of Reality theory. This is that in connec-tion with the objects of intellection (section (b) of the diagram of the Divided Line: the objects studied by geometry) Plato does not appear to specify anything but the *Forms* as objects (for example, the Circle itself, the Diagonal itself). Great scholars, most famously Adam 1902, vol. II: 156ff., have nevertheless not hesi-tated to leap to the defense of this Degrees of Reality theory, suggesting that the objects studied by geometry are not such Forms as the Circle itself, but rather certain "mathematicals" which Aristotle speaks of. (There is only one Circle itself; but the first proposition of Euclid refers to two absolutely equal circles; they are obviously not perceptible circles, and equally obviously not Forms, since there is only one of each Form. These are Aristotle's "mathematicals.") This defense of Adam's *would* solve the problem, if there were the slightest indication that the "Circle itself" and "Diagonal itself" refer in this passage not to Forms but to "mathematicals." But there isn't.

There are other problems for the Degrees of Reality. Consider, in the parallel allegory of the Cave, the four kinds of objects perceived by the chained prisoner in his successively improved forms of cognition:

(d) the black shapes moving on the rock,
(c) the stone objects that cast the shadows on the rock,
(b) the animals of which the stone objects are statues, and
(a) the Sun, through which one sees best what the animals are as well as what the Sun is.

Is what we have allegorized here objects of four different degrees of reality, and four forms of cognition of the corresponding objects, as the Degrees of Reality theory requires? This would give the question "What are you seeing?" four different interpretations (or even, four different senses) with four different four kinds of objects as answers:

- What do you see on the rock? (black shapes)
- What do you see when freed? (shaped rocks carried in front of a fire)
- What do you see in reflections outside the cave? (perceptible animals) and
- What do you see in the sky outside the cave? (stars, and above all the Sun).

Each answer would be perfectly correct as answer to the corresponding question, even though at higher stages in the ascent, the objects turn out to be "more real" (*mallon onta*: 515d4; *aléthestera*, truer: 515d7). Such a question-and-answer scheme suggests that Plato recognizes that at the lowest stage of the Cave the prisoner has at least the knowledge that certain black shapes are moving across the rock – empirical knowledge as we now say (and compare the uncanny anticipation of Humean "constant conjunction" at 516c–d). Plato would be granting that there is such a thing as empirical knowledge, even while denying that it is in touch with highest realities.

But this suggestion of four different questions corresponding to four different interpretations of "What are you seeing?" will not work. Let me explain why.

So far as the text is concerned, the chained prisoner is asked two questions. The first is,

What are the passing things [in the current situation] (515b).[33]

The prisoner's answer is "The [black shapes] I see on the rock". (Notice the connection with the "What is it?" questions that appear in (F2) and (F3) above, as well as "What each of them is?" and (twice) "What the truth is [about what you are seeing]" at 515c–d.)[34] And the second question is,

What is speaking?

We have seen how the first question is interpreted in the Degrees of Reality theory: as a one of four different interpretations of (or four different senses of) "What is it that you are seeing?" At the lowest stage, this Degrees of Reality interpretation yields:

What are the black shapes you are seeing? (And by the way, never mind what the causal history of these black shapes is.)

I do not believe this is the question we are asking when we ask the freed prisoner: "What are the passing things [in this situation]?"

This interpretation is utterly refuted by the prisoner's successive answers to the second question, "What is it (that causes the sound in this situation)?" When still chained, he answers "The black shapes I see." But when he has been freed and has become used to the dazzle of the fire, we do not have a new interpretation of the question. It is the very same question, the prisoner now recognizes to be the question which, in its first asking, he had answered wrongly. It was not the black shapes on the rock but the statue-holders who were speaking. Applying this result to the first question, there are *not* two different "What is it?" questions, the answers to each of which are perfectly correct, given the degree of reality of their respective objects. Instead there is the *same* question (What are the passing things [in this situation]?) with different answers – the black shapes and the statues (or statue-holders that were shadowed on the rock) – *one falser than the other.*

Notice the exquisite consequence – inconsistent with empiricism, Hume, Kant, positivism, and "the linguistic turn" – that the chained prisoners are not restricted to intending to refer to things they can conceptualize, that is, to things in their "world." What they intend to speak of is, unbeknownst to themselves, the statue-movers on the parapet behind themselves. Indeed for them to want to speak of the actual causes of the sound they hear coming off the rock is for them to have a notion of correctness that goes beyond anything they can actually conceptualize. Plato would, quite correctly, have had nothing to do with Kant's "Copernican revolution."

We get a similar result when we consider the two highest levels of the Line. It is not that there are two objects and two faculties of cognition, one for "mathematicals," one for Forms, so that there is a "What is it?" question for each level, and a corresponding answer that is as correct as it can be given its degree of reality. Let me quote this rather tangled passage.

510c2 I think you are aware that students of geometry and reckoning and such subjects first hypothesize the odd and the even, and the various figures and three kinds of angles and other things akin to these in each branch of science. They regard them as known; and, treating them as hypotheses, do not deign to render any further account of them to themselves or others, taking it for granted that **d1** they are obvious to everybody.[35] They take their start from these, and pursuing the inquiry from this point on consistently conclude with that for the investigation of which they set out . . . **d5** And do you not also know that they further make use of these visible forms [e.g., drawn squares at stage (c) of the Line] and talk about them, though they are not thinking of those [drawn squares] but of those things of which the [drawn squares] are a likeness, pursuing their inquiry for the sake of the Square itself and the Diagonal itself **e1**, and not for the sake of the image of

it which they draw . . . **a4**. This, then, is the kind [of cognition] I have called intelligible (*noêton*),[36] it is true, but with the reservation first that the soul is compelled
to employ hypotheses in the investigation of it, not proceeding to a principle
because of its inability to extricate itself from and rise above its hypotheses, and
second, that it uses as images or likenesses the very [drawn figures] that are themselves copied and adumbrated by the class below them [shadows, reflections, and
so forth of physical objects, drawn squares, and so forth] where [the hypotheses],
in comparison with these [drawn squares], are esteemed as clear **a9** and held in
honor . . . [i.e. the things] that fall under geometry and **a10** the kindred arts. (trans.
adapted from Shorey)

(If *imitation* in Plato implies Self-Predication, then the mathematicals will themselves be, for example, perfectly square, as will the Form itself.[37])

Is there any mention of mathematicals here as objects of geometry? Or
mention of anything else the geometer uses or thinks of but (a) perceptibles
(drawn figures) which they use even though their thought is not directed towards
them, and (b) the odd and the even, the kinds of angles, the Square itself, and
the Diagonal itself which they *hypothesize* and *treat as known*, though at that stage
they do *not* know them, since they merely hypothesize them? On the Degrees
of Reality theory, why *wouldn't* geometers have mathematical knowledge of the
mathematicals, even if mathematicals are not as real as Forms? (Compare on
"empirical knowledge" just above.) To get to knowledge of the subject matter
of geometry, we have to ascend from these hypotheses (axioms and definitions),
and come to a full understanding of such things as the Square itself. It is not
said here that the geometer knows certain propositions concerning the objects
of geometry (the mathematicals) to the extent such knowledge is possible, which
propositions can be known without knowing the corresponding Forms. The
objects of geometry aren't mathematicals at all. They are such Forms as the
Square itself. Of that Form the geometer does *not* have knowledge, even though,
while he is working with the perceptible drawn figures used in the geometer's
theorems, he is *thinking* of that Form – of course without knowing what it is.
So there are not two "What is it?" questions, one for each of these upper two
levels of the line, each with its own answer (the mathematicals and the Forms).
Rather there is just one question, "What is the square?" and just one object (the
Square itself); and to the one question there are two answers, one inferior to
the other. The geometer's answer is based upon mere hypotheses ("postulates"
as we now say), which are not themselves known. And, as Plato points out at
Theaetetus 201e ff. – at any rate, by implication – if you don't have *knowledge*
of the axioms, then the proofs don't give you knowledge of the so-called theorems.[38] On the other hand, at the top level, where there is knowledge of the
Square itself – that is, knowledge of *what the square is* – the dialectician gives
the fully adequate answer that is given by the Forms.

Putting together our discussions of the lower two stages of the Cave and the
Line, I infer that we do not have four different "What is it?" question about

objects of four different degrees of reality, but just one "What is it?" question, for example "What is the square?," to which people offer four successively more adequate answers. Extrapolating a little, for the Line, this one question might be "What is the square?" The four answers – three of them being reductionist answers – would be

A1: The square is nothing more than these images, shadows;

A2: The square is nothing more than these square objects and drawn squares;

A3: The square is nothing more than the objects – whatever they might be – defined by our axioms; and

A4: The square is what is given by the Form.

Only the fourth (non-reductionist) answer gives us the knowledge of the answer to the one question. This shows us why Plato says the geometer does not have knowledge of geometry. It also shows us why we cannot say that the chained prisoner knows (empirically) at least that black shapes are moving across the rock.[39]

Let me further, if briefly, defend this Platonic attack on "empirical" knowledge of the black shapes. What are these black shapes? Are not these black shapes (d) *shadows* of (c) *shaped rocks* which are in fact statues of (b) certain *perceptible things outside the cave*, which are what they are (horses, say) only because they embody (a) a certain abstract structure, the real nature of the horse, or of equinity – *the Horse Itself*. So how could you know the answer to the question "What is the real nature of the horse?" if you thought that all there was to the real nature of a horse was black shapes moving on the rock; or these shaped rocks being carried on the parapet; or some plurality of physical (perceptible) horses? But now, suppose that in the cave, not only those at the highest stage, but also the chained prisoners, are referring to (intend to refer to) not just black-shapes-whatever-their-causal-history but to (d) shadows of (c) statues of (b) horses partaking in (a) the Form of Horse (if that is what the black shapes really are). Then whether they know it or they are really referring to shadows of statues of . . . There is no such thing in Plato as knowledge, empirical or not, of the "proposition" that *the black shapes are moving across the rocks* that is compatible with almost total ignorance of what the black shapes *are*.

I emphasize a point already made above. Contrary to modern logic and "the linguistic turn," Plato takes it that to know what someone is saying, it is not enough to know what "proposition" the person's sentence expresses. One must know what the things are that the person intends to refer to. Thus what the prisoner intends to refer to when he talks about the black shapes moving on the rock is *whatever those black shapes really are*; even if, unbeknownst to him, they are (d) shadows of (c) statues of (b) animals which embody (a) the Form, he does not know that his claim is true. Hence when he says "The black shapes are moving on the rock" he does not know *what* claim he is making. (*A fortiori*, he does not have knowledge, even "empirical knowledge," that his claim is true.)

Contrast the common logical notion that while we do not always know whether what we are saying is true, we do in general know what we are saying (what "proposition" we are expressing).

In sum, what the Cave and Line images give us is an expansion of the same anti-reductionism as we saw earlier with those who are "awake" as opposed to the "dreamers" (compare [F3] above). This time Plato is claiming that

F5: The square cannot be reduced to any shadows, to any physical objects or drawn squares, or even any entities of the sort a geometer might postulate as implicitly defined by the axioms of geometry. There are four different degrees of *truth* about what the square is, only one of which, when apprehended, gives us the actual truth (*alêtheia*) about the square. There are, if you will, four different degrees of grasp of what the square *is* (*einai, on*). There are not four different degrees of reality. And there are no "mathematicals" in the Divided Line.

Not different degrees of *reality* in different *objects*, but different degrees of *truth* in different *conceptions* of one object. The threat to (F1)–(F4) from the talk of "degrees of reality" is removed.

10   Conclusion

This completes our brief survey of passages on the Forms in the *Republic*. I have argued that believing that there exist, antecedently to our thought and language, real natures or Forms is no more extraordinary than believing there are, antecedently to our thought and language, certain laws of nature which give the underlying structure of the universe. In a way this is an idea so elementary as to be almost taken for granted by those, such as myself, who take this realist approach to science. No wonder, then, that Plato gives us no full-dress exposition of the "Theory of Forms." His failure to do so should tell us something about a great many other bizarre accounts of the Theory of Forms.

Notes

1   An example of this method: actually attributing to Socrates in the early dialogues just such a strictly deductive method, the so-called "Socratic elenchus." For my utter repudiation of this method – both as philosophy and as interpretation – see Penner forthcoming, a.

2   Similarly, at *Phaedo* 74a–c, the Form of the equal is taken to be perfectly equal – not equal to *this* or equal to *that*, but (preposterously!) equal *period*. The Form of Largeness seems itself (even more preposterously!) to be *a large object* if the famous

"Third Man Argument" (*Parmenides* 132a) is to get off the ground as a formalizable argument. (See Penner 1987, Clarifications VI–VII.) Notice that no interpreter
was so much as *tempted* to find anything so preposterous as "Self-Predication"
in Plato prior to the discovery of the logicist/formalist difficulties with self-
membership in the Russell Paradox. See Taylor 1915–16, Wedberg 1955, with
Vlastos 1965, as well as the discussion at Penner 1987, Clarifications VI–VII.

3 See the brilliant but implausible Rawlsian move in White 1979: 35–7, 44, 54, 58–60,
along with the difficulties he bravely faces at p. 48 ("the good of the city is . . . more
of an unqualified good than one's own good"!!). On the other hand, compare Morris
1934–5, who managed, *without* Self-Predication, to suggest that the Form of
the Good was a moral good as metaphysically radical as the Kantian Categorical
Imperative.

4 I use "science," "expertise," "knowledge," and "understanding" interchangeably here
for Plato's use, interchangeably, of *epistême* and *technê*. These expertises are for the
most part intended by Socrates and Plato to be technologies, each with a specific
end (e.g. health) where the relevant expert aims at finding *means* (e.g., healing) to
realize the end. In my view – a controversial one – if, as Socrates holds, virtue is
knowledge, i.e., the science of the good, then the end of virtue is happiness, and
goodness in a person is being good at the means to securing that end. (For Plato
in the *Republic*, virtue is also, in its main part, a science of the good, though, unlike
Socrates, Plato thinks this one science is not achievable by purely intellectual means,
since extensive prior training of *character* is required.) See also the second last paragraph of section 6 with n. 30 below.

5 We find laws-of-nature accounts in the British idealists and Kantians: see Penner
1987: 330 nn. 18–20, as well as the index under "laws of nature." See also the
attractive, if far too Kantian, far too Aristotelian Natorp 1903. (Laws of nature would
of course be teleological for Plato – as in Aristotelian biology – and so will be construed in terms of means and ends, functions, and so forth.)

6 It is symptomatic of the best modern work in philosophical logic, in its preoccupa-
tion with formalization, that the only use it has for "context" is in connection with
interpreting words like "here," "now," "I," etc. Thus the person intended by the
speaker, if (as often) it does not follow from what the *sentence* says, is not part of
the context!

7 It is a city constructed "in words" (see, for example, 369a). Compare also "as if in a
fable" vs. "into the realm of truth" at *Timaeus* 26c–d. See also Penner forthcoming, b.

8 The constitution of a city (*polis*) is the way in which the parts of the city (actually
the three classes: ruling intellectuals, soldiers, workers) interact with each other within
the way the city as a whole carries on (*polit-eia*). But then, to speak of an *identity
of constitution* between ideal city and just soul is surely surprising. For the three parts
of the city each have a plurality of members, while the three parts of the soul certainly do not. Hence one speaks only of an *analogy* between ideal city and just soul.
But it is evidently Plato's intention that what counts as the *constitution* of the ideal
city should abstract from any such differences, and actually be *identical* with the constitution of the just soul. Notice also (Schofield 2001: 199) that the word for the
constitution of both city and soul is *politeia*. The title of the *Republic* is actually
"About the Constitution" in Greek. When Cicero translated it as *De Republica*, he

was probably thinking of the work as primarily a work of utopian-political theory. But, *pace* many modern interpreters, it is only secondarily that, being primarily a work about whether the constitution of a just soul makes an individual happy.

9 See Santas 2001: 66ff.

10 See Penner forthcoming, b, as well as n. 11.

11 The argument of 444e–445bb is just that as life is not worth living for a sick body – one whose parts are not well-adjusted to each other – no matter how much food, drink, etc. it can have, so life is not worth living for a *soul* whose parts are not well-adjusted to each other. There are similar uses of the body/soul analogy at *Crito* 47d–48a and *Gorgias* 504e–505b.

12 There are three elements in the comparisons within Books VIII–IX: (a) the individual soul of a given degree of injustice *in no matter what city*, (b) depicted cities of that degree of injustice, and (c) depicted typical citizens *in those cities*. We do Plato no service if we confuse (a) the just soul *in no matter what city* with (b) the soul of the just citizen *of the ideal city*.

13 Similar questions about the discussion of primary education in the ideal city in Books II–III are not so serious; for that discussion applies *mutatis mutandis* to the primary education of individuals.

14 Notice that on this account, the inadequacy of the argument of Book IV is not an actual *error*. (Books VIII–IX, indeed, give no indication of any such error.) All we have in Book IV is a gap concerning the good that the rational part of a just person looks to, a gap which is filled by looking to the Form of the Good.

15 It will become clear from the underlinings that *what justice is* = *what Justice itself is*. (Notice that things partake in *what justice is*.)

16 Sometimes translated "becoming." "Coming-to-be" is closer to the Greek in that one can't become *period* (without becoming *something*), whereas one can come-to-be *period*.

17 For the question whether that ideal city might come-to-be, see 450c, 452e, 456c, 457d, 458b, 461e, 466d, 471c–473e. It seems plain that Plato does not confuse the ideal man and the ideal city. He simply feels free here, as in Books VIII–IX, to go back and forth between ideal city (or unjust city) and individuals whose souls have the same constitution. See nn. 8, 12 above.

18 Compare Aristotle's criticism in (3) of section 1 above, reinforcing (2) and (5).

19 See VI.484b–485b, 501b–e, 540a–b (the painter or sculptor looking to the Form to embody the Form of Justice in the ideal city, in the ideal man, and in the souls of humans), as well as 477c, 500b–e ,477d, 500b, 515d, 518d, 527d, 532b–c. Even in earlier dialogues, where the Form is not often spoken of, there is something a science or expertise *looks to* in doing its work.

20 E.g., Kraut 1992: 316–23 and 2003: 238–9, on the Forms as intrinsically good *because* ordered, unified, and harmonious.

21 As for God creating the Forms (presumably at some point in time), this suggestion about the (eternal!) Forms is quite un-Platonic. (See also *Timaeus* 28a–b, 28e–29b.) In interpreting what Socrates is saying here, we should attend not to what his *words* would say, taken by themselves, but rather try to work out from the wider context what *Socrates* is trying to convey by means of these words. Isn't God brought in here simply to have an artisan to parallel the carpenter and the painter? Isn't what

is important the objects in question: painting (made by painter), artifact (made by carpenter), Form (made by God)? That this is so will become clearer below when we come to a later doublet of the present passage.

22 As for why the Form of the Good is "beyond being," the analogy with the Sun (first among perceptibles, surely) tells us that the point is simply that the Form of the Good is non-identical with any of the subordinate beings that make up the realm of being. Nothing more is required.

23 See Penner 1987: 57–69 with 20–6, 40–3 on non-identities as sometime existence claims, and on the strong confirmation of this anti-nominalist picture of Plato's arguments for the Forms in the "Argument from the Sciences" which Aristotle attributes to Plato.

24 Conceptualism or Constructivism holds that all abstract objects whatever are created by us. (Thus laws of nature, as construed above, would not exist till rational beings such as humans exist.)

25 Indeed on the present showing, the opposites are the Forms of opposites. See Penner 1987: 86–95.

26 There is no knowledge of any Form without knowledge of the Form of the Good (section 6, second last paragraph). But presumably no one has a full grasp on the Form of the Good. (See 505d–506a, 504b–505b, 533b, 534b–c.) Propositions, on the other hand, are supposed to be the sorts of things we can know. (Those who say the *Republic* works with a "mathematical model" of knowledge, have geometers knowing *many propositions*. But the attribution to the *Republic* of this account of mathematical certainty is indefensible. See the discussion of 510c2ff. in section 9 below.)

27 This is one reason that there is no knowledge of perceptible flutes; for (looked at omni-temporally) what they are is *not* flutes, but rather pieces of wood that are temporarily flutes. Indeed, not only may anything at all happen to flutes to make them stop being flutes (them? bits of wood?); anything at all may happen to bits of wood. What is the *it* here that is temporarily this piece of wood, this flute? What knowledge do we have of *it*? (Thus, for Plato, does flux undo knowledge of things in this world. Similarly, Socrates is not unchangeably taller [than Phaedo]. When Phaedo grows, Socrates, without changing, becomes shorter [than Phaedo]. So being taller, like being a flute, does not attach unchangeably to any perceptible.)

28 What we translate, at 505a6, as "[this]" and "this," ignorance of which will make nothing else of any use, surely refers back to the 'it' at 505a5 and the Form of the Good at 505a2. But "the good" at 505b1 and 505b3 surely refers back to "this." Hence these occurrences of "this," "it," and "the good" here cannot stand for a Form of the Good which is distinct from the good. When the many say "Pleasure is the good" (505b, 506b with 505d–506a, 509a), they are not saying, surely, that pleasure is a certain Form of the Good which is distinct from the good. The only solution is to suppose that in such passages as the present one, Plato uses "the good" and "the Form of the Good" interchangeably – identifying them, indeed.

29 Given that the Idea or Form of the Good that we seek knowledge of, and which makes other things useful and beneficial, is the good, we may note that it is also the knowledge of the good that makes things useful and beneficial at *Euthydemus* 280a–281e, *Meno* 88c–e, suggesting there is no ethically relevant distinction between the good in the early dialogues and the Form of the Good in the *Republic*. This

identity of the Form of the Good and the good of which we seek knowledge can also be seen at 505a vs. 505b–c and 506b; also at 506d7–8 and 506e vs. 506d4.

30 I admit that it is less easy to see how knowing what the Forms of Square and Diagonal are requires knowledge of the Form of the Good. However we are to see this, it must fit with *Euthydemus* 290b–c, where dialectic is certainly said to be the superordinate science which uses what the geometer hunts, while at *Cratylus* 390d, dialectic is said to be the superordinate science which uses name-legislation (the science of assigning of words to things).

31 "How can we all desire the same thing, if I desire my good, and you desire your good?" I suggest that for me to seek *my* happiness and for you to seek *your* happiness = for us both to seek the same happiness (I that it be instantiated in my life, you that it be instantiated in your life) = for us both to seek (to have our lives partake in) the same Form of the Good.

32 Both features are present in the "Argument from the Sciences" which Aristotle attributes to Plato (Penner 1987: 245–7, 43; 2003: 197–207).

33 The text at 515b is disputed. Another text makes the question rather "What are the real things?" (Answer: The black shapes I see.)

34 See Penner 1987: 116–21 on four more occurrences of the "What is it?" questions at 523d, 524a, 524c, 524e.

35 We may have here a hint of self-evidence of the sort that may also appear in the *Meno* and *Phaedo*, though not elsewhere in Plato, before it reappears in Aristotle.

36 The reservations that follow make clear this is a *part* of the intelligible, as just below at 511b2. (The intelligible covers both what the geometer studies and what is studied by one who knows the Forms.)

37 An impossible suggestion, given *Phaedrus* 247c, which says that Forms are colorless and shapeless. How could a Square itself, which is self-predicationally square, be shapeless?

38 Think of "simples" in this passage as axioms and "complexes" as theorems. What is proved is not thereby known, since in the end there are no proofs of axioms. Given then that there is no such thing as self-evidence, the common talk of proofs providing knowledge is entirely misguided. Might proofs then really be proofs that *if* the axioms are true, *then* the theorems are true (Russell)? Not unless logic is itself self-evident.

39 Why does Plato bother with the shadows and reflections at the bottom of the Line? Because Plato is preparing for the upcoming Allegory of the Cave. For the shadows of justice at the bottom of the Cave are the actual laws of the city and the things insisted on by the citizens. Plato thinks it important to disagree emphatically with those who wish to reduce *what justice is* to justice *as commonly and plausibly conceived*.

References

Adam, J. (1902) *The Republic of Plato*, 2 vols., Cambridge: Cambridge University Press.

Kraut, R. (1992) "The defense of justice in Plato's *Republic*," in R. Kraut (ed.) *The Cambridge Companion to Plato*, Cambridge: Cambridge University Press.

——(2003) "Penner's anti-paradeigmatism," in *The Modern Schoolman* 80, pp. 235–43.

Morris, C. R. (1934–5) "Plato's theory of the good man's motives," *Proceedings of the Aristotelian Society* 34, pp.129–42.

Natorp, Paul (1903) *Plato's Theory of Ideas: An Introduction to Idealism*; trans. (2004) V. Politis and J. Connolly, Sankt Augustin, Germany: Academia.

Penner, T. (1987) *The Ascent from Nominalism*, Dordrecht: Reidel.

——(2003) "The Forms, the Form of the Good, and the desire for good in Plato's *Republic*," *The Modern Schoolman* 80, pp. 191–233.

——(forthcoming, a) "Logic, language, and the so-called 'Socratic elenchus'," *Proceedings of the 2004 Meetings of the International Plato Society*.

——(forthcoming, b) "Platonic justice and the meaning of 'Justice'," online in *Plato: The Journal of the International Plato Society*, 2005 (http:/www.nd.edu/~plato).

Santas, G. (2001) *Goodness and Justice: Plato, Aristotle, and the Moderns*, Malden, MA: Blackwell.

Schofield, M. (2001) "Approaching Plato's *Republic*," in C. Rowe and M. Schofield (eds.) *The Cambridge History of Greek and Roman Thought*, Cambridge: Cambridge University Press.

Taylor, A. E. (1915–16) "Parmenides, Zeno, and Socrates," in *Proceedings of the Aristotelian Society* 16; repr. in *Philosophical Studies*, London: Macmillan, 1934.

Vlastos, G. (1954) "The Third Man Argument in the *Parmenides*," in *Philosophical Review* 63; repr. (1965) in R. E. Allen (ed.) *Studies in Plato's Metaphysics*, New York: Humanities Press.

Wedberg, A. (1955) *Plato's Philosophy of Mathematics*, Stockholm: Almquist and Wiksell.

White, N. P. (1979) *A Companion to Plato's Republic*, Indianapolis: Hackett Publishing.

13

Plato's Defense of Justice in the *Republic*

Rachel G. K. Singpurwalla

We have a strong intuition that considerations of moral rightness or justice play a central role in the good life – an intuition, that is, that it is always in our interest to be just. We fear, however, that there might be no justification for our intuition. This worry is only deepened when we attempt to substantiate the idea that it is always in our interest to be just and find that the most obvious and immediate justifications suggest that it is only in our interest to be just some of the time. For example, one justification for the claim that justice is always in my interest is that if I am just, I can reap the rewards of having a reputation for justice, and avoid the negative consequences of having a reputation for injustice. But clearly this response suggests that it is only in our interest to be just some of the time. What about those circumstances where I can engage in immoral behavior without detection? Certainly I have plenty of opportunities to cheat or steal without getting caught. Or, what about circumstances where I think that the goods gained by engaging in immoral behavior outweigh the social disapprobation associated with that behavior? After all, I won't be shunned by an entire community for seducing someone else's partner, or for investing in a company with exploitive practices. Is there any reason for thinking that being just in these circumstances is in my interest?

Plato's aim in the *Republic* is to demonstrate that we do have a reason to be just in all circumstances, for being just is always in our best interest. To accomplish this goal, Plato must show three things. First, he must put forth an account of justice, since we cannot evaluate whether or not justice is always in our interest without knowing what, at least in large measure, justice is. Second, he must show that justice itself, and not merely having the reputation for justice, is beneficial. Finally, he must show that the intrinsic value of justice is so great that it is always and in every circumstance in our best interest to be just.

In section I of this essay, I explicate Plato's defense of justice; and in section II, I raise a standard objection that has been levied against his account.[1] In short,

Plato defines justice as a state of an individual's soul or psyche where each part of the soul performs its proper function, with the result that the individual attains psychological harmony; Plato proceeds to argue that this state is essential to our happiness. The problem for Plato's defense of justice, however, is that his account of justice appears to have nothing to do with justice in the ordinary sense of the term, which at the least implies acting with some regard for the good of others. This is deeply problematic, since doubts about the value of justice in terms of our own happiness arise because we view justice as requiring that we act for the sake of the good of others, often at our own perceived expense. Thus, Plato cannot assuage our worries about justice by giving an account of it that ignores this essential other-regarding aspect of justice.

In sections III and IV of the essay, I present two broad strategies for trying to show that, despite the initial appearances, there is a connection between Plato's account of justice and justice in the ordinary sense of the term, and I point out the major weaknesses for each approach. In section V, I describe a third general strategy for drawing a connection between Plato's account of justice and justice in the ordinary sense of the term. Although this third general strategy is in broad outline defensible, it has so far not received its best formulation. I close the paper, then, by providing such a formulation, which I suggest is the most promising way of explicating Plato's defense of justice. Although my aim is not to establish this final interpretation conclusively, I do hope, having canvassed the main alternatives currently proposed, to highlight some of its advantages. In any event, once armed with an awareness of the main strategies for addressing Plato's defense of justice, students of Plato may want to return to the *Republic* in order to determine for themselves which approach, if any, should be endorsed.

I

Prior to determining whether or not justice is always in our interest, Plato must provide an account of justice. His strategy is to start with his description of the relationship between functioning or doing well and virtue. In *Republic* I, Socrates, Plato's mouthpiece throughout the *Republic*, claims that each thing has a function, which he defines as that which only it can do or it can do best; for example, the function of the eyes is to see and the function of a pruning knife is to prune (352e–353b).[2] Socrates goes on to argue that a thing performs its function well by means of its own peculiar virtue and poorly by means of its own peculiar vice (353b–c). Accordingly, one way to discover the virtue of a particular thing is to imagine what it would be for it to function well, or in other words, be good, and then find the condition that enables it to function well; this condition is the virtue appropriate to that thing.

Socrates holds that justice is a virtue appropriate to both cities and individuals, and the nature or form of justice is the same in both (435a). Accordingly,

Socrates' strategy for finding the nature of justice is first to describe the perfectly functioning or perfectly good city. Since the city is perfectly good, and since it is by means of its own peculiar virtues that a thing is good, the city must contain all of the virtues appropriate to a city. By isolating those features of a city that enable it to be good, Socrates hopes to uncover the nature of the virtues of a city, including, most importantly, justice.

This account of justice is only provisional, however, until it is shown that the same account of justice applies to the individual. Thus, Socrates needs to show that the same account of justice explains our ascriptions of justice in the individual. If the same account of justice does apply to the individual, then the nature of justice will be revealed, and Socrates will be in a position to answer the question of the *Republic*, namely, whether or not it is in our interest to give considerations of justice a central place in our deliberations.

Socrates begins, then, by envisioning the perfectly good city; according to him, the perfectly good city is the city that provides the greatest possible happiness for all of its citizens (420b). Socrates argues that cities are formed when individuals come together as partners and helpers to provide each other with the many things that each needs (369b). Socrates goes on to argue that the needs of the individuals that make up a city are best fulfilled when each individual does that work for which he or she is best suited by nature (370a–c). Some individuals, for example, have natural tendencies towards excellence in the traditional crafts, such as farming, building, selling, medical treatment and the like; these individuals should perform the role of provisioning the city in various ways (370c–373d). Other individuals are best at activities that demand physical strength and spirit; these individuals should constitute the auxiliary class of the city: the class that does the work of defending the city against internal and external enemies (374a–375b). Finally, some individuals are well suited for developing and living in accordance with their rational capacities and it is these individuals, the guardians, who ought to rule the city (412c–414b). Socrates believes that a city organized in such a fashion is possible if its citizens receive the proper early education, one that emphasizes both a love of one's fellow citizens (377d–379a, 386a) and a love and development of traditional ethical ideals such as courage (386a–388e) and moderation (388e–391c).[3]

Having described the perfectly functioning or good city, Socrates is able to define or identify the excellences or virtues of the city, or those qualities that enable the city to flourish; the virtues appropriate to a city are wisdom, bravery, moderation, and justice. He identifies the wisdom of the city with the guardians' knowledge of what is best for the city and of how to maintain good internal and external relations (428c–429a). He identifies the bravery of the city with the auxiliaries' ability to preserve the correct beliefs about what ought and ought not be feared (429b–430c). The moderation of the city lies in the fact that each class has the same belief about which individuals are naturally wise and so ought to rule and make decisions for the city (432a). Finally, Socrates thinks that the condition that most enables the city to flourish is that each citizen does his or her own work and does not attempt to do the work of another; he identifies this condition with the justice of the city (433a–d).

To confirm that this condition truly is justice, Socrates argues that this conception of justice has links with our ordinary understanding of justice. Thus, he notes that a predominant commonsense notion of justice is that justice is doing one's own work and not meddling with what is not one's own (433a). He also notes that everyone would want the sole aim of the rulers in delivering just judgments to be that no citizen should have what belongs to another or be deprived of what is his own (433e). If what is most importantly a citizen's own is his work, and if when he does his work he is guaranteed to get what he deserves, then Socrates' account of justice, while distinctive, does have links with commonsense notions of justice.

Socrates says, though, that we cannot be secure in this account of justice until we are sure that the same account explains justice in the individual (434d). There is, however, an immediate problem for thinking that the same account of justice applies to the individual: if the same account is to apply, the individual, like the city, must have parts, each of which is best suited for playing a certain role in the individual's life. But is there any *independent* reason to think that an individual's soul or psyche has the same parts as the city?

Socrates thinks there is. He notes that we often experience mental conflict; that is, we often have the experience of wanting something, for example, a drink, but at the same time fervently wishing that we did not want that drink (439a–c). Or, sometimes we desperately want to exact revenge on someone whom we believe has wronged us, and yet believe that acting on such anger is not appropriate (441b–c). In such cases, we struggle against ourselves, and many times we take actions that we later regret. According to Socrates, we can only explain this phenomenon by appealing to the idea that the psyche has "parts" or distinct sources of motivation that can come into conflict. He attributes at least three parts to the psyche: the appetitive part, the spirited part and the reasoning part.[4]

According to Socrates, the parts of the soul represent the values that motivate all of our actions. Thus, in *Republic* IX, Socrates characterizes each part of the soul as loving a certain object. For example, he states that the appetitive part loves money, since this is the easiest means for satisfying whatever strong desires we happen to have (580d–e). We might conclude, then, that humans value acquiring things that simply occur as pleasant or desirable.[5] Socrates characterizes the spirited part as loving honor (581a–b). Since we are honored when we live up to our own or others' ideals, we can conclude that we value having a positive conception of ourselves by living up to those ideals.[6] Finally, he describes the reasoning part of the soul as loving learning and wisdom (580d–581c). He is arguing, then, that we value both acquiring and acting on knowledge.[7]

Socrates thinks that all of our actions spring from these values, but that each of these values gives rise to specific actions in different ways. If, for example, we are motivated by the appetitive part of the soul, which values acquiring things that simply appear pleasant or desirable, then the particular ends of our actions are the result of mere perceptions of what appears good or worth pursuing, and not on any more sophisticated form of reasoning; thus Socrates sometimes characterizes the appetitive part as non-rational (439d). If we are motivated by the spirited part of the soul, which values having a positive conception of ourselves by living up to certain ideals, then our particular goals in action are the result of reasoning about whether certain actions are *consistent* with these ideals, regardless of how those ideals may have been acquired. Accordingly, Socrates compares the spirited part to a dog who obeys the commands of its ruler (440d). Finally, if we are motivated by the reasoning part of the soul, which values acting wisely, then our actions are the result of rational deliberation about what is *truly* advantageous for the soul as a whole (439c–d, 441e, 442c).

According to Socrates, these distinct and powerful sources of motivation explain mental conflict (436b–441c). We experience conflict because we can arrive at conclusions about what to do from the perspective of reason, spirit, or appetite; since these conclusions are generated both from different conceptions of the ends that ought to be pursued and by more and less limited forms of reasoning, they can clash. We regret our actions when we fail to act from the perspective of reason, since only reason can determine what is truly best for each aspect of ourselves and for ourselves as a whole.

With this independently motivated picture of our moral psychology in place, Socrates can now see if the definition of justice in the city applies to the individual. According to him, just as justice in the city occurs when each individual does the work for which he or she is best suited, justice in the individual occurs when each part of the soul does the work for which it is best suited. Thus, reason, since it alone is able to acquire knowledge of what is best for each part of the soul and the soul as a whole ought to rule (441e, 442c). The spirited part of the soul, since it is capable of being emotionally forceful when it comes to making the individual live up to his or her ideals, ought to ally itself with reason, and endeavor to make sure that the individual lives up to rational ideals (441e, 442b). And finally, although Socrates does not explicitly characterize the proper function of the appetites, we may presume, on the analogy between the soul and the city, that the appetitive part ought to provide the motivation for meeting the more basic needs of the individual.

Socrates confirms this account of justice by noting that just as justice in his city has links with commonsense notions of justice, his analysis of justice in the individual has links with commonsense platitudes about justice. In particular, Socrates thinks that his definition of justice can explain our ordinary ascriptions of justice. Thus he notes that we would never think that the individual with a just soul would engage in actions typically considered unjust, such as embezzling, temple robberies, thefts, betrayals of friends in private and public life, breaking promises, adultery, disrespect of parents, and neglect of the gods (442e–443a). Socrates takes these observations, then, to secure the account.

Having uncovered the nature of justice, Socrates proceeds to describe and compare the life of the individual with a just soul with the life of an individual with an unjust soul. The discussion culminates in *Republic* IX, where Socrates provides an image of the soul that is intended to illustrate the fact that having a just soul enables a person to flourish, for it is only in the just soul that the individual is friendly and at peace with herself (588a–e). The individual with the just soul has such inner harmony because she is ruled by reason, and only reason can engage in the sort of rational reflection necessary to ensure that all parts of ourselves are satisfied. In sum, it is only when acting wisely is the dominant value in our lives that *all* of our values are allowed their proper expression, and thus that we can achieve a state of inner harmony and friendship.

In a similar vein, Socrates argues that the unjust person is not happy, for injustice is a state of discord and enmity within oneself (588e–589a). Again, he thinks that such discord occurs when reason fails to rule because only reason knows how to harmoniously realize all of our values. If we are motivated by spirited or appetitive values, then our actions will not be the result of rational reflection on what is best for the soul as a whole; rather, our actions will be the result of what appears desirable or of ungrounded opinions about ideals. But if we are guided simply by what appears to be pleasant or desirable or by ungrounded opinions about the proper ideals, then it will not be the case that all of our values are allowed expression. As such, we will feel deprived and incomplete and so resent those aspects of ourselves that are causing the deprivation; the result is a perpetual state of inner conflict and hostility towards oneself. Socrates concludes, then, that injustice, whether detected or not, is never in one's interest.

II

Should we accept Socrates' defense of justice? Certainly we can agree with Socrates that if justice is a state of the soul where each part performs its proper function with the result that the individual achieves psychic harmony, then justice *is* beneficial in itself or independently of the rewards of having a reputation for justice. Some may even agree with the more controversial claim that if justice is such a state, then justice is more important than anything else in terms of our own happiness. But is Socrates' account of justice correct? More specifically, can we be sure that an individual with a just soul will refrain from unjust actions?

It is precisely this point in Socrates' defense of justice that has drawn a great deal of attention, for many commentators think that Socrates has not given us any reason for thinking that the individual with a just soul will refrain from unjust actions.[8] Socrates describes the individual with the just soul as having excellent inner relations, or relations with herself; accordingly, he makes no reference at all to our relations with other people. But it is our relationship with others that is the terrain of ordinary justice. Consequently, on Socrates' account it seems possible to have a good relationship with yourself, to act in accordance with what you rationally determine to be best for all aspects of yourself as whole, and yet fail to treat others rightly.

We should be clear that Socrates does not take himself to have to show that the just person will refrain from all of the actions typically considered unjust. After all, lying is typically considered unjust, but Socrates thinks that the just person will lie to the citizens of the ideal city when he or she believes it is for their own good (414c–415e; 459c–e). There need not, then, be a complete overlap between the actions of the individual with the just soul and actions typically considered just. At the very least, though, justice requires that we do not wantonly disregard the good of others. But again, what reason has Socrates given us for thinking that the individual with a just soul will refrain from actions that display disregard for the good of others?

This question is pressing, because if Socrates has not shown us that the individual with the just soul will not violate the good of others – if, that is, there is a gap between having a just soul and taking just actions – then he has failed to answer the central question of the *Republic*, for while he certainly has given us a reason to have a just or harmonious soul, he still has not given us a reason to give the good of others a central place in our deliberations. In sum, then, if the conception of justice on which Socrates' defense of it relies bears no relation to the other-regarding elements of the ordinary conception, then we will have to reject his defense of justice.

The resolution of this issue is the concern of the remainder of this essay. In the following two sections, I sketch and evaluate two predominant interpretive strategies for closing the gap between the just soul and just actions. I hope that by getting clear on the problems for each approach the criteria for a philosophically promising interpretation of Socrates' defense of justice will be brought to light.

III

The first strategy that I consider for closing the gap between the just soul and just actions – which I call the indirect justice strategy – appeals to the fact that the individual with a just soul acts on certain values and desires the satisfaction of which happen to be incompatible with unjust actions.[9] More precisely, the individual with a just soul is dedicated to acquiring knowledge of what is truly best and acting on it; according to the indirect justice approach, having the ability to act in this way requires that one lack the sorts of desires that typically lead to unjust actions. Thus the individual with a just soul simply will not have an interest in committing unjust actions and the gap between the just individual and just action is closed.

Socrates claims that the individual who lives in accordance with the value of acquiring and acting on the knowledge of what is best will live a life devoted to learning, since, first, an individual who values living in accordance with her conception of the truth about what is best is likely to have intellectual proclivities and to value intellectual pursuits (485a–d; 486c–487a). Secondly, and more importantly, Socrates thinks that acquiring knowledge of the good requires a dedication to intellectual pursuits, for in order to know the truth about what is best one must have knowledge of the Forms, and in particular, knowledge of the Form of the Good (504e–505b). I will have more to say about the Form of the Good later, but for now it is sufficient to note that Socrates thinks that arriving at knowledge of the Form of the Good requires fifteen years of study in highly abstract fields, such as mathematics (522d–529), astronomy (527d–530d), harmonics (530d–531c), and dialectic (532a–535a). Thus, according to Socrates' conception of goodness, satisfying the desire for knowledge of the good requires enormous intellectual effort.

In *Republic* VI, Socrates says that when one's desires flow towards one thing, such as learning, one has less desire for other things, such as the acquisition of objects or experiences that require a great deal of money, or living up to certain prevalent ideals, for example, having power over others. Since these excessive appetitive and spirited desires are the sorts of desires that typically lead to unjust actions, and since the individual with a just soul is not the type of person who has such desires, that individual would never, according to Socrates, be unreliable or unjust (485d–486b). In short, then, Socrates thinks that the individual who is ruled by reason will have all of her desires channeled towards the acquisition of knowledge, with the result that she simply will not have the sorts of unruly appetitive or spirited desires that motivate unjust acts.

In addition, according to this account of Socrates' defense of justice, he also provides individuals who aspire to have a just soul with a reason for refraining from indulging the sorts of desires that typically lead to unjust actions, for such desires are incompatible with acquiring knowledge of the good. Indeed, even if we query Socrates' idea of the sort of study that is required for attaining knowledge of the good, we ought to agree that knowledge of what's truly valuable and of what particular courses of action we ought to pursue, is hard to come by, because of the effort required and also the impediments, particularly strong desires and self-deception, to honestly attempting to discover what is best. Books VIII and IX of the *Republic* describe with remarkable psychological acuity how unruly spirited and appetitive desires ruin one's ability to think clearly about one's own good (see especially 559e–561c). If, then, we want to be the type of person who can acquire knowledge of what is truly good for herself, we ought to avoid indulging the sorts of disorderly desires that detract from our ability to attain and act on this knowledge. But, again, it is precisely these disorderly desires that typically lead to unjust actions. Thus, the indirect justice interpretation of

Socrates' defense of justice offers both an explanation of why the individual with the just soul will not engage in unjust actions, as well as a psychologically plausible reason for those of us who want just souls to avoid unjust actions.

Despite the psychological insights of the indirect justice interpretation, however, the account is problematic since it is open to counterexamples. The indirect justice approach holds that the individual with the just soul simply will not have the sorts of desires that lead to unjust actions because these desires are incompatible with satisfying the desire to acquire and act on knowledge of what is best. But are all unjust actions motivated by desires that are incompatible with satisfying the desire to acquire and act on our knowledge of the good? It seems not. Suppose, for example, that in order to satisfy her desire for knowledge, an individual with a just soul needs to acquire money, equipment, or time. Why should we think that an individual with a just soul, an individual, that is, who is ruled by the desire to acquire knowledge, would refrain from committing unjust acts, such as stealing or enslaving others, in order to satisfy this desire for knowledge?[10]

Furthermore, and perhaps more importantly, we must keep in mind that some injustice, as Socrates himself acknowledges, occurs by omission. In *Republic* VII, Socrates describes the philosophers, the individuals with just souls, as preferring pure intellectual pursuits to ruling the city; nonetheless, these philosophers take their turn ruling the city simply because they realize that failing to do so would be unjust (519c–521b). But it is unclear why, on the indirect justice interpretation, the just individual would refrain from the unjust act of failing to rule the city, since failing to rule the city would not at all interfere with satisfying her desire for knowledge; indeed, it looks as if ruling the city would actually hinder the satisfaction of her desire for knowledge.[11]

The indirect justice approach is susceptible to these kinds of problems because its explanation for the fact that the individual with a just soul refrains from unjust actions makes absolutely no reference to the idea that the individual with a just soul considers the good of others in her decision-making. The fact that the individual with a just soul refrains from unjust acts is simply a by-product of her interest in satisfying her own desire to attain and act on her knowledge. Not only, then, does this feature of the indirect justice approach leave Socrates' claim that the individual with the just soul will refrain from unjust actions open to counterexamples, it violates our intuition that the just individual's motivation for refraining from unjust acts should have something to do with regard for the good of others.

IV

The problems for the indirect justice approach have prompted Plato's commentators to search for another way of closing the gap between the individual with a just soul and just actions, one that argues for a direct relation between the just individual's motives for action and the good of others. According to this approach – which I call the impartial justice approach – the individual with a just soul knows what is objectively good and is directly motivated to bring about the objective good in the world.[12]

Recall that the just individual, the one who is ruled by reason, aims to have and act on the knowledge of what is truly good. The object of such knowledge, according to Socrates, is the Form of the Good. Furthermore, this knowledge is impersonal: it is not knowledge of what is good for a particular individual, or of what is good in relation to a particular context or in reference to a particular desire; rather, it is knowledge of what is good *simpliciter* (479a–e). Defenders of the impartial justice approach argue that the just individual's knowledge of the good directly motivates her to bring about the good in the world. The primary evidence for this claim is that it explains why the philosopher, the paradigmatic just individual, is motivated to rule the city despite the fact that it will interfere with her intellectual pursuits: she realizes that by doing so she will bring about the objective good. Moreover, this interpretation explains the philosopher's activity in ruling the city: the philosopher aims not at his own personal good, but at instantiating goodness in the city (500b–501c). In sum, then, the impartial justice approach holds that the just individual is directly motivated to bring about the good; since actions motivated by the aim of creating such objective goodness in the world could not, according to Socrates, be unjust (505a), we have forged a connection between justice in the soul and just actions.[13]

This approach to Socrates' defense of justice in the *Republic* has the advantage that its explanation for the fact that the just individual takes just actions appeals to the fact that the just individual is directly motivated to bring about the good, including the good of others, and thus it is not open to the sorts of counterexamples and explanatory problems that plagued the indirect justice approach. The impartial justice approach, however, faces at least one serious objection. Socrates set out to show that justice is in our own interest. He argued that justice is in our interest because it involves having a certain type of soul, one that is organized such that all of our values can be harmoniously realized, with the result that we are friendly and at peace with ourselves. But then Socrates argues that having such a soul – one ruled by reason – involves knowledge of the good and that having such knowledge entails that we are motivated to create goodness in the world, not goodness for ourselves, but simply, goodness. What, though, does creating goodness in the world have to do with having all of our own particular values realized? Indeed, couldn't the goals of creating goodness in the world, and meeting our own particular, individual needs come into conflict? If all this is true, then it looks as if it is possible that the just individual might have to sacrifice her own particular self-interest in order to create goodness *simpliciter*.

Indeed, some commentators think that Socrates acknowledges such results in the *Republic* itself.[14] As we have seen, Socrates describes the philosophers, the individuals with just souls, as preferring pure intellectual pursuits to ruling the city; nonetheless, these philosophers take their turn ruling the city simply because they realize that it is just to do so. Thus it does seem that the just individual sacrifices her self-interest for the sake of the good. But this is a result that should give us serious pause, for the goal of the *Republic* is to show that justice is always in our best interest. In sum, the impartial justice approach appears to close the gap between the just soul and just actions only to reopen the gap between self-interest and just actions.

The dilemma that we are faced with thus far can be posed as follows: the indirect justice interpretation stressed the connection between having a just soul and being happy. The just individual knows what is good for her and is able to act on this knowledge. The just individual refrains from unjust actions because the desires that motivate such actions are incompatible with her ability to acquire and act on knowledge of what is good for her. The weakness of this interpretation, though, is that the just individual is not directly motivated to refrain from unjust actions – her reasons for refraining from injustice have nothing to do with concern for the good of others – with the result that we cannot be certain that the just individual will always refrain from unjust actions.

The impartial justice interpretation attempts to remedy this situation by showing that there is a direct connection between the just person's motives and regard for the good of others. On this account, the individual with a just soul is motivated to bring about the objective good and such actions could never involve treating others wrongly. This approach, however, faces the problem that it appears to allow for cases where an individual sacrifices her own self-interest for the sake of bringing about the objective good, and thus on this approach Socrates fails to explain why it is always in our best interest to be just.

The successful approach to Socrates' defense of justice, then, should resolve this dilemma. The obvious way to do so is to show that the just person has a very important desire or value, the realization of which requires that she consider the good of others. In other words, we must show that the just individual sees her good as realized in having regard for the good of others; I call this strategy the self-interested justice approach. In the next section, I consider and raise objections to one version of this approach. In the following section, I suggest what I take to be a more promising, yet neglected formulation of the self-interested justice approach.

V

What important value could the just individual have that requires that she consider the good of others in her deliberations? Many commentators have found the answer to this question in the just individual's – the philosopher's – love of the Forms.[15] Recall that the individual who is ruled by reason loves wisdom, and wants to discover and act in accordance with her knowledge of what is best. According to Socrates, this love of wisdom will transform into a love of the Forms, since the Forms are what make knowledge possible, and since he thinks that if someone truly loves something, then he loves everything akin to it (474c–475c, and 479e–480a).

Many commentators argue that Socrates thinks that the love of Forms inspires in the just individual not just a desire to contemplate them, but also a desire to imitate them (500b–d; also *Symposium* 209a–b, 212a–b), for if someone loves something, particularly an ideal, she deeply wants to act in ways that are consistent with that ideal, and thus she sees failing to act in such a way as against her self-interest. Moreover, the philosopher sees the Forms as the greatest possible good. Since happiness consists in "possessing" good things (*Symposium* 204e–205a), it follows that the philosopher will take her relationship with the Forms to be the greatest good, and her desire to act in accordance with them as essential to her self-interest or happiness.

Accordingly, adherents of the self-interested justice approach argue that Socrates *does* think that it is in the philosopher's interest to rule, despite the fact that it conflicts with her desire to pursue purely intellectual activities, for by ruling the philosopher is imitating the Forms. Socrates states that the Forms themselves constitute a just order (500b–c); thus, to imitate the Forms we must be just. Since he says that it is just for the philosophers to rule, the philosophers must perform the just act of ruling in order to imitate the Forms and so act in their own self-interest.

Despite the fact that this attempt at articulating the self-interested justice approach nicely solves the dilemma that we posed at the end of the last section, this interpretation of Socrates' defense is open to a serious objection: namely, the ideal of the just person that he encourages us to aspire to is unattainable for most individuals. Socrates began with the idea that to be a just person one must care for the truth and for being the kind of person who leads her life in accordance with wisdom. But then he argues that in order to be such a person one must be devoted to highly theoretical intellectual pursuits. He argues in addition that one who loves such intellectual pursuits will also love the objects of such pursuits, the Forms, and thus will be loath to do anything that contradicts them, and this is the just individual's reason to act justly. As Socrates himself admits, however, the knowledge required for attaining this ideal is possible for only a very select few.

This observation poses a serious challenge for Socrates' defense of justice, for his aim is to show that, despite the appearances, we do have a reason to be just. His model of the just person, though, turns out to be unattainable (and perhaps even unappealing) to many. But if Socrates' model of the just person is unattainable for us, then we no longer have a reason to be just; that is, while the fact that the ideal of the just person is unattainable for many does not necessarily make the ideal false, it does make the ideal inappropriate to the task at hand, namely, to show that everyone has a reason to be just.

One might argue, however, that we can save Socrates' defense of justice by focusing on the spirit of his defense, and not on the details. The spirit of this interpretation of Socrates' defense of justice is that we have a love of abstract ideals, such as justice and goodness, and so we value acting in accordance with them. But loving such ideals need not involve a devotion to intellectual pursuits or knowledge of the Forms; it is certainly possible to love such ideals, and to try to bring them about, without being able to give a philosophical account of their nature.

Indeed, this is how Socrates envisions the non-philosophers in the ideal society. Recall that the aim of the ideal education is to instill in the citizens a love of ethical ideals (386a–391c).[16] Once an individual loves such ideals, she sees acting in accordance with the ideals as in her self-interest for the same reasons that the philosopher sees it as in her own interest to act in accordance with the Forms. On this approach, then, the ideal of the just person does not depend on acquiring knowledge of the Forms and is thus not in principle unattainable for many.

This approach assumes, though, that we love ideals such as justice and goodness. But what if we do not already love these ethical ideals? Socrates might respond that all of us, owing to acculturation, have an attachment to ethical ideals, and thus we do have a reason to act in accordance with these ideals. If, however, we are asking the question of why be moral at all, then we are questioning the value of our attachment to these ethical ideals. Why should we aspire to be the kind of person who has a devotion to ethical ideals? Why shouldn't we, as Thrasymachus recommends, throw off the shackles of such an attachment and unabashedly pursue our own self-interest? To answer this question, Socrates needs to give us a reason to endorse, as opposed to shake off, our attachment to ethical ideals.

Socrates could respond that we should endorse our attachment to ethical ideals because loving such ideals helps us attain the psychic harmony that we all desire. Loving justice prevents us from acting on our unruly spirited and appetitive desires, and thus prevents us from strengthening those parts of the soul that jeopardize our psychic harmony. On this picture an individual values justice not because she sees something worthwhile in considering the good of others, but because loving justice is a means to psychic harmony. Now, however, we are back to an approach similar to the indirect justice approach, where the reason for being just has nothing to do with concern for the good of others.

In sum, then, the first articulation of the self-interested justice approach faces the following problem: if we have the sort of nature that is amenable to and capable of knowing and loving the Forms, then we have a self-interested reason to consider the good of others. If, however, we are not amenable to or capable of knowing and loving the Forms, then at most we have an indirect reason to be just. But then, for the majority of individuals, the reason to be just has nothing to do with concern for the good of others. And, again, this violates our intuition that the justification for being moral ought to make some reference to concern for the good of others. Does Socrates have the resources to give every-one a self-interested justification for being moral that makes some reference to having concern for the good of others? In what follows, I will suggest that he does.

VI

In this section, I suggest an alternative but neglected way of understanding Socrates' defense of justice. On my interpretation, the *Republic* does provide us with the tools to argue that the just individual has a self-interested reason to be concerned with the good of others; moreover, the ideal on which Socrates' defense relies is available and appealing to everyone. On my view, Socrates thinks that we have a reason to behave justly because behaving justly is necessary for fulfilling a deeply important need that we all as social creatures have, namely, the need to be connected or unified with other people.

In what follows, I will argue first that Socrates thinks that our happiness resides, at least in part, in being unified with other people. I will then argue that he thinks that being unified with others requires that we consider their own good in our decision-making; specifically, it requires that we see their good as our own good. Accordingly, behaving unjustly, which at the very least involves disregard-ing the good of another, is incompatible with being unified with others, and thus, incompatible with our own happiness.

What evidence is there for thinking that Socrates holds that being unified with others is essential to our happiness? Since he thinks that we all want the good (505d–e), and that happiness consists in having good things (*Symposium* 204e–205a), the best place to look for his conception of happiness is in his con-ception of the Form of the Good. While Socrates' account of the good is not fully developed, most commentators agree that the good is unity or harmony. The primary evidence for this interpretation is the fact that the claim that the good is unity or harmony explains a number of metaphysical, epistemological, political, and ethical claims in the *Republic*.[17] For example, the claim accounts for Socrates' assertion that the good explains the nature of the Forms, for the Forms, both individually and as a whole, are characterized as unified and har-monious (475a; 479a–e; 500c–e). The assertion that the good is unity or harmony also explains Socrates' claim that the good is responsible for the knowa-bility of the Forms, for the Forms are knowable because they never exhibit contradictory features and as such are unified and harmonious (479a–e). The contention that the good is unity also explains his claim that the greatest good for a city is that which "binds it together and makes it one," and the greatest evil that which "tears it apart and makes it many instead of one" (462a–b). And finally, the thought that the good is unity explains Socrates' claim that the most desirable soul is the soul that is "entirely one, moderate and harmonious" (443e), and the most undesirable souls are those that lack unity (see especially 554d–e, 560a, 573a–577e).

If happiness consists in having good things, and if the good is unity, then it follows that happiness consists in having unity and harmony in our lives. The desire for a unified soul is an important illustration of the general desire to possess unity and harmony. Another important example of the desirability of unity and harmony that Socrates emphasizes in the *Republic*, and one that I think has been neglected in discussions of his' defense of justice, is the desirability of being unified with and having harmonious relationships with others.

One might object, however, to the claim that Socrates thinks that unity with others is essential for our happiness by arguing that there are two senses of having unity; according to the first sense, having unity simply means being unified yourself, and according to the second sense, having unity also involves being part of instances of unity, for example, being part of unified relationships. The objector might continue that while there is evidence that Socrates thinks that unity in the first sense is integral to happiness, there is no evidence that unity in the second sense is part of his conception of happiness. This objection fails, however, since there *is* evidence that Socrates thinks that being part of unified relationships is an essential part of our happiness.

First, Socrates' critique of the tyrannical individual is largely dependent on an appeal to the poor quality of his relationships with others. The tyrant is surrounded by individuals whom he does not trust and who mistrust and even hate him (567a–580a). In attempting to convince us that the tyrant, the supremely unjust individual, is not happy, Socrates describes his life as follows: "So someone with a tyrannical nature lives his whole life without being friends with anyone, always a master to one man or slave to another and never getting a taste of either true freedom or true friendship" (576a). Thus, just as there is war, conflict, servitude, and enmity within the parts of the tyrant's soul, there is war, conflict, enmity, and servitude in the tyrant's external community. The tyrant lacks both internal and external unity, and Socrates characterizes *both* deficiencies as contributing to his unhappiness.

Second, Socrates describes the tyrannical city as unhappy because of the conflict between the individuals in the city (566d–569c), and he characterizes the ideal city as happy because of the unity found between the individuals in the city (462a–465b). One might object here that he is saying that the happiness of *the city* is due to unity, and by this he is not making any claims about the happiness of the citizens. It is clear, however, that in calling the city happy, Socrates is referring to the happiness of the citizens, for he repeatedly says that in fashioning the happy city, the goal is not to make one group happy, but all of the citizens happy (420b–c; 466a); thus he thinks that the happiness of the city is due to the happiness of the citizens. If, then, he argues that the city is happy because of the unified relationships between its citizens, and if the city's happiness is due to the citizen's happiness, then it follows that the citizen's happiness, at least qua citizen, is due to the fact that they have unified relationships with one another. Thus, there is evidence in the *Republic* that Socrates thinks that our happiness crucially involves having unified relationships with the members of our community.

But what reason do we have for thinking that Socrates holds that considering the good of others is necessary for having unified and harmonious relationships? While I cannot give a full account here of what it is for something to be unified, Socrates' discussion of the unified city in *Republic* V does provide us with some sense of what unity between individuals involves and some minimal conditions for unity. In *Republic* V, Socrates argues that when people are unified they share in each other's successes and failures and pleasures and pains (462b–e, 463e–464d). He goes on to argue that this is possible when individuals do not see their own concerns as separate or distinct from the concerns of others (462c; 463e–464d). Conversely, when individuals are not unified their pleasures and pains are privatized; that is, the welfare of one citizen or group of citizens does not affect the welfare of any other citizen or groups of citizens (462b); this privatization occurs when individuals do not see the concerns of others as having anything to do with their own concerns (462c). We can conclude, then, that a necessary condition of being unified with others is seeing their good as your own good.

Socrates' discussion of the happiness of the guardians in the ideal city in *Republic* IV provides further evidence for the claim that he thinks that our happiness consists in being unified with others and that this involves seeing their good as our good. When Adeimantus asks Socrates why we should think that the guardians are happy, he replies that the happiness of individuals in a city cannot be determined independently of their nature qua citizen or member of a community (420c–421a). One's nature qua citizen is determined by the role one best plays in making the city as a whole happy. Socrates seems to be suggesting, then, that the happiness of an individual citizen cannot be achieved independently of his fulfilling his role in making the community of which he is a part happy, or in other words, in making his fellow citizens happy (420d–421b). But why should Socrates think this?

One sensible answer is this: Socrates thinks that the happiness of individuals consists, at least in part, in being unified with other individuals, and that being unified with other individuals involves taking their own good into account, or seeing their good as one's own good. Thus, if the good of an individual's fellow citizens requires that he does the work for which he is best suited in the city, then doing that work will enable him to be unified with the members of his community and thus will contribute to his happiness. And indeed, Socrates says that the concern of the ideal city is to "spread happiness throughout the city by bringing the citizens into harmony with each other through persuasion or compulsion and by making them share with each other the benefit that each class can confer on the community" (519e).

It should be clear, then, that treating others unjustly is incompatible with being unified with them. Treating another unjustly involves, at the least, ignoring the other's good and this in turn involves seeing the other as separate from and unimportant to your own welfare, or as a tool to be used for your own ends. Moreover, once you have treated someone unjustly, or intentionally ignored his own good in your actions, you are likely to see the one you have wronged as a potential enemy, an individual who might want to avenge himself on you, and who will certainly ignore your own good. All of these attitudes are incompatible with being unified with others. Finally, those who act unjustly tend to view others in the world as having a similar disregard for the good of others, even those who have not given them reason to be suspicious, and thus, the unjust individual is likely to feel disconnected or estranged from others in this way as well. The lack of unity that the unjust individual cultivates between himself and others, as Socrates notes in his discussion of the unjust souls in *Republic* VIII and IX, results in feelings of isolation, suspicion and fear – experiences that are incompatible with happiness.

Furthermore, Socrates argues that when individuals are unified, they actually feel the pleasures and pains of those they are unified with; he is pointing out by this that being unified with others involves having empathy for them (462b–464d). Accordingly, in order to avoid feeling the pain of someone you have wronged, you must psychologically separate yourself from that person; you must see him as utterly distinct and different than you – as an entity with radically different psychological responses from your own. Viewing others in this way results in thinking of yourself as fundamentally different and disconnected from those around you, and this in turn leads to feelings of alienation, which are, again, incompatible with happiness.

This interpretation of Socrates' defense of justice has the advantage of showing that the just individual sees it as in her interest to consider the good of others in her deliberations: it is in her interest because considering the good of others is necessary for being unified with others, and being unified with others is part of what constitutes her happiness. Accordingly, this view, like the first version of the self-interested justice strategy, can explain why the philosopher sees it as in her interest to rule the city: she realizes that her happiness requires that she is unified with her fellow citizens, and this in turn requires that she consider their good, which is for her to rule the city.

One might argue, however, that while my interpretation has the advantages of the self-interested justice strategy, it is also subject to the same objection, namely, on my account, the ideal of the just individual is unattainable to many. On my view, the individual with a just soul knows the Form of the Good, and it is this knowledge that motivates her to act justly. But if having a just soul requires having knowledge of the good, and if I must have a just soul to have a reason to act justly, then, again, Socrates has failed to give the average individual a reason to be just, since the average individual simply does not have the willingness or the capacity to attain knowledge of the good.

I hope it is obvious, however, that this objection fails, since unity and connection with others is a fundamental and universal human value. The desirability of having unity with others is not something that only the just individual recognizes; rather, it is something that we all intuitively recognize and experience. This is why Socrates' description of the tyrant is so effective: we see the value in being genuinely connected with others, and we recoil from the thought of being surrounded by people with whom we lack this sort of connection. Thus, we all have a reason to be just.

I do not mean to suggest by this that Socrates thinks that the philosopher's motivation to take just actions is exactly the same as a non-philosopher's motivation to take just actions. We can see the difference by distinguishing two senses of being ruled by reason. According to the first sense, an individual is ruled by reason if she knows the Form of the Good; if an individual is ruled by reason in this sense then her motivation for acting justly will be based, among other things, on a very abstract comprehension of why unity, including unity with others, is part of the good life. According to the second sense of being ruled by reason, an individual is ruled by reason if she is free to deliberate and act on her determinations of what is best without interference from non-rational passions and impulses. Socrates could argue that one who is ruled by reason in this sense will be able to clearly intuit and act in accordance with the idea that unity with others is necessary for the good life. On this final interpretation, then, while the philosopher and the non-philosopher have, respectively, clearer and dimmer apprehensions of the good, both are motivated by the idea that their interest is realized in acting out of concern for the good of others.

Obviously this interpretation of Socrates' defense of justice should not be accepted without a full consideration of both the textual evidence for and against it, as well as possible objections, which I do not consider here. I do hope, though, to have alerted readers of the *Republic* to an unexplored and potentially fruitful way of justifying Socrates' defense of justice. In addition, I hope that by canvassing the various approaches to Socrates' account of justice, I have left the reader not only with an awareness of the broad strategies for approaching the *Republic*, but of the possible routes for arguing more generally that justice is a central component of the good life.

Notes

1 In fact, Plato offers several defenses of justice in the *Republic*. The first defense spans from *Republic* IV to IX, and consists in a comparison between the lives of the supremely just and the supremely unjust individual. Plato also provides two arguments in *Republic* IX for the claim that the life of the just individual is more pleasant than the life of the unjust individual (580d–588a). In this essay, I will focus on Plato's first and primary defense of justice – the one that compares the lives of the just and the unjust individuals.

2 For the remainder of the essay, I will refer to the ideas expressed in the *Republic* as those of Socrates, since he is the main speaker. I do not mean to suggest by this that the *Republic* expresses the views of the historical Socrates.

3 There is some controversy over whether or not the craftspeople receive the moral education that Plato describes in the *Republic*. See, for example, Reeve 1988: 186–91.
4 At 443d–e Socrates suggests that there may be other, distinct sources of motivation in the soul as well.
5 See Cooper 1984 for a defense of this interpretation of the appetitive part of the soul.
6 See Annas 1981: 126–8, for a defense of this interpretation of the spirited part of the soul.
7 See Cooper 1984 for more on this interpretation of the reasoning part of the soul.
8 Sachs initiated the contemporary concern with this problem in his 1963 article.
9 Kraut 1973, Kraut 1992b, and Brown 2004 also appeal to the indirect justice approach to bolster different accounts of Socrates' defense of justice.
10 See Annas 1978: 440–2; Dahl 1991: 822–4, and Kraut 1973: 215, for discussions of possible counterexamples to the claim that the individual with a just soul will not commit unjust acts because he simply will not have any motivation to do so.
11 According to Reeve (1988: 202–3) the just individual is motivated to rule the city because she realizes that this is the best way to ensure that she lives in the type of city that will allow her the rational activity that she desires. Thus, on this picture of the just individual's reason for ruling the city, the indirect justice approach could in fact explain the philosopher's motivation to rule. As Kraut (1992a: 50–1) notes, however, this interpretation is based on the dubious empirical claim that the philosopher could more fully pursue knowledge by taking her turn ruling in the ideal city rather than by leaving for another city. Additionally, this solution makes no appeal to the fact that Socrates claims that the philosophers rule *because* they recognize that it is just to do so in return for the education they receive from the city (520a–e).
12 Adherents of this interpretive strategy include Annas (1981: 260–71; Cooper (1977) (but see n. 15 below); White (1979: 9–60, 189–96 and 1986). Waterlow (1972) also argues that the just individual is directly concerned with the good of others. Her approach, however, does not emphasize the just individual's knowledge of the good, but the fact that the just individual is ruled by reason: as a rational person, the just individual realizes that her good is no different, and thus no more privileged, than the good of another.
13 Brown (2004) has argued against such an interpretation of the link between the just soul and just actions on the grounds that there is insufficient evidence in the *Republic* for the claim that the philosopher's knowledge of the objective good motivates her to do anything other than get the good for herself.
14 See White 1986 for the most explicit defense of the view that Plato thinks the rulers sacrifice their own self-interest for the sake of the good.
15 See, for example, Demos 1964; Dahl 1991; Irwin 1995: 298–317; Kraut 1992b and 1992a. Cooper 1977 appears to go back and forth between the impartial justice approach and the self-interested justice approach. The first part of this section of the paper relies most heavily on Kraut's formulation of the self-interested justice approach.
16 See Brown 2004 for a much fuller defense of the notion that Plato's theory of education plays a key role in his defense of justice.

17 Different commentators call the property that Plato is trying to isolate by different names, such as "order," "harmony," and "unity"; despite the slight variation in language all of these commentators are pointing to the same thing. See, for example, Brown 2004; Dahl 1991: 828; Cooper 1977: 144; Fine 1999; Hitchcock 1985; Irwin 1995: 272–3; Reeve 1988: 81–95; White 1979: 35–43. For an alternative, although not, in my view, incompatible account of the form of the good, see Santas 2001: ch. 5.

I would like to thank Eric Brown, William Larkin, Gerasimos Santas, Clerk Shaw, Christopher Shields, Paul Studtmann, Daniel Sturgis, Matt Warren, and Shelley Wilcox for their insightful comments on earlier versions of this article.

References

Annas, J. (1978) "Plato and common morality," *Classical Quarterly* 28, pp. 437–51.

——(1981) *An Introduction to Plato's* Republic, Oxford: Oxford University Press.

Brown, E. (2004) "Minding the gap in Plato's *Republic*," *Philosophical Studies* 117, pp. 275–302.

Cooper, J. (1977) "The psychology of justice in Plato," *American Philosophical Quarterly* 14, pp. 151–7; repr. in J. Cooper (1999) *Reason and Emotion: Essays on Ancient Moral Psychology and Ethical Theory*, Princeton, NJ: Princeton University Press.

——(1984) "Plato's theory of human motivation," *History of Philosophy Quarterly* 1, pp. 3–21; repr. in J. Cooper (1999) *Reason and Emotion: Essays on Ancient Moral Psychology and Ethical Theory*, Princeton, NJ: Princeton University Press.

Dahl, N. (1991) "Plato's defense of justice," *Philosophy and Phenomenological Research* 51, pp. 809–34; repr. in G. Fine (ed.) (1999) *Plato 2: Ethics, Politics, Religion and the Soul,*. Oxford: Oxford University Press.

Demos, R. (1964) "A fallacy in Plato's *Republic?*," *Philosophical Review* 73, pp. 395–8.

Fine, G. (1999) "Knowledge and belief in *Republic* V–VII," in G. Fine (ed.) *Plato 1: Metaphysics and Epistemology*, Oxford: Oxford University Press.

Hitchcock, D. (1985) "The good in Plato's *Republic*," *Aperion* 19, pp. 65–93.

Irwin, T. (1995) *Plato's Ethics*, Oxford: Oxford University Press.

Kraut, R. (1973) "Reason and justice in Plato's *Republic*," in E. N. Lee, A. P. D. Mourelatos, and R. M. Rorty (eds.) *Exegesis and Argument: Studies in Greek Philosophy, Phronesis* Supplement 1, pp. 207–24.

——(1992a) "Return to the Cave: *Republic* 519–521," *Proceedings of the Boston Area Colloquium in Ancient Philosophy* 7, pp. 43–61.

——(1992b) "The defense of justice in Plato's *Republic*," in R. Kraut (ed.) *The Cambridge Companion to Plato's* Republic, Cambridge: Cambridge University Press.

Reeve, C. D. C (1988) *Philosopher-Kings*, Princeton, NJ: Princeton University Press.

Sachs, D. (1963) "A fallacy in Plato's *Republic*," *Philosophical Review* 72, pp. 141–58.

Santas, G. (2001) *Goodness and Justice*, Oxford: Blackwell.

Waterlow, S. (1972) "The good of others in Plato's *Republic*," *Proceedings of the Aristotelian Society* 72, pp. 19–36.

White, N. (1979) *A Companion to Plato's* Republic, Indianapolis: Hackett Publishing.

——(1986) "The ruler's choice," *Archiv für Geschichte der Philosophie* 68, pp. 22–46.

General Bibliography

Adam, James, *The* Republic *of Plato*, 2 vols. (Cambridge, 1902)

Allen, R. E., *Studies in Plato's Metaphysics* (New York, 1965)

Andersson, T. J., *Polis and Psyche: A Motif in Plato's* Republic (Stockholm, 1971)

Annas, Julia, *An Introduction to Plato's* Republic (Oxford, 1981)

Anton, John P. (ed.) *Science and the Sciences in Plato* (Delmar, NY, 1980)

Bloom, A., *The* Republic *of Plato* (New York, 1968)

Blosser, N., *Dialogform und Argument: Studien zu Platons Politeia* (Stuttgart, 1997)

Bobonich, Christopher, *Plato's Utopia Recast* (Oxford, 2002)

Burnyeat, M., "Culture and society in Plato's *Republic*," in *The Tanner Lectures on Human Values* 20 (Salt Lake City, 1999)

Cooper, John, *Reason and Emotion* (Princeton, NJ, 1999)

Cornford, F. M., *The* Republic *of Plato* (Oxford, 1941)

Cross, R. C., and A. D. Woozley, *Plato's* Republic (London, 1964)

Everson, S. (ed.) *Companions to Ancient Thought* 1: *Epistemology* (Cambridge, 1990)

Ferrari, G. R. F. (ed.) *Plato: Republic*, trans. Tom Griffith (Cambridge, 2000)

—— *City and Soul in Plato's* Republic (Sankt Augustin, Germany, 2003)

Fine, Gail, *On Ideas: Aristotle's Criticisms of Plato's Theory of Forms* (Oxford, 1993)

—— (ed.) *Plato 1: Metaphysics and Epistemology* (Oxford, 1999)

—— (ed.) *Plato 2: Ethics, Politics, Religion and the Soul* (Oxford, 1999)

Gill, C. (ed.) *The Person and the Human Mind: Issues in Ancient and Modern Philosophy* (Oxford, 1990)

Gosling, J. C. B., and C. C. W. Taylor, *The Greeks on Pleasure* (Oxford, 1984)

Griswold, C. L. (ed.) *Platonic Writings, Platonic Readings* (New York, 1988)

Grote, George, *Plato and the Other Companions of Socrates*, 4th edn., 4 vols. (London, 1888)

Guthrie, W. K. C., *A History of Greek Philosophy*, vol. 4 (Cambridge, 1975)

Hoffe, O. (ed.) *Platon: Politeia* (Berlin, 1997)

Irwin, T., *Classical Thought* (Oxford, 1989)

—— *Plato's Ethics* (Oxford, 1995)

Irwin, T., and M. Nussbaum (eds.) *Virtue, Love, and Form* (Edmonton, Alta., 1993)

Joseph, H. W. B., *Essays in Ancient and Modern Philosophy* (Oxford, 1935)

Jowett, B., and L. Campbell (eds.) *The* Republic *of Plato*, 3 vols. (Oxford, 1894)

Kahn, C., *Plato and the Socratic Dialogue* (Cambridge, 1996)

Keyt, D., and F. Miller (eds.) *A Companion to Aristotle's* Politics (Oxford, 1991)

Klagge, J. C., and N. D. Smith, *Methods of Interpreting Plato and his Dialogues* (Oxford, 1992)

Klosko, G., *The Development of Plato's Political Theory* (London, 1986)

Kraut, Richard (ed.) *The Cambridge Companion to Plato* (Cambridge, 1992)

── (ed.) *Plato's* Republic: *Critical Essays* (New York, 1997)

Mayhew, R., *Aristotle's Criticisms of Plato's* Republic (Lanham, MD, 1997)

Miller, F., *Nature, Justice, and Rights in Aristotle's* Politics (Oxford, 1995)

Mitchell, Basil, and J. R. Lucas, *An Engagement with Plato's* Republic (Burlington, VT, 2003)

Moravcsik, J., *Plato and Platonism* (Oxford, 1992)

Moravcsik, J., and P. Temko (eds.) *Plato on Beauty, Wisdom and the Arts* (Totowa, NJ, 1982)

Murdoch, I., *The Fire and the Sun: Why Plato Banished the Artists* (Oxford, 1997)

Murphy, N. R., *The Interpretation of Plato's* Republic (Oxford, 1951)

Nettleship, Richard, *Lectures on the* Republic *of Plato* (London, 1962)

Nussbaum, M., *The Fragility of Goodness* (Cambridge, 1986)

Penner, T., *The Ascent from Nominalism* (Dordrecht, 1987)

Popper, K., *The Open Society and its Enemies*, vol. 1 (London, 1945)

Price, A. W., *Love and Friendship in Plato and Aristotle* (Oxford, 1989)

── *Mental Conflict* (London, 1995)

Reale, Giovanni, and Samuel Scolnicov (eds.) *Dialogues on Plato: The Idea of the Good* (Sankt Augustin, Germany, 2002)

Reeve, C. D. C., *Philosopher-Kings: The Argument of Plato's* Republic (Princeton, NJ, 1988)

Reshotko, N. (ed.) *Desire, Identity and Existence* (Kelowna, BC, 2003)

Rowe, C. J., and M. Schofield (eds.) *The Cambridge History of Greek and Roman Political Thought* (Cambridge, 2000)

Santas, Gerasimos, *Goodness and Justice: Plato, Aristotle, and the Moderns* (Oxford, 2001)

Schofield, M., *Saving the City: Philosopher-Kings and Other Classical Paradigms* (London, 1999)

Shorey, Paul (trans.) *The Republic*, 2 vols. (Cambridge, MA, 1978)

Vigetti, M. di, *Platone: La Republica* (Naples, 1998)

Vlastos, Gregory (ed.) *Plato*, 2 vols. (Garden City, NJ, 1971)

── *Platonic Studies*, 2nd edn. (Princeton, NJ, 1981)

── *Socrates, Ironist and Moral Philosopher* (Ithaca, NY, 1991)

── *Studies in Greek Philosophy*, 2 vols. (Princeton, NJ, 1994)

Waterfield, R., *Plato:* Republic (Oxford, 1994)

White, N. P., *A Companion to Plato's* Republic (Indianapolis, 1979)

Index